WEBER'S
time
to
grill

// BY JAMIE PURVIANCE
PHOTOGRAPHY BY TIM TURNER

AUTHOR
Jamie Purviance

MANAGING EDITOR
Marsha Capen

PHOTOGRAPHY
Tim Turner, Photographer and Photo Art Direction
Takamasa Ota, Digital Guru
Christy Clow, Photo Assistant
Michael Anton Herbert, Photo Assistant

FOOD STYLING
Lynn Gagné, Food Stylist
Nina Albazi, Assistant Food Stylist

INDEXER
Becky LaBrum

COLOR IMAGING AND IN-HOUSE PREPRESS
Weber Creative Services

CONTRIBUTORS
Nina Albazi, Monica Bhide, Lena Birnbaum,
Carolynn Carreño, April Cooper, Sarah Epstein,
Heather Fogarty, Lynn Gagné, Susan Hoss,
Lillian Kang, Patty Mastracco, Selma Morrow,
Rick Rodgers, Cheryl Sternman Rule,
Jess Thomson, Lucy Vaserfirer, Amy Vogler,
Kate Washington, Molly Watson

DESIGN AND PRODUCTION
rabble+rouser, inc.:
Christina Schroeder, Chief Rouser
Marsha Capen, Editorial Director
Shum Prats, Creative Director
Elaine Chow, Art Director
R. Matthew Thomas, Illustrator
Erin Beth Bosik, Copywriter

WEBER-STEPHEN PRODUCTS LLC
Mike Kempster Sr., Executive Vice President
Sherry L. Bale, Director, Public Relations
Brooke Jones, Marketing Manager

ROUND MOUNTAIN MEDIA
Susan Maruyama, Consulting Publishing Director

OXMOOR HOUSE, INC.
Jim Childs, Vice President and Publishing Director
Fonda Hitchcock, Brand Manager
Bob Doyle, Contributing Editor

10 9 8 7 6 5 4 3 2 1

ISBN 10: 0-376-02060-1
ISBN 13: 978-0-376-02060-4
Library of Congress Control Number: 2010929144

Weber Customer Service: 1.800.446.1071

www.weber.com®
www.sunset.com
www.oxmoorhouse.com
www.rabbleandrouser.com

About this book.

Let's face it. Life is complicated and some days are crazier than others. We lead busy, action-packed lives and time is of the essence. Some days we travel at the speed of light and dinner needs to happen without delays and without hassles. Other days we roll along at a more relaxed pace, so spending a few extra minutes in the kitchen is no big deal.

Whatever your speed, this book is all about options. Half the recipes are easy. They require only about fifteen minutes of active prep time and about ten ordinary supermarket ingredients. The other half of the recipes are a bit more adventurous. They involve a few more ingredients and a little more prep time so that you can try some interesting variations. As you flip through the recipes, you will find an easy one on the left side of every spread and an adventurous variation on the right. Each pairing shares a common set of ingredients or flavors.

The direction you take on any given day is totally up to you. Go the easy route and you'll get in, get out, and get grilling in no time flat. Or take the scenic route and enjoy the ride. Throughout the book you'll find helpful tips for shaving off precious time, even with traditional barbecue classics. Now let's get to it. It's time to grill.

To make your life even easier, this book comes with free mobile tools you can access on any smartphone or Web-enabled mobile device. Get a grocery list for each recipe in this book, add items that are on your general grocery list, and email it to a friend. Rate your favorite recipes, read comments from other users, and look up grilling times and temperatures for dozens of your favorite foods. There's even a grilling timer. You'll find all these tools and more at timetogrill.mobi.

TABLE OF // contents

// stocking your pantry

Really, the hardest part of making dinner is shopping for dinner. If you have to shop for more than half the ingredients in a recipe you want to make today, you are in trouble. But if you have an inventory of wisely chosen items, most of the ingredients in any given recipe will already be at home and ready to go. Now you are starting from a position of strength. Now you just need to shop a couple times a week to add fresh foods and replenish your pantry. The key is that you always keep your shopping a few days ahead of your grilling schedule so you never have to buy more than a handful of ingredients at a time.

So what should be in your pantry? For seasonings, you will obviously need salt and pepper. These seem so ordinary that it is easy to skip over them and focus on more unusual ingredients, but don't underestimate the enormous value of good kosher salt and ground black peppercorns (preferably Tellicherry peppercorns), especially when you are making simple food. Grinding peppercorns seconds before you add them to a recipe would be ideal, though it takes quite a bit of time to grind more than a fraction of a teaspoon, so go ahead and grind a few tablespoons at a time in a spice mill or coffee grinder, and keep the grounds in a little bowl or glass jar. The flavors will remain strong for a few days.

> **The key is that you always keep your shopping a few days ahead of your grilling schedule so you never have to buy more than a handful of ingredients at a time.**

You will also need some dried herbs and spices—not every type and species grown under the sun, but just a selection of the basics. The spices most useful for grilling are ground cumin, chile powder, granulated garlic, paprika, and cayenne pepper. These create the basis of many barbecue spice rubs and they are featured prominently in the world's most exciting grilling cultures. Some of the most versatile dried herbs are oregano, thyme, rosemary, and dill. You can work them into spice rubs and use them to flavor lots of marinades and sauces.

To make marinades, pastes, sauces, glazes, etc., you will need some other pantry items, especially oils (at least olive oil and canola oil), vinegars (balsamic and white wine), and a few concentrated condiments (like Dijon mustard, soy sauce, and Worcestershire sauce). If you want some simple, no-cook options for sauces, keep some bottled salsa and barbecue sauce in your pantry. What could be easier on a busy night than pouring a good salsa or sauce over something simple like chicken breasts or steaks that you have quickly oiled, seasoned, and grilled?

a well-stocked pantry

The items in the "good to have" list may not be as important day after day as the essentials, but they are still really helpful for making quick meals more interesting. Imagine, for instance, that it's Tuesday night and you need something to jazz up grilled pork chops or shrimp. If you toss a few roasted red peppers and a couple sun-dried tomatoes in a food processor or blender with some oil and vinegar, and then season the puree with salt and pepper, there's your dipping sauce. To fill out the plate, add some angel hair pasta lightly coated with pesto or maybe some creamy white beans warmed in a bit of tomato sauce seasoned with crushed red pepper flakes. See how easy dinner can be with a well-stocked pantry?

Your freezer can be a treasure chest and a real time saver, too. Sausages, boneless chicken pieces, and individually wrapped steaks take just a few hours to defrost. The quickest method is to submerge them (still tightly wrapped in plastic) in a bowl of cold water. Change the water every half hour for safety reasons. Plan on one to two hours per pound to defrost most individual servings of meats and poultry. They will thaw even faster if you use a thick stainless steel skillet instead of a mixing bowl, because the thick metal does a better job of conducting the heat of the room through the water and into the meat. No kidding. Nonstick and cast-iron skillets don't work nearly as well as the heavy stainless steel ones. As tempting as it is to use a microwave oven for defrosting meats, don't do it. The outer surfaces of the meat will actually begin to cook before the interior is soft.

// ESSENTIALS

CONDIMENTS
- ☐ balsamic vinegar
- ☐ barbecue sauce
- ☐ Dijon mustard
- ☐ salsa in a jar
- ☐ soy sauce
- ☐ white wine vinegar
- ☐ Worcestershire sauce

OIL AND SPICES
- ☐ canola oil
- ☐ dried herbs
- ☐ extra-virgin olive oil
- ☐ ground black pepper
- ☐ kosher salt
- ☐ spices

//GOOD TO HAVE

CONDIMENTS
- ☐ capers
- ☐ chicken broth/stock
- ☐ chili sauce
- ☐ hoisin sauce
- ☐ honey
- ☐ mayonnaise
- ☐ mustards
- ☐ peanut sauce
- ☐ pesto
- ☐ pickles
- ☐ pitted olives
- ☐ prepared horseradish
- ☐ tomato sauce
- ☐ vinegar

OIL AND SPICES
- ☐ flavored oils
- ☐ spice rubs

//GOOD TO HAVE (CONT.)

FRESH PRODUCE
- ☐ bags of pre-chopped vegetables and salads:
  - bell peppers
  - broccoli florets
  - coleslaw
  - mixed greens
  - trimmed green beans
- ☐ fresh salsas

MEAT/POULTRY/SEAFOOD
- ☐ boneless chicken pieces
- ☐ chops
- ☐ sausages/brats
- ☐ shrimp (peeled and deveined)
- ☐ steaks

DAIRY
- ☐ ice cream
- ☐ grated cheeses

OTHER
- ☐ bread crumbs
- ☐ canned beans
- ☐ canned chipotle chiles in adobo sauce
- ☐ cornmeal/polenta
- ☐ dried pasta
- ☐ hot fudge sauce
- ☐ peeled garlic cloves in plastic containers
- ☐ refrigerated pizza dough
- ☐ rice
- ☐ roasted red bell peppers in a jar
- ☐ salad dressing
- ☐ slivered almonds
- ☐ sugar, granulated and brown
- ☐ sun-dried tomatoes packed in oil

Access this grocery list on your mobile device. timetogrill.mobi.

// stocking your pantry

Another smart strategy for saving time and money is to buy meat in bulk or "value packs." You can grill what you want right away and freeze the rest for later. Meats freeze better than vegetables or fish because they are sturdier and don't hold as much water. Water expands in the freezer and can break the cell structure of food, which can leave tender vegetables and fish limp and unappealing when they are thawed and then cooked. Meats stand up relatively well, but don't leave them in the freezer for too long. After a few months, the quality deteriorates. Besides, if you are using this strategy properly, you should defrost meats every few weeks and replenish your freezer supply with fresh ones.

// FREEZING INDIVIDUAL CUTS OF MEAT

Buying chicken and other meats in bulk or "value packs" saves more than money. It can also save you the time required to run to the store on a busy day, if you have frozen servings waiting for you in the freezer. The key is to wrap each individual portion separately in plastic wrap, and then store all the wrapped portions in a heavy-duty, resealable freezer bag. That way, you can defrost just the number of servings you need that day. Be sure to mark the bag with the date when the meat was first frozen, and try to use all the portions within a few weeks.

// must-have tools

Tongs
Look for heavy-duty tongs that are about 16 inches long, feel comfortable in your hand, have sturdy metal pincers, and are dishwasher safe. A locking mechanism is nice for keeping them closed when not in use.

Spatula
The material should be solid, heavy-gauge metal with a thin yet rigid blade about 4 inches wide. Look for a bent (offset) neck that puts the blade lower than the handle. The total length should be about 16 inches.

Grill Brush
Spring for a solid, sturdy, long-handled brush with stiff stainless steel bristles.

Perforated Grill Pan
Get a thick metal pan that is big enough to accommodate the food in a single layer. The holes should be wide enough to allow heat and smoke to reach the food directly, and the rim of the pan should be low enough that you can slide a spatula under the food.

Timer
The best ones have extra large digits for easy reading, loud alarms, belt clips, and the flexibility to count up from zero as well as down from whatever time you pick.

Instant-read Thermometer
You can buy an inexpensive thermometer with a dial face or a more expensive one with a digital face. Ideally the sensor will be very close to the tip so you can easily pinpoint the area of the food you want to measure.

Insulated Barbecue Mitts
Invest in a pair with good-quality materials and workmanship that will hold up well over time.

// NICE TO HAVE

Sheet Pans
Portable surfaces for oiling and seasoning foods. Convenient landing pads for food coming hot off the grill.

Cast-iron Skillet
Once it gets hot on the grill, you can sauté, stew, pan-roast, or bake just about anything in it without ever worrying that the skillet will discolor or deteriorate. Get one that is at least 10 inches in diameter.

Chimney Starter
The simple design lets you start charcoal quickly and evenly without using lighter fluid. Look for one with two handles—one heatproof side handle for lifting and a hinged top handle for support—and a capacity to hold at least 5 quarts of briquettes (about 80 to 100 pieces).

Basting Brush
You can now find brushes with silicone bristles that are dishwasher safe. Much better than synthetic/natural boar bristles that you have to wash by hand.

Skewers
Bamboo skewers are always an option for kabobs, though flat metal skewers or double-pronged ones do a better job of holding the food in place.

GRILLING BASICS

// knives

Good grilling requires a good set of knives. How much you spend on each knife is not nearly as important as how comfortable it feels in *your* hand. Uncomfortable knives sit in a drawer or knife block doing no good at all, no matter how much they cost. A comfortable knife at any price is a pleasure to use often, especially when you are using the right knife for the right job.

1 // Sharpening Steel
This special metal rod grinds and realigns the edges of a knife blade.

2// Serrated Knife
Its jagged edge is great at sawing through crusty bread, slicing through tender vegetables, and carving meats.

3 // Chef's Knife
This is your number one, most important tool for slicing, dicing, and carving almost anything.

4// Santoku Knife
A good all-purpose knife for smaller hands. Oval cutouts along the edge help to reduce friction, which prevents foods from sticking to the blade.

5// Boning Knife
The thin, somewhat flexible blade moves easily along the edges of bones and in between tight spaces.

6 // Paring Knife
A short tool that is especially effective at peeling, trimming, and mincing vegetables.

// USING A SHARPENING STEEL —THE BUTCHER'S METHOD

All knives lose their sharp edges when you run them across cutting boards again and again. They turn dull just from cutting food. If your knives are dull, you'll need to work harder and longer to cut your food, raising the chances that you will slip while exerting too much force.

A steel doesn't sharpen a knife as much as it straightens the crooked edges. The safest way to do this is with the "butcher's method," shown to the left.

Point the narrow end of the steel facing down on a cutting board. Position the heel of your knife somewhere between 15 and 20 degrees near the handle of the steel. Swipe the blade down one side of the steel, pulling the knife toward you at the same time so that every part of the blade—from heel to tip—runs along the steel. Repeat the swiping action on the opposite side of the steel. Continue to swipe on both sides of the steel a few times, or until the knife can easily cut through a piece of paper.

// prep school

If you intend to reduce the amount of time it takes you to make dinner, get some quick recipes but also get serious about speeding up your prep time. For each recipe in this book, the prep time refers to the number of minutes you're actively getting your food ready to grill. It includes hands-on prep work like slicing, dicing, seasoning, and mixing, all of which can go faster or slower, depending on your level of organization and knife skills.

Before you pull any food out of the refrigerator or start chopping, read the whole recipe from start to finish. People typically skip this step and discover too late that they don't have a required ingredient or tool, or they realize that a certain step, like marinating or simmering, will take much more time than they expected. Suddenly dinner is in trouble, or at least delayed.

Also, begin with a clean kitchen. Cluttered countertops and dirty dishes in the sink are major obstacles to efficient prep work. Taking some time to clear your work spaces before you start will save you time later.

And continue to clean as you go. In the process of almost every recipe, there are idle minutes when you are waiting for something to happen—like the grill temperature to rise or an ingredient to reach room temperature. These are moments when you can wipe down your cutting boards, rinse your utensils, or just put away some unused ingredients so you have plenty of counter space and you are ready to go for the next step.

Give yourself as much room as possible to do your slicing and dicing. Your cutting boards should be at least 16 inches in length and width, and ideally you will have at least two of them: one for raw meats, poultry, and fish, and one for everything else. Finally, make sure you have a trash can nearby for your scraps, or put a bowl near your cutting board to collect the scraps and discard them later.

// CHOPPING AN ONION

1 2 3
4 5 6
7 8 9
10 11 12

Cut the onion in half through the stem and root ends. Peel off the skin and possibly one layer of each half with a paring knife. Trim about ½ inch from the stem end of each half, but during the rest of the chopping, keep the root end on each half intact; otherwise the onion will fall apart. Lay each half, flat side down, on a cutting board. Hold the onion steady with the fingertips of one hand. With the other hand, make a series of horizontal cuts from the stem toward the root end but not through it. Then make a series of vertical cuts, with the tip of the knife cutting almost but not quite through the root end. Then cut each half crosswise to create an evenly sized dice. The size of the dice depends on how far apart you make each horizontal, vertical, and crosswise cut.

// prep school

// PREPPING AN ONION FOR KABOBS

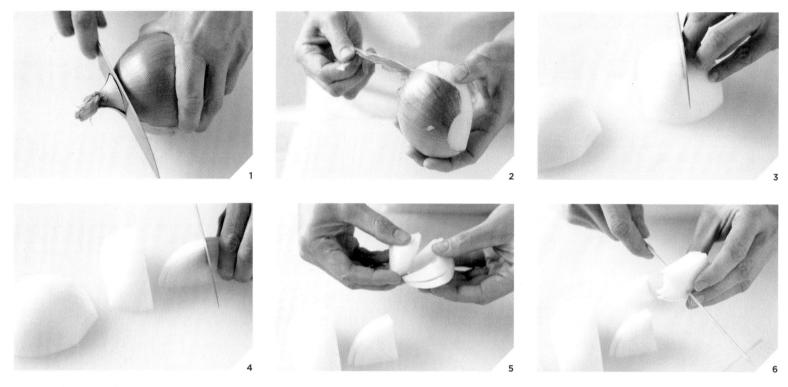

First trim the stem and root ends from the onion and cut it in half lengthwise. Peel each half and then set the onion on one of the cut sides. Cut each half into four equal quarters. The innermost layers of each quarter are too small for kabobs—they would fall off the skewers. Use the outer two or three layers of each quarter as a section of onion to slide onto a skewer.

// SLICING AN ONION

A round onion tends to move on a cutting board, which can be dangerous, so use one hand to hold it firmly in place. Use the other hand to cut straight down. You want thick, even slices. Slices thinner than one-third of an inch often fall apart on the grill, and slices that are not the same thickness from edge to edge cook unevenly and fall apart.

// prep school

// PEELING AND MINCING GARLIC

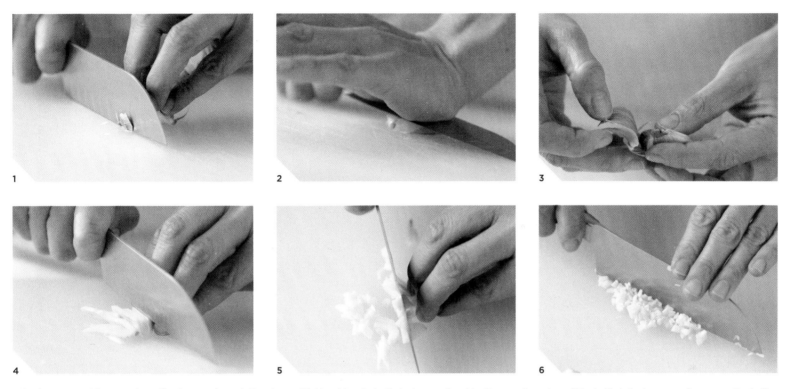

1

2

3

4

5

6

Trim the root end from each garlic clove and crush the clove with the side of a knife to loosen the skin. Be sure the edge of the knife is facing away from you. Peel off the skin. For a very even mince, cut the clove into thin slices first, and then line up the slices in a row so you can cut across the slices. Repeat with all the cloves and finally rock your knife over the chopped garlic until all of it is minced as finely as you want.

// DICING AN AVOCADO

1

2

3

Cut a ripe avocado lengthwise around the pit and then twist the halves in opposite directions. Tap the exposed pit with the heel of a chef's knife. It will pull out from the avocado. Carefully push the pit off the blade of the knife. You can chop the avocado right in the skin by crosshatching it and then scooping the little pieces into a bowl with a spoon.

// prep school

// MINCING A JALAPEÑO CHILE PEPPER

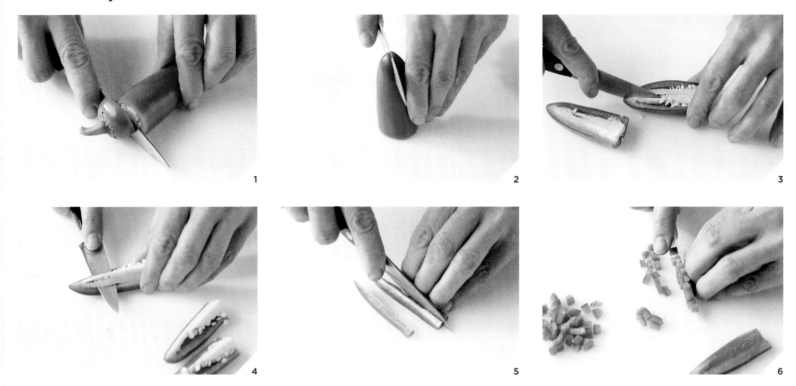

With a paring knife, trim off the stem end and cut the pepper in half lengthwise. Most of the chile pepper's heat is in the whitish veins and seeds. Remove as much of those as you want by cutting each half in half and running your knife under the seeds and discarding them, always with the edge of the knife facing away from you. Then cut the pepper into thin strips. Line up the strips and cut across them to create minced peppers. People with sensitive skin should do this wearing rubber gloves.

// DICING A PLUM TOMATO

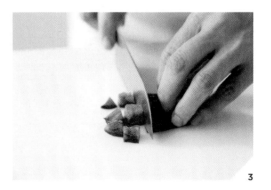

Quarter the tomato lengthwise to expose the seeds and watery pulp. Using a paring knife, scoop just under the pulp in each quarter and discard it. Always face the edge of the knife blade away from you. Then, with the skin side facing down, cut each quarter into thin strips. Line up the thin strips and cut across them to dice the tomato, leaving behind any bits of the stem.

// prep school

// PREPPING A BELL PEPPER

1

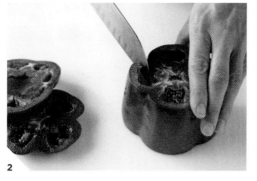
2

3

4

5

6

The goal is to create a uniform piece of bell pepper that will lie flat on the grill. Begin by trimming off the stem and bottom ends. Stand the pepper up and cut an opening down one side. Put the pepper on its side, with the opening facing up. Position your knife inside so you can make a cut between the inner wall of the pepper and the undesirable core/seeds. Go back and trim any whitish areas off the inner wall of the pepper. Now you have lots of surface area you can lay flat on the hot cooking grate, where it will caramelize or char evenly.

// MINCING GINGER

1

2

3

The skin of fresh ginger is quite fibrous, so scrape it off with the edge of a spoon. A spoon will create less waste than a vegetable peeler or paring knife. Then rub the peeled ginger along the tiny, sharp blades of a handheld grater, which is also an efficient tool for grating garlic cloves, the zest of citrus fruits, and hard cheeses.

// prep school

// CUTTING MEAT FOR KABOBS

1 2 3

The primary goal is to cut chunks of meat that will cook evenly on skewers. Start by cutting slices at least one inch thick, and then cut each slice into chunks at least one inch in all directions. Smaller chunks tend to overcook and turn dry quickly. Also be careful not to cram the chunks together on skewers. They cook more evenly when you leave a bit of space between them.

// BUTTERFLYING A PORK CHOP

1 2 3

Begin with a boneless center-cut pork chop at least one inch thick. Cut into the middle of the fat side to within about one-half inch of the other side, so that the chop opens up like a butterfly. Flatten the meat with the palm of your hand and trim off any excess fat. Lay the chop between two large sheets of plastic wrap. Use the flat side of a meat tenderizer (or the bottom of a small, heavy skillet) to flatten the meat to an even thickness of about one-fourth inch. This creates a *paillard*.

// REMOVING SILVER SKIN FROM A PORK TENDERLOIN

1 2 3

The thin layer of sinew on the surface of a pork tenderloin is called silver skin. Slip the tip of a sharp, thin boning knife under one end of the silver skin. Grab the loosened end with your fingertips. Then slide the knife away from you just underneath the silver skin, with the knife blade angled slightly upward. The "cleaned" tenderloins should have hardly any visible silver skin or surface fat.

// prep school

// SKINNING A FISH FILLET

1

2

3

Along one end of the fillet, cut a slit all the way through the skin large enough to get your finger though. Holding the skin steady with your finger in the slit, angle the blade of a large, sharp chef's knife inside the seam between the flesh and skin. Cut away from you and over the top of the skin, always with the knife angled slightly downward so you don't cut into the fish fillet.

// PEELING AND DEVEINING SHRIMP

1

2

3

4

5

6

To peel each shrimp, grab the shell just above the tail and break it loose. Peel off the shell along with all the little legs. With a sharp paring knife, make a shallow slit along the back of each shrimp, being careful not to cut too deep. Lift any black vein out of the slit and discard it. Whether you leave the tail on or not is up to you. Some people like to use it as a handle.

// prep school

// BUTTERFLYING A WHOLE CHICKEN

 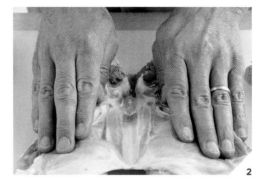 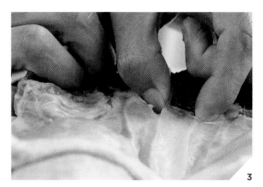

 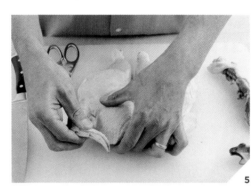 

Pull out and discard the loose clumps of fat that are typically just inside the chicken. Turn the chicken over so that the back is facing up and the neck end is closest to you. Use poultry shears to cut along both sides of the backbone and then discard it. Open the chicken like a butterfly spreading its wings, and press down to flatten it. Run your fingertips along both sides of the breastbone to expose it. Dig your fingers along the breastbone until it comes loose from the meat. Then pull it out and discard it. Fold the wing tips behind the chicken's back to prevent them from burning. Now you have overcome one of the key cooking challenges of a whole chicken: an uneven shape. By butterflying (or spatchcocking) the bird, you have created a relatively even shape.

// BUTTERFLYING A CHICKEN BREAST

Lay the breast lengthwise on the board, with the narrow end farthest from you and the slightly thicker side to your right. Use one hand to hold the breast in place. With the blade of your knife running parallel to the board, make a shallow slit halfway up the thicker side of the breast, but do not cut into the narrow end. Using the tip of your knife, make the cut deeper and deeper until you are almost but not all the way to other side of the breast. Now you have a pocket suitable for filling.

// prep school

// TRUSSING A CHICKEN

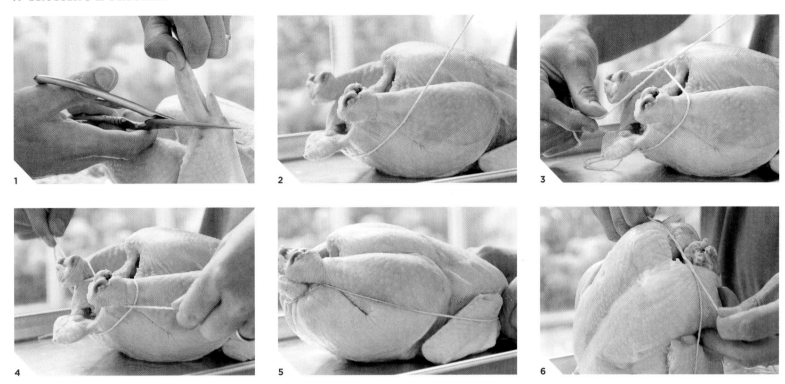

The wing tips have almost no meat and they tend to burn, so remove them at the joint with poultry shears. Slide a four-foot length of butcher's twine under the legs and back. Lift both ends of the twine and cross them between the legs. Then run one end under one drumstick. Run the other end under the other drumstick and pull both ends to draw the drumsticks together. Bring the twine along both sides of the chicken so that it holds the legs and wings against the body. Tie a knot in the ends between the neck and the top of the breast. If necessary, push the breast down a little to expose more of the neck.

// SETTING A CHICKEN ON A ROTISSERIE

Position one set of fork prongs on the far end of the center rod (spit) and slide the spit into the opening between the neck and the knotted twine, though the chicken, and out the other side, just underneath the drumsticks. Slide the other set of fork prongs on the spit and drive the prongs into the back of the chicken. Make sure the chicken is centered on the spit before tightening the fork prongs into place.

// gas vs. charcoal

// WHAT SIZE WORKS BEST?

The size of your grill will also affect your timing. If you use a grill that is too small for the amount of food you want to cook, you will have to cook the food in batches, which of course takes more time and runs the risk of some of the food turning cold before all of it is cooked.

Remember that frequently you will want to grill two or three items at once. That might require having two or three zones of heat, and each zone needs to have enough room for the number of people you are feeding.

Here are recommendations based on the number of people eating.

GAS

 : A GRILL WITH ONE OR TWO BURNERS

: A GRILL WITH THREE OR FOUR BURNERS

⁺: A GRILL WITH SIX BURNERS

CHARCOAL

: AN 18½"–DIAMETER GRILL

: A 22½"–DIAMETER GRILL

⁺: A 26¾"–DIAMETER GRILL

Gas

Let's settle one issue right up front. Gas is quicker than charcoal. Lighting a gas grill, in most cases, is as simple as lifting the lid, turning on the gas, and igniting the burners. After you have opened the valve on your propane tank all the way (or turned on the gas at the source), wait a minute for the gas to travel through the gas line, and then turn each burner to high, making sure one burner has ignited before turning on the next.

Charcoal

Sure, gas grills start up faster than charcoal grills, and turning a knob is easier than raking coals, but there are compelling reasons why some people will grill only with charcoal and other people will choose charcoal over gas whenever they have a little time available.

The amount of time required to fire up a charcoal grill can be as little as 15 to 20 minutes, if you are using certain equipment.

1// The easiest method involves a chimney starter, which is an upright metal cylinder with a handle on the outside and a wire rack inside. You simply fill the space under the wire rack with a few sheets of wadded-up newspaper or a few paraffin cubes, and then fill the space above the rack with briquettes.

1

2

3

2// Once you light the newspaper, some impressive thermodynamics channel the heat evenly throughout the briquettes.

3// When the briquettes are lightly covered with white ash, put on two insulated barbecue mitts and grab hold of the two handles on the chimney starter. The swinging handle is there to help you lift the chimney starter and safely aim the coals just where you want them.

// grilling time

// DIRECT HEAT

Direct heat works great for small, tender pieces of food that cook quickly, such as hamburgers, steaks, chops, boneless chicken pieces, fish fillets, shellfish, and sliced vegetables. It sears the surface of these foods, developing flavors, textures, and caramelization while it cooks the food all the way to the center.

// INDIRECT HEAT

Indirect heat works better for larger, tougher foods that require longer cooking times, such as roasts, whole chickens, and ribs. It is also the proper way to finish cooking thicker foods or bone-in cuts that have been seared or browned first over direct heat.

1

2

Heat Configurations

1// The most flexible charcoal configuration is a two-zone fire. That means the coals are spread out on one side of the charcoal grate and the other side has no coals at all. This allows you to cook with both direct and indirect heat.

You can set up a similar configuration on a gas grill by leaving some of the burners on and turning one or two of them off.

How hot your charcoal grill is depends on how much charcoal you use and how long it has been burning. The coals are at their hottest when they are newly lit. Over time they gradually lose heat. The heat of your gas grill depends of course on how you adjust the burners.

After the coals or gas burners are fully lit, close the lid and wait for about 10 minutes so the temperature rises to at least 500°F on the lid's thermometer. This makes the cooking grate much easier to clean and it improves the grill's ability to sear.

Wearing an insulated barbecue mitt, use a long-handled grill brush to scrape off any bits and pieces that may be stuck to the grate.

There is no need to oil the grate before grilling. Oil would just drip into the grill and potentially cause flare-ups. You can avoid wasting oil and improve the chances of food releasing more easily by oiling the food, not the grate.

2// Once your grill is preheated and brushed clean, bring out all the food and other supplies you will need and organize them on a tray. If you have everything chopped and measured beforehand, the cooking will go faster and you won't have to run back into the kitchen. Don't forget clean plates and platters for serving the grilled food.

Keep the Lid Closed as Much as Possible

Whether using a charcoal grill or a gas grill, keeping the lid closed as much as possible is really important. The grill's lid limits the amount of air getting to the fire, thus preventing flare-ups, and it helps to cook food on the top and bottom simultaneously. While the bottom of the food is almost always exposed to more intense heat, the lid reflects some heat down and speeds up the overall cooking time. Without the lid, the fire would lose heat more quickly and many foods would take much longer to cook, possibly drying out.

↗ *A few flames flickering under your food for a few seconds are to be expected in grilling. Don't worry. But if the flames last longer and threaten to burn your food, move the food to a cooler part of the grill until the flames subside.*

// doneness

// CHECKING STEAKS FOR DONENESS

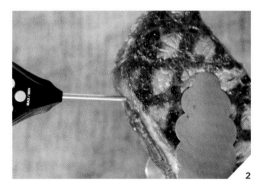

Steaks get firmer as they grill, so one way to judge their doneness is by pressing the surface of a steak with your fingertip. When the meat is no longer soft, but is not yet firm either, it has reached a doneness somewhere near medium rare (see below for more specifics with the "hand test"). A more scientific approach is to use an instant-read thermometer. If you are sure to position the thermometer sensor right in the middle of the steak, you'll have a perfectly accurate reading of doneness (see page 285 for a doneness chart). Perhaps the most straightforward approach is to have a look at the color of the meat inside the steak. On the underside of the steak (the side that will face the plate), cut a little slit down to the center of the meat and peek inside. When it's cooked just the way you want it, turn the steak over and press the surface with your fingertip. Note how it feels so that next time you won't need to cut into your steak.

// USING THE HAND TEST

Most raw steaks are as soft as the base of your thumb when your hand is relaxed. If you touch your first finger and thumb together, and then press the base of your thumb, that's how most steaks feel when they are rare. If you touch your middle finger and thumb together, and then press the base of your thumb, that's how most steaks feel when they are medium rare.

// doneness

// CHECKING DONENESS OF POPULAR GRILLED FOODS

Pork Chops. The one on the left, with raw meat in the center, is clearly under cooked. The chop on the right, with a dry, gray appearance, is overcooked. The chop in the middle, with a little bit of pink in the center, is cooked to 150°F, which is just right. The meat gives a little under the pressure of a fingertip.

Chicken. The meat near the bone usually takes the longest to cook. If the juices near the bone are clear and the meat there is no longer pink, the chicken is done.

Ribs. If you bend a rack of ribs backwards, with the bone side facing up, and the meat tears easily along the bone, the meat is done.

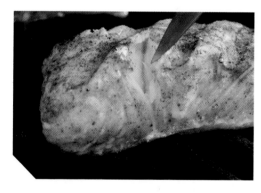

Fish Fillet. With almost every kind of fish, you should get it off the grill before it flakes from over-cooking. You are looking for an internal temperature of 125° to 130°F, but that's sometimes difficult to measure with fillets or steaks, so look at the internal appearance. The whitish color should be opaque (not translucent) all the way to the center.

Shrimp. As shrimp cook, the meat tightens up and turns opaque. The shrimp on the left is under cooked (still a little translucent). The shrimp on the right is overcooked (shrunken and dry). The shrimp in the middle is just right.

Scallops. After grilling, the interior of a scallop should be barely opaque, like the one in the center. The scallop on the left is a little under cooked and the scallop on the right is overcooked.

// rubs

A rub is a mixture of spices, herbs, and other seasonings (often including sugar) that can quickly give a boost of flavors to foods before grilling. This page and the next provide some mighty good examples, along with recommendations for which foods they complement, but dare to be different. One of the steps toward developing your own style at the grill is to concoct a signature rub recipe or two. Only you will know exactly what ingredients are blended in your special jar of "magic dust."

A word about freshness: Ground spices lose their aromas in a matter of months (8 to 10 months maximum). If you have been holding on to a little jar of coriander for years, waiting to blend the world's finest version of curry powder, forget about it. Dump the old, tired coriander and buy some freshly ground. Better yet, buy whole coriander seeds and grind them yourself. Whatever you do, store your spices and spice rubs in airtight containers away from light and heat, to best preserve their flavors and fragrances.

How Long?

If you leave a rub on for a long time, the seasonings intermix with the juices in the meat and produce more pronounced flavors, as well as a crust. This is good to a point, but a rub with a lot of salt and sugar will draw moisture out of the meat over time, making the meat tastier, yes, but also drier. So how long should you use a rub? Here are some guidelines.

// CLASSIC BARBECUE SPICE RUB

MAKES: ABOUT ⅓ CUP

4	teaspoons kosher salt
2	teaspoons pure chile powder
2	teaspoons packed light brown sugar
2	teaspoons granulated garlic
2	teaspoons paprika
1	teaspoon celery seed
1	teaspoon ground cumin
½	teaspoon ground black pepper

1. In a small bowl mix the ingredients.

// CAJUN RUB

MAKES: ABOUT ⅓ CUP

2	teaspoons granulated garlic
2	teaspoons granulated onion
2	teaspoons dried thyme
2	teaspoons dried oregano
2	teaspoons kosher salt
2	teaspoons paprika
1½	teaspoons packed light brown sugar
1	teaspoon smoked paprika
1	teaspoon ground black pepper

1. In a small bowl mix the ingredients.

// TOASTED CUMIN RUB

MAKES: ABOUT ¼ CUP
SPECIAL EQUIPMENT: SPICE MILL

2	teaspoons cumin seed
1	teaspoon mustard seed
1	teaspoon coriander seed
2	teaspoons paprika
2	teaspoons kosher salt
2	teaspoons packed brown sugar
½	teaspoon granulated garlic
½	teaspoon ground cayenne pepper

1. In a medium skillet over medium-high heat, toast the cumin, mustard, and coriander seed until fragrant, 2 to 3 minutes, shaking the pan occasionally. Transfer the seeds to a spice mill. Add the remaining ingredients and pulse until finely ground.

// CARIBBEAN RUB

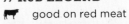

MAKES: ABOUT ¼ CUP

1	tablespoon packed light brown sugar
1	tablespoon granulated garlic
1	tablespoon dried thyme
2½	teaspoons kosher salt
¾	teaspoon ground black pepper
¾	teaspoon ground allspice

1. In a small bowl combine the ingredients.

TIME	TYPES OF MEAT
Up to 15 minutes:	Small foods, such as shellfish, cubed meat for kabobs, and vegetables
15 to 30 minutes:	Thin cuts of boneless meat, such as chicken breasts, fish fillets, pork tenderloin, chops, and steaks
30 minutes to 1½ hours:	Thicker cuts of boneless or bone-in meat, such as leg of lamb, whole chickens, and beef roasts
2 to 8 hours:	Big or tough cuts of meat, such as racks of ribs, whole hams, pork shoulders, and turkeys

// RUB LEGEND

- good on red meat
- good on pork
- good on poultry
- good on seafood
- good on vegetables

// rubs

// FRENCH ROAST SPICE RUB

MAKES: ABOUT 3½ TABLESPOONS

- 2 tablespoons coarsely ground French roast coffee beans
- 2 teaspoons kosher salt
- 1 teaspoon packed light brown sugar
- ¾ teaspoon ground black pepper
- ½ teaspoon granulated garlic

1. In a small bowl mix the ingredients.

// STEAK HOUSE RUB

MAKES: ABOUT 3 TABLESPOONS
SPECIAL EQUIPMENT: SPICE MILL

- 2 teaspoons black peppercorns
- 2 teaspoons mustard seed
- 2 teaspoons paprika
- 1 teaspoon granulated garlic
- 1 teaspoon kosher salt
- 1 teaspoon packed light brown sugar
- ¼ teaspoon pure chile powder

1. Using a spice mill crush the peppercorns and mustard seed. Pour into a small bowl and add the remaining ingredients. Mix thoroughly.

// SANTA FE SPICE RUB

MAKES: ABOUT 2 TABLESPOONS

- 1½ teaspoons kosher salt
- 1 teaspoon ground black pepper
- 1 teaspoon ground cumin
- 1 teaspoon packed light brown sugar
- ½ teaspoon ancho chile powder
- ½ teaspoon dried oregano

1. In a small bowl mix the ingredients.

// NEW ORLEANS BARBECUE RUB

MAKES: ABOUT 3 TABLESPOONS

- 1 tablespoon smoked paprika
- 1 teaspoon granulated garlic
- 1 teaspoon granulated onion
- 1 teaspoon dried oregano
- 1 teaspoon dried thyme
- 1 teaspoon kosher salt
- ¼ teaspoon ground cayenne pepper

1. In a small bowl mix the ingredients.

// BEEF RUB

MAKES: ABOUT ⅓ CUP

- 4 teaspoons kosher salt
- 1 tablespoon pure chile powder
- 1 tablespoon granulated onion
- 1½ teaspoons granulated garlic
- 1 teaspoon paprika
- 1 teaspoon dried marjoram
- ½ teaspoon ground cumin
- ½ teaspoon ground black pepper
- ¼ teaspoon ground cinnamon

1. In a small bowl mix the ingredients.

// PORK RUB

MAKES: ABOUT ¼ CUP

- 2 teaspoons pure chile powder
- 2 teaspoons ground black pepper
- 2 teaspoons kosher salt
- 2 teaspoons ground cumin
- 2 teaspoons dried oregano
- 1 teaspoon granulated garlic

1. In a small bowl mix the ingredients.

// CHICKEN AND SEAFOOD RUB

MAKES: ABOUT ⅓ CUP

- 4 teaspoons granulated onion
- 4 teaspoons granulated garlic
- 1 tablespoon kosher salt
- 2 teaspoons prepared chili powder
- 2 teaspoons ground black pepper

1. In a small bowl mix the ingredients.

// MAGIC RUB

MAKES: 2 TABLESPOONS

- 1 teaspoon dry mustard
- 1 teaspoon granulated onion
- 1 teaspoon paprika
- 1 teaspoon kosher salt
- ½ teaspoon granulated garlic
- ½ teaspoon ground coriander
- ½ teaspoon ground cumin
- ½ teaspoon ground black pepper

1. In a small bowl mix the ingredients.

// ASIAN RUB

MAKES: ABOUT ¼ CUP

- 2 tablespoons paprika
- 2 teaspoons kosher salt
- 2 teaspoons ground coriander
- 2 teaspoons Chinese five-spice powder
- 1 teaspoon ground ginger
- ½ teaspoon ground allspice
- ½ teaspoon ground cayenne pepper

1. In a small bowl mix the ingredients.

Access the grocery list for these rub recipes on your mobile device. timetogrill.mobi.

// marinades

Marinades work more slowly than rubs, but they can seep in a little deeper. Typically, a marinade is made with some acidic liquid, some oil, and some combination of herbs and spices. These ingredients can "fill in the gaps" when a particular meat, fish, or vegetable (yes, vegetable) lacks enough taste or richness. They can also give food characteristics that reflect regional/ethnic cooking styles.

If indeed your marinade includes some acidic liquid, be sure to use a non-reactive container. This is a dish or bowl made of glass, plastic, stainless steel, or ceramic. A container made of aluminum, or some other metals, will react with acids and add a metallic flavor to food.

How Long?

The right times vary depending on the strength of the marinade and the food you are marinating. If your marinade includes intense ingredients, such as soy sauce, liquor, or hot chiles and spices, don't overdo it. A fish fillet should still taste like fish, not a burning-hot, salt-soaked piece of protein. Also, if an acidic marinade is left too long on meat or fish, it can make the surface mushy or dry. Here are some general guidelines to get you going.

// LEMON-MINT MARINADE

MAKES: ABOUT ⅓ CUP

- 3 tablespoons extra-virgin olive oil
- 1 teaspoon finely grated lemon zest
- 2 tablespoons fresh lemon juice
- 1 tablespoon finely chopped fresh mint leaves
- 1 teaspoon minced garlic
- 1 teaspoon kosher salt
- ½ teaspoon ground black pepper

1. In a small bowl whisk the ingredients.

// TANDOORI MARINADE

MAKES: ABOUT ⅔ CUP

- 1 cup plain yogurt
- ¼ cup fresh lemon juice
- 1 tablespoon minced fresh ginger
- 1 tablespoon minced garlic
- 1 tablespoon paprika
- 2 teaspoons ground cumin
- 2 teaspoons kosher salt
- 1 teaspoon ground turmeric
- ½ teaspoon ground cayenne pepper

1. In a small bowl combine the ingredients.

// CREOLE MUSTARD MARINADE

MAKES: ABOUT ⅔ CUP

- 3 tablespoons Creole mustard
- 3 tablespoons extra-virgin olive oil
- 3 tablespoons red wine vinegar
- 2 teaspoons Worcestershire sauce
- 2 teaspoons minced garlic
- 1 teaspoon dried thyme
- ½ teaspoon kosher salt
- ½ teaspoon ground black pepper

1. In a small bowl whisk the ingredients.

// SWEET BOURBON MARINADE

MAKES: ABOUT 2 CUPS

- ½ cup bourbon
- ½ cup packed brown sugar
- ⅓ cup soy sauce
- ⅓ cup fresh lemon juice
- 2 tablespoons Worcestershire sauce
- 2 teaspoons finely chopped garlic
- 2 teaspoons finely chopped fresh thyme leaves

1. In a medium bowl whisk the ingredients.

TIME	TYPES OF MEAT
15 to 30 minutes:	Small foods, such as shellfish, fish fillets, cubed meat for kabobs, and tender vegetables
1 to 3 hours:	Thin cuts of boneless meat, such as chicken breasts, pork tenderloin, chops, and steaks, as well as sturdy vegetables
2 to 6 hours:	Thicker cuts of boneless or bone-in meat, such as leg of lamb, whole chickens, and beef roasts
6 to 12 hours:	Big or tough cuts of meat, such as racks of ribs, whole hams, pork shoulders, and turkeys

// MARINADE LEGEND

 good on red meat
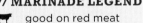 good on pork
good on poultry
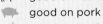 good on seafood
good on vegetables

// marinades

// PROVENÇAL MARINADE

MAKES: ABOUT 1½ CUPS

- 1 small yellow onion, roughly chopped
- ½ cup loosely packed fresh Italian parsley leaves and tender stems
- ¼ cup fresh rosemary leaves
- 4 large garlic cloves
- 2 tablespoons Dijon mustard
- 2 tablespoons tomato paste
- 2 teaspoons kosher salt
- ½ teaspoon ground black pepper
- ½ cup dry white wine
- ¼ cup extra-virgin olive oil

1. In a food processor or blender process the ingredients, except the wine and oil, until finely chopped. Add the wine and oil and process until fairly smooth.

// GREEK ISLAND MARINADE

MAKES: ABOUT ⅔ CUP

- ½ cup roughly chopped fresh Italian parsley leaves
- ¼ cup dry white wine
- ¼ cup extra-virgin olive oil
  Grated zest and juice of ½ lemon
- 1 teaspoon granulated garlic
- 1 teaspoon dried oregano
- 1 teaspoon paprika
- ¾ teaspoon kosher salt
- ¼ teaspoon ground black pepper

1. In a small bowl whisk the ingredients.

// WORCESTERSHIRE PASTE

MAKES: ABOUT ¼ CUP

- 2 tablespoons extra-virgin olive oil
- 2 tablespoons Worcestershire sauce
- 2 teaspoons cracked black pepper
- 2 teaspoons granulated garlic
- 1½ teaspoons kosher salt
- 1 teaspoon smoked paprika
- 1 teaspoon ground cumin
- ½ teaspoon ground cinnamon

1. In a small bowl whisk the ingredients.

// TERIYAKI MARINADE

MAKES: ABOUT 1¼ CUPS

- ¼ cup extra-virgin olive oil
- ¼ cup soy sauce
- ¼ cup packed brown sugar
- 2 tablespoons rice wine (mirin)
- 1 large shallot, grated
- 1 tablespoon sesame seeds
- 1 tablespoon grated fresh ginger
- 2 garlic cloves, grated or minced
- 1 teaspoon toasted sesame oil
- 1 teaspoon ground black pepper

1. In a medium bowl whisk the ingredients.

// BEER MARINADE

MAKES: ABOUT 1¼ CUPS

- 1 cup dark beer
- 2 tablespoons toasted sesame oil
- 1 tablespoon finely chopped garlic
- 1 teaspoon dried oregano
- 1 teaspoon kosher salt
- ½ teaspoon ground black pepper
- ¼ teaspoon ground cayenne pepper

1. In a medium bowl whisk the ingredients.

// MOJO MARINADE

MAKES: ABOUT 1 CUP

- ½ cup fresh orange juice
- 2 tablespoons fresh lime juice
- 2 tablespoons soy sauce
- 2 tablespoons extra-virgin olive oil
- 1 tablespoon minced garlic
- ½ teaspoon hot pepper sauce
- ½ teaspoon ground cumin
- ¼ teaspoon kosher salt
- ¼ teaspoon ground black pepper

1. In a small bowl whisk the ingredients.

// COCONUT-GINGER MARINADE

MAKES: ABOUT 2½ CUPS

- 1 cup loosely packed fresh cilantro leaves and tender stems
- 10 garlic cloves
- 1 four-inch section fresh ginger, cut into thin slices
- 1 can (13.5 ounces) unsweetened coconut milk, stirred
- ¾ cup low-sodium soy sauce
- ¼ cup honey

1. In a food processor or blender combine the cilantro, garlic, and ginger. Process until the ingredients are finely chopped. Transfer to a large bowl and add the remaining ingredients. Mix well.

Access the grocery list for these marinade recipes on your mobile device. timetogrill.mobi.

// sauces

Sauces open up a world of flavors for grillers. They offer us almost limitless ways for distinguishing our food and making it more interesting. Once you have learned some of the fundamentals about balancing flavors and some of the techniques for holding sauces together, you are ready to develop your own. A little more of this. A little less of that. Maybe a few more minutes simmering over the fire. Sauces are playgrounds for discovery. Learn the basics and build from there.

// SMOKED PAPRIKA BUTTER

MAKES: ABOUT ½ CUP
SPECIAL EQUIPMENT: SPICE MILL

- 2 teaspoons coriander seed *or*
  1 tablespoon ground coriander
- ½ cup (1 stick) butter, softened
- 2 teaspoons smoked paprika
- ¼ teaspoon ground cayenne pepper

1. In a small skillet over medium heat, toast the coriander seed until aromatic and slightly darker in color, about 2 minutes, stirring occasionally. Transfer to a spice mill and pulse until ground. Pour into a small bowl and mix thoroughly with the butter, paprika, and cayenne pepper.

// SAUCE LEGEND

- good on red meat
- good on pork
- good on poultry
- good on seafood
- good on vegetables

// TEN-MINUTE BARBECUE SAUCE

MAKES: ABOUT ¾ CUP

- ½ cup ketchup
- ¼ cup water
- 1 tablespoon Worcestershire sauce
- 1 tablespoon red wine vinegar
- 1 teaspoon packed light brown sugar
- 1 teaspoon prepared chili powder
- 1 teaspoon granulated onion
- ¼ teaspoon ground black pepper

1. In a small saucepan whisk the ingredients. Simmer over low heat for about 10 minutes to allow the sugar to fully dissolve and all of the flavors to blend, stirring occasionally.

// RED WINE SAUCE

MAKES: ABOUT ¾ CUP

- 2 tablespoons minced shallot
- 1½ cups dry red wine
- 1 tablespoon tomato paste
- 2 teaspoons balsamic vinegar
- ½ teaspoon Worcestershire sauce
- 3 tablespoons unsalted butter, cut into 3 pieces
  Kosher salt
  Ground black pepper

1. In a small saucepan over high heat, bring the shallot and wine to a boil. Then immediately reduce the heat to medium and simmer until the wine has reduced to about ½ cup, 15 to 20 minutes. Add the tomato paste, vinegar, and Worcestershire sauce. Remove from the heat and add the butter piece by piece, whisking to incorporate the butter into the sauce. Season with salt and pepper.

// BOURBON-BACON SAUCE

MAKES: ABOUT 2 CUPS

- 4 slices bacon, cut into ½-inch dice
- 1 cup finely chopped yellow onion
- 1 tablespoon minced garlic
- ½ cup ketchup
- ¼ cup dark molasses
- ¼ cup yellow mustard
- ¼ cup bourbon
- 2 tablespoons packed brown sugar
- 2 tablespoons Worcestershire sauce
- ⅛ teaspoon hot pepper sauce

1. In a medium saucepan over medium heat, cook the bacon until crisp, about 10 minutes, stirring occasionally. Reduce the heat to low, add the onion and garlic, and cook until soft, about 5 minutes. Add the remaining ingredients and simmer for about 5 minutes. Remove from the heat and let cool.

// AVOCADO SAUCE

MAKES: ABOUT 1½ CUPS

- 1 medium Hass avocado, diced
- ½ cup finely diced English cucumber
- ¼ cup sour cream
- ¼ cup thinly sliced scallions (white and light green parts only)
- ¼ cup roughly chopped fresh dill
- 2 tablespoons fresh lime juice
- ¼ teaspoon Tabasco® sauce
  Kosher salt

1. In a food processor or blender puree all the ingredients, except the salt, until smooth. Season with salt. Pour the sauce into a medium bowl, cover, and refrigerate until ready to use.

// sauces

// ROOT BEER BARBECUE SAUCE

MAKES: ABOUT 3 CUPS

- 1 tablespoon extra-virgin olive oil
- 1 cup finely chopped yellow onion
- 1 teaspoon minced garlic
- ½ teaspoon peeled, grated fresh ginger
- 1 cup root beer
- 1 cup ketchup
- ½ cup fresh orange juice
- 2 tablespoons Worcestershire sauce
- 2 tablespoons packed light brown sugar
- ½ teaspoon grated lemon zest
  Kosher salt
  Ground black pepper

1. In a medium saucepan over medium heat, warm the oil. Add the onion and cook until tender but not browned, 3 to 4 minutes, stirring occasionally. Add the garlic and ginger and cook until fragrant, about 1 minute. Add the root beer, ketchup, orange juice, Worcestershire sauce, and brown sugar, whisking until smooth. Simmer over medium-low heat until the sauce is thick and coats the back of a wooden spoon, 20 to 30 minutes, stirring occasionally. Remove the saucepan from the heat and stir in the lemon zest. Season with salt and pepper.

// ORANGE-GINGER SAUCE

MAKES: ABOUT ¾ CUP

- ½ cup orange marmalade
- 2 tablespoons cider vinegar
- 1 tablespoon soy sauce
- 2 teaspoons peeled, grated fresh ginger
- ⅛ teaspoon ground black pepper

1. In a small saucepan over medium heat, mix the ingredients. Cook the sauce until liquefied and bubbling, 3 to 4 minutes, stirring occasionally. Remove from the heat and allow to cool to room temperature before serving.

// TOMATO-CHIMICHURRI SAUCE

MAKES: ABOUT 1 CUP

- 1 cup loosely packed fresh Italian parsley leaves
- ½ cup extra-virgin olive oil
- ⅓ cup loosely packed fresh cilantro leaves
- ¼ cup oil-packed sun-dried tomatoes, drained
- 3 garlic cloves
- ¾ teaspoon crushed red pepper flakes
  Kosher salt
  Ground black pepper

1. In a food processor or blender combine all the ingredients except the salt and pepper. Pulse until you get a semi-smooth consistency. Season with salt and pepper. Transfer to a small bowl and set aside until ready to use.

// CREAMY MUSTARD SAUCE

MAKES: ABOUT ¾ CUP

- 1 tablespoon unsalted butter
- 2 tablespoons minced shallot
- 2 tablespoons cognac *or* brandy (optional)
- ½ cup low-sodium beef broth
- ¾ cup heavy whipping cream
- 3 tablespoons whole-grain mustard
  Kosher salt

1. In a medium skillet over medium heat, melt the butter. Add the shallot and cook until softened, 1 to 2 minutes, stirring often. Add the cognac, if using, and cook until reduced to a glaze, about 30 seconds. Add the broth and bring to a boil over high heat. Cook until the broth reduces by half, 2 to 3 minutes. Add the cream and bring to a simmer (not a boil). Whisk in the mustard and simmer until the sauce is reduced to ¾ cup and is thick enough to coat the back of a spoon, 3 to 5 minutes. Season with salt.

// HORSERADISH-LEMON CREAM SAUCE

MAKES: ABOUT 1½ CUPS

- 1 cup sour cream
- 2 tablespoons plus 1 teaspoon prepared horseradish
- ¼ teaspoon finely grated lemon zest
- 2 tablespoons fresh lemon juice
- 2 tablespoons minced shallot
- 1 tablespoon finely chopped fresh Italian parsley leaves
- 2 teaspoons Worcestershire sauce
- ½ teaspoon kosher salt
- ½ teaspoon ground black pepper

1. In a medium bowl combine the ingredients and stir until well blended. The sauce should have the consistency of thick cream.

// BASIL-ARUGULA PESTO

MAKES: ABOUT ½ CUP

- 1½ cups loosely packed baby arugula
- ½ cup loosely packed fresh basil leaves
- 2 tablespoons roughly chopped toasted walnuts
- 1 garlic clove
- ½ teaspoon finely grated lemon zest
- ¼ cup extra-virgin olive oil
  Kosher salt
  Ground black pepper

1. In a food processor or blender combine the arugula, basil, walnuts, garlic, and lemon zest and pulse until coarsely chopped. With the machine running, gradually add the oil and process until well blended. Season with salt and pepper.

Access the grocery list for these sauce recipes on your mobile device. timetogrill.mobi.

// dressings

Dressings serve many of the same purposes as sauces. Essentially they coat grilled and non-grilled ingredients in layers of moist, delicious flavors. But dressings tend to be simpler than sauces, because usually the ingredients require no cooking at all. You just mix them in a bowl or blender. Any of these can be made a few hours before you plan to serve them.

// CUMIN VINAIGRETTE

MAKES: ABOUT ¾ CUP

- 2 tablespoons red wine vinegar
- 1 teaspoon Dijon mustard
- 1 teaspoon honey
- 1 teaspoon ground cumin
- ¼ teaspoon crushed red pepper flakes
- ½ cup extra-virgin olive oil
- ½ teaspoon kosher salt
- ¼ teaspoon ground black pepper

1. In a small bowl or in a blender whisk or pulse the vinegar, mustard, honey, cumin, and red pepper flakes. Slowly drizzle in the oil while whisking until the dressing has emulsified. Season with the salt and pepper.

// RED WINE VINAIGRETTE

MAKES: ABOUT ½ CUP

- ¼ cup extra-virgin olive oil
- 2 tablespoons red wine vinegar
- 1 teaspoon minced garlic
- ½ teaspoon kosher salt
- ¼ teaspoon ground black pepper

1. In a small bowl whisk the ingredients.

// ORANGE-FENNEL DRESSING

MAKES: ABOUT ½ CUP
SPECIAL EQUIPMENT: SPICE MILL

- ¾ teaspoon fennel seed
- ¼ teaspoon kosher salt
- ⅓ cup extra-virgin olive oil
- 1 teaspoon finely grated orange zest
- 2 tablespoons fresh orange juice
- 1 tablespoon white wine vinegar
- 1 tablespoon minced shallot

1. Put the fennel seed and salt in a spice mill and process until finely ground. Pour into a small bowl and add the remaining ingredients. Whisk until emulsified.

// BLUE CHEESE DRESSING

MAKES: ABOUT ½ CUP

- ¼ cup crumbled blue cheese
- 2 tablespoons sour cream
- 2 tablespoons mayonnaise
- 1 tablespoon buttermilk
- ½ teaspoon cider vinegar

1. In a small bowl combine the ingredients. Cover and refrigerate until ready to serve.

// BASIL VINAIGRETTE

MAKES: ABOUT ⅔ CUP

- ½ cup loosely packed fresh basil leaves
- ¼ cup loosely packed fresh Italian parsley leaves and tender stems
- 1 tablespoon fresh lemon juice
- 1 tablespoon red wine vinegar
- 1 small garlic clove, minced
- ⅓ cup extra-virgin olive oil
- ½ teaspoon kosher salt
- ¼ teaspoon ground black pepper

1. In a food processor or blender pulse the basil, parsley, lemon juice, vinegar, and garlic until coarsely chopped. With the machine running, slowly add the oil. Transfer to a small bowl and season with the salt and pepper.

// HONEY-LIME DRESSING

MAKES: ABOUT 1 CUP

- ¼ cup fresh lime juice
- 3 tablespoons honey
- 2 tablespoons minced shallot
- 1 tablespoon Dijon mustard
- 1 tablespoon minced fresh rosemary leaves
- 1 teaspoon kosher salt
- ½ teaspoon ground black pepper
- ⅓ cup extra-virgin olive oil

1. In a small bowl whisk the lime juice, honey, shallot, mustard, rosemary, salt, and pepper. Slowly whisk in the oil to make a smooth dressing.

// DRESSING LEGEND

- good on red meat
- good on pork
- good on poultry
- good on seafood
- good on vegetables

// dressings

// HERB AND SHALLOT VINAIGRETTE

MAKES: ABOUT ⅔ CUP

- ¼ cup extra-virgin olive oil
- 3 tablespoons white wine vinegar
- 3 tablespoons finely chopped fresh herbs, such as basil, chives, Italian parsley, or your favorite combination
- 1 teaspoon minced shallot
- ½ teaspoon Dijon mustard
- ¼ teaspoon kosher salt
- ⅛ teaspoon ground black pepper

1. In a small bowl whisk the ingredients.

// CREAMY DILL DRESSING

MAKES: ABOUT ⅔ CUP

- ½ cup mayonnaise
- 2 tablespoons finely chopped fresh dill
- 2 teaspoons fresh lemon juice
- ½ teaspoon kosher salt
- ¼ teaspoon ground black pepper

1. In a small bowl whisk the ingredients.

// SESAME-SOY DRESSING

MAKES: ABOUT ½ CUP

- ¼ cup canola oil
- 2 tablespoons fresh lime juice
- 1 tablespoon soy sauce
- 2 teaspoons packed light brown sugar
- 2 teaspoons toasted sesame oil
- ½ teaspoon peeled, grated fresh ginger
- ¼ teaspoon crushed red pepper flakes

1. In a small bowl whisk the ingredients.

// LEMON-OREGANO DRESSING

MAKES: ABOUT 1 CUP

- ½ cup extra-virgin olive oil
- ¼ cup fresh lemon juice
- ¼ cup finely chopped fresh oregano leaves
- 1 tablespoon minced garlic
- 2 teaspoons coarsely ground black pepper
- ½ teaspoon kosher salt

1. In a small bowl whisk the ingredients.

// BUTTERMILK DRESSING

MAKES: ABOUT ¾ CUP

- ⅓ cup buttermilk
- ⅓ cup mayonnaise
- 2 tablespoons finely chopped fresh dill
- ½ teaspoon finely grated lemon zest
- 2 tablespoons fresh lemon juice
- 2 teaspoons granulated sugar
- 2 teaspoons Dijon mustard

1. In a small bowl whisk the ingredients.

// SHERRY VINAIGRETTE

MAKES: ABOUT 1¼ CUPS

- ¾ cup extra-virgin olive oil
- ¼ cup sherry vinegar
- 2 tablespoons minced shallot
- 1½ tablespoons finely chopped fresh marjoram leaves
- 1 tablespoon Dijon mustard
- ½ teaspoon kosher salt
- ¼ teaspoon ground black pepper

1. In a medium bowl whisk the ingredients.

// MINTY FETA DRESSING

MAKES: ABOUT ½ CUP

- 3 ounces feta cheese
- ¼ cup loosely packed fresh mint leaves
- 2 tablespoons extra-virgin olive oil
- 2 tablespoons water
- 1 tablespoon white wine vinegar
- 1 small garlic clove, roughly chopped
  Kosher salt
  Ground black pepper

1. In a food processor or blender combine all the ingredients except the salt and pepper. Blend until thick and smooth, scraping down the sides as needed. Season with salt and pepper.

// LEMON-MUSTARD DRESSING

MAKES: ABOUT 1 CUP

- 3 tablespoons red wine vinegar
- 1½ tablespoons minced shallot
- 2 teaspoons fresh lemon juice
- 1 tablespoon Dijon mustard
- ⅔ cup extra-virgin olive oil
  Kosher salt
  Ground black pepper

1. In a small bowl whisk the vinegar, shallot, lemon juice, and mustard. Slowly whisk in the oil until it is emulsified. Season with salt and pepper.

Access the grocery list for these dressing recipes on your mobile device. timetogrill.mobi.

APPETIZERS

Glazed and crunchy pecans are nice to have on hand for snacking. They can also add a sweet note to salads and even morning cereal. To make cleanup faster and easier, transfer the warm nuts to a cooling rack set over a sheet of aluminum foil. The warm dates make an impressive starter that marries the creaminess and saltiness of the blue cheese with the nuttiness of pecans all held together inside the sticky, gooey dates. Get yourself organized ahead of time by stuffing the dates and skewering them hours before grilling. For an extra-special appetizer, wrap them, without the oil, in prosciutto.

Balsamic Caramelized Toasted Pecans

SERVES: 👤👤👤👤👤👤

PREP TIME: 5 MINUTES

GRILLING TIME: 11 TO 15 MINUTES

SPECIAL EQUIPMENT: 12-INCH CAST-IRON SKILLET

¾ cup granulated sugar
¼ cup balsamic vinegar
1 pound raw pecan halves
½ teaspoon kosher salt

1. Prepare the grill for direct cooking over medium heat (350° to 450°F).

2. In a cast-iron skillet mix the sugar with the vinegar until the sugar is evenly moistened. Place the skillet on the grill over *direct medium heat*, close the lid, and cook until the sugar has dissolved and the mixture comes to a strong simmer, 5 to 7 minutes, stirring occasionally.

3. Add the pecans, stir to coat them evenly, and continue cooking over *direct medium heat*, with the lid closed, until the liquid has reduced to a thick glaze that coats the nuts and almost no liquid remains on the bottom of the skillet, 6 to 8 minutes. Sprinkle the salt over the pecans and stir to coat evenly. Carefully transfer the nuts to a cooling rack, spreading them into one thin layer.

4. Let the nuts cool for 10 minutes, then break apart the clusters into individual nuts. Let cool completely, and then serve. Can be stored in an airtight container for up to 3 days.

Access the grocery list for this recipe on your mobile device. timetogrill.mobi.

Warm Dates Stuffed with Blue Cheese and Pecans

SERVES: ♈♈♈♈♈♈

PREP TIME: **20** MINUTES

GRILLING TIME: ABOUT **1** MINUTE

SPECIAL EQUIPMENT: 12 METAL OR BAMBOO COCKTAIL SKEWERS (IF USING BAMBOO, SOAK IN WATER FOR AT LEAST 30 MINUTES)

// GLAZE
1 cup balsamic vinegar
½ cup granulated sugar

// DATES
3 ounces soft blue cheese
½ cup finely chopped pecans (about 2 ounces)
24 medjool dates, about 1 pound
Canola oil spray

1. **Prepare the grill for direct cooking over medium heat (350° to 450°F).**

2. **In a small saucepan combine the vinegar and sugar.** Bring to a simmer and cook until the mixture coats the back of a spoon, about 10 minutes, stirring occasionally. Set aside.

3. **In a small bowl mash the blue cheese and pecans together with a fork.** Make a small slice the length of each date and pull out the pit. Stuff each date with about 1 teaspoon of the cheese mixture, pressing it closed as much as possible. Thread two dates on each skewer so that the skewer goes through both halves of each date. Lightly spray with the canola oil.

4. **Brush the cooking grates clean.** Grill the dates over *direct medium heat*, with the lid closed, until heated through, about 1 minute.

5. **Arrange the dates on a platter and let cool for 10 minutes.** Serve the dates warm with the glaze.

Access the grocery list for this recipe on your mobile device. timetogrill.mobi.

SERVES: 👤👤👤👤👤👤

PREP TIME: **15** MINUTES

BOILING TIME: **5** TO **10** MINUTES

GRILLING TIME: **6** TO **8** MINUTES

Kosher salt
12 baby artichokes
    Juice of ½ lemon
½ cup plus 1 tablespoon extra-virgin olive
    oil, divided
    Ground black pepper

⅓ cup loosely packed fresh basil leaves
¼ cup freshly grated Parmigiano-
    Reggiano® cheese
2 tablespoons pine nuts,
    preferably toasted
1 garlic clove, minced

EASY

1. Bring a medium saucepan of lightly salted water to a boil. Rinse the artichokes under cold running water. Snap off the dark green outer leaves of the artichokes to reveal the yellowish leaves with pale green tips. Lay each artichoke on its side. With a sharp knife cut off the stem end and the sharp tip of each artichoke. Cut each artichoke in half lengthwise. Pare off the green skin from the base and stem. After each artichoke is trimmed, place in a medium bowl of water mixed with lemon juice.

2. Prepare the grill for direct cooking over medium heat (350° to 450°F).

3. Drain the artichokes. Cook in the boiling water just until tender when pierced with the tip of a knife, 5 to 10 minutes. Drain and rinse under cold water. Transfer to a bowl and toss with 1 tablespoon of the oil. Season with salt and pepper.

The beauty of baby artichokes is that each one is so tender that you can eat the whole thing, meaning you don't need to bother scooping out the purplish chokes. Grilling brings out the natural sweetness of artichokes, which is delicious with something rich like this basil dipping oil. The crab fondue is also rich and lends itself well to a party. You can serve the fondue in one bowl to share or in a small, single ramekin for each person. Either way, provide toothpicks or small forks to spear the artichokes so your guests don't have to use their fingers. If baby artichokes are not in season, use artichoke hearts for either recipe.

Baby Artichokes
WITH BASIL OIL

4. In a food processor pulse the basil, cheese, pine nuts, and garlic until the basil is minced. With the machine running, add the remaining ½ cup oil through the feed tube. Season with ¼ teaspoon salt and ⅛ teaspoon pepper. Pour into a small bowl.

5. Brush the cooking grates clean. Grill the artichokes over *direct medium heat*, with the lid closed as much as possible, until golden brown, 6 to 8 minutes, turning occasionally. Remove from the grill and serve warm with the dip.

Access the grocery list for this recipe on your mobile device. timetogrill.mobi.

1. **Bring a medium saucepan of lightly salted water to a boil.** Rinse the artichokes under cold running water. Snap off the dark green outer leaves of the artichokes to reveal the yellowish leaves with pale green tips. Lay each artichoke on its side. With a sharp knife cut off the stem end and the sharp tip of each artichoke. Cut each artichoke in half lengthwise. Pare off the green skin from the base and stem. After each artichoke is trimmed, place in a medium bowl of water mixed with the juice of one-half of the lemon. Juice the other lemon half and set aside to use for the dip.

2. **Prepare the grill for direct cooking over medium heat (350° to 450°F).**

3. **Drain the artichokes.** Cook in the boiling water just until tender when pierced with the tip of a knife, 5 to 10 minutes. Drain and rinse under cold water. Transfer to a bowl and toss with the oil. Season with salt and pepper.

4. **Brush the cooking grates clean.** Grill the artichokes over *direct medium heat*, with the lid closed as much as possible, until golden brown, 6 to 8 minutes, turning occasionally. Remove from the grill and set aside while you make the fondue.

5. **In a medium saucepan over medium-low heat, melt the butter.** Whisk in the flour and cook, without browning, for 1 to 2 minutes, whisking often. Add the milk and bring to a simmer while whisking over medium heat. Cook until the mixture thickens and the flour taste has cooked out, about 10 minutes, whisking occasionally. Reduce the heat to low and keep warm. Rinse the crabmeat in a sieve. Add the crabmeat, cheese, Tabasco, basil, and 1 teaspoon of the reserved lemon juice. Season with salt and pepper. Stir to combine. Pour into a small bowl and serve with the baby artichokes.

Access the grocery list for this recipe on your mobile device. timetogrill.mobi.

Baby Artichokes
WITH CRAB FONDUE

SERVES: 👤👤👤👤👤👤

PREP TIME: **20** MINUTES

BOILING TIME: **5** TO **10** MINUTES

GRILLING TIME: **6** TO **8** MINUTES

Kosher salt
12 baby artichokes
 1 lemon
 1 tablespoon extra-virgin olive oil
    Ground black pepper

// FONDUE
 1 tablespoon unsalted butter
 1 tablespoon all-purpose flour
1½ cups whole milk
 6 ounces canned crabmeat,
    any cartilage removed
½ cup freshly grated Parmigiano-
    Reggiano® cheese
3–4 dashes Tabasco® sauce
 2 tablespoons finely chopped fresh
    basil leaves

Roasting whole peppers on the grill involves turning them every few minutes to blacken their skins evenly. It works great, but the technique here of cutting the peppers open before grilling them speeds up the procedure, as they don't need turning. Once roasted and peeled, they can be turned into a colorful and appetizing salad with Mediterranean flavors that you can serve warm or at room temperature. Or take the same roasted peppers and roll them up with good tuna and serve them with greens as a first course or light lunch. The roulades fit nicely on an antipasto platter or on toasted bread slices as hors d'oeuvres. For the most authentic Italian flavor, use tuna packed in olive oil.

Roasted Red Pepper Salad
WITH PINE NUTS

SERVES: 👤👤👤👤👤👤

PREP TIME: 15 MINUTES

GRILLING TIME: 6 TO 8 MINUTES

6 medium bell peppers, preferably 2 red, 2 yellow, and 2 orange
2 tablespoons pine nuts
2 teaspoons red wine vinegar
1 garlic clove, minced
3 tablespoons extra-virgin olive oil
¼ teaspoon kosher salt
¼ teaspoon ground black pepper
2 tablespoons nonpareil capers, rinsed
1 tablespoon chopped fresh oregano leaves

1. **Prepare the grill for direct cooking over high heat (450° to 550°F).**

2. **Working with one pepper at a time, use a sharp knife to cut off the top and bottom of each pepper to make "lids."** Remove and discard the stem. Cut each pepper down the side, and open each up into a large strip. Cut away the ribs and seeds (see page 15).

3. **Brush the cooking grates clean.** Grill the pepper strips and lids, shiny skin side down, over *direct high heat*, with the lid closed, until the skin is blackened and blistered, 6 to 8 minutes (do not turn). Place the pepper strips in a bowl and cover with plastic wrap to trap the steam. Let stand for 5 to 10 minutes.

4. **Preheat a small skillet over medium heat.** Add the pine nuts and cook until toasted, about 3 minutes, stirring often. Transfer to a plate.

5. **Remove the peppers from the bowl and peel away and discard the charred skins.** Cut the long pepper strips into 1-inch-wide pieces and coarsely chop the "lids." Arrange on a platter.

6. **In a small bowl whisk the vinegar and garlic.** Gradually whisk in the oil, and then season with the salt and pepper. Drizzle the vinaigrette over the peppers. Top with the toasted pine nuts, capers, and oregano. Serve warm or at room temperature.

Access the grocery list for this recipe on your mobile device. timetogrill.mobi.

SERVES: 🧍🧍🧍🧍🧍🧍

PREP TIME: **30** MINUTES

GRILLING TIME: **6** TO **8** MINUTES

2 cans (5 ounces each) chunk light tuna in olive oil, drained

2 tablespoons nonpareil capers, rinsed

2 tablespoons minced red onion

1 tablespoon chopped fresh oregano leaves
Zest and juice of 1 lemon, divided

¼ teaspoon crushed red pepper flakes
Kosher salt

6 medium bell peppers, preferably 2 red, 2 yellow, and 2 orange

// VINAIGRETTE

2 tablespoons fresh lemon juice

¼ teaspoon ground black pepper

¼ cup extra-virgin olive oil

5 ounces mixed spring greens (mesclun)

 Roasted Red Pepper Roulades
WITH ITALIAN TUNA

1. Prepare the grill for direct cooking over high heat (450° to 550°F).

2. In a medium bowl flake the tuna with a fork and then mix in the capers, onion, oregano, lemon zest, and red pepper flakes. Season with salt and set aside.

3. Working with one pepper at a time, use a sharp knife to cut off the top and bottom of each pepper (save for another use). Cut each pepper down the side, and open each up into a large strip. Cut away the ribs and seeds (see page 15).

4. Brush the cooking grates clean. Grill the pepper strips, shiny skin side down, over *direct high heat*, with the lid closed, until the skin is blackened and blistered, 6 to 8 minutes (do not turn). Place the peppers in a bowl and cover with plastic wrap to trap the steam. Let stand for 5 to 10 minutes.

5. Remove the peppers from the bowl and peel away and discard the charred skins. Cut each pepper strip in half to make 12 rectangles about 3 inches long. Place in a bowl and drizzle with the juice of one lemon to coat all the peppers. Spread the tuna mixture evenly among the pepper strips. Roll up the pepper strips and secure with

toothpicks. Transfer to a plate, cover with plastic wrap, and refrigerate for at least 15 minutes or up to 12 hours.

6. In a small bowl whisk the lemon juice, pepper, and ¼ teaspoon salt. Gradually whisk in the oil. In a large bowl toss the greens with half of the vinaigrette.

7. To serve, divide the dressed greens and roulade pieces evenly among six serving plates. Drizzle the roulades with the remaining vinaigrette.

Access the grocery list for this recipe on your mobile device. timetogrill.mobi.

You are probably aware of how acidic liquids like lime juice can essentially "cook" raw fish for a Latin American dish called seviche, which is often flavored with tomatoes, onions, and herbs. Here that idea gets an added dimension of flavor from the grill, as halibut spends a few minutes over searing hot flames before being broken into pieces and acidified. You can also take grilled halibut in a completely different (Vietnamese) direction by wrapping it in rice paper with very thinly sliced vegetables and herbs, and dipping the rolls in a lemongrass-and-lime sauce. Slicing the vegetables by hand is very time consuming, but a plastic mandoline cutter will do the job in just a few minutes.

1. **Prepare the grill for direct cooking over high heat (450° to 550°F).**

2. **Brush the halibut fillets on both sides with oil.**

3. **Brush the cooking grates clean.** Grill the halibut over *direct high heat*, with the lid closed as much as possible, just long enough to sear both sides, 4 to 5 minutes, turning once. Remove from the grill and let cool. Break into ½-inch pieces and place in a bowl with ¾ cup lime juice, or enough to cover the fish. Cover and refrigerate for 2 hours or until the fish is opaque, stirring once or twice.

4. **Drain and discard the liquid from the bowl and then stir in the remaining ingredients (if not serving immediately, add radishes just before serving to keep the seviche from turning pink).** Serve immediately or cover and chill for several hours. Serve cold with tortilla chips.

Access the grocery list for this recipe on your mobile device. timetogrill.mobi.

Grilled Halibut Seviche

SERVES: 🧍🧍🧍🧍 TO 🧍🧍🧍🧍🧍🧍

PREP TIME: **20** MINUTES

MARINATING TIME: ABOUT **2** HOURS

GRILLING TIME: **4** TO **5** MINUTES

EASY

1	pound skinless halibut fillets, about 1 inch thick
	Extra-virgin olive oil
¾–1	cup fresh lime juice (from 6 to 8 limes)
1	medium tomato, seeded and diced
⅓	cup minced red onion
3	small radishes, trimmed and cut into very thin wedges
½–1	jalapeño chile pepper, stemmed, seeded, and minced
1	garlic clove, minced
¼	teaspoon kosher salt
⅛	teaspoon granulated sugar
1	bag (12 ounces) tortilla chips

Summer Rolls
WITH HALIBUT, LEMONGRASS, AND RADISHES

SERVES: 🚶🚶🚶🚶 TO 🚶🚶🚶🚶🚶🚶

PREP TIME: **45** MINUTES

GRILLING TIME: **6** TO **7** MINUTES

// SPRING ROLLS

12 ounces halibut fillets, about 1 inch thick
3 tablespoons hot chili-garlic sauce, such as Sriracha, divided
 Extra-virgin olive oil
8 large round rice paper wrappers
1 English cucumber, cut into very thin julienne strips
1 carrot, cut into very thin julienne strips
2 radishes, cut into very thin julienne strips
2 scallions (white and light green parts only), cut into very thin julienne strips
3 ounces roughly chopped lettuce leaves (2 cups)
3 tablespoons chopped fresh mint leaves
3 tablespoons chopped fresh cilantro leaves

// SAUCE

½ cup fresh lime juice (from about 4 limes)
2 tablespoons granulated sugar
4½ teaspoons fish sauce *or* 1 tablespoon soy sauce
1 tablespoon minced lemongrass
1 teaspoon peeled, grated fresh ginger
1 garlic clove, minced

!

// Rice paper wrappers will stick together once softened in water. Soak them one at a time as you're assembling, then separate the prepared rolls with plastic wrap to avoid any sticking.

1. Prepare the grill for direct cooking over high heat (450° to 550°F).

2. Brush the fillets on both sides with 2 tablespoons of the chili-garlic sauce and then brush with oil.

3. Brush the cooking grates clean. Grill the fillets over *direct high heat*, with the lid closed as much as possible, until you can lift them off the cooking grate without sticking, about 4 minutes for steaks, slightly less for fillets. Turn the fillets over and cook until the center is opaque, 2 to 3 minutes. Remove and discard any skin. Break the fish into ½-inch chunks. Lightly toss with the remaining 1 tablespoon of chili-garlic sauce.

4. To assemble the spring rolls, work with one rice paper wrapper at a time. Soak the wrapper in hot (but not boiling) water for 30 seconds, or until softened. Carefully lift out of the water. Place on a cutting board, blot dry, and place a few pieces of halibut in a horizontal line just below the center of the wrap. Top the halibut with the julienned vegetables, lettuce, mint, and cilantro. Fold the bottom of the wrapper over the filling and then fold in the sides; roll up tightly. Repeat with the remaining wrappers and fillings. Rolls may be covered and refrigerated for several hours at this point.

5. In a small bowl combine the sauce ingredients. Cut the spring rolls in half on the bias, and serve with the sauce for dipping.

Access the grocery list for this recipe on your mobile device. timetogrill.mobi.

Calamari, also known as squid, cooks up tender and tasty in just a few minutes, which is obviously convenient, but the real key for saving time in these recipes is buying the tubes and tentacles already cleaned and skinned. On a hot grill the tubes tend to curl up and shrink, so to help prevent that, you should either lay foil-wrapped bricks on top of them while they are grilling, as described in the easy recipe, or score them with a knife beforehand, as described in the adventurous recipe.

SERVES: 🧍🧍🧍🧍 TO 🧍🧍🧍🧍🧍🧍

PREP TIME: **15** MINUTES

GRILLING TIME: **2** TO **4** MINUTES
PER BATCH

SPECIAL EQUIPMENT:
2 FOIL-WRAPPED BRICKS

// SAUCE

- 1 medium navel orange, about 8 ounces
- 2 tablespoons white wine vinegar
- 1 tablespoon Dijon mustard
  Extra-virgin olive oil
  Kosher salt

- 2 pounds calamari, tubes and tentacles, cleaned and patted dry
- ½ teaspoon ground black pepper

- 2 medium navel oranges, each about 8 ounces, cut crosswise into ¼-inch slices

Calamari
WITH ORANGE DIPPING SAUCE

1. Slice off the top and bottom of one orange. Stand the orange on one flat end and, using a sharp paring knife, slice off the rind and all the whitish pith in curved, vertical strips. Rotate the orange as you go, following the curve as you slice downward. Cut the orange in half and remove any seeds. In a blender or food processor whirl the orange halves with the vinegar and mustard. With the motor running, slowly add in ¾ cup oil and process until the sauce is smooth and emulsified. Season with ½ teaspoon salt.

2. Prepare the grill for direct cooking over high heat (450° to 550°F).

3. Place the calamari in a bowl. Add 3 tablespoons oil, 1 teaspoon salt, and the pepper and toss to coat evenly.

4. Brush the cooking grates clean. Making two rows, place about four calamari tubes in a line over *direct high heat* so they can be weighted under the bricks. Place the bricks on top of the tubes, with the smooth side of the foil facing down, and grill, with the lid closed as much as possible, until the tubes easily lift off the cooking grate, 1 to 2 minutes. Wearing insulated barbecue mitts and using tongs, carefully tilt the bricks onto their sides off of the tubes. Turn the tubes over, and set the bricks back in place over the tubes. Close the lid and grill for an additional 1 to 2 minutes. Transfer the tubes to a platter. Repeat with the remaining tubes, brushing the cooking grates clean after each batch. At the same time, grill the tentacles and orange slices over *direct high heat* beside the bricks for about 4 minutes, turning once. Serve the calamari warm with the sauce and grilled orange slices.

Access the grocery list for this recipe on your mobile device. timetogrill.mobi.

SERVES: 🧍🧍🧍🧍 TO 🧍🧍🧍🧍🧍🧍

PREP TIME: **25** MINUTES

GRILLING TIME: **2** TO **4** MINUTES

// VINAIGRETTE

- 2 medium jalapeño chile peppers, cut in half lengthwise, seeds and veins removed
- 1 tablespoon finely grated orange zest
- ¼ cup fresh orange juice
- 2 tablespoons white wine vinegar
- ½ teaspoon paprika
  Kosher salt
  Extra-virgin olive oil

- 1 can (15 ounces) chickpeas (garbanzo beans), rinsed
- 1 cup small cherry or grape tomatoes, each one cut in half
- 1 whole shallot, thinly sliced into rings

- 1½ pounds calamari, tubes and tentacles, cleaned and patted dry
- ½ teaspoon ground black pepper

- ¼ cup roughly chopped fresh mint leaves

Spicy Calamari and Chickpea Salad
WITH ORANGE VINAIGRETTE

1. In a food processor or blender process the jalapeños until finely chopped. Add the orange zest and juice, vinegar, paprika, and 2 teaspoons salt. Process to combine. With the motor running, slowly add in ¼ cup oil and process until the vinaigrette is smooth and emulsified.

2. Prepare the grill for direct cooking over high heat (450° to 550°F).

3. In a large bowl combine the chickpeas, tomatoes, and shallot. Toss with ¼ cup of the vinaigrette and set aside.

4. Slide a knife into each tube and make horizontal cuts on one side of the calamari (the knife inside the tube allows you to score each tube without cutting all the way through). Place the calamari in a bowl. Add 2 tablespoons oil, 1 teaspoon salt, and the pepper and toss to coat evenly.

5. Brush the cooking grates clean. Grill the calamari over *direct high heat*, with the lid closed as much as possible, until opaque and cooked through, 2 to 4 minutes, turning once. Remove from the grill and slice the tubes into ½-inch rings. Add the tubes and tentacles to the salad and drizzle with the remaining vinaigrette. Toss gently to combine. Top with the mint. Serve immediately.

Access the grocery list for this recipe on your mobile device. timetogrill.mobi.

Sweet and salty create a forever-popular combination that you can put together in about fifteen minutes or about thirty minutes, depending on which recipe you pick here. The quicker appetizer features grilled pears and grilled prosciutto (your sweet and salty elements) stacked on toasted bread smeared with ricotta and blue cheeses. The slightly longer recipe puts grilled, diced pears in a simmering chutney with cranberries, lemon, and cinnamon. The sweet chutney works as a dunking sauce for grilled shrimp wrapped in prosciutto. Make the chutney as far in advance as you like, but the shrimp is best served hot off the grill.

Pear and Prosciutto Bruschetta

SERVES: 6 TO 8

PREP TIME: 10 MINUTES

GRILLING TIME: 9 TO 12 MINUTES

2 ripe pears, such as Bosc, about ¾ pound total
1 tablespoon fresh lemon juice
Extra-virgin olive oil
1 baguette, cut into 20 slices
4 thin slices prosciutto

1 cup ricotta cheese
⅓ cup crumbled blue cheese
3 tablespoons honey

1. **Prepare the grill for direct cooking over medium heat (350° to 450°F).**

2. **Peel the pears, cut them into quarters, and core them.** Put the pears in a medium bowl, add the lemon juice, and toss to coat. Lightly brush the pears on all sides with oil.

3. **Lightly brush one side of each baguette slice with oil.**

4. **Brush the cooking grates clean.** Grill the pears over *direct medium heat*, with the lid closed as much as possible, until crisp-tender, 8 to 10 minutes, turning occasionally. Remove from the grill and cut each pear quarter into about eight slices.

5. **Grill the baguette slices and the prosciutto over *direct medium heat*, with the lid open, until the bread is lightly toasted (grill one side only) and the prosciutto is crisp, 1 to 2 minutes.** Remove from the grill and chop the prosciutto.

6. **In a small bowl combine the ricotta and blue cheese.** Spread about 1 tablespoon of the cheese mixture on the grilled side of each baguette slice. Place about three pear slices on top of the cheese and add some chopped prosciutto. Finish with a drizzle of honey.

Access the grocery list for this recipe on your mobile device. timetogrill.mobi.

EASY

SERVES: 6 TO 8

PREP TIME: **20** MINUTES, PLUS 20 TO 30 MINUTES FOR THE CHUTNEY

GRILLING TIME: **10** TO **14** MINUTES

// CHUTNEY

3–4 ripe pears, such as Bosc, about 1½ pounds total
    Extra-virgin olive oil
½ cup packed brown sugar
⅓ cup dried cranberries
¼ cup finely chopped shallot
¼ cup sherry vinegar
2 tablespoons grated lemon zest
2 tablespoons fresh lemon juice
1 tablespoon minced crystallized ginger
1 tablespoon unsalted butter
1 cinnamon stick
½ teaspoon kosher salt
⅛ teaspoon ground cayenne pepper

4 ounces prosciutto, about 10 slices
1 pound extra-large shrimp (16/20 count), peeled and deveined, tails left on

 # Prosciutto-Wrapped Shrimp
WITH PEAR CHUTNEY

1. Prepare the grill for direct cooking over medium heat (350° to 450°F).

2. Peel the pears, cut them into quarters, core them, and lightly brush all sides with oil.

3. Brush the cooking grates clean. Grill the pears over *direct medium heat*, with the lid closed as much as possible, until crisp-tender, 8 to 10 minutes, turning once or twice. Remove from the grill and, when cool enough to handle, put them in a food processor and pulse about 10 times (or cut them into a small dice). In a medium saucepan over medium heat, combine the pears and the rest of the chutney ingredients. Cook until slightly thickened, 20 to 30 minutes, stirring occasionally. Cool to room temperature.

4. Increase the temperature of the grill to high heat (450° to 550°F).

5. Cut the prosciutto slices in half lengthwise. Starting at one end, lay the shrimp on the prosciutto and roll the prosciutto around the shrimp. Lightly brush with oil.

6. Grill the shrimp over *direct high heat*, with the lid closed as much as possible, until lightly charred, firm to the touch, and just turning opaque in the center, 2 to 4 minutes. Remove from the grill and serve warm with the chutney.

Access the grocery list for this recipe on your mobile device. timetogrill.mobi.

Oysters need only a few minutes on the grill to warm up their briny juices. How long it takes to get them to the grill depends mostly on how quickly you can shuck them (open their shells). The keys there are to save as much of the natural oyster juices as possible and to prevent any pieces of broken shell from falling into the oysters. In the first recipe even simpler accompaniments would be lemon wedges, hot sauce, and cocktail sauce. The other recipe is a take on a New Orleans classic called Oysters Rockefeller, for which the oysters are traditionally broiled on the half shell with sautéed spinach and bread crumbs. This liberated version is done on the grill with Parmesan cheese and crispy bacon.

SERVES: 👤👤👤👤 TO 👤👤👤👤👤👤

PREP TIME: 5 MINUTES, PLUS ABOUT 30 MINUTES TO SHUCK THE OYSTERS

GRILLING TIME: 2 TO 4 MINUTES

SPECIAL EQUIPMENT: OYSTER KNIFE

// MIGNONETTE

- 3 tablespoons finely chopped shallot
- ½ cup cider vinegar
- ¼ cup apple cider
- 1 tablespoon finely chopped fresh tarragon leaves
- ⅛ teaspoon kosher salt
- ⅛ teaspoon ground black pepper

- 2 dozen large, fresh oysters, each about 3 inches long

Oysters
WITH APPLE-TARRAGON MIGNONETTE

1. In a small bowl whisk the mignonette ingredients. Refrigerate until ready to use.

2. Shuck the oysters: Grip each oyster, flat side up, in a folded kitchen towel. Find the small opening between the shells near the hinge and pry it open with an oyster knife. Try not to spill the delicious juices, known as the "oyster liquor," in the bottom shell. Cut the oyster meat loose from the top shell and then loosen the oyster from the bottom shell by running the oyster knife carefully under the body. Discard the top, flatter shell, keeping the oyster and juices in the bottom, deeper shell.

3. Prepare the grill for direct cooking over high heat (450° to 550°F).

4. Brush the cooking grates clean. Grill the oysters, shell sides down, over **direct high heat**, with the lid closed as much as possible, until the oyster juices start to bubble and the edges curl, 2 to 4 minutes. (The oysters should be warmed but not actually cooked through.) Using tongs, carefully remove the oysters from the grill. Serve with the apple-tarragon mignonette.

Access the grocery list for this recipe on your mobile device. timetogrill.mobi.

SERVES: 🧍🧍🧍🧍 TO 🧍🧍🧍🧍🧍🧍

PREP TIME: **30** MINUTES, PLUS ABOUT 15 MINUTES TO SHUCK THE OYSTERS

GRILLING TIME: **2** TO **4** MINUTES

SPECIAL EQUIPMENT: OYSTER KNIFE

¼ cup finely chopped bacon (from 2 thick strips)
1 cup panko bread crumbs
2 tablespoons unsalted butter
2 tablespoons finely chopped shallot
2 teaspoons finely chopped garlic
¼ teaspoon kosher salt
⅛ teaspoon ground black pepper
1 bag (5 ounces) baby spinach, roughly chopped
1 teaspoon hot pepper sauce

1 dozen large, fresh oysters, each about 3 inches long

¼ cup finely grated Parmigiano-Reggiano® cheese
2 tablespoons finely chopped fresh tarragon leaves
Finely grated zest and juice of ½ lemon

Oysters
WITH SPINACH AND BACON BREAD CRUMBS

1. In a large skillet over medium heat, cook the bacon until crisp, about 8 minutes, stirring occasionally. Stir the bread crumbs into the skillet, letting them soak up the bacon fat. Cook until they are golden and crispy, about 2 minutes. Set aside.

2. In a large skillet over medium heat, melt the butter. Add the shallot and cook until soft, about 5 minutes, stirring occasionally. Add the garlic, salt, and pepper, and cook for 1 minute, stirring occasionally. Add the spinach and cook until completely wilted, folding the leaves over with tongs as you go, and then cook until all the liquid has evaporated, about 5 minutes. Add the hot sauce, mix, and set aside.

3. Shuck the oysters: Grip each oyster, flat side up, in a folded kitchen towel. Find the small opening between the shells near the hinge and pry it open with an oyster knife. Try not to spill the delicious juices, known as the "oyster liquor," in the bottom shell. Cut the oyster meat loose from the top shell and then loosen the oyster from the bottom shell by running the oyster knife carefully under the body. Discard the top, flatter shell, keeping the oyster and juices in the bottom, deeper shell.

4. Prepare the grill for direct cooking over high heat (450° to 550°F).

5. Arrange the shucked oysters on a large sheet pan. Divide the spinach mixture between the oysters, spreading some right over the flesh of each oyster. Top with the bread crumb mixture, gently pressing it into the spinach to help it adhere. Evenly top each oyster with the cheese.

6. Brush the cooking grates clean. Grill the oysters, shell sides down, over **direct high heat**, with the lid closed as much as possible, until the bread crumbs have browned and the juices are bubbling, 2 to 4 minutes. Using tongs, carefully remove the oysters from the grill. Evenly top each oyster with tarragon, lemon zest, and lemon juice. Serve right away.

Access the grocery list for this recipe on your mobile device. timetogrill.mobi.

Not too long ago, there was a popular Bloody Mary variation made with clam juice. This first recipe revives this bright idea with a zippy sauce for clams hot off the grill. Similar flavors come to play in cioppino, a beloved fish stew first prepared by Italian fishermen in San Francisco, and often considered a cold-weather dish. But it is never better than in the summer, when red bell peppers and plum tomatoes, not to mention clams, are at their peak. The heat of grilling concentrates the fresh vegetable juices, adding incredible flavor to the broth. Don't despair if peppers and tomatoes are not in season. Substituting a twenty-eight-ounce can of diced tomatoes and bottled, fire-roasted red peppers will yield a somewhat lighter but still delicious sauce.

Clams
WITH BLOODY MARY COCKTAIL SAUCE

SERVES: 👤👤👤👤👤👤

PREP TIME: 10 MINUTES

GRILLING TIME: 10 TO 15 MINUTES

SPECIAL EQUIPMENT: LARGE DISPOSABLE FOIL PAN

EASY

1. Prepare the grill for direct cooking over medium heat (350° to 450°F).

2. In a small bowl combine the sauce ingredients. Cover and refrigerate until ready to serve.

3. Arrange the clams in a large disposable foil pan. Cover the pan tightly with heavy-duty aluminum foil (to trap the steam and cook the clams).

4. Brush the cooking grates clean. Set the pan over *direct medium heat*, close the lid, and cook for 10 minutes. Carefully lift the cover off the pan and check to see if the clams are open. If not, replace the foil, close the grill lid, and cook for 3 to 5 minutes longer.

5. Wearing barbecue mitts, carefully remove the pan from the grill, supporting the bottom with a sheet pan if necessary. Discard any unopened clams. Spoon equal amounts of the clams and their juices into deep bowls. Serve with the sauce for dipping, the lemon wedges, and plenty of crackers or crusty bread.

Access the grocery list for this recipe on your mobile device. timetogrill.mobi.

// SAUCE

  1 cup ketchup-style chili sauce
  1 small rib celery (with leaves), minced
  ¼ cup vodka
  1 tablespoon prepared horseradish
  ½ teaspoon Worcestershire sauce
  ⅛ teaspoon hot pepper sauce, such
     as Tabasco®

4–6 dozen littleneck clams, scrubbed under
    cold running water
  1 lemon, cut into wedges
    Soda crackers *or* crusty bread

Grilled Clam and Shrimp Cioppino

SERVES:

PREP TIME: **20** MINUTES

GRILLING TIME: **45** TO **48** MINUTES

SPECIAL EQUIPMENT: DUTCH OVEN OR OVENPROOF COVERED CASSEROLE

2½ pounds ripe plum tomatoes
1 large red bell pepper
1 pound large shrimp (21/30 count), peeled and deveined, tails left on
Extra-virgin olive oil
Kosher salt
Ground black pepper
3 ounces pancetta, diced
1 medium yellow onion, finely chopped
2 ribs celery, finely chopped
2 garlic cloves, minced
1 cup dry white wine
1 cup water
1 tablespoon tomato paste
¼ teaspoon crushed red pepper flakes
4 dozen littleneck or manila clams, each about 2 inches in diameter, scrubbed under cold running water

1. **Prepare the grill for direct cooking over high heat (450° to 550°F).**

2. **Brush the cooking grates clean.** Grill the tomatoes and pepper over **direct high heat**, with the lid closed as much as possible, until the tomato skins are blackened and split and the pepper skin is charred, 7 to 10 minutes for the tomatoes and 10 to 12 minutes for the peppers, turning occasionally to char all sides. As the vegetables are ready, transfer them to a platter. Let cool until they are easy to handle.

3. **Lightly brush the shrimp with oil and season evenly with salt and pepper.** Grill the shrimp over **direct high heat**, with the lid closed as much as possible, until almost cooked through, 2 to 3 minutes, turning once. Set aside.

4. **Reduce the temperature of the grill to medium heat (350° to 450°F).** Peel, core, and seed the tomatoes, working over a sieve set in a bowl to collect the juices. Discard the solids remaining in the sieve. Chop the tomatoes, and add any juices from the cutting board to the bowl. Peel, seed, and chop the bell pepper.

5. **Place an ovenproof Dutch oven on the grill over direct medium heat.** Add the pancetta and 1 tablespoon oil. Cook until the pancetta is lightly browned, about 6 minutes, stirring occasionally. Add the onion, celery, and garlic and cook until the onion is tender, about 5 minutes. Pour in the wine and cook for 1 minute. Add the tomatoes with their juices, the bell pepper, water, tomato paste, and red pepper flakes. Simmer until slightly reduced, about 10 minutes. Keep the lid closed as much as possible during grilling.

6. **Arrange the clams in the Dutch oven and cover with the pot lid.** Close the grill lid and cook until the clams have opened, about 10 minutes, stirring the clams once. Discard any clams that don't open. Add the shrimp and cook for another minute. Carefully remove the Dutch oven from the grill. Serve warm in soup bowls.

Access the grocery list for this recipe on your mobile device. timetogrill.mobi.

Chicken wings are a super simple way to begin a casual barbecue. All you really need to do is brown them over direct heat for ten minutes or so and then finish them over indirect heat for about the same length of time. If they cook over indirect heat for five or ten minutes more, no big deal. It's pretty hard to overcook them, and if any get a little too charred, use the sweet hot sauce here to gloss over the crispy edges. Satays feel a little more sophisticated, but because these feature lean breast meat, you should be vigilant about not overcooking them. Buying chicken tenders will save you the time required to slice the breasts in thin strips.

Chicken Wings
WITH HOT HONEY BARBECUE SAUCE

SERVES: 🍴🍴🍴🍴 TO 🍴🍴🍴🍴🍴🍴

PREP TIME: **10** MINUTES

GRILLING TIME: **20** TO **25** MINUTES

// SAUCE

¾ cup ketchup
¼ cup honey
2 tablespoons spicy brown mustard
3 tablespoons cider vinegar
1 teaspoon ground cayenne pepper

3 pounds chicken wings, each cut in half at the joint, wing tips removed
¾ teaspoon garlic powder
½ teaspoon kosher salt

1. Prepare the grill for direct and indirect cooking over medium heat (350° to 450°F).

2. In a small saucepan combine the sauce ingredients. Cook over medium heat until the sauce comes to a simmer, stirring occasionally. Simmer for about 30 seconds to blend in the honey, stirring often, and then remove the saucepan from the heat.

3. Season the chicken wings evenly with the garlic powder and salt.

4. Brush the cooking grates clean. Grill the wings over *direct medium heat*, with the lid closed as much as possible, until golden brown, 10 to 15 minutes, turning once or twice. Move the wings over *indirect medium heat* and continue grilling until the skin is dark brown and crisp and the meat is no longer pink at the bone, about 10 minutes more. During the final 5 minutes of grilling, brush the wings evenly with the sauce, turning once or twice. Serve warm.

Access the grocery list for this recipe on your mobile device. timetogrill.mobi.

SERVES: 👤👤👤👤 TO 👤👤👤👤👤👤

PREP TIME: **20** MINUTES

GRILLING TIME: **4** TO **6** MINUTES

SPECIAL EQUIPMENT: METAL
OR BAMBOO SKEWERS (IF USING
BAMBOO, SOAK IN WATER FOR AT
LEAST 30 MINUTES)

// GLAZE

¼ cup honey
¼ cup soy sauce
2 tablespoons rice vinegar
1 tablespoon peeled, grated fresh ginger
2 teaspoons minced garlic
½–1 teaspoon hot chili-garlic sauce,
such as Sriracha

2 pounds chicken breast tenders *or*
boneless, skinless chicken breasts, cut
into ½-inch strips
Vegetable oil
½ teaspoon kosher salt
½ teaspoon ground black pepper

1 lime, cut into wedges

// This glaze is also delicious on shrimp.
Mix it with a little mayonnaise to make
an interesting sandwich spread or
dressing for chicken or shrimp salad.

Honey-Ginger Chicken Satays

1. Prepare the grill for direct and indirect cooking over high heat (450° to 550°F).

2. In a small saucepan over medium-high heat, combine the glaze ingredients and bring to a boil. Reduce the heat to low and simmer for about 3 minutes. Set aside.

3. Thread the pieces of chicken lengthwise onto skewers, making sure the skewers run through the center of each piece. Lightly coat the chicken with oil and season evenly with the salt and pepper.

4. Brush the cooking grates clean. Grill the chicken over ***direct high heat***, with the lid closed as much as possible, until nicely marked, 2 to 3 minutes, turning once. Move the chicken over ***indirect high heat***, brush with the glaze on both sides, and continue grilling until the chicken is cooked through and the glaze looks glossy, 2 to 3 minutes, turning once. Remove from the grill and serve warm with the lime wedges.

Access the grocery list for this recipe on your mobile device. timetogrill.mobi.

RED MEAT

When you are making something as iconic as a hamburger with just a handful of ingredients, the quality of every ingredient is paramount, so buy the best you can. For example, rather than relying on a generic blue cheese, splurge on some English Stilton, Italian Gorgonzola, or Maytag blue from Iowa. The same principle holds true for the meatball recipe. Look for a true Greek feta cheese made from sheep's or goat's milk to use in the dressing. Inferior versions are made with cow's milk and they are not worth the cost savings.

SERVES:

PREP TIME: 15 MINUTES

GRILLING TIME: 6 TO 8 MINUTES

1½ pounds ground chuck (80% lean)
6 ounces coarsely crumbled blue cheese, divided
Kosher salt
Ground black pepper

8 slices red onion, each about ¼ inch thick and 3 inches in diameter
Extra-virgin olive oil
8 small soft rolls, cut in half
½ cup loosely packed baby arugula

Blue Cheese Burgers
WITH RED ONIONS

1. **Prepare the grill for direct cooking over medium heat (350° to 450°F).**

2. **Divide the ground chuck into eight equal portions.** Split each portion in half and shape into two patties, each 3 inches in diameter. Arrange eight patties on a work surface and place a tablespoon of the cheese in the center of each. Top with a second patty and squeeze the edges together, sealing the cheese inside. Season evenly with salt and pepper.

3. **Keeping the onion slices intact, brush them with oil and season with salt and pepper.**

4. **Brush the cooking grates clean.** Grill the patties and onion slices over **direct medium heat**, with the lid closed as much as possible, until the meat is cooked to medium and the onions are slightly charred, 6 to 8 minutes, turning once. During the last minute of grilling time, toast the cut side of the rolls over direct heat.

5. **Build the burgers with some arugula, a patty, more blue cheese, and an onion slice.** Serve warm.

Access the grocery list for this recipe on your mobile device. timetogrill.mobi.

Meatballs with Grilled Romaine
AND FETA DRESSING

SERVES: 4

PREP TIME: **30** MINUTES

GRILLING TIME: ABOUT **8** MINUTES

// MEATBALLS
- 1 pound ground chuck (80% lean)
- 1 cup grated mozzarella cheese (4 ounces)
- ½ cup dry bread crumbs
- 2 large eggs
- 2 tablespoons ketchup
  Kosher salt
  Ground black pepper

- 2 hearts of romaine, each cut in half lengthwise

// DRESSING
- ½ cup buttermilk
- ¼ cup mayonnaise
- 2 ounces feta cheese
  Juice of ½ lemon
- ½ teaspoon ground black pepper

- 1 tablespoon minced fresh chives
- 1 teaspoon minced fresh thyme leaves

1. **Prepare the grill for direct cooking over medium heat (350° to 450°F).**

2. **In a medium bowl using your hands, gently mix the meatball ingredients, including ½ teaspoon salt and ½ teaspoon pepper.** Do not overwork the mixture or the meatballs will be tough. Shape into 12 balls, and then flatten the meatballs with the palm of your hand.

3. **Drizzle oil on the cut sides of the romaine and season evenly with salt and pepper.**

4. **In a food processor combine the dressing ingredients and process until smooth.** Add the chives and thyme. Set aside.

5. **Brush the cooking grates clean.** Grill the meatballs and the romaine over *direct medium heat*, with the lid closed as much as possible, until the meatballs are cooked to medium doneness and the lettuce just starts to wilt and has nice grill marks, turning once. The meatballs will take about 8 minutes and the lettuce will take about 2 minutes. Remove from the grill as they are done.

6. **Spoon about ¼ cup of the dressing on each plate and top with a grilled romaine half and three meatballs.** Drizzle with a little more dressing and serve immediately.

Access the grocery list for this recipe on your mobile device. timetogrill.mobi.

No doubt you've had plenty of renditions of spaghetti and meatballs. Have you ever tried grilling the meatballs? When the meat drips a little fat into the sizzling hot grill, it creates an aromatic smoke that lifts an old, familiar dish to a new, more interesting level. And what about meat loaf? Chances are that your mother did not grill hers. It's fun to reinvent these old-time classics.

Spaghetti and Meatballs

SERVES: 4

PREP TIME: **15** MINUTES

GRILLING TIME: ABOUT **10** MINUTES

// MEATBALLS
- 1 pound ground chuck (80% lean)
- ½ cup panko bread crumbs
- 1 large egg
- 2 tablespoons finely chopped fresh Italian parsley leaves
- 1 tablespoon finely chopped fresh oregano leaves
- ½ teaspoon kosher salt
- ¼ teaspoon ground black pepper
- ¼ teaspoon garlic powder

- 1 jar (24 ounces) tomato-basil pasta sauce
- 1 pound dried spaghetti
  Freshly grated Parmigiano-Reggiano® cheese

1. Prepare the grill for direct cooking over medium heat (350° to 450°F).

2. Bring a large pot of water to a boil for the pasta.

3. In a large bowl thoroughly but gently blend the meatball ingredients. Using ¼ cup of the mixture for each, gently make eight meatballs slightly larger than a golf ball.

4. **Brush the cooking grates clean.** Grill the meatballs over *direct medium heat*, with the lid closed as much as possible, until cooked on all sides, about 10 minutes, turning two or three times.

5. **Meanwhile, in a 3- to 4-quart saucepan over low heat, heat the pasta sauce.** Cook the spaghetti in the large pot of boiling water according to package instructions. When the meatballs are done, add them to the hot pasta sauce and simmer gently while the pasta finishes cooking. Drain the pasta, toss it with the sauce and meatballs, and serve hot with freshly grated cheese.

Access the grocery list for this recipe on your mobile device. timetogrill.mobi.

EASY

SERVES: 👤👤👤👤👤👤

PREP TIME: **30** MINUTES

GRILLING TIME: **45** MINUTES TO **1** HOUR

SPECIAL EQUIPMENT:
9-BY-5-INCH LOAF PAN,
12-INCH CAST-IRON SKILLET

Extra-virgin olive oil
1 medium yellow onion, finely chopped
4 garlic cloves, minced
1½ tablespoons finely chopped fresh thyme leaves
1 tablespoon finely chopped fresh rosemary leaves
1 pound ground chuck (80% lean)
½ pound ground pork
½ pound ground lamb
1 cup panko bread crumbs
¾ cup freshly grated Parmigiano-Reggiano® cheese
1¼ cups canned tomato sauce, divided
2 large eggs
½ teaspoon kosher salt
¼ teaspoon ground black pepper

2 large tomatoes, about 1 pound total, roughly chopped
2 tablespoons dry red wine *or* balsamic vinegar
1 teaspoon crushed red pepper flakes
2 garlic cloves, minced

Not Your Mother's Meat Loaf

1. Prepare the grill for direct cooking over medium-low heat (300° to 400°F).

2. Heat a 12-inch cast-iron skillet on the stove top over medium heat. When hot, add 1 tablespoon oil and the onion and cook until the onion is soft, about 5 minutes, stirring occasionally. Add the garlic and herbs. Cook for another minute and then transfer the mixture to a large bowl. (No need to clean the skillet; it will be reused.) Add the ground chuck, pork, lamb, bread crumbs, cheese, ½ cup of the tomato sauce, the eggs, salt, and pepper to the bowl and blend well.

3. Line a 9-by-5-inch loaf pan by placing a 9-inch-wide strip of aluminum foil across the pan, leaving some foil hanging over the sides. There is no need to line the short ends of the pan. Pat the meat loaf into the lined pan. Brush the cooking grates clean. Turn the loaf pan upside-down onto the grill, lift off the loaf pan and carefully remove the foil by pulling gently on what was the foil overhang.

Grill the meat loaf over ***direct medium-low heat***, with the lid closed, until one side begins to brown, about 15 minutes.

4. Meanwhile, mix the remaining ¾ cup tomato sauce, the tomatoes, wine, red pepper flakes, garlic, and 1 tablespoon oil in the cast-iron skillet. Push the tomato chunks to the edges of the pan. Using a long spatula, lift the meat loaf off the grill and turn it into the cast-iron skillet, grilled side up. Spoon some of the sauce over the top of the meat loaf. Place the skillet over ***direct medium-low heat***, close the lid, and cook until the meat is cooked through and the sauce is thick, 30 to 45 minutes, spooning the sauce over the meat every 15 minutes. Wearing insulated barbecue mitts, carefully remove the skillet from the grill. Cut the meat loaf into thick slices and serve hot topped with the sauce.

Access the grocery list for this recipe on your mobile device. timetogrill.mobi.

Ordinary mushroom cheeseburgers put the mushroom on top, but this one has you finely chopping the portabello mushrooms and blending the pieces into the meat along with chopped roasted peppers and seasonings. The flavorful moisture of the vegetables makes for wonderfully juicy burgers. They taste even better with a relatively new condiment on supermarket shelves, sun-dried tomato spread. In place of lettuce, try baby arugula that's been drizzled with a little olive oil and balsamic vinegar. The arugula gives the burgers an extra peppery bite. If you prefer to forgo the bun altogether, use the bowled shape of portabello mushrooms to hold a filling that looks and tastes a lot like meat loaf draped in melted cheese.

Portabello Mushroom Cheeseburgers

SERVES: 👤👤👤👤

PREP TIME: **10** MINUTES

GRILLING TIME: **8** TO **10** MINUTES

// PATTIES

1½ pounds ground chuck (80% lean)

½ cup finely chopped
   portabello mushrooms

¼ cup finely chopped roasted red bell
   pepper (from a jar)

1 teaspoon dried Italian herb seasoning

1 teaspoon garlic salt

½ teaspoon ground black pepper

4 thin slices provolone cheese

4 ciabatta *or* hamburger rolls

¼ cup sun-dried tomato spread

4 leaves red or green lettuce

1. **Prepare the grill for direct cooking over high heat (450° to 550°F).**

2. **In a large bowl gently combine the patty ingredients and shape into four patties of equal size and thickness, each about ¾ inch thick.** With your thumb or the back of a spoon, make a shallow indentation about 1 inch wide in the center of each patty. This will help the patties cook evenly and prevent them from puffing on the grill.

3. **Brush the cooking grates clean.** Grill the patties over *direct high heat*, with the lid closed as much as possible, until cooked to medium doneness, 8 to 10 minutes, turning them once when the patties release easily from the grate without sticking. During the last minute of grilling time, place a slice of cheese on each patty to melt and toast the rolls, cut side down. Build each burger with sun-dried tomato spread and lettuce.

Access the grocery list for this recipe on your mobile device. timetogrill.mobi.

Beef and Sun-Dried Tomato Stuffed Mushrooms

SERVES: 👤👤👤👤

PREP TIME: **30** MINUTES

GRILLING TIME: **19** TO **26** MINUTES

// MARINADE

- 6 tablespoons extra-virgin olive oil
- 1 tablespoon balsamic vinegar
- ¾ teaspoon garlic salt
- ¼ teaspoon ground black pepper

- 4 large portabello mushrooms, each 4 to 5 inches in diameter

// FILLING

- 1 pound ground chuck (80% lean)
- ½ cup panko bread crumbs
- ¼ cup minced sweet onion
- 3 tablespoons finely chopped fresh parsley leaves
- 3 tablespoons finely chopped oil-packed sun-dried tomatoes
- 1 large egg
- 1 teaspoon Worcestershire sauce
- ½ teaspoon garlic salt
- ¼ teaspoon ground black pepper

- ½ cup grated fontina cheese (2 ounces)

!

// To extend the life of fresh herbs, place a damp paper towel in the bottom of a storage container. Place the herbs on top and seal the container.

1. In a medium bowl whisk all of the marinade ingredients.

2. Wipe the mushrooms clean with a damp cloth or paper towel. Remove and discard the stems. With a teaspoon, carefully scrape out and discard the gills from the mushroom caps. Place the mushrooms, gill side up, on a sheet pan and brush them on both sides with the marinade. Set aside at room temperature while you make the filling and prepare the grill for direct and indirect cooking over medium heat (350° to 450°F).

3. In a medium bowl gently combine the filling ingredients until evenly incorporated.

4. Brush the cooking grates clean. Grill the mushrooms, gill side down, over **direct medium heat**, with the lid closed, until the mushrooms begin to soften, 4 to 6 minutes. Turn the mushrooms over and move them over **indirect medium heat**. Spoon equal amounts of the filling on top of each mushroom and continue grilling until a thermometer inserted horizontally through the top of each registers 160°F, 15 to 20 minutes. During the last minute of grilling time, top each mushroom with an equal amount of the cheese. Remove from the grill and serve with grilled bread, if desired.

Access the grocery list for this recipe on your mobile device. timetogrill.mobi.

Green Chile Lamb Burgers

SERVES:

PREP TIME: **10** MINUTES

GRILLING TIME: **8** TO **10** MINUTES

// **PATTIES**
- 1 pound ground lamb
- ¼ cup canned diced green chiles, drained
- 1 tablespoon paprika
- 1 teaspoon crushed red pepper flakes
- 1 teaspoon kosher salt
- ½ teaspoon ground black pepper

- 4 onion buns
- 4 leaves Boston lettuce
- 1 beefsteak tomato, cut into 4 slices
  Mayonnaise (optional)

Ground lamb is just as quick and easy to grill as ground beef, yet people look past it day after day. It could be that they think the flavor is too gamy, but today's lamb is raised to taste much milder than it did even ten years ago. Mixed with some dry seasonings and pre-cooked chiles, it makes a nice alternative to hamburgers. If you have the time to dial up lamb burgers to another level altogether, try the adventurous recipe here, which blends ground lamb with sautéed chorizo (fresh pork sausage). Hours before grilling the burgers, arrange them on a sheet pan lined with plastic wrap, and refrigerate them. That way, after the burgers are grilled, you can peel off the plastic wrap and set your burgers on a clean, portable tray.

1. **Prepare the grill for direct cooking over medium heat (350° to 450°F).**

2. **In a large bowl gently mix the patty ingredients.** Shape the mixture into four patties of equal size and thickness, each about ¾ inch thick. With your thumb or the back of a spoon, make a shallow indentation about 1 inch wide in the center of each patty. This will help the patties cook evenly and prevent them from puffing on the grill.

3. **Brush the cooking grates clean.** Grill the patties over *direct medium heat*, with the lid closed as much as possible, until cooked to medium doneness, 8 to 10 minutes, turning once. During the last minute of grilling time, toast the buns over direct heat.

4. **Build the burgers with a lettuce leaf, a tomato slice, and mayonnaise, if desired.** Serve warm.

Access the grocery list for this recipe on your mobile device. timetogrill.mobi.

Lamb and Chorizo Burgers

WITH JACK CHEESE AND POBLANO CHILES

SERVES: 6

PREP TIME: 30 MINUTES

GRILLING TIME: 14 TO 18 MINUTES

// MAYONNAISE

- ½ cup mayonnaise
- ½ cup plain Greek yogurt
- 1 tablespoon finely grated lime zest
- 2 teaspoons fresh lime juice
- Kosher salt
- Ground black pepper

- 1 pound fresh (raw) pork chorizo sausages, casings removed, *or* bulk chorizo
- 1 pound ground lamb
- 2 tablespoons water
- Extra-virgin olive oil
- 3 large poblano chile peppers
- 12 thin slices Monterey Jack cheese
- 12 small pita pockets, tops cut off
- 6 thin slices sweet onion

1. **In a small bowl combine the mayonnaise ingredients.** Season with salt and pepper.

2. **In a heavy, medium skillet over medium heat, sauté the chorizo until it is cooked through, breaking the meat into ½-inch chunks, about 8 minutes, stirring occasionally.** Transfer the chorizo to a large sieve set over a bowl. Drain and reserve the drippings.

3. **Prepare the grill for direct cooking over medium-high heat (400° to 500°F).**

4. **In a large bowl combine the lamb, water, ½ teaspoon salt, ¼ teaspoon pepper, and 1 tablespoon of the chorizo drippings.** Mix thoroughly. Add the drained chorizo and blend gently, taking care not to overwork the mixture. Using wet hands, form the mixture into 12 patties, each about ½ inch thick. Lightly brush both sides with oil.

5. **Brush the cooking grates clean.** Grill the chiles over ***direct medium-high heat***, with the lid closed as much as possible, until charred and beginning to soften, 8 to 10 minutes, turning occasionally. Transfer the chiles to a bowl and cover with plastic wrap to trap the steam.

6. **Grill the patties over *direct medium-high heat*, with the lid closed as much as possible, until cooked to medium doneness, 6 to 8 minutes, turning once or twice.** During the last minute of grilling time, place a slice of cheese on top of each patty to melt.

7. **Remove the chiles from the bowl and peel off and discard the skin, stems, and seeds.** Cut each chile into four pieces. Serve the burgers in pita with the mayonnaise, a few rings of onion, and a slice of chile.

Access the grocery list for this recipe on your mobile device. timetogrill.mobi.

Kofta is a Turkish preparation of ground meat, usually lamb, mixed with herbs and spices, rolled into little balls or ovals, and then grilled or fried. The recipe here calls for lettuce to hold the grilled meat, but the kofta can also be served in pita bread like a falafel or lined up on a section of baguette like an Italian meatball sandwich. They can even be hors d'oeuvres served with the yogurt sauce for dipping. Feel free to shape the kofta one day ahead and keep them covered in the refrigerator. Seasoned lamb can also make a fantastic style of sausage to combine with tomatoes, eggplants, olives, and mozzarella cheese on grilled pizzas. Purchasing store-bought dough will save you hours of prep time. If you let the dough sit at room temperature for thirty minutes or so, it will be much easier to roll out.

Lamb Kofta

SERVES: 👤👤👤👤

PREP TIME: **15** MINUTES

GRILLING TIME: ABOUT **6** MINUTES

SPECIAL EQUIPMENT: 16 METAL OR BAMBOO SKEWERS (IF USING BAMBOO, SOAK IN WATER FOR AT LEAST 30 MINUTES)

1. In a medium bowl mix the yogurt, mint, and lemon juice.

2. Prepare the grill for direct cooking over medium-high heat (400° to 500°F).

3. In a large bowl combine the *kofta* ingredients, blending well. Wet your hands with water and shape rounded tablespoons of the mixture into 24 balls or ovals. Thread three *kofta* onto each skewer. Lightly brush with oil.

4. Brush the cooking grates clean. Grill the *kofta* over **direct medium-high heat**, with the lid closed as much as possible, until they are nicely charred on the outside and the centers are still slightly pink, about 6 minutes, turning once or twice. Remove from the grill.

5. Place two lettuce leaves on each of four plates. Slide three *kofta* onto each lettuce leaf. Serve warm with the mint yogurt.

Access the grocery list for this recipe on your mobile device. timetogrill.mobi.

// YOGURT
- ¾ cup plain Greek yogurt
- 1 tablespoon finely chopped fresh mint leaves
- 1 tablespoon fresh lemon juice

// KOFTA
- 1¼ pounds ground lamb
- 1 medium onion, coarsely grated
- 2½ teaspoons ground cumin
- 1¼ teaspoons kosher salt
- 3 large garlic cloves, minced
- ¾ teaspoon ground black pepper

- Vegetable oil
- 8 leaves romaine lettuce

SERVES: 👤👤👤👤

PREP TIME: **30** MINUTES

GRILLING TIME: **12** TO **20** MINUTES

// SAUSAGE

½	pound ground lamb
1	teaspoon fennel seed
1	teaspoon paprika
½	teaspoon ground cumin
½	teaspoon kosher salt
¼	teaspoon ground cayenne pepper

1¼ pounds pre-made pizza dough
    Vegetable oil

1	package (12 ounces) grape tomatoes
1	small globe eggplant, cut crosswise into ¼-inch slices
2	cups grated mozzarella cheese (8 ounces)
24	kalamata olives

 Lamb Sausage Pizzas

1. In a small skillet combine the sausage ingredients and sauté the mixture until the lamb is cooked through, about 10 minutes. Remove the sausage with a slotted spoon and set aside until ready to use.

2. Prepare the grill for direct cooking over medium heat (350° to 450°F).

3. Divide the dough into four equal pieces. Lightly brush four 9-inch squares of parchment paper on one side with oil. Using your fingers, flatten each piece of dough on a sheet of parchment paper to create four rounds. Each round should be about 8 inches in diameter and ¼ inch thick. Lightly brush the tops with oil. Let the rounds stand at room temperature for 5 to 10 minutes.

4. Brush the cooking grates clean. Grill the tomatoes and eggplant over **direct medium heat**, with the lid closed as much as possible, until the tomato skins burst and the flesh becomes very soft and the eggplant is tender, turning once or twice. The tomatoes will take about 5 minutes and the eggplant will take 8 to 10 minutes. Remove from the grill as they are done. Put the tomatoes in a bowl and crush with a spoon. When the eggplant is cool enough to handle, cut into a ½-inch dice.

5. Place the dough on the cooking grate with the paper sides facing up. Grill over **direct medium heat**, with the lid closed as much as possible, until the dough is well marked and firm on the underside, 2 to 5 minutes, rotating as needed for even cooking. Peel off and

discard the parchment paper. Transfer the crusts to a work surface with the grilled sides facing up.

6. Evenly divide the sausage, tomatoes, eggplant, cheese, and olives over the crusts. Return the pizzas to the grill and cook over **direct medium heat**, with the lid closed as much as possible, until the cheese is melted and the bottoms of the crusts are crisp, 2 to 5 minutes, rotating the pizzas occasionally for even cooking. Transfer to a cutting board and cut into wedges. Serve warm.

Access the grocery list for this recipe on your mobile device. timetogrill.mobi.

You've seen dozens of versions of North American hot dogs, arguably the easiest food ever to grill and one that lends itself easily to "accessorizing" with toppings and condiments. But have you seen all that South Americans do with cured sausage? One brilliant idea from the other hemisphere is to top them with a smooth guacamole followed by the crunch of slivered white onions and crushed potato chips. Or, with a bit more time, you can smother the dogs with a bacon-studded, chipotle-infused chili crowned with cheese.

1. Prepare the grill for direct cooking over medium heat (350° to 450°F).

2. Cut the avocados in half, remove the pits, and scoop the flesh into a medium bowl. Add the remaining guacamole ingredients and mash together with a fork. Cover with plastic wrap, placing the wrap directly on the surface of the guacamole to prevent it from browning. Refrigerate until ready to serve.

3. Cut a few shallow slashes in each hot dog.

4. Brush the cooking grates clean. Grill the hot dogs over *direct medium heat*, with the lid closed as much as possible, until lightly marked on the outside and hot all the way to the center, 5 to 7 minutes, turning occasionally. During the last minute of grilling time, toast the buns, cut sides down, over direct heat.

5. Place the hot dogs in buns. Top each with the guacamole, slivered onions, tomatoes, and crushed potato chips. Serve warm.

Access the grocery list for this recipe on your mobile device. timetogrill.mobi.

Hot Dogs with Avocado and Chips

EASY

SERVES: 8

PREP TIME: 10 MINUTES

GRILLING TIME: 5 TO 7 MINUTES

// GUACAMOLE

2 ripe Hass avocados
1 tablespoon fresh lime juice
½ teaspoon kosher salt
¼ teaspoon ground black pepper

8 all-beef hot dogs, each about 4 ounces
8 hot dog buns
1 small white onion, cut into slivers
2 ripe plum tomatoes, seeded and cut into ¼-inch dice
1 cup crushed potato chips

Hot Dogs with Bacon and Chipotle Chili

SERVES: 8

PREP TIME: 15 MINUTES, PLUS
ABOUT 20 MINUTES FOR THE CHILI

GRILLING TIME: 5 TO 7 MINUTES

// CHILI

- 2 slices bacon, finely chopped
- 1 medium white onion,
  finely chopped, divided
- 1 tablespoon minced jalapeño chile pepper
- 2 teaspoons minced garlic
- 1 pound ground sirloin (85% lean)
- 1 canned chipotle chile in adobo sauce,
  chopped, *or* 1 teaspoon chipotle
  chile powder
- 1 teaspoon smoked paprika
- ½ teaspoon ground cumin
- ½ teaspoon kosher salt
- 1 can (8 ounces) tomato sauce
- ½ cup lager beer *or* beef broth *or* water

- 8 all-beef hot dogs, each about 4 ounces
- 8 hot dog buns
- 1 cup grated sharp cheddar cheese
  (4 ounces)

1. In a large skillet over medium heat, heat the bacon and one-half of the onion until the bacon is crisp and browned, about 5 minutes, stirring occasionally. Add the jalapeño and garlic and cook until fragrant, about 1 minute. Add the ground sirloin and cook until the meat loses its raw look, about 5 minutes, stirring and breaking up the meat with the side of a spoon. Add the chipotle chile, paprika, cumin, and salt and mix well. Stir in the tomato sauce and beer and bring to a simmer. Reduce the heat to medium-low and simmer, stirring occasionally, until the liquid thickens, about 10 minutes. Keep the chili warm.

2. While the chili simmers, prepare the grill for direct and indirect cooking over medium heat (350° to 450°F).

4. Cut a few shallow slashes in each hot dog. Wrap the hot dog buns in a foil packet.

5. Brush the cooking grates clean. Grill the hot dogs over *direct medium heat*, with the lid closed as much as possible, until lightly marked on the outside and hot all the way to the center, 5 to 7 minutes, turning occasionally. During the last 3 minutes of grilling time, warm the packet with the buns over *indirect medium heat*.

6. Place the hot dogs in buns. Top each with chili, cheese, and the remaining chopped onion. Serve warm.

Access the grocery list for this recipe on your mobile device. timetogrill.mobi.

how charcoal // IS MADE

1   2   3

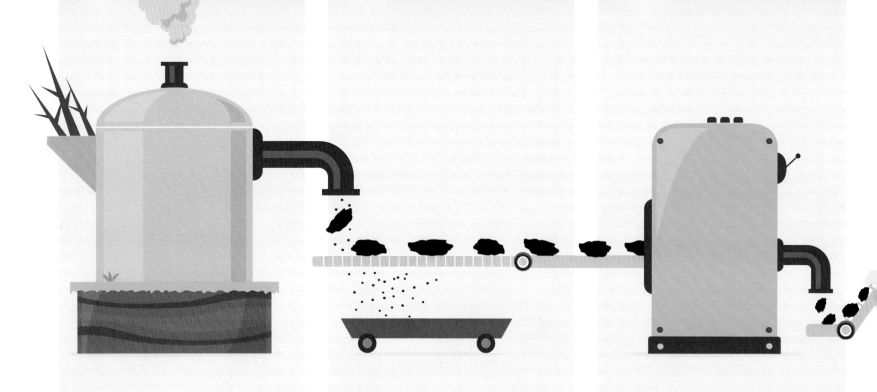

STEP 1
Hardwood logs are placed in an oxygen-deprived environment, like a kiln or underground pit. The logs are set on fire and covered loosely to allow a slow burn over several weeks.

STEP 2
Over time, the water and resins burn out of the log leaving behind big chunks of combustible carbon. These chunks are then broken into smaller lumps, hence the name "lump charcoal." This is also known as charwood.

STEP 3
To form the briquettes, the charcoal lumps are pulverized and mixed with sawdust and other binders such as starch (made from wheat or corn).

DID YOU KNOW ?

In the 1920s, Henry Ford invented a process that burned leftover scrap wood and sawdust from Model T manufacturing and turned it into charcoal briquettes.

Barbecuing began over a wood fire, which gives great flavor, but also has its drawbacks. A wood log fire tends to create huge amounts of smoke and often requires waiting up to an hour or more for the flames to die down and the embers to reach a manageable level of heat. Charcoal is essentially pre-burned wood, which means it reaches ideal grilling temperatures faster than wood and with much less smoke. There are two kinds of charcoal: lump and briquette.

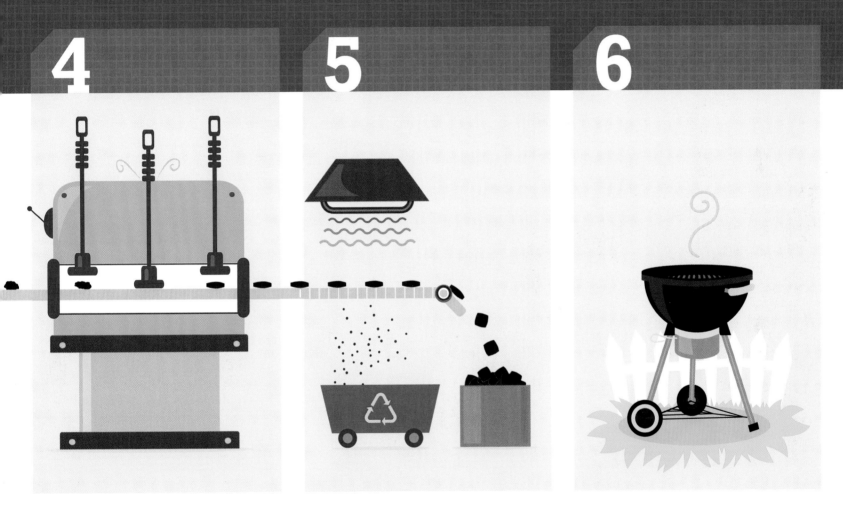

4

5

6

STEP 4
This mixture is poured into giant presses that use high pressure to form the mixture into pillow-shaped briquettes.

STEP 5
From there, the briquettes are dried and sent through a sifter to ensure no broken pieces go into packaging. All fragments and dust are collected and recycled through the process again.

Now the briquettes are ready for packaging and distribution to retailers everywhere.

STEP 6
Grilling enthusiasts around the world use charcoal briquettes to fuel the fire in their backyards—whether it's in a charcoal grill or a smoker. Charcoal provides a versatile fuel source that can be arranged and rearranged to create the perfect heat intensity inside a grill. Plus, it's affordable and ... well ... fun.

One of the surest and fastest ways to elevate the taste of steak is with a well-balanced dry rub. This one stars sultry, smoky ancho chile flavors in combination with the sweetness of brown sugar and the fragrance of Mexican oregano, which tends to be a little "mintier" than Mediterranean oregano—both taste great, so use whichever variety you have on hand. Now, if today you are feeling more adventurous, slather your steaks with an oregano-mustard paste before grilling, and drape them with those same ancho flavors in another form, which involves softening whole dried chiles in red wine and blending them into a smooth, mahogany-colored sauce.

Rib Eye Steaks
WITH ANCHO DRY RUB

SERVES: 🧍🧍🧍🧍

PREP TIME: **5** MINUTES

GRILLING TIME: **6** TO **8** MINUTES

// RUB
- 1 tablespoon ancho chile powder
- 2 teaspoons packed brown sugar
- 2 teaspoons kosher salt
- 1 teaspoon ground cumin
- 1 teaspoon dried Mexican oregano
- 1 teaspoon ground black pepper

- 4 boneless rib eye steaks, each 8 to 10 ounces and about 1 inch thick, trimmed of excess fat
  Extra-virgin olive oil

1. **Prepare the grill for direct cooking over high heat (450° to 550°F).**

2. **In a small bowl mix the rub ingredients.**

3. **Lightly coat the steaks on both sides with oil and season evenly with the rub.** Allow the steaks to stand at room temperature for 15 to 30 minutes before grilling.

4. **Brush the cooking grates clean.** Grill the steaks over *direct high heat*, with the lid closed as much as possible, until cooked to your desired doneness, 6 to 8 minutes for medium rare, turning once (if flare-ups occur, move the steaks temporarily over indirect heat). Remove from the grill and let rest for 3 to 5 minutes. Serve warm.

Access the grocery list for this recipe on your mobile device. timetogrill.mobi.

EASY

SERVES: 👤👤👤👤

PREP TIME: **15** MINUTES, PLUS ABOUT 30 MINUTES FOR THE SAUCE

GRILLING TIME: **6** TO **8** MINUTES

// SAUCE

1 medium dried ancho chile pepper, about ¼ ounce
1½ cups dry red wine
2 medium garlic cloves
½ cup ketchup
2 teaspoons Worcestershire sauce
½ teaspoon ground cumin

// PASTE

2 tablespoons extra-virgin olive oil
1 tablespoon Dijon mustard
1 tablespoon finely chopped fresh oregano leaves
2 teaspoons kosher salt
1 teaspoon ground black pepper

4 boneless rib eye steaks, each 8 to 10 ounces and about 1 inch thick, trimmed of excess fat

Rib Eye Steaks
WITH ANCHO CHILE SAUCE

1. **Cut off and discard the stem of the chile, cut it open, and knock out and discard the seeds.** In a small saucepan combine the chile, wine, and garlic. Bring the mixture to a boil over medium-high heat. Cook until about ¾ cup of wine remains, 5 to 10 minutes. Set aside for 20 minutes, keeping the chile submerged so that it softens completely.

2. **Pour the contents of the saucepan into a food processor.** Process for 1 full minute to puree the chile. Pour the mixture into a small saucepan along with the remaining sauce ingredients. Mix well and then heat the sauce over medium heat for about a minute. Set aside.

3. **In a small bowl mix the paste ingredients.** Smear the steaks evenly on both sides with the paste. Allow the steaks to stand at room temperature for 15 to 30 minutes before grilling.

4. **Prepare the grill for direct cooking over high heat (450° to 550°F).**

5. **Brush the cooking grates clean.** Grill the steaks over ***direct high heat***, with the lid closed as much as possible, until cooked to your desired doneness, 6 to 8 minutes for medium rare, turning once or twice (if flare-ups occur, move the steaks temporarily over indirect heat). Remove from the grill and let rest for 3 to 5 minutes. While the steaks rest, warm the sauce over low heat. Serve the steaks warm with the sauce.

Access the grocery list for this recipe on your mobile device. timetogrill.mobi.

Most people think of a vinaigrette as an oil-and-vinegar dressing to use on salad, and that's true, but if you add some quartered cherry tomatoes and crumbled blue cheese, it can also be a substantial topping for grilled steaks. Of course, steak and blue cheese play so well together that we've given you another variation on that theme. The steaks are first marinated with red wine and concentrated tomato paste. The Gorgonzola sauce that goes on top is mighty rich, so lighten the rest of the plate with some fresh vegetables.

SERVES:

PREP TIME: 15 MINUTES

GRILLING TIME: 6 TO 8 MINUTES

4 New York strip steaks, each 10 to 12 ounces and about 1 inch thick, trimmed of excess fat
Extra-virgin olive oil
Kosher salt
Ground black pepper

// VINAIGRETTE

1 tablespoon minced shallot
2 teaspoons red wine vinegar
1 teaspoon Dijon mustard
2 cups (about 20) cherry tomatoes, each cut into quarters
¼ cup finely chopped fresh basil leaves
2 ounces crumbled Gorgonzola cheese (½ cup)

Strip Steaks
WITH TOMATO AND BLUE CHEESE VINAIGRETTE

1. Prepare the grill for direct cooking over high heat (450° to 550°F).

2. Lightly brush the steaks on both sides with oil and season evenly with salt and pepper. Allow the steaks to stand at room temperature for 15 to 30 minutes before grilling.

3. In a medium bowl whisk the shallot, vinegar, mustard, ¼ teaspoon salt, and ¼ teaspoon pepper. Slowly whisk in 2 tablespoons of oil, forming a smooth vinaigrette. Add the tomatoes and basil. Mix well.

4. Brush the cooking grates clean. Grill the steaks over **direct high heat**, with the lid closed as much as possible, until cooked to your desired doneness, 6 to 8 minutes for medium rare, turning once or twice (if flare-ups occur, move the steaks temporarily over indirect heat). Remove from the grill and let rest for 3 to 5 minutes. Add the cheese to the vinaigrette. Mix gently. Serve the steaks warm with the vinaigrette spooned over the top.

Access the grocery list for this recipe on your mobile device. timetogrill.mobi.

Marinated Strip Steaks with Gorgonzola Sauce

SERVES: 👤👤👤👤

PREP TIME: **20** MINUTES

MARINATING TIME: **2** TO **4** HOURS

GRILLING TIME: **6** TO **8** MINUTES

// MARINADE

- 2 cups beef broth
- 1 cup dry red wine
- 1 medium yellow onion, finely chopped
- 2 tablespoons tomato paste

- 4 New York strip steaks, each 10 to 12 ounces and about 1 inch thick, trimmed of excess fat
  Extra-virgin olive oil
  Kosher salt
  Ground black pepper

// SAUCE

- 1 tablespoon unsalted butter
- 2 tablespoons minced shallot
- 1 cup sour cream
- 4 ounces crumbled Gorgonzola cheese (1 cup)

- 1 tablespoon finely chopped fresh chives (optional)

1. In a large glass baking dish combine the marinade ingredients. Whisk to dissolve the tomato paste. Submerge the steaks in the marinade. Cover and refrigerate for 2 to 4 hours.

2. Prepare the grill for direct cooking over high heat (450° to 550°F).

3. Lift the steaks from the dish and pat dry with paper towels. Discard the marinade. Lightly brush the steaks with oil and season evenly with salt and pepper. Allow to stand at room temperature for 15 to 30 minutes before grilling. Meanwhile, make the sauce.

4. In a medium saucepan over medium heat, melt the butter. Add the shallot and cook until tender, about 2 minutes, stirring often.

Mix in the sour cream and cheese and cook until the sauce begins to simmer and the cheese has melted, about 3 minutes, stirring occasionally. Remove from the heat, add ¼ teaspoon pepper, and cover to keep warm.

5. Brush the cooking grates clean. Grill the steaks over **direct high heat**, with the lid closed as much as possible, until cooked to your desired doneness, 6 to 8 minutes for medium rare, turning once or twice (if flare-ups occur, move the steaks temporarily over indirect heat). Remove from the grill and let rest for 3 to 5 minutes. Serve warm with the sauce. Garnish with chives, if desired.

Access the grocery list for this recipe on your mobile device. timetogrill.mobi.

The commonly available assortment of dried herbs called herbes de Provence will save you big amounts of time and money you might otherwise spend finding and blending basil, fennel seed, lavender, marjoram, rosemary, sage, summer savory, and thyme. Keep a jar of it in your spice cabinet and use it for a nice, sophisticated touch on grilled steaks paired with foil-roasted shallots. If you really love the food of Provence, take the time to roast some diced summer vegetables, including shallots, with fresh garlic and rosemary in a disposable foil pan right alongside your grilled steaks.

Provençal Strip Steaks
WITH CARAMELIZED SHALLOTS

EASY

SERVES: ♟♟♟♟

PREP TIME: **15** MINUTES

GRILLING TIME: **28** TO **35** MINUTES

1 tablespoon herbes de Provence
  Kosher salt
  Ground black pepper
4 New York strip steaks, each 10 to 12 ounces and about 1 inch thick, trimmed of excess fat
  Extra-virgin olive oil
8-10 ounces shallots, peeled and cut into ¼-inch rings
4 small zucchini, cut in half lengthwise
1 tablespoon finely chopped fresh Italian parsley leaves
¼ teaspoon sherry vinegar

1. **Prepare the grill for direct cooking over medium heat (350° to 450°F).**

2. **In a small bowl mix the herbes de Provence with 2 teaspoons salt and ½ teaspoon pepper.** Lightly coat the steaks on both sides with oil and season evenly with the herb mixture. Allow the steaks to stand at room temperature for 15 to 30 minutes before grilling.

3. **In a medium bowl mix the shallots with 2 tablespoons oil.** Spread the shallots in a single layer on one end of a sheet of aluminum foil, about 12 by 24 inches. Fold the foil over the shallots and bring the ends together to secure them, folding them down tightly. Fold and tightly secure the two remaining sides to create a foil packet. Brush the zucchini with oil.

4. **Brush the cooking grates clean.** Grill the shallot packet over *direct medium heat*, with the lid closed as much as possible, until the shallots are tender, 12 to 15 minutes, turning the package once or twice. Carefully open the package with tongs and continue to cook the shallots until golden brown, 10 to 12 minutes more, stirring them once or twice. During the last 4 to 6 minutes of grilling time, grill the zucchini over *direct medium heat* until crisp-tender, turning once. Remove from the grill and set aside. Increase the temperature of the grill to high heat (450° to 550°F).

5. **Grill the steaks over *direct high heat*, with the lid closed as much as possible, until cooked to your desired doneness, 6 to 8 minutes for medium rare, turning once or twice (if flare-ups occur, move the steaks temporarily over indirect heat).** Remove from the grill and let rest for 3 to 5 minutes.

6. **Transfer the shallots to a small bowl.** Add the parsley and vinegar and season with salt and pepper. Mix well. Cut the zucchini on the diagonal into bite-sized pieces. Serve the shallots and zucchini warm with the steaks.

Access the grocery list for this recipe on your mobile device. timetogrill.mobi.

New York Strip Steaks with Provençal Vegetables

SERVES: 👤👤👤👤

PREP TIME: **30** MINUTES

GRILL TIME: **18** TO **23** MINUTES

SPECIAL EQUIPMENT: LARGE
DISPOSABLE FOIL PAN

4 New York strip steaks, each 10 to
  12 ounces and about 1 inch thick,
  trimmed of excess fat
  Extra-virgin olive oil
  Kosher salt
  Ground black pepper

// VEGETABLES

1 large zucchini, cut into ½-inch dice
  (about 2 cups)
1 medium Italian eggplant, cut into ½-inch
  dice (about 2 cups)
1 red bell pepper, cut into ½-inch dice
  (about 1½ cups)
4 ounces shallots, peeled and cut into
  ¼-inch rings
¼ cup finely chopped oil-packed
  sun-dried tomatoes
2 tablespoons oil from the jar of
  sun-dried tomatoes
1 tablespoon minced garlic
1 tablespoon extra-virgin olive oil
2 teaspoons finely chopped fresh
  rosemary leaves
1 teaspoon herbes de Provence

1. Prepare the grill for direct cooking over medium heat (350° to 450°F).

2. Lightly brush the steaks on both sides with oil and season evenly with salt and pepper. Allow the steaks to stand at room temperature for 15 to 30 minutes before grilling.

3. In a large disposable foil pan combine the vegetable ingredients and mix thoroughly.

4. Brush the cooking grates clean. Grill the vegetables in the foil pan over *direct medium heat*, with the lid closed as much as possible, until the vegetables are tender, 12 to 15 minutes, stirring occasionally. Wearing insulated barbecue mitts, remove the pan from the grill. Increase the temperature of the grill to high heat (450° to 550°F).

5. Grill the steaks over *direct high heat*, with the lid closed as much as possible, until cooked to your desired doneness, 6 to 8 minutes for medium rare, turning once or twice (if flare-ups occur, move the steaks temporarily over indirect heat). Remove from the grill and let rest 3 to 5 minutes. Season the vegetables with salt and pepper. Serve the steaks warm with the vegetables.

Access the grocery list for this recipe on your mobile device. timetogrill.mobi.

Today you can find dried porcini mushrooms at most supermarkets, usually in the produce section. They are also available at Italian markets and at specialty foods stores. Here, in the easy recipe, they are ground to a powder and used to coat steaks before grilling, giving the meat great earthiness and depth. A simple pan sauce tops the steaks before serving. In the adventurous recipe they are rehydrated in hot water before being chopped and added to a simple cream sauce. If steak and mushrooms are your thing, now you've got two ways to enjoy them.

Porterhouse Steaks
WITH PORCINI CRUST

SERVES: 🧍🧍🧍🧍 TO 🧍🧍🧍🧍🧍🧍

PREP TIME: **15** MINUTES, PLUS 10 TO 15 MINUTES FOR THE SAUCE

GRILLING TIME: **6** TO **8** MINUTES

SPECIAL EQUIPMENT: SPICE MILL

¼ cup (¼ ounce) crumbled, dried porcini mushrooms
2 tablespoons plus 2 teaspoons finely chopped fresh rosemary leaves, divided
Kosher salt
Ground black pepper
4 porterhouse steaks, each about 1 pound and 1 inch thick, trimmed of excess fat
Extra-virgin olive oil
4 tablespoons (½ stick) unsalted butter, chilled, divided
2 small shallots, about 1½ ounces total, finely chopped (about ⅓ cup)
1 cup low-sodium beef broth
⅓ cup dry red wine

1. In a spice mill grind the mushrooms to a fine powder. Transfer to a small plate and mix with 2 tablespoons of the rosemary, 2 teaspoons salt, and 1 teaspoon pepper. Lightly coat the steaks on both sides with oil and season evenly with the porcini mixture. Allow the steaks to stand at room temperature for 15 to 30 minutes before grilling.

2. Prepare the grill for direct cooking over high heat (450° to 550°F).

3. In a medium nonstick skillet over medium heat, melt 1 tablespoon of the butter. Add the shallots and the remaining 2 teaspoons of rosemary and cook until the shallots are tender and beginning to brown, 2 to 3 minutes, stirring occasionally to prevent burning. Add the broth and wine and boil until the mixture is reduced to about ½ cup, 5 to 10 minutes. Remove the skillet from the heat.

4. Brush the cooking grates clean. Grill the steaks over **direct high heat**, with the lid closed as much as possible, until cooked to your desired doneness, 6 to 8 minutes for medium rare, turning once or twice (if flare-ups occur, move the steaks temporarily over indirect heat). Remove from the grill and let rest for 3 to 5 minutes.

5. While the steaks rest, reheat the sauce over medium-high heat and whisk in the remaining 3 tablespoons butter, 1 tablespoon at a time, until melted. Season the sauce with salt and pepper. Serve the steaks warm with the sauce spooned over the top.

Access the grocery list for this recipe on your mobile device. timetogrill.mobi.

EASY

SERVES: 4 TO 6

PREP TIME: 15 MINUTES, PLUS ABOUT 25 MINUTES FOR THE SAUCE

GRILLING TIME: 6 TO 8 MINUTES

Porterhouse Steaks

WITH CREAMY PORCINI SAUCE

- 1 package (½ ounce) dried porcini mushrooms
- 1 cup boiling water
- 1 tablespoon unsalted butter
- ⅓ cup minced yellow onion
- 2 tablespoons plus 2 teaspoons finely chopped fresh thyme leaves, divided
- 1 cup heavy whipping cream

- 4 porterhouse steaks, each about 1 pound and 1 inch thick, trimmed of excess fat
- Extra-virgin olive oil
- Kosher salt
- Ground black pepper

- 2 tablespoons finely grated Parmigiano-Reggiano® cheese
- 2 tablespoons finely chopped fresh Italian parsley leaves

1. **In a medium bowl soak the mushrooms in the boiling water until they are soft, about 15 minutes.** Drain, reserving the soaking liquid. Finely chop the mushrooms.

2. **In a medium saucepan over medium heat, melt the butter.** Add the onion and 2 teaspoons of the thyme and cook until the onion is tender and just beginning to brown, 3 to 5 minutes. Add the reserved soaking liquid and cream and bring to a simmer. Add the mushrooms. Simmer the sauce until 1 to 1½ cups remain, about 15 minutes. Remove from the heat.

3. **Prepare the grill for direct cooking over high heat (450° to 550°F).**

4. **Lightly coat the steaks on both sides with oil and season evenly with the remaining 2 tablespoons thyme, 2 teaspoons salt, and 1 teaspoon pepper.** Allow the steaks to stand at room temperature for 15 to 30 minutes before grilling.

5. **Brush the cooking grates clean.** Grill the steaks over ***direct high heat***, with the lid closed as much as possible, until cooked to your desired doneness, 6 to 8 minutes for medium rare, turning once or twice (if flare-ups occur, move the steaks temporarily over indirect heat). Remove from the grill and let rest for 3 to 5 minutes.

6. **While the steaks rest, reheat the sauce over medium heat.** Add the cheese to the sauce and stir. Season with salt and pepper. Serve the steaks warm with the sauce spooned over the top and garnished with the parsley.

Access the grocery list for this recipe on your mobile device. timetogrill.mobi.

A full-blown béarnaise sauce requires a reduction of vinegar, shallots, and tarragon followed by a delicate, whisked emulsion of egg yolks and butter that usually strikes fear into the minds of amateur cooks. The adventurous recipe here involves a blender version that reduces the anxiety level considerably. The easy recipe employs a sauce that is not technically a béarnaise sauce, but it melds some of the same essential ingredients. If you prep and measure all your ingredients ahead of time, you can make the brown butter sauce in the time it takes to rest your steaks.

SERVES:

PREP TIME: **15** MINUTES

GRILLING TIME: **8** TO **10** MINUTES

1½ tablespoons extra-virgin olive oil
2½ tablespoons finely chopped fresh
      tarragon leaves, divided
      Kosher salt
      Ground black pepper
  4 filet mignon steaks, each about 8 ounces
      and 1¼ inches thick

  6 tablespoons (¾ stick) unsalted butter,
      cut into 4 pieces
  ¼ cup chopped walnuts, preferably toasted
  1 tablespoon white wine vinegar

EASY

Filet Mignon Steaks
WITH BROWN BUTTER SAUCE

1. Prepare the grill for direct cooking over medium heat (350° to 450°F).

2. In a small bowl mix the oil, 1½ tablespoons of the tarragon, ¾ teaspoon salt, and ¼ teaspoon pepper. Smear the paste on both sides of the steaks. Allow the steaks to stand at room temperature for 15 to 30 minutes before grilling.

3. Brush the cooking grates clean. Grill the steaks over *direct medium heat*, with the lid closed as much as possible, until cooked to your desired doneness, 8 to 10 minutes for medium rare, turning once or twice (if flare-ups occur, move the steaks temporarily over indirect heat). Remove the steaks from the grill and let rest while you make the sauce.

4. In a small skillet over medium heat, melt the butter. Let it foam and cook until it turns a light golden brown, 4 to 6 minutes, swirling the skillet occasionally to prevent the butter from burning. Remove the skillet from the heat. Add the nuts, vinegar (be careful, it will bubble up), and the remaining 1 tablespoon tarragon. Season with salt and pepper. Serve immediately with the steaks (the sauce will separate if it sits for more than a few minutes).

Access the grocery list for this recipe on your mobile device. timetogrill.mobi.

SERVES: 👤👤👤👤

PREP TIME: **30** MINUTES

GRILLING TIME: **36** TO **43** MINUTES

Whole Tenderloin with Béarnaise
AND ASPARAGUS

1 center-cut beef tenderloin roast, about
  2 pounds, trimmed of excess fat and
  silver skin
  Extra-virgin olive oil
  Kosher salt
  Ground black pepper
1 pound asparagus, woody ends discarded

// SAUCE

2 tablespoons minced shallot
1 tablespoon finely chopped fresh
  tarragon leaves
¼ cup dry white wine *or* dry vermouth
¼ cup white wine vinegar
1 cup (2 sticks) unsalted butter
4 large egg yolks (see note)

1. **Prepare the grill for direct and indirect cooking over medium heat (350° to 450°F).**

2. **Lightly brush the roast on all sides with oil and season evenly with salt and pepper.** Lightly coat the asparagus with oil. Allow the roast to stand at room temperature for 15 to 30 minutes before grilling.

3. **Brush the cooking grates clean.** Sear the roast over *direct medium heat*, with the lid

// Using raw egg yolks to make the sauce could cause salmonella poisoning. To avoid that risk, use yolks from pasteurized eggs.

closed as much as possible, until well marked, about 15 minutes, turning a quarter turn every 3 to 4 minutes. Continue grilling over *indirect medium heat*, with the lid closed, until cooked to your desired doneness, 15 to 20 minutes for medium rare, turning once. Meanwhile, make the sauce.

4. **In a small saucepan over high heat, bring the shallot, tarragon, wine, and vinegar to a boil.** Cook until the liquid is reduced to about 2 tablespoons, 4 to 6 minutes. Strain through a wire sieve into a small bowl; set the wine mixture and the shallot mixture aside.

5. **In another saucepan over medium heat, melt the butter until it's bubbling hot (so that it will cook the egg yolks).** In a blender combine the yolks and the wine mixture. Pulse to combine. With the blender running, in a slow, steady stream, pour one-third of the hot

butter into the blender and process until the sauce has emulsified. Then add the remaining butter and blend on high for 5 seconds until it is thick and smooth. Transfer to a heatproof bowl. Stir in the reserved shallot mixture and season with salt and pepper. Place the bowl in a skillet of hot (but not simmering) water over very low heat to keep warm.

6. **Remove the roast from the grill and let rest for 5 to 10 minutes.** Meanwhile, grill the asparagus over *direct medium heat*, with the lid closed as much as possible, until browned in spots but not charred, 6 to 8 minutes, rolling the spears a couple of times.

7. **Cut the roast crosswise into slices.** Serve warm with the asparagus and sauce.

Access the grocery list for this recipe on your mobile device. timetogrill.mobi.

A lot of kabob recipes rely on time-consuming marinades to penetrate the meat, but here is an easy recipe you can whip up and grill immediately. The combination of four different peppercorns, sold as mixed peppercorns, and a simple mustard sauce gives the kabobs plenty of kick. The adventurous recipe also stars kabobs, this time inspired by the intriguing cooking of Peru, where a tangy red pepper-based puree does double duty as a marinade and as a sauce.

Peppered Beef Sirloin Kabobs
WITH DIJON CREAM

SERVES: 👤👤👤👤 TO 👤👤👤👤👤👤

PREP TIME: **15** MINUTES

GRILLING TIME: **6** TO **8** MINUTES

SPECIAL EQUIPMENT: SPICE MILL, METAL OR BAMBOO SKEWERS (IF USING BAMBOO, SOAK IN WATER FOR AT LEAST 30 MINUTES)

1 tablespoon four-color mixed peppercorns (black, white, pink, and green) *or* 2 teaspoons black peppercorns
  Kosher salt
½ teaspoon ground cumin
2 pounds top sirloin, about 1¼ inches thick, cut into 1¼-inch cubes
  Extra-virgin olive oil
2 medium zucchini, each cut lengthwise and then crosswise into ½-inch pieces
2 large red bell peppers, cut into 1¼-inch squares

// CREAM
½ cup crème fraîche *or* sour cream
2 tablespoons Dijon mustard
2 tablespoons finely chopped fresh chives
1 tablespoon red wine vinegar

1. Prepare the grill for direct cooking over high heat (450° to 550°F).

2. In a spice mill coarsely grind the peppercorns. Pour the pepper into a large bowl and mix in 1½ teaspoons salt and the cumin. Place the meat in the large bowl with the spices and add enough oil to coat the cubes lightly; toss to coat evenly. In another bowl lightly coat the zucchini and bell peppers with oil and season evenly with salt. Thread each skewer alternately with zucchini, meat cubes, and bell pepper.

3. In a small bowl whisk the cream ingredients. Cover and refrigerate until ready to serve.

4. Brush the cooking grates clean. Grill the kabobs over **direct high heat**, with the lid closed as much as possible, until the vegetables are crisp-tender and the meat is cooked to your desired doneness, 6 to 8 minutes for medium rare, turning occasionally. Remove the skewers from the grill and serve warm with the cream.

Access the grocery list for this recipe on your mobile device. timetogrill.mobi.

EASY

Peruvian Beef Sirloin Kabobs
AND CORN

1. **Prepare the grill for direct cooking over medium heat (350° to 450°F).**

2. **Brush the cooking grates clean.** Grill two red peppers over *direct medium heat*, with the lid closed as much as possible, until the skins are blackened and blistered all over, 12 to 15 minutes, turning occasionally. Place the peppers in a bowl and cover with plastic wrap to trap the steam. Let stand for 10 to 15 minutes. Remove the peppers from the bowl and peel away and discard the charred skins, stems, and seeds.

3. **In a food processor combine the roasted peppers, garlic, vinegar, cumin, paprika, salt, and pepper.** Pulse until the peppers are chopped. With the machine running, gradually add the oil through the feed tube to make a thick paste.

4. **Place the meat in a large bowl and pour in one-third of the paste.** Turn to coat the meat evenly. Reserve the remaining paste to use to brush on the corn and serve as a sauce. Thread the meat and pepper squares alternately onto skewers. Allow the kabobs to stand at room temperature for 15 to 30 minutes before grilling.

5. **Lightly brush the corn with some of the remaining paste.** Grill the corn over *direct medium heat*, with the lid closed as much as possible, until browned in spots and tender, 10 to 15 minutes, turning several times. At the same time, grill the kabobs over *direct medium heat* until the peppers are crisp-tender and the meat is cooked to your desired doneness, 6 to 8 minutes for medium rare, turning occasionally. Remove from the grill as they are done. Serve the kabobs and corn warm with the remaining paste.

Access the grocery list for this recipe on your mobile device. timetogrill.mobi.

SERVES: 👤👤👤👤👤👤

PREP TIME: **30** MINUTES

GRILLING TIME: **22** TO **30** MINUTES

SPECIAL EQUIPMENT: METAL OR BAMBOO SKEWERS (IF USING BAMBOO, SOAK IN WATER FOR AT LEAST 30 MINUTES)

// **PASTE**

- 2 medium red bell peppers
- 6 garlic cloves, coarsely chopped
- 2 tablespoons red wine vinegar
- 2 teaspoons ground cumin
- 1 teaspoon smoked paprika
- 1 teaspoon kosher salt
- ½ teaspoon ground black pepper
- ½ cup extra-virgin olive oil

- 2 pounds top sirloin, about 1¼ inches thick, cut into 1¼-inch cubes
- 3 ears fresh corn, husked, each ear cut crosswise into 6 pieces
- 1 large red bell pepper, cut into 1¼-inch squares

This first recipe could be titled Tuesday Night Top Sirloin, because it lets you get a decent dinner on the table without a long list of ingredients. Bring on an inexpensive steak marinated at room temperature while you preheat the grill, and grill some fresh vegetables as a side dish. The second recipe is a messy, gooey sandwich in all the very best ways. Its horseradish cream can be used to make deviled eggs, a seafood dip, or a topping for baked potatoes. The marmalade is great on crostini with goat cheese or as a filling for omelets.

1. Prepare the grill for direct cooking over medium heat (350° to 450°F).

2. In a small bowl whisk the vinegar, horseradish, pepper, ¼ cup oil, and ½ teaspoon salt. Place the steak in the bowl and marinate at room temperature for 15 to 30 minutes.

3. Remove the steak from the bowl and discard the marinade. Brush the cooking grates clean. Grill the steak over *direct medium heat*, with the lid closed as much as possible, until cooked to your desired doneness, 12 to 14 minutes for medium rare, turning once or twice (if flare-ups occur, transfer the steak temporarily to indirect heat). Remove from the grill and let rest for 3 to 5 minutes. Cut into thin slices.

4. Lightly brush the broccolini and onion slices with oil and season them with salt. Grill them over *direct medium heat*, with the lid closed as much as possible, until the vegetables are tender, about 8 minutes. Remove from the grill and chop the onion.

5. Divide the steak slices and broccolini among four plates and top with the onions.

Access the grocery list for this recipe on your mobile device. timetogrill.mobi.

Top Sirloin with Broccolini

SERVES: 👤👤👤👤

PREP TIME: **10** MINUTES

MARINATING TIME: **15** TO **30** MINUTES

GRILLING TIME: **20** TO **22** MINUTES

EASY

// MARINADE

2 tablespoons balsamic vinegar
1 teaspoon prepared horseradish
¼ teaspoon ground black pepper
Extra-virgin olive oil
Kosher salt

1¼ pounds top sirloin steak, about 1 inch thick

1 bunch thin broccolini, about ½ pound
1 red onion, cut crosswise into ⅓-inch slices

Steak Sandwiches
WITH ONION MARMALADE

SERVES: 👤👤👤👤

PREP TIME: **30** MINUTES

GRILLING TIME: **10** TO **12** MINUTES

// CREAM
- ½ cup mayonnaise
- 2 tablespoons prepared horseradish
- ½ teaspoon dry mustard powder

- Extra-virgin olive oil
- 1 pound red onions, thinly sliced
- 2 teaspoons minced garlic, divided
- 1 teaspoon packed dark brown sugar
- ¼ cup balsamic vinegar
- Kosher salt
- Ground black pepper

- 1¼ pounds top sirloin steak, about
  1 inch thick

- 2 tablespoons white wine vinegar
- 1 bag (8 ounces) shredded green cabbage
- 1 raw golden beet, about 2 inches
  diameter, peeled, coarsely grated

- 8 slices sourdough bread, each about
  6 by 3 inches and ½ inch thick
- 4 thin slices Gruyère cheese

1. In a small bowl combine the cream ingredients. Cover and chill.

2. In a large, heavy nonstick skillet over medium-high heat, warm 2 tablespoons oil. Add the onions, 1 teaspoon of the garlic, and the brown sugar. Cover the skillet and cook until the onions are deep golden brown, about 12 minutes, stirring occasionally. Add the vinegar and stir, uncovered, until it is absorbed, 2 to 3 minutes. Remove from the heat and season with salt and pepper.

3. Prepare the grill for direct cooking over medium-high heat (400° to 500°F).

4. Brush the steak on both sides with oil and season evenly with salt and pepper. Allow the steak to stand at room temperature for 15 to 30 minutes before grilling.

5. In a medium bowl whisk 3 tablespoons oil, the vinegar, and the remaining 1 teaspoon of garlic. Add the cabbage and the beet. Toss to coat well. Season with salt and pepper. Let stand at room temperature for 15 to 20 minutes.

6. Brush the cooking grates clean. Grill the steak over *direct medium-high heat*, with the lid closed as much as possible, until cooked to your desired doneness, 8 to 10 minutes for medium rare, turning once or twice (if flare-ups occur, transfer the steak temporarily to indirect heat). Remove from the grill and let rest for 3 to 5 minutes.

7. While the steak rests, grill the bread slices over *direct medium-high* heat until the bottoms are crispy and golden, about 1 minute. Turn them over and arrange the cheese on top of four slices. Close the lid and grill until the cheese is melted and the bottoms are crispy and golden, about 1 minute. Transfer to a work surface.

8. Cut the steaks into thin slices. Build the sandwiches with equal amounts of the cream, steak, and marmalade. Serve with the slaw.

Access the grocery list for this recipe on your mobile device. timetogrill.mobi.

Some store-bought salsas pack a lot of punch. Why not direct all those tomatoes, onions, chiles, and garlic into a steak marinade and save a bunch of prep time? Slicing flank steak before marinating with the salsa will speed up the time required to flavor the meat, meaning you can have juicy, flavorful fajitas in a matter of minutes. If you have a little more time to spare, pack many of the same fajita ingredients, along with cheese, into a homemade masa harina crust and make a nice warm tamale casserole on the grill.

Steak Fajitas
WITH CUMIN SOUR CREAM

SERVES: ♦♦♦♦

PREP TIME: **15** MINUTES

MARINATING TIME: **20** TO **30** MINUTES

GRILLING TIME: **4** TO **6** MINUTES PER BATCH

SPECIAL EQUIPMENT: PERFORATED GRILL PAN

1. In a small bowl whisk all of the marinade ingredients.

2. Place the vegetables and steak slices in a large, resealable plastic bag and pour in the marinade. Press the air out of the bag and seal tightly. Turn the bag to distribute the marinade, and marinate at room temperature for 20 to 30 minutes before grilling.

3. Prepare the grill for direct and indirect cooking over high heat (450° to 550°F) and preheat the grill pan.

4. Divide the tortillas into 2 piles and wrap each pile in foil. Set aside.

5. In a small bowl mix the sour cream, cumin, and salt. Set aside.

6. Spread the steak and vegetables (mixed together) in a single layer on the grill pan (you will need to do two or three batches). Grill over *direct high heat*, with the lid closed as much as possible, until the vegetables are crisp-tender and the meat is lightly charred, 4 to 6 minutes, stirring occasionally. Transfer to a serving plate and keep warm while you grill the remaining steak and vegetables.

7. Alongside the grill pan, warm the foil-wrapped tortillas over *indirect high heat* for 2 to 4 minutes, turning each package once or twice. Serve the steak and vegetables with warm tortillas, cumin sour cream, and lime wedges.

Access the grocery list for this recipe on your mobile device. timetogrill.mobi.

// MARINADE
  1 cup prepared green or red salsa, preferably medium or hot
  ¼ cup vegetable oil
  ¼ cup fresh lime juice
  1 tablespoon kosher salt

  2 bell peppers, any color, about 12 ounces total, cut into ¼-inch strips
  1 red onion, about 10 ounces, cut in half and then into ¼-inch strips
  1 flank steak, about 1½ pounds and ¾ inch thick, cut in half lengthwise, and then cut crosswise into ¼-inch slices

12 flour tortillas (6 to 8 inches)

  1 cup sour cream
  1 teaspoon cumin
  ½ teaspoon kosher salt
  1 lime, cut into wedges

EASY

SERVES: 6 TO 8

PREP TIME: 30 MINUTES

GRILLING TIME: 53 MINUTES TO 1 HOUR

SPECIAL EQUIPMENT: 12-INCH CAST-IRON SKILLET

// RUB

1 teaspoon kosher salt
1 teaspoon prepared chili powder
½ teaspoon ground cumin
¼ teaspoon ground black pepper

1 flank steak, 1 to 1¼ pounds and about ¾ inch thick
Vegetable oil

// DOUGH

2 cups masa harina corn flour
1 teaspoon kosher salt
1 teaspoon ground cumin
½ teaspoon baking powder
2 cups water
¼ cup (½ stick) unsalted butter, melted

1 cup prepared red or green salsa, preferably medium or hot
½ cup chopped roasted red peppers
2½ cups grated pepper jack cheese (10 ounces), divided

// You could use the pre-shredded blend of four Mexican-style cheeses instead of the pepper jack to make it more kid friendly.

Steak and Cheese Tamale Casserole

1. In a small bowl combine the rub ingredients. Lightly brush the steak on both sides with oil and season evenly with the rub. Allow the steak to stand at room temperature for 15 to 30 minutes before grilling.

2. Prepare the grill for direct and indirect cooking over medium heat (350° to 450°F).

3. Brush the cooking grates clean. Grill the steak over *direct medium heat*, with the lid closed as much as possible, until cooked to your desired doneness, 8 to 10 minutes for medium rare, turning once or twice (if flare-ups occur, move the steak temporarily over indirect heat). Remove from the grill and let rest for 3 to 5 minutes. Cut the steak into ½-inch pieces.

4. In a large bowl mix the corn flour, salt, cumin, and baking powder. Pour in the water and melted butter and then stir with a spoon until the dough is thick and pasty, 2 to 3 minutes.

5. Lightly brush the inside of a cast-iron skillet with oil. Spoon the dough into the skillet and spread it out evenly to cover the bottom and about one inch up the sides of the skillet.

6. In a large bowl combine the steak pieces, salsa, roasted peppers, and 2 cups of the cheese. Pour into the prepared skillet, spreading the filling evenly but not all the way to the outer edge. Leave a one-half-inch rim of the crust uncovered.

7. Grill the casserole over *indirect medium heat*, with the lid closed as much as possible, until the crust begins to brown, about 40 minutes, rotating the skillet as necessary for even cooking. Top the casserole with the remaining ½ cup of cheese and cook until the cheese is melted and the crust turns golden brown along the edges, 5 to 10 minutes. Carefully remove the skillet from the grill. Let cool for 10 minutes. Cut into wedges.

Access the grocery list for this recipe on your mobile device. timetogrill.mobi.

If you are looking for a quick-cooking steak, you can't do much better than skirt steak. Typically it is only about one-half inch thick, so it is on and off the grill in about five minutes, which is about all the time you need to cut up some fresh tomatoes and creamy avocados. Add tortillas and dinner is done. With just a few extra minutes to spend cooking, you could create some fully loaded nachos with an extra oomph from the steak. They are great for a snack or appetizer but also substantial enough for a meal.

Skirt Steak
WITH MEXICAN FLAVORS

SERVES: 4

PREP TIME: **10** MINUTES

GRILLING TIME: **4** TO **6** MINUTES

// RUB

1½ teaspoons pure chile powder
1 teaspoon packed brown sugar
1 teaspoon granulated garlic
½ teaspoon kosher salt
¼ teaspoon ground cumin

1½ pounds skirt steak, ½ to ¾ inch thick, trimmed of excess surface fat, cut into foot-long pieces
1 tablespoon extra-virgin olive oil

EASY

1. **Prepare the grill for direct cooking over high heat (450° to 550°F).**

2. **In a small bowl mix the rub ingredients.** Lightly brush the steaks on both sides with the oil and season evenly with the rub. Allow the steaks to stand at room temperature for 15 to 30 minutes before grilling.

3. **Brush the cooking grates clean.** Grill the steaks over *direct high heat*, with the lid closed as much as possible, until cooked to your desired doneness, 4 to 6 minutes for medium rare, turning once or twice (if flare-ups occur, move the steaks temporarily over indirect heat). Remove from the grill and let rest for 3 to 5 minutes.

4. **Cut the steaks across the grain into ½-inch slices.** Serve immediately with chopped tomatoes and avocado, and warm tortillas, if desired.

Access the grocery list for this recipe on your mobile device. timetogrill.mobi.

Cheesy Nachos
WITH STEAK AND BLACK BEANS

SERVES: **6** TO **8**;

12 TO **15** AS AN APPETIZER

PREP TIME: **30** MINUTES

GRILLING TIME: **14** TO **16** MINUTES

SPECIAL EQUIPMENT: LARGE
SHEET PAN

// PASTE

- 1 tablespoon extra-virgin olive oil
- 1 tablespoon minced garlic
- 1 teaspoon pure chile powder
- 1 teaspoon packed brown sugar
- ½ teaspoon kosher salt
- ½ teaspoon chipotle chile powder
- ¼ teaspoon ground cumin

- 1½ pounds skirt steak, ½ to ¾ inch thick, trimmed of excess surface fat, cut into foot-long pieces

// SALSA

- 2 ripe Hass avocados, diced
- 3 ripe plum tomatoes, diced
- ⅓ cup minced red onion
- ⅓ cup finely chopped fresh cilantro leaves
- 2-3 pickled jalapeño chile peppers, minced
- 3 tablespoons fresh lime juice
- 1 tablespoon minced garlic
  Kosher salt

- 1 bag (12 ounces) tortilla chips
- 1 can (15 ounces) black beans, rinsed
- 2 cups grated sharp cheddar cheese (8 ounces)
- 2 cups grated Monterey Jack cheese (8 ounces)

1. In a small bowl mix the paste ingredients. Spread the paste on both sides of each steak. Allow the steaks to stand at room temperature for 15 to 30 minutes before grilling.

2. In a medium bowl combine the salsa ingredients and then season with salt. To fully incorporate the flavors, let the salsa sit at room temperature for about 30 minutes.

3. Prepare the grill for direct cooking over high heat (450° to 550°F).

4. Brush the cooking grates clean. Grill the steaks over **direct high heat**, with the lid closed as much as possible, until cooked to your desired doneness, 4 to 6 minutes for medium rare, turning once or twice (if flare-ups occur, move the steaks temporarily over indirect heat). Remove from the grill and let rest for 3 to 5 minutes. Cut the steak into bite-sized pieces.

5. Working in two batches, layer tortilla chips, steak, black beans, and cheese on a large sheet pan. Place the sheet pan over **direct high heat**, close the lid, and cook until the cheese is melted, about 5 minutes. Remove from the grill and serve immediately with the salsa.

Access the grocery list for this recipe on your mobile device. timetogrill.mobi.

What skirt steak lacks in tenderness, it certainly overcomes with rich beefy flavor, particularly if you smear it with a quick spice paste. While the steaks sizzle on one side of the grill, roast some plum tomatoes brushed with the same paste on the other side. Then slice the steaks nice and thin so no one notices its "chewiness." Another good approach is to sear it first and then simmer it for about an hour or so in a dark, tomato-based chili made with ale.

Southern Steak
WITH ROASTED TOMATOES

SERVES: 🧍🧍🧍🧍

PREP TIME: **15** MINUTES

GRILLING TIME: **16** TO **21** MINUTES

// PASTE
¼ cup extra-virgin olive oil
1 tablespoon cider vinegar
1 tablespoon pure chile powder
1 tablespoon smoked paprika
2 teaspoons garlic powder
1 teaspoon ground cumin
½ teaspoon ground black pepper
   Kosher salt

2 pounds skirt steak, about ¾ inch thick, trimmed of excess fat, cut into foot-long pieces
4 medium plum tomatoes, each cored and halved lengthwise
2 tablespoons finely chopped fresh Italian parsley or basil leaves (optional)

1. **Prepare the grill for direct and indirect cooking over medium heat (350° to 450°F).**

2. **In a small bowl whisk the paste ingredients, including 1½ teaspoons salt.** Put 2 tablespoons of the paste in a medium bowl and set aside.

3. **Spread the remaining paste on both sides of the steaks.** Allow the steaks to stand at room temperature 15 to 30 minutes.

4. **Add the tomatoes to the medium bowl with the paste and toss to coat them lightly.** Brush the cooking grates clean. Grill the tomatoes over *indirect medium heat*, with the lid closed as much as possible, until they turn very soft and begin to darken in spots, 12 to 15 minutes, turning once. Remove from the grill and season with salt.

5. **Grill the steaks over *direct medium heat*, with the lid closed as much as possible, until cooked to your desired doneness, 4 to 6 minutes for medium rare, turning once or twice (if flare-ups occur, move the steaks temporarily over indirect heat).** Remove from the grill and let rest for 3 to 5 minutes.

6. **Cut the steaks across the grain into ⅓-inch slices.** Serve warm with the roasted tomatoes and fresh herbs, if desired.

Access the grocery list for this recipe on your mobile device. timetogrill.mobi.

Steak and Ale Chili
WITH BEANS

SERVES: 6 TO 8

PREP TIME: 30 MINUTES

GRILLING TIME: 4 TO 6 MINUTES, PLUS 1 TO 1¼ HOURS TO SIMMER THE CHILI

// RUB

2 teaspoons ground cumin
  Kosher salt
  Ground black pepper

1 pound skirt steak, about ¾ inch thick, trimmed of excess fat, cut into foot-long pieces
  Vegetable oil

// CHILI

1½ cups finely chopped yellow onion
1 tablespoon minced garlic
2 tablespoons pure chile powder
2 teaspoons dried oregano
2 cans (16 ounces each) chili beans, such as pinto beans, with liquid
1 can (28 ounces) diced tomatoes
1 bottle (12 ounces) stout beer
2 tablespoons cider vinegar
½ teaspoon Worcestershire sauce

2 cups finely grated cheddar cheese (8 ounces)

1. **Prepare the grill for direct cooking over medium heat (350° to 450°F).**

2. **In a small bowl combine the cumin, 1 teaspoon salt, and 1 teaspoon pepper.** Lightly brush the steaks on both sides with oil and season evenly with the rub. Allow the steaks to stand at room temperature for 15 to 30 minutes before grilling.

3. **Brush the cooking grates clean.** Grill the steaks over **direct medium heat**, with the lid closed as much as possible, until cooked to medium-rare doneness, 4 to 6 minutes, turning once. Remove from the grill and let rest for 3 to 5 minutes. Cut the steaks into ½-inch pieces.

4. **In a large saucepan over medium heat, heat 1 tablespoon oil.** Add the onion and garlic and cook until the onion is tender, about 5 minutes, stirring occasionally. Stir in the chili powder and oregano and cook until fragrant, 1 to 2 minutes. Add the remaining chili ingredients and increase the heat to bring the chili to a boil. Reduce the heat to low, add the steak, cover, and simmer for 20 minutes. Uncover the pan and continue to simmer until the chili thickens to the consistency you like, 40 to 50 minutes, stirring to the bottom of the pan occasionally. Season with salt and pepper. Serve warm topped with grated cheese.

Access the grocery list for this recipe on your mobile device. timetogrill.mobi.

One brilliantly convenient item to have on hand for dressing up a simple steak is compound butter, which is nothing more than softened butter mixed with whatever ingredients you like. In this first recipe, the butter gains depth and "tanginess" from goat cheese and tomato paste. Make a double batch and keep some in the refrigerator for any kind of steak or other grilled meats. The adventurous recipe makes good use of the affinities between steak and goat cheese, but it also adds quickly pickled red onions and a tangle of roasted peppers and baby greens for extra elegance and texture.

Flat Iron Steaks
WITH GOAT CHEESE-TOMATO BUTTER

SERVES: 🧍🧍🧍🧍🧍🧍

PREP TIME: **20** MINUTES, PLUS ABOUT 1 HOUR TO CHILL THE BUTTER (OPTIONAL)

GRILLING TIME: **4** TO **6** MINUTES

¼ cup (½ stick) unsalted butter, softened
2 ounces goat cheese, at room temperature
1 tablespoon tomato paste
¼ teaspoon minced fresh thyme leaves
Kosher salt
Ground black pepper

6 flat iron steaks, each 6 to 8 ounces and about ¾ inch thick, excess fat and any gristle removed
Extra-virgin olive oil
½ teaspoon granulated garlic

1. **In a small bowl blend the butter, cheese, tomato paste, thyme, ⅛ teaspoon salt, and ⅛ teaspoon pepper.** The butter mixture is now ready to serve by smearing it with a knife on grilled steaks, but for a more elegant presentation, transfer the butter mixture to a sheet of plastic wrap and roll into a log about 1½ inches thick. Refrigerate until firm, about 1 hour.

2. **Prepare the grill for direct cooking over direct medium heat (350° to 450°F).**

3. **Lightly brush the steaks on both sides with oil and season evenly with the granulated garlic and salt and pepper.** Allow the steaks to stand at room temperature for 15 to 30 minutes before grilling.

4. **Brush the cooking grates clean.** Grill the steaks over **direct medium heat**, with the lid closed as much as possible, until cooked to your desired doneness, 4 to 6 minutes for medium rare, turning once or twice (if flare-ups occur, move the steaks temporarily over indirect heat). Remove from the grill and let rest for 3 to 5 minutes. Cut the steaks across the grain into thin slices. Serve immediately with a smear or slice of the goat cheese-tomato butter.

Access the grocery list for this recipe on your mobile device. timetogrill.mobi.

Flat Iron Steaks
WITH PICKLED ONIONS AND ARUGULA

SERVES: 👤👤👤👤

PREP TIME: 30 MINUTES

GRILLING TIME: 16 TO 21 MINUTES

½ small red onion, thinly sliced
½ cup red wine vinegar
1 teaspoon granulated sugar
   Kosher salt

¾ teaspoon granulated garlic
¾ teaspoon minced fresh thyme leaves
¼ teaspoon ground black pepper

4 flat iron steaks, each 6 to 8 ounces and
   about ¾ inch thick, excess fat and any
   gristle removed
   Extra-virgin olive oil

1 large red bell pepper
2 ounces baby arugula
1 log (5 ounces) goat cheese,
   at room temperature

1. In a small bowl combine the onion, vinegar, sugar, and ¼ teaspoon salt. Set aside to marinate at room temperature until ready to serve.

2. Prepare the grill for direct cooking over medium heat (350° to 450°F).

3. In a small bowl combine the granulated garlic, thyme, pepper, and ½ teaspoon salt. Lightly brush the steaks on both sides with oil and season evenly with the rub. Allow the steaks to stand at room temperature for 15 to 30 minutes before grilling.

4. Brush the cooking grates clean. Grill the pepper over *direct medium heat*, with the lid closed as much as possible, until blackened and blistered all over, 12 to 15 minutes, turning occasionally. Place the pepper in a small bowl and cover with plastic wrap to trap the steam. Set aside for at least 10 minutes. Remove the pepper from the bowl and peel away and discard the charred skin. Cut off the top, remove the seeds, and cut into small pieces.

5. Grill the steaks over *direct medium heat*, with the lid closed as much as possible, until cooked to your desired doneness, 4 to 6 minutes for medium rare, turning once or twice (if flare-ups occur, move the steaks temporarily over indirect heat). Remove from the grill and let rest for 3 to 5 minutes. Cut the steaks across the grain into thin slices.

6. Arrange equal amounts of pickled onions, steak slices, arugula, pepper, and crumbled cheese among four serving plates. Season with salt and pepper. Serve while the steak is still warm.

Access the grocery list for this recipe on your mobile device. timetogrill.mobi.

When time is short, lean on the simple flavor combinations that have stood the test of time, like lamb chops with mint and lemon. Add a tangy little yogurt sauce to balance out the richness of the meat and maybe some grilled endive, and you are good to go in about 15 minutes. Now, if you really want to impress some dinner guests, grill a whole rack of lamb and serve the carved chops on a bed of quick-cooking bulgur wheat mixed with pistachios and dried fruits. Take some minutes off your prep time by asking the butcher to French the bones and trim the rack so all the fat and membrane is removed from the meat. In this adventurous recipe, two lamb chops make a portion. For bigger eaters, double the paste and grill two racks.

1. Prepare the grill for direct cooking over medium heat (350° to 450°F).

2. In a large bowl whisk 1 tablespoon of the mint, 1 teaspoon of the lemon juice, the cumin, 1 tablespoon oil, ½ teaspoon salt, and ½ teaspoon pepper. Add the lamb chops to the bowl and allow to stand at room temperature for 15 to 30 minutes before grilling. Brush the endive on both sides with oil and season evenly with salt and pepper.

3. In a small bowl combine the yogurt, the remaining 2 teaspoons mint, and the remaining 1 teaspoon lemon juice.

4. Remove the chops from the bowl and discard the marinade. Brush the cooking grates clean. Grill the lamb chops and the endive over **direct medium heat**, with the lid closed as much as possible, until the lamb is cooked to medium rare and the endive is tender, about 6 minutes, turning once or twice. Remove from the grill and let the lamb rest for 3 to 5 minutes. Serve the lamb warm with endive halves and yogurt sauce.

Access the grocery list for this recipe on your mobile device. timetogrill.mobi.

Rib Lamb Chops

SERVES: 👤👤👤👤

EASY

PREP TIME: **15** MINUTES

GRILLING TIME: ABOUT **6** MINUTES

1 tablespoon plus 2 teaspoons minced fresh mint leaves, divided
2 teaspoons fresh lemon juice, divided
1 teaspoon ground cumin
Extra-virgin olive oil
Kosher salt
Ground black pepper
16 rib lamb chops, each about ¾ inch thick, trimmed of excess fat
4 heads Belgium endive, each one cut in half lengthwise
½ cup plain Greek yogurt

Turkish Rack of Lamb
WITH TABBOULEH

SERVES: 🧍🧍🧍🧍

PREP TIME: **40** MINUTES

GRILLING TIME: **15** TO **20** MINUTES

// TABBOULEH

- 1 teaspoon kosher salt
- 1 cup whole-grain, quick-cooking bulgur wheat, such as Bob's Red Mill®
- ¾ cup (3 ounces) shelled dry roasted, unsalted pistachios
- ½ cup chopped fresh mint leaves
- ⅓ cup currants
- ⅓ cup chopped dried apricots

// DRESSING

- 3 tablespoons extra-virgin olive oil
- 3 tablespoons fresh lemon juice
- ¾ teaspoon ground cumin
- ¼ teaspoon ground cinnamon

// PASTE

- 2 tablespoons extra-virgin olive oil
- 1 tablespoon dried mint leaves
- ½ teaspoon ground cumin
- ¼ teaspoon ground cinnamon
- ¼ teaspoon kosher salt
- ¼ teaspoon ground black pepper

- 1 lamb rack, 8 bones and about 1½ pounds, frenched and trimmed of excess fat

To pop open a tightly closed pistachio, wedge the pointed end of a half shell into the small opening and twist.

1. Fill a large saucepan two-thirds full with water and bring to a boil. Add the salt and bulgur. Boil until the bulgur is tender but still slightly chewy, about 14 minutes, stirring occasionally. Drain, rinse under cold water to cool quickly, and drain again. Squeeze one handful of bulgur at a time to remove the excess water, transferring the dried grains to a large bowl. Add the remaining tabbouleh ingredients and stir to combine.

2. In a small bowl whisk the dressing ingredients. Pour the dressing over the tabbouleh and mix thoroughly.

3. Prepare the grill for direct cooking over medium heat (350° to 450°F).

4. In a small bowl combine the paste ingredients. Spread the paste all over the lamb. Allow to stand at room temperature for 15 to 30 minutes before grilling.

5. Brush the cooking grates clean. Grill the lamb, bone side down first, over **direct medium heat**, with the lid closed as much as possible, until cooked to your desired doneness, 15 to 20 minutes for medium rare, turning once or twice and moving the racks over indirect heat if flare-ups should occur. Remove from the grill and let rest for 3 to 5 minutes. Cut the rack between the bones into individual chops. Serve warm with the tabbouleh.

Access the grocery list for this recipe on your mobile device. timetogrill.mobi.

Bottled teriyaki sauce should be a staple in any busy cook's pantry. In that dark liquid lies a powerful combination of saltiness, sweetness, and most importantly, umami, which is a savory, mouth-filling taste developed when soybeans are fermented in the process of making teriyaki. In the easy recipe, the sauce benefits from the aromatics in orange zest and toasted sesame seeds, making it a really nice, shiny glaze for lamb chops and scallions. Alternatively, you can whip up your own teriyaki sauce based on low-sodium soy sauce and use it to marinate racks of lamb. Mixing a little of the reserved sauce with rice vinegar gives you a dressing for a grilled and chopped eggplant salad.

Teriyaki Lamb Chops

SERVES: ♦♦♦♦

PREP TIME: **5** MINUTES

GRILLING TIME: **8** TO **10** MINUTES

½ cup teriyaki sauce, such as Kikkoman®
Finely grated zest of 1 small orange
8 scallions, root ends trimmed
8 lamb loin chops, each about
1½ inches thick
2 teaspoons toasted sesame seeds

1. Prepare the grill for direct cooking over medium heat (350° to 450°F).

2. In a small bowl whisk the teriyaki sauce and orange zest.

3. Place the scallions on a plate and brush with some of the teriyaki mixture.

4. Allow the lamb chops to stand at room temperature for 15 to 30 minutes before grilling.

5. Brush the cooking grates clean. Grill the chops over **direct medium heat**, with the lid closed as much as possible, until the meat is cooked to your desired doneness, 8 to 10 minutes for medium rare, turning and brushing with the teriyaki mixture once. During the last 2 to 3 minutes of grilling time, grill the scallions over **direct medium heat** just until marked by the grill and slightly wilted, turning once or twice. Remove the chops and scallions from the grill and let the chops rest for 3 to 5 minutes.

6. Place two chops and two scallions on each dinner plate and top with the sesame seeds. Serve warm with rice, if desired.

Access the grocery list for this recipe on your mobile device. timetogrill.mobi.

SERVES: 👤👤👤👤

PREP TIME: **30** MINUTES

MARINATING TIME: **4** TO **6** HOURS

GRILLING TIME: **21** TO **28** MINUTES

// MARINADE

1 cup low-sodium soy sauce
½ cup packed light brown sugar
⅓ cup rice vinegar
2 tablespoons toasted sesame oil
2 tablespoons finely chopped garlic
2 tablespoons grated fresh ginger

2 lamb racks, each 8 bones and about
1½ pounds, frenched and trimmed of
excess fat

3 long, slender Japanese eggplants,
about 12 ounces total
2 bell peppers, 1 red and 1 yellow
1 tablespoon rice vinegar
¼ cup thinly sliced scallions (white and
light green parts only)
¼ cup finely chopped fresh cilantro leaves
2 teaspoons toasted sesame seeds

Rack of Lamb
WITH EGGPLANT-BELL PEPPER SALAD

1. In a small bowl whisk the marinade ingredients until the sugar is dissolved. Place the lamb racks in a large, resealable plastic bag and pour in 1¼ cups of the marinade, reserving the remainder. Press the air out of the bag and seal tightly. Turn the bag to distribute the marinade and refrigerate for 4 to 6 hours, turning the bag once or twice. Remove the bag from the refrigerator 15 to 30 minutes before grilling the lamb.

2. Cut the eggplants into lengthwise quarters; if the wedges are thicker than ¾ inch, cut into eighths. Stem and seed the peppers and cut into ¾-inch strips. Place the vegetables in a large bowl and add ¼ cup of the reserved marinade; toss to coat.

3. Prepare the grill for direct cooking over medium heat (350° to 450°F).

4. Brush the cooking grates clean. Grill the eggplants and peppers over **direct medium heat**, with the lid closed as much as possible, until tender and lightly charred, 6 to 8 minutes, turning once or twice. Transfer to a shallow dish and cover with foil to keep warm.

5. Remove the lamb from the bag and discard the marinade. Grill the lamb, bone side down first, over **direct medium heat**, with the lid closed as much as possible, until cooked to your desired doneness, 15 to 20 minutes for medium rare, turning once or twice (if flare-ups occur, move the racks

temporarily over indirect heat). Transfer to a platter, tent loosely with foil, and let rest for 5 to 10 minutes.

6. When the vegetables are cool enough to handle, peel away and discard any blackened skin and then coarsely chop.

7. In a large bowl whisk the remaining ¼ cup reserved marinade with the rice vinegar. Add the eggplant, peppers, scallions, cilantro, and sesame seeds; toss to combine. Serve the lamb warm with the salad.

Access the grocery list for this recipe on your mobile device. timetogrill.mobi.

Here are a couple great options for a buffet. Leg of lamb is a little like roast beef in that it is best served warm, but it also tastes mighty good at room temperature. Pesto alone is a classic accompaniment for grilled lamb. Make your own or buy a store-bought version and dial it up with a little fresh garlic and mayonnaise. This makes a terrific sandwich spread, by the way. The adventurous recipe pulls apart the essentials of a pesto—basil, garlic, Parmesan cheese, and pine nuts—and arranges them almost like a composed salad with tomatoes and olives.

1. In a small bowl combine the aioli ingredients. Set aside.

2. Coat the lamb on all sides with the oil and season evenly with the salt and pepper. Allow the lamb to stand at room temperature for 15 to 30 minutes before grilling.

3. Prepare the grill for direct and indirect cooking over medium heat (350° to 450°F).

4. Brush the cooking grates clean. Sear the lamb over *direct medium heat*, with the lid closed as much as possible, until nicely browned on both sides, 10 to 15 minutes, turning once. Slide the lamb over *indirect medium heat* and cook, with the lid closed, to your desired doneness, 20 to 30 minutes for medium rare. Remove from the grill and let rest for 5 to 10 minutes.

5. Cut the lamb crosswise into ¼-inch slices. Serve warm with the aioli.

Access the grocery list for this recipe on your mobile device. timetogrill.mobi.

Butterflied Leg of Lamb
WITH PESTO AIOLI

EASY

SERVES: 6 TO 8

PREP TIME: 15 MINUTES

GRILLING TIME: 30 TO 45 MINUTES

// AIOLI
¾ cup prepared pesto
½ cup mayonnaise
1 garlic clove, minced

1 boneless leg of lamb, about 3 pounds, butterflied and trimmed of excess fat
3 tablespoons extra-virgin olive oil
1 tablespoon kosher salt
1½ teaspoons ground black pepper

Leg of Lamb
WITH DECONSTRUCTED PESTO

SERVES: **6** TO **8**

PREP TIME: **30** MINUTES

GRILLING TIME: **30** TO **45** MINUTES

3 tablespoons extra-virgin olive oil
8 garlic cloves, minced
1 boneless leg of lamb, about 3 pounds, butterflied and trimmed of excess fat
1 tablespoon kosher salt
1½ teaspoons ground black pepper

3 plum tomatoes, thinly sliced
1 cup fresh basil leaves, torn into small pieces
1 cup pitted kalamata olives, each one cut in half
1 chunk, about 2 ounces, Parmigiano-Reggiano® cheese
⅓ cup toasted pine nuts

1. In a small bowl mix the oil and garlic. Coat the lamb all over with the oil mixture and season evenly with the salt and pepper. Allow the lamb to stand at room temperature for 15 to 30 minutes before grilling.

2. Prepare the grill for direct and indirect cooking over medium heat (350° to 450°F).

3. Brush the cooking grates clean. Sear the lamb over **direct medium heat**, with the lid closed as much as possible, until nicely browned on both sides, 10 to 15 minutes, turning once. Slide the lamb over **indirect medium heat**, close the lid, and cook to your desired doneness, 20 to 30 minutes for medium rare. Remove from the grill and let rest for 5 to 10 minutes.

4. Cut the lamb crosswise into ¼-inch slices and divide evenly among serving plates. Top with tomato slices, basil, and olives. Using a vegetable peeler, shave wide ribbons of cheese over each serving, and garnish with the pine nuts. Serve immediately.

Access the grocery list for this recipe on your mobile device. timetogrill.mobi.

In order to grill the whole leg evenly, you need to make the thickest parts thinner. You do that by making angled cuts at the thickness you want and spreading the meat open like a book.

Tri-tip gets a lot of positive attention out west. Oddly enough, it is not well known in other parts of the country. Because it is so flavorful and relatively inexpensive, it shows up at a lot of big California barbecues. One easy and fantastic way to serve it is with grilled onions and peppers that are finished in a pan with cream and herbs. A more traditional way, which takes some more time, is to serve it with black beans, grilled corn salsa, and a salty Mexican cheese called cotija. If you can't find that cheese, try using feta cheese instead.

Tri-Tip
WITH CREAMY ONIONS AND POBLANO RAJAS

SERVES: 4 TO 6

PREP TIME: 15 MINUTES

GRILLING TIME: 33 TO 45 MINUTES

3 medium poblano chile peppers
3 tablespoons extra-virgin olive oil, divided
1 teaspoon prepared chili powder
  Kosher salt
  Ground black pepper
1 tri-tip roast, 1½ to 2 pounds, excess fat and silver skin removed
1 medium red onion, quartered and cut into ⅓-inch strips
½ cup heavy whipping cream
¼ teaspoon dried oregano

1. **Prepare the grill for direct and indirect cooking over medium heat (350° to 450°F).**

2. **Brush the cooking grates clean.** Grill the chile peppers over *direct medium heat*, with the lid closed as much as possible, until charred and blackened on all sides, 10 to 15 minutes, turning occasionally. Transfer to a bowl, cover with plastic wrap, and set aside for at least 10 minutes. Remove the peppers from the bowl and peel away and discard the charred skins. Cut off the tops and remove the seeds. Cut into ⅓-inch-wide strips.

3. **In a small bowl combine 2 tablespoons of the oil, the chili powder, 1 teaspoon salt, and ½ teaspoon pepper.** Smear the paste all over the roast. Allow the roast to stand at room temperature for 15 to 30 minutes before grilling.

4. **Meanwhile, in a heavy, large skillet over medium-high heat, heat the remaining 1 tablespoon oil.** Add the onion and the chile strips and cook, stirring often, until tender, 5 to 10 minutes. Stir in the cream and oregano and season with salt and pepper. Simmer until the cream is slightly thickened and coats the chile and onion strips, 3 to 5 minutes. Remove the skillet from the heat.

5. **Grill the roast over *direct medium heat*,** with the lid closed as much as possible, until well marked on both sides, 8 to 10 minutes, turning once. Then move the roast over *indirect medium heat*, close the lid, and cook to your desired doneness, 15 to 20 minutes for medium rare. Remove from the grill and let rest for about 5 minutes. Reheat the chile-and-onion mixture over medium heat. Cut the meat across the grain into thin slices and serve warm with the chile-and-onion mixture.

Access the grocery list for this recipe on your mobile device. timetogrill.mobi.

Tri-Tip
WITH BLACK BEANS, CORN SALSA, AND COTIJA CHEESE

SERVES: 4 TO 6

PREP TIME: **30** MINUTES

GRILLING TIME: **33** TO **45** MINUTES

// SALSA

2 ears fresh corn, husked

½ pint cherry tomatoes, each cut into quarters

⅓ cup finely chopped red onion

2 tablespoons finely chopped fresh basil *or* cilantro leaves

2-3 teaspoons minced serrano chile pepper

2 teaspoons fresh lime juice
Extra-virgin olive oil
Kosher salt
Ground black pepper

1 teaspoon ancho chile powder

1 teaspoon ground cumin

1 tri-tip roast, 1½ to 2 pounds, excess fat and silver skin removed

1 can (15 ounces) black beans, rinsed

1½ cups thinly sliced hearts of romaine

2 ounces crumbled cotija cheese (½ cup)

1. **Prepare the grill for direct and indirect cooking over medium heat (350° to 450°F).**

2. **Brush the cooking grates clean.** Grill the corn over *direct medium heat*, with the lid closed as much as possible, until browned in spots and tender, 10 to 15 minutes, turning occasionally. Remove from the grill and, when cool enough to handle, cut the kernels off the cobs over a medium bowl. Stir in the remaining salsa ingredients, including 2 tablespoons oil, ½ teaspoon salt, and ¼ teaspoon pepper. (The salsa can be made 6 hours ahead. Cover and refrigerate. Let stand at room temperature 1 hour before serving.)

3. **In a small bowl mix 2 tablespoons oil with the chile powder, cumin, 1 teaspoon salt, and ½ teaspoon pepper.** Smear the mixture all over the roast. Let stand at room temperature for 15 to 30 minutes before grilling.

4. **Grill the roast over *direct medium heat*, with the lid closed as much as possible, until well marked on both sides, 8 to 10 minutes, turning once.** Move over *indirect medium heat*, close the lid, and cook to your desired doneness, 15 to 20 minutes for medium rare. Remove from the grill and let rest for about 5 minutes. Cut the meat across the grain into thin slices.

5. **In a heavy medium saucepan over low heat, cook the beans with 1 tablespoon oil until warm, about 5 minutes, stirring once or twice.** Remove from the heat and season with salt and pepper.

6. **Serve the steak with black beans, lettuce, cheese, and salsa.**

Access the grocery list for this recipe on your mobile device. timetogrill.mobi.

When properly grilled, a tri-tip yields tender, succulent slices of meat. That means searing it over direct heat for about ten minutes and then roasting it over indirect heat for twenty minutes or so. Then you can slice it to make these terrific steak sandwiches. If that seems like too much time today, grill thinner steaks, like New York strips or a flank steak, which cook in less than ten minutes. On the other hand, if you have some time to spare, season your tri-tip with a dry marinade for a couple hours, grill the meat, and then serve it with some braised Swiss chard and spinach drizzled with the smoky meat juices.

SERVES:

PREP TIME: **10** MINUTES

GRILLING TIME: **28** TO **40** MINUTES

// MAYONNAISE

½ cup mayonnaise
1½ teaspoons curry powder
1 teaspoon minced garlic
1 teaspoon fresh lemon juice
   Kosher salt

1 tri-tip roast, 1½ to 2 pounds and about 1½ inches thick, fat and silver skin removed
½ teaspoon ground black pepper

4 ciabatta rolls, cut in half lengthwise
4 cups baby arugula *or* fresh watercress
½ small red onion, thinly sliced

EASY

Tri-Tip Sandwiches
WITH CURRIED MAYONNAISE

1. In a medium bowl mix the mayonnaise ingredients, including ½ teaspoon salt. Refrigerate until ready to use.

2. Season the roast evenly with ¾ teaspoon salt and the pepper. Allow the roast to stand at room temperature for 15 to 30 minutes before grilling.

3. Prepare the grill for direct and indirect cooking over medium heat (350° to 450°F).

4. Brush the cooking grates clean. Grill the roast over ***direct medium heat***, with the lid closed as much as possible, until well marked on both sides, 8 to 10 minutes, turning once. Move the roast over ***indirect medium heat***, close the lid, and continue to cook to your desired doneness, 20 to 30 minutes for medium rare. During the last minute of grilling time, toast the rolls over direct heat. Remove the roast and rolls from the grill and let the roast rest for 3 to 5 minutes. Cut the meat across the grain into thin slices.

5. Assemble the sandwiches on rolls with the mayonnaise, meat, arugula, and onion.

Access the grocery list for this recipe on your mobile device. timetogrill.mobi.

Tri-Tip with Braised Greens

SERVES: 👤👤👤👤 TO 👤👤👤👤👤

PREP TIME: **20** MINUTES

MARINATING TIME: **2** HOURS

GRILLING TIME: **28** TO **40** MINUTES

SPECIAL EQUIPMENT: SPICE MILL

2 teaspoons black peppercorns
1 teaspoon crushed red pepper flakes
1 teaspoon granulated sugar
2½ teaspoons kosher salt, divided

1 tri-tip roast, 1½ to 2 pounds and 1½ inches thick, fat and silver skin removed

2 bunches Swiss chard
¼ cup extra-virgin olive oil
1 red onion, halved and thinly sliced
2 tablespoons minced garlic
6 ounces baby spinach (about 8 packed cups)

1. **Coarsely grind the peppercorns and pepper flakes in a spice mill.** Pour into a small bowl and stir in the sugar and 1 teaspoon of the salt.

2. **Season the roast evenly with the spices, gently pressing the mixture into the meat.** Wrap the roast with plastic wrap and refrigerate for about 2 hours. Allow to stand at room temperature for 15 to 30 minutes before grilling.

3. **Strip the chard leaves from the stems and then tear the leaves into large pieces.** Trim off and discard the very ends of the stems and thinly slice the rest of the stems.

4. **In a large sauté pan over medium-high heat, warm the oil.** Add the chard stems, onion, and garlic; season with ¾ teaspoon of the salt. Sauté until tender, 8 to 10 minutes, adding a splash of water if the pan gets dry. Add the chard leaves and spinach, season with the remaining ¾ teaspoon salt, and fold them in with the onions to coat the leaves with the oil. Add 1 cup of water and cook until wilted and soft and the water has evaporated, about 15 minutes. Remove from the heat.

5. **Prepare the grill for direct and indirect cooking over medium heat (350° to 450°F).**

6. **Brush the cooking grates clean.** Grill the roast over *direct medium heat*, with the lid closed as much as possible, until well marked on both sides, 8 to 10 minutes, turning once. Move the roast over *indirect medium heat*, close the lid, and continue to cook to your desired doneness, 20 to 30 minutes for medium rare. Remove from the grill and let rest for 3 to 5 minutes. Cut the meat across the grain into thin slices. Transfer to a serving platter and drizzle any juices left on the cutting board over the meat. Serve warm with the braised greens.

Access the grocery list for this recipe on your mobile device. timetogrill.mobi.

↓ **EASY**   **ADVENTUROUS** ↗

PORK

Italian sausages are never better than when they are cooked on the grill. Whether you use pork or poultry sausages, sweet or hot, they drip luscious juices into the grill and cook in clouds of aromatic smoke. And what could be better with sausages than peppers and onions? In the easy recipe the vegetables are prepared in a "confit" style, that is, cooked in their own juices. Wrapped in foil with garlic and herbs, they turn tender and moist with very little attention. Another way to enjoy this classic Italian combination is to stuff the sausage in hollowed out "boats" of zucchini with a warm pepper puree poured over the top. It requires more ingredients and more time, but it is something you could make on a relaxed Sunday afternoon.

Italian Sausages with Peppers and Onions

SERVES: ♟♟♟♟

PREP TIME: **10** MINUTES

GRILLING TIME: **28** TO **33** MINUTES

2 tablespoons extra-virgin olive oil
1 tablespoon minced garlic
1 teaspoon kosher salt
½ teaspoon dried oregano
¼ teaspoon crushed red pepper flakes

3 bell peppers, 1 red, 1 yellow,
   and 1 orange, each cut into planks
1 medium yellow onion, cut crosswise into
   ¼-inch slices

5 fresh Italian sausages, each about
   4 ounces, pierced a few times with a fork

1. Prepare the grill for direct and indirect cooking over medium heat (350° to 450°F).

2. In a medium bowl whisk the oil, garlic, salt, oregano, and pepper flakes. Add the peppers and onion slices and turn to coat them evenly.

3. Brush the cooking grates clean. Grill the peppers and onion over *direct medium heat*, with the lid closed as much as possible, until tender, about 8 minutes, turning once or twice. Remove from the heat and cut the peppers into thin strips and cut the onions in half or separate into rings.

4. Grill the sausages over *indirect medium heat*, with the lid closed as much as possible, until thoroughly cooked, 20 to 25 minutes, turning occasionally. If you'd like to brown the sausages, cook them over *direct medium heat* during the last 3 to 5 minutes of grilling time, turning once. Remove from the grill and cut each sausage into three pieces. Put the peppers and onions on a platter and pile the sausage pieces on top. Serve warm.

Access the grocery list for this recipe on your mobile device. timetogrill.mobi.

SERVES: 🧍🧍🧍🧍 TO 🧍🧍🧍🧍🧍🧍

PREP TIME: **30** MINUTES

GRILLING TIME: **25** TO **30** MINUTES

// PUREE

- 4 large plum tomatoes, about 1 pound total
- 1 small yellow onion, cut crosswise into ½-inch slices
- 2 small bell peppers, 1 red and 1 yellow
- 2 tablespoons finely chopped fresh basil leaves
- 2 tablespoons finely chopped fresh oregano leaves
- 2 garlic cloves
- 2 tablespoons red wine vinegar
- 1 teaspoon kosher salt
- ¼ teaspoon ground black pepper
- ¼ cup extra-virgin olive oil

- 4 medium zucchini, about 2 pounds total, each one cut in half lengthwise
- 1 pound bulk Italian sausage meat *or* 1 pound uncooked Italian sausages, casings removed
- 1 cup grated Romano cheese
- ⅓ cup panko bread crumbs

1. Prepare the grill for direct cooking over medium heat (350° to 450°F).

2. Brush the cooking grates clean. Grill the tomatoes, onion, and peppers over *direct medium heat*, with the lid closed as much as possible, until the tomatoes and onions are soft and the peppers are blackened and blistered, turning every few minutes. The tomatoes and onions will take 8 to 10 minutes, and the peppers will take 10 to 15 minutes. Remove the vegetables from the grill as they are done. Place the peppers in a bowl and cover with plastic wrap to trap the steam. Let stand for about 10 minutes.

Sausage Stuffed Zucchini
WITH ROASTED PEPPER PUREE

3. When the vegetables are cool enough to handle, pull the skins from the tomatoes and cut out the stem ends. Peel, core, and seed the peppers. In the bowl of a food processor combine the tomatoes, onion, peppers, basil, oregano, garlic, vinegar, salt, and pepper. Pulse until a semi-smooth puree is created. With the motor running, slowly add the oil. In a medium saucepan over low heat, warm the puree until slightly thickened, 3 to 5 minutes, stirring occasionally. Remove from the heat.

4. With the cut sides of the zucchini facing up, lightly score the flesh ⅛ to ¼ inch in from the edges all the way around. Using a small spoon or melon baller, and using the scored edges as guides, carefully scoop out and discard the flesh and seeds, leaving what looks like a boat with uniformly thick walls.

5. In a medium bowl gently combine the sausage meat, cheese, bread crumbs, and ½ cup of the puree. Divide the mixture evenly between the zucchini boats, spreading it and lightly pressing it to fill the shells completely.

6. Brush the cooking grates clean. Grill the zucchini boats over *direct medium heat*, with the lid closed as much as possible, until the sausage is cooked through and no longer pink, about 15 minutes. Using a wide spatula under the zucchini for support, carefully remove them from the grill. Serve on a bed of rice or pasta, if desired, and top each with some of the warm puree. Pass any remaining puree.

Access the grocery list for this recipe on your mobile device. timetogrill.mobi.

Spanish-style chorizo sausages are often cured and smoked before they get to you, so they need only a few minutes on the grill. As far as sausages go, they are relatively spicy, and this chimichurri sauce has quite a kick of garlic and red pepper flakes, so the easy dish is for folks who like their food big and bold. Serve the skewers over white or red rice. The adventurous recipe also features chorizo, but here it is in the company of a traditional black bean salad from South America, pork tenderloin, and boneless, skinless chicken breasts. You could also substitute or add turkey or lamb in this recipe. That's the spirit of Brazilian churrasco—a mouthwatering variety of meats seared over open flames.

Chorizo and Beef Skewers
WITH CHIMICHURRI

SERVES: ♙♙♙♙

PREP TIME: **10** MINUTES

GRILLING TIME: **4** TO **6** MINUTES

SPECIAL EQUIPMENT: METAL OR BAMBOO SKEWERS (IF USING BAMBOO, SOAK IN WATER FOR AT LEAST 30 MINUTES)

EASY

// CHIMICHURRI

　1　cup firmly packed fresh Italian parsley leaves and tender stems
　2　medium garlic cloves
　¼　cup extra-virgin olive oil
　2　tablespoons white wine vinegar
　1　tablespoon water
　½　teaspoon crushed red pepper flakes
　　　Kosher salt
　　　Ground black pepper

　1　pound top sirloin, about 1 inch thick, trimmed of excess fat, cut into 1-inch cubes
　12　ounces fully cooked Spanish-style chorizo sausages, cut crosswise into 1-inch pieces

1. In a food processor whirl the parsley and garlic until finely chopped. With the machine running, add the oil, vinegar, and water in a steady stream. Season with the red pepper flakes, ½ teaspoon salt, and ½ teaspoon pepper. Pour about half of the chimichurri into a small bowl.

2. Prepare the grill for direct cooking over high heat (450° to 550°F).

3. Season the cubed beef with ¼ teaspoon salt and ⅛ teaspoon pepper. Thread the beef and chorizo pieces alternately onto skewers. Brush the meat with the chimichurri sauce left in the food processor.

4. Brush the cooking grates clean. Grill the skewers over *direct high heat*, with the lid closed as much as possible, until the steak is cooked to your desired doneness, 4 to 6 minutes for medium rare, turning 2 to 3 times (watch for flare-ups). Serve warm with the reserved chimichurri spooned over the top.

Access the grocery list for this recipe on your mobile device. timetogrill.mobi.

Churrasco Mixed Grill
WITH TOMATO-CITRUS BLACK BEANS

SERVES: 🧍🧍🧍🧍🧍🧍

PREP TIME: **30** MINUTES

MARINATING TIME: **1** HOUR

GRILLING TIME: **15** TO **20** MINUTES

// BEANS

- 2 cans (15 ounces each) black beans, rinsed
- 2 cups grape tomatoes, about 10 ounces, each cut in half
- 1 cup finely diced white onion, rinsed under cold water
- ½ cup finely chopped fresh Italian parsley leaves
- 2 tablespoons extra-virgin olive oil
- 1 tablespoon fresh lime juice
- 2 teaspoons minced garlic
  Grated zest of 1 orange
- ½ teaspoon smoked paprika
- ½ teaspoon kosher salt

// MARINADE

- ½ cup finely chopped fresh Italian parsley leaves
- ¼ cup extra-virgin olive oil
- ¼ cup fresh orange juice
- 1 tablespoon fresh lime juice
- 1 tablespoon minced garlic
- 2 teaspoons kosher salt
- 1 teaspoon ground black pepper

- 1 pork tenderloin, ¾ to 1 pound, trimmed of excess fat and silver skin
- 3 boneless, skinless chicken breast halves, each about 6 ounces
- 8 ounces fully cooked Spanish-style chorizo sausages

1. In a large bowl gently mix the bean ingredients. Set aside at room temperature for at least 45 minutes.

2. In a medium bowl whisk the marinade ingredients. Pour half of the marinade into another medium bowl. Add the pork tenderloin to the first bowl and the chicken breasts to the second bowl. Turn to coat the meat evenly. Cover and refrigerate for 1 hour.

3. Prepare the grill for direct cooking over medium heat (350° to 450°F).

4. Brush the cooking grates clean. Remove the pork and chicken from the bowls and let any excess marinade drip back into the bowls.

Discard the marinade. Grill the pork, chicken, and chorizo over *direct medium heat*, with the lid closed as much as possible, until the pork is evenly seared and the centers are barely pink, the chicken is firm to the touch and opaque all the way to the center, and the chorizo is browned, turning occasionally. The pork will take 15 to 20 minutes, the chicken will take 8 to 12 minutes, and the chorizo will take about 8 minutes. Remove from the grill as they are done.

5. Cut the meat into ½-inch slices. Serve warm with the bean salad.

Access the grocery list for this recipe on your mobile device. timetogrill.mobi.

Literally meaning "melted cheese," this easy dish is rich and hearty—something like a chunky Mexican fondue. Scoop it up with sturdy tortilla chips or spoon it into warm tortillas and roll them up like soft tacos. In some supermarkets, chorizo is sold in plastic-wrapped rolls, and the product is softer and considerably more fatty than the fresh, firm chorizo in casings. For the right texture in the queso fundido and the black bean cakes, you want the fresh, firm chorizo. Handle the black bean cakes delicately, because they are fragile until fully cooked (chilling them for 30 minutes helps them stay together), but the final results are wonderful. The heat of the chile sauce makes a nice bridge between the savory cakes and the sweet salsa.

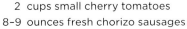

Queso Fundido
WITH CHORIZO

SERVES: 👤👤👤👤 TO 👤👤👤👤👤👤

PREP TIME 15 MINUTES

GRILLING TIME: 17 TO 23 MINUTES

SPECIAL EQUIPMENT: 10- OR 12-INCH CAST-IRON SKILLET

EASY

2 cups small cherry tomatoes
8–9 ounces fresh chorizo sausages (see headnote)
¾ cup thinly sliced scallions (white and light green parts only)
2 cups coarsely grated Monterey Jack cheese (8 ounces)
1 tablespoon all-purpose flour
½ cup low-sodium chicken broth, divided
½ cup crumbled cotija cheese
¼ cup finely chopped fresh cilantro leaves
1–2 tablespoons hot pepper sauce, such as Cholula®
1 bag (12 ounces) tortilla chips

1. Prepare the grill for direct cooking over medium heat (350° to 450°F).

2. Brush the cooking grates clean. Grill the tomatoes and chorizo over *direct medium heat*, with the lid closed as much as possible, until the tomatoes are slightly charred and beginning to break down and the chorizo is cooked through, turning occasionally. The tomatoes will take 4 to 6 minutes and the chorizo will take 12 to 15 minutes. Transfer the tomatoes to a 10- or 12-inch cast-iron skillet and the chorizo to a cutting board. Cut the chorizo into ½-inch slices and then cut each slice into quarters.

3. Add the chorizo and scallions to the skillet with the tomatoes and set the skillet on the cooking grate over *direct medium heat*. Cook, with the lid open, until the scallions wilt, 4 to 6 minutes, stirring occasionally. In a medium bowl toss the Monterey Jack cheese with the flour; add to the skillet and then pour in ¼ cup of the broth. Stir and cook, with the lid closed as much as possible, until the cheese melts and the sauce is smooth, 1 to 2 minutes. Add the cotija cheese and the cilantro. Add as much hot sauce as you like. Stir the sauce just until the cotija softens but remains in separate lumps, about 15 seconds. Stir in as much as ¼ cup of the remaining chicken broth to thin the cheese, if desired. Serve directly from the hot skillet with tortilla chips.

Access the grocery list for this recipe on your mobile device. timetogrill.mobi.

SERVES: 👤👤👤👤

PREP TIME: **25** MINUTES

CHILLING TIME: **30** MINUTES

GRILLING TIME: ABOUT **12** MINUTES

// SAUCE

1½ ounces dried New Mexico *or guajillo*
      chiles, stemmed, seeded, coarsely torn
1¼ cups low-sodium chicken broth
1½ tablespoons packed dark brown sugar
1½ tablespoons balsamic vinegar
 1   teaspoon ground cumin
      Kosher salt
      Ground black pepper

      Extra-virgin olive oil
 1   tablespoon fresh lime juice
 1   large, ripe mango, peeled, pitted, diced
 1   large Hass avocado, diced

 6   ounces fresh chorizo sausages,
      casings removed (see headnote)
 1   can (15 ounces) black beans, drained
 1   egg
 ½ cup panko bread crumbs
 ¼ cup finely chopped fresh cilantro leaves
 2   scallions (white and light green parts
      only), finely chopped
 ¼ cup sour cream

Chorizo and Black Bean Cakes
WITH RED CHILE SAUCE

1. In a small saucepan over high heat, bring the chiles and broth to a boil. Reduce the heat to medium-low, cover, and simmer until the chiles are softened, about 10 minutes. Pour the mixture into a blender. Add the brown sugar, vinegar, and cumin. Blend until the sauce is smooth, scraping down the sides as needed. Season with salt and pepper. Pour back into the saucepan.

2. In a medium bowl whisk 2 tablespoons oil and the lime juice. Add the mango and avocado and toss gently to coat. Season with

salt and pepper. Set the salad aside at room temperature.

3. Prepare the grill for direct cooking over medium-high heat (400° to 450°F).

4. In a medium skillet over medium-high heat, crumble the chorizo and sauté it until it is cooked through, 4 to 6 minutes, breaking it up and stirring it with the back of a fork. Reserve ¼ cup of the beans and place the remainder in a food processor. Whirl the beans until a thick paste forms, scraping down the sides as needed. Add the chorizo with any accumulated pan juices, the egg, bread crumbs, cilantro, and scallions. Pulse until blended but not completely pureed. There should be some texture, but the chorizo should be in small pieces. Transfer to a medium bowl and stir in the reserved beans. Using wet hands, shape the mixture into four firm patties, each about 3½ inches in diameter and ¾ inch thick. Place on a sheet pan, cover with plastic wrap, and refrigerate for about 30 minutes to firm up the patties.

5. Brush the cooking grates clean. Lay a sheet of heavy-duty aluminum foil, large enough to accommodate all four patties, on the cooking grate. Brush the top of each bean cake generously with oil and turn them, oil side down, onto the foil. Grill the bean cakes over *direct medium-high heat*, with the lid closed as much as possible, for 6 minutes. Brush the tops of the cakes with oil and gently slide a wide spatula under each patty, using another spatula to support the back of it if necessary (the bean cakes will be fragile at this point but will firm up as they continue to cook). Turn the patties over and grill them until they are cooked through, about 6 minutes. Remove the bean cakes from the grill and place them on individual serving dishes.

6. Reheat the chile sauce over medium heat and then drizzle each bean cake with equal amounts of the sauce. Serve with sour cream and the mango and avocado salad.

Access the grocery list for this recipe on your mobile device. timetogrill.mobi.

EASY

There's a delicious, down-home southern quality about grilled pork with whiskey and mustard. You can have a taste of that in a matter of minutes by brushing some pork chops with a sweet boozy glaze and grilling them along with tart apples. Or you can go for a deeper effect by brining the chops first in buttermilk. The salt in the brine penetrates the meat, taking the flavors and moisture of the buttermilk and mustard all the way inside. If only all pork chops could be this juicy.

SERVES: ††††

PREP TIME: **15** MINUTES

GRILLING TIME: **12** TO **16** MINUTES

// GLAZE
- ¼ cup whiskey
- ¼ cup packed brown sugar
- 2 tablespoons whole-grain mustard
- 1 teaspoon pure vanilla extract

- 4 bone-in pork loin chops, each about 8 ounces and 1 inch thick, trimmed of excess fat
  Vegetable oil
- 1 teaspoon kosher salt
- ½ teaspoon ground black pepper
- 4 Granny Smith apples, cored and cut into ½-inch wedges
- 1 tablespoon finely chopped fresh tarragon leaves

Whiskey-Mustard Pork Chops
WITH GRILLED APPLES

1. In a small bowl whisk the glaze ingredients until the brown sugar dissolves. Reserve 3 tablespoons of the glaze in a large bowl.

2. Lightly coat the pork chops on both sides with oil, season evenly with salt and pepper, and brush with the whiskey glaze in the small bowl. Allow the chops to stand at room temperature for 15 to 30 minutes before grilling.

3. Prepare the grill for direct cooking over medium heat (350° to 450°F).

4. Lightly coat the apple slices on both sides with oil.

5. Brush the cooking grates clean. Grill the apples over *direct medium heat*, with the lid closed as much as possible, until crisp-tender and lightly charred, 4 to 6 minutes, turning once or twice. Transfer the apple slices to the large bowl with the reserved whiskey glaze, add the tarragon, and toss to coat.

6. Grill the chops over *direct medium heat*, with the lid closed as much as possible, until they are still slightly pink in the center, 8 to 10 minutes, turning once or twice. Remove from the grill and let rest for 3 to 5 minutes. Serve the chops warm with the grilled apples.

Access the grocery list for this recipe on your mobile device. timetogrill.mobi.

Buttermilk-Brined Pork Chops
WITH WHISKEY-BRAISED CABBAGE AND APPLES

SERVES: ††††

PREP TIME: **30** MINUTES

BRINING TIME: **1** TO **1½** HOURS

GRILLING TIME: **8** TO **10** MINUTES

// BRINE

- 2 cups cold buttermilk
- 1 cup water
- ½ cup kosher salt
- 1 tablespoon whole-grain mustard
- 1 tablespoon finely chopped fresh tarragon leaves

- 4 boneless pork loin chops, each about 8 ounces and 1 inch thick, trimmed of excess fat
  Extra-virgin olive oil

- 2 tablespoons unsalted butter
- 4 cups shredded red cabbage
- 2 cups coarsely grated tart green apples, such as Granny Smith
- ⅓ cup whiskey
- 2 tablespoons balsamic vinegar
- ¼ teaspoon celery seed
- ¾ teaspoon kosher salt
- ¼ teaspoon ground black pepper

1. In a medium bowl whisk the brine ingredients until the salt dissolves.

2. Put the chops in a large, resealable plastic bag and pour in the brine. Press the air out of the bag and seal tightly. Place the bag in a bowl or a rimmed dish and refrigerate for 1 to 1½ hours, turning the bag every 30 minutes.

3. Remove the chops from the bag and discard the brine. Rinse the chops under cold water and pat dry with paper towels. Lightly brush or spray the chops on both sides with oil and allow to stand at room temperature for 15 to 30 minutes before grilling.

4. Prepare the grill for direct cooking over medium heat (350° to 450°F).

5. In a large skillet over medium-high heat, melt the butter. Add the cabbage and apples and sauté until the cabbage just starts to wilt, 2 to 3 minutes. Stir in the whiskey, vinegar, and celery seed. Cover and cook until the cabbage is tender, 10 to 12 minutes, stirring occasionally. Remove from the heat, season with the salt and pepper, and cover to keep warm.

6. Brush the cooking grates clean. Grill the chops over *direct medium heat*, with the lid closed as much as possible, until they are still slightly pink in the center, 8 to 10 minutes, turning once or twice. Remove the chops from the grill and let rest for 3 to 5 minutes. Serve warm with the braised cabbage and apples.

Access the grocery list for this recipe on your mobile device. timetogrill.mobi.

Complex flavors come together quickly if all you really need to do is pour them out of a spice jar. That's the case here in the easy recipe, where some bold spices like turmeric and cumin make ordinary pork chops a lot more interesting, particularly with some grilled fresh fruit for a bit of extra juiciness and sweetness. The spice rub includes a fair amount of sugar, so use low heat to grill the pork chops without burning them. Working along similar lines, the adventurous recipe uses an aromatic rub but also makes an impressive stuffing for the inside of the chops, with dried fruits, white wine, and toasted almonds. If you are not feeling up to splitting open the pork chops, just spoon the "stuffing" over the top of the grilled chops.

Moroccan-Spiced Pork Chops
WITH APRICOTS

SERVES: 🧍🧍🧍🧍

PREP TIME: **15** MINUTES

GRILLING TIME: **16** TO **18** MINUTES

// RUB
Finely grated zest of 1 large lemon
1 tablespoon packed brown sugar
1 teaspoon kosher salt
1 teaspoon ground turmeric
1 teaspoon ground cumin
¾ teaspoon ground black pepper
½ teaspoon ground cinnamon
½ teaspoon ground ginger

4 boneless pork loin chops, each about 6 ounces and 1 inch thick, trimmed of excess fat
Extra-virgin olive oil

4 fresh apricots, each cut in half
¼ cup golden raisins

1. Prepare the grill for direct cooking over low heat (250° to 350°F).

2. In a small bowl mix the rub ingredients. Lightly brush the chops on both sides with oil and season evenly with the rub. Marinate the chops at room temperature for 15 to 30 minutes while the grill preheats.

3. Brush the cooking grates clean. Grill the apricots, cut side down, over *direct low heat*, with the lid closed as much as possible, until heated through, 6 to 8 minutes, turning once.

Cooking times will vary depending on the ripeness of the apricots. Remove from the grill and, when cool enough to handle, cut into bite-sized pieces. Place in a bowl and add the raisins; stir to combine. Set aside while you grill the chops.

4. Grill the chops over *direct low heat*, with the lid closed as much as possible, until they are still slightly pink in the center, about **10 minutes, turning once or twice.** Remove from the grill and let rest for 3 to 5 minutes. Serve warm with the apricot-raisin mixture.

Access the grocery list for this recipe on your mobile device. timetogrill.mobi.

SERVES: ♦♦♦♦♦♦

PREP TIME: **30** MINUTES

GRILLING TIME: **12** TO **16** MINUTES

// RUB

- 1 tablespoon mild curry powder
- 2 teaspoons packed brown sugar
- ¾ teaspoon kosher salt
- ½ teaspoon ground ginger
- ½ teaspoon ground black pepper

- 6 boneless pork loin chops, each about 8 ounces and 1¼ inches thick, trimmed of excess fat
  Extra-virgin olive oil

// STUFFING

- ½ cup finely chopped dried apricots
- ¼ cup golden raisins
- ½ medium onion, finely chopped
- 2 teaspoons minced garlic
- ½ teaspoon curry powder
- ¼ teaspoon ground coriander
- ¼ teaspoon kosher salt
- ⅛ teaspoon ground black pepper
- ¼ cup dry white wine
- ¼ cup panko bread crumbs
- ⅓ cup toasted slivered almonds

Pork Chops
STUFFED WITH APRICOTS AND RAISINS

1. In a small bowl mix the rub ingredients.

2. **Using a small, sharp knife, cut each pork chop almost all the way in half, so that it opens like a book, with the fatty part as its spine.** Splay the chops open and lay them on a work surface with the cut sides down. Lightly brush the outsides with oil and season evenly with the rub. Allow the chops to stand at room temperature for 15 to 30 minutes before grilling.

3. **Prepare the grill for direct and indirect cooking over medium heat (350° to 450°F).**

4. **Meanwhile, in a small bowl combine the apricots and raisins.** Add enough boiling water to cover the fruit; set aside to soften for 5 minutes and then drain.

5. **Heat a large skillet over medium heat.** When the skillet is hot, add 1 tablespoon oil and the onion. Cook until the onion begins to soften, about 5 minutes, stirring occasionally. Add the garlic, curry powder, coriander, salt, pepper, and drained fruit and cook for 2 minutes, stirring to combine. Add the wine, bring to a simmer, and cook until the wine has evaporated, 2 to 3 minutes. Remove the pan from the heat and mix in the bread crumbs and almonds.

6. **Turn the chops over so the insides face up.** Spoon some of the stuffing on each chop, leaving a rim without stuffing at the edges. Gently press the chop together to close.

7. **Brush the cooking grates clean.** Grill the chops over *direct medium heat*, with the lid closed as much as possible, until nicely seared on both sides, 8 to 10 minutes, turning once or twice. Move the chops over *indirect medium heat* and continue to grill until they are still slightly pink in the center, 4 to 6 minutes. Remove from the grill and let rest for 3 to 5 minutes. Serve warm.

Access the grocery list for this recipe on your mobile device. timetogrill.mobi.

SERVES: 🧍🧍🧍🧍

PREP TIME: **15** MINUTES

GRILLING TIME: **8** TO **10** MINUTES

SPECIAL EQUIPMENT: PERFORATED GRILL PAN

¼ cup white miso paste (sometimes labeled *shiro* miso)

2 tablespoons peeled, grated fresh ginger

2 tablespoons soy sauce, divided

2 tablespoons toasted sesame oil, divided

4 boneless pork loin chops, each about 6 ounces and 1 inch thick, trimmed of excess fat

½ teaspoon wasabi paste

1 pound fresh green beans, trimmed

1 tablespoon sesame seeds (black, white, or a combination)

Vegetable oil

Boneless pork chops are almost infinitely versatile. Here they are in two Asian-inspired variations. The first uses a Japanese miso-ginger paste that grows sweeter on the meat as it grills. The second is a Chinese stir-fry done right on the grill in a cast-iron skillet. Once you begin to stir-fry, you need to stay next to the grill and keep the food moving almost constantly, so have all the ingredients prepared and within reach. If you don't have a fine grater for the ginger, chop it very finely with a knife.

Miso-Ginger Pork Chops
WITH SESAME GREEN BEANS

1. In a small bowl combine the miso, ginger, 1 tablespoon of the soy sauce, and 1 tablespoon of the sesame oil. Spread the chops on both sides with the paste and marinate at room temperature for 15 to 30 minutes.

2. Prepare the grill for direct cooking over medium heat (350° to 450°F) and preheat the grill pan.

3. In a large bowl combine the remaining 1 tablespoon soy sauce, the remaining 1 tablespoon sesame oil, and the wasabi paste. Add the green beans and turn to coat them thoroughly. Sprinkle the sesame seeds over the beans and toss gently to distribute the seeds evenly.

4. Brush the cooking grates clean. Wipe almost all of the paste from the chops and lightly brush with vegetable oil. Grill the chops over **direct medium heat**, with the lid closed as much as possible, until they are still slightly pink in the center, 8 to 10 minutes, turning once or twice. At the same time, spread the green beans in a single layer on the grill pan, reserving any dressing that remains in the bowl, and grill over **direct medium heat** until they are browned in spots and crisp-tender,

5 to 7 minutes, turning occasionally. Remove the chops and beans from the grill and let the chops rest for 3 to 5 minutes.

5. Drizzle the beans with the reserved dressing and serve with the pork chops.

Access the grocery list for this recipe on your mobile device. timetogrill.mobi.

EASY

Stir-Fried Pork with Broccoli and Snow Peas

SERVES: 🧍🧍🧍🧍

PREP TIME: **30** MINUTES

GRILLING TIME: **9** TO **12** MINUTES

SPECIAL EQUIPMENT: WOK OR
12-INCH CAST-IRON SKILLET

// SAUCE

- ¾ cup water
- ¼ cup reduced-sodium soy sauce
- 2 tablespoons peeled, grated fresh ginger
- 1 tablespoon toasted sesame oil
- 2½ teaspoons cornstarch
- 2 teaspoons minced garlic
- ¾ teaspoon hot chili-garlic sauce, such as Sriracha

// STIR-FRY

- 2 tablespoons peanut oil *or* canola oil
- 3 boneless pork loin chops, each about 6 ounces and 1 inch thick, trimmed of all fat, cut into ¼-inch strips
- 2 cups bite-sized broccoli florets
- 1 cup snow peas, 2 to 3 ounces, each trimmed and cut diagonally in half
- 5 scallions (white and light green parts only), cut into 1-inch pieces
- 1 large red bell pepper, cut into bite-sized pieces

- 3 cups cooked rice

1. In a medium bowl whisk the sauce ingredients. Set aside.

2. Prepare the grill for direct cooking over high heat (450° to 550°F).

3. Brush the cooking grates clean. Place the wok or skillet on the cooking grate and preheat it for 5 minutes. Have all the stir-fry ingredients prepared and together at the grill.

4. When the wok is hot, add the oil, then the pork, separating the slices as they are added to the wok. The pork may spatter a bit. Grill over **direct high heat**, with the lid closed as much as possible, until the meat starts to brown and releases easily from the wok, about 2 minutes. Add the vegetables all at once. Stir to combine them with the pork and cook for another 3 minutes, with the lid closed as much as possible, stirring once or twice. Add the sauce, close the grill lid, and cook until the sauce comes to a simmer, 1 to 2 minutes. Simmer until the sauce is thick enough to coat the vegetables, 3 to 5 minutes, stirring occasionally. Remove from the grill and serve immediately over warm rice.

Access the grocery list for this recipe on your mobile device. timetogrill.mobi.

This easy recipe calls for pork chops that have been butterflied, which means the butcher made a deep cut into the side of each pork chop and spread the meat open to look like a butterfly with its wings spread out. You can find these chops at big supermarkets now, and the benefit for grillers is that they have increased surface area to put in direct contact with the hot cooking grate, creating more opportunity for browning the meat. A minty plum salsa with a bit of jalapeño is all you need to complement the chops. The adventurous recipe plays with many of the same flavors but also takes advantage of what happens to a pork loin when you salt it twelve to twenty-four hours before cooking it. Initially the salt draws moisture out of the meat, and then the salty juices are reabsorbed into the meat, making it tastier than before. The spicy mint sauce adds a kick to both the pork and the sweet grilled plums.

Butterflied Pork Chops
WITH PLUM, MINT, AND JALAPEÑO SALSA

SERVES: 🧍🧍🧍🧍 TO 🧍🧍🧍🧍🧍🧍

PREP TIME: **15** MINUTES

GRILLING TIME: **8** TO **10** MINUTES

4 center-cut butterflied pork loin chops, each about 10 ounces and ¾ to 1 inch thick, trimmed of excess fat
1¼ teaspoons kosher salt, divided
4 ripe plums, cut into bite-sized pieces
½ medium jalapeño chile pepper, seeded and minced
⅓ cup finely chopped fresh mint leaves
1½ teaspoons granulated sugar
¼ teaspoon ground coriander
¼ teaspoon ground black pepper
2 teaspoons extra-virgin olive oil

1. Season the pork chops on both sides with 1 teaspoon of the salt. Allow the chops to stand at room temperature for 15 to 30 minutes.

2. Prepare the grill for direct cooking over medium heat (350° to 450°F).

3. In a medium bowl gently combine the plums, jalapeño, mint, sugar, coriander, pepper, and the remaining ¼ teaspoon salt. Set aside.

4. Lightly brush the pork chops on both sides with the oil. Brush the cooking grates clean. Grill the chops over **direct medium heat**, with the lid closed as much as possible, until they are stilll slightly pink in the center, 8 to 10 minutes, turning once or twice. Remove from the grill and let rest for 3 to 5 minutes. Serve warm topped with the salsa.

Access the grocery list for this recipe on your mobile device. timetogrill.mobi.

1. **Sprinkle the roast all over with 1 teaspoon of the salt.** Place it in a bowl, cover, and refrigerate for 12 to 24 hours.

2. **Remove the roast from the bowl and pat dry with paper towels.** Coat the roast all over with 1 teaspoon of the vegetable oil and allow to stand at room temperature for about 30 minutes before grilling.

3. **Prepare the grill for direct and indirect cooking over high heat (450° to 550°F).**

4. **Brush the cooking grates clean.** Sear the roast over *direct high heat*, with the lid closed as much as possible, until the surface is well marked but not burned, 10 to 12 minutes, turning occasionally. Watch for flare-ups, especially when searing the fatty side. Move the roast over *indirect high heat* and cook, fat side up, with the lid closed, until the internal temperature reaches 145° to 150°F, 25 to 35 minutes. Transfer to a cutting board, tent loosely with aluminum foil, and let rest for about 15 minutes.

5. **Remove and discard the stem from the chile pepper and cut it into a few large pieces (if a milder sauce is preferred, remove the seeds).** In a blender or food processor whirl the chile pepper, mint, ginger, garlic, lemon juice, olive oil, and the remaining 1 teaspoon of salt until smooth. Set aside.

6. **Brush both sides of the plums with the remaining 1 teaspoon vegetable oil.** Grill the plums, cut side down, over *indirect high heat*, with the lid closed as much as possible, until grill marks appear and the plums are tender when poked with the tip of a knife, 8 to 10 minutes; do not turn the plums. Remove from the grill and cut each plum half in half.

7. **Cut the roast crosswise into ½-inch slices.** Serve warm with the grilled plums and the mint sauce.

Access the grocery list for this recipe on your mobile device. timetogrill.mobi.

Roasted Pork Loin
WITH PLUMS AND MINT SAUCE

SERVES: 6 TO 8

PREP TIME: **30** MINUTES

DRY BRINING TIME: **12** TO **24** HOURS

GRILLING TIME: **43** TO **57** MINUTES

SPECIAL EQUIPMENT:
INSTANT-READ THERMOMETER

1 boneless center-cut pork loin roast, 3 to 4 pounds
2 teaspoons kosher salt, divided
2 teaspoons vegetable oil *or* canola oil, divided
1 medium serrano chile pepper
2 cups loosely packed fresh mint leaves
2 teaspoons peeled, grated fresh ginger
2 garlic cloves
2 tablespoons fresh lemon juice
6 tablespoons extra-virgin olive oil
6 ripe plums, each one cut in half

Grilling pork chops with the bone still attached will always give you a little extra flavor, and taste buds will really light up when the pork is rubbed with a fragrant combination of rosemary, sage, and garlic. This Mediterranean blend opens the door to several French and Italian side dishes, from beans to grilled vegetables. Fans of French cuisine might recognize the adventurous dish as a deconstructed cassoulet, a rib-sticking casserole that can take days to make. Here, the basic elements, including a hearty bean ragout, a garlicky bread crumb topping, and deeply flavored pork, are tweaked for big flavor with little effort.

SERVES:

PREP TIME: **10** MINUTES

GRILLING TIME: **8** TO **10** MINUTES

Pork Chops with Herb-Garlic Rub

EASY

// RUB

- 2 medium garlic cloves
- 1 teaspoon kosher salt
- 3 tablespoons extra-virgin olive oil
- 2 teaspoons fresh rosemary leaves
- 2 teaspoons fresh sage leaves
- ½ teaspoon ground black pepper

- 4 bone-in pork loin chops, each about 8 ounces and 1 inch thick, trimmed of excess fat

1. Prepare the grill for direct cooking over medium heat (350° to 450°F).

2. Smash the garlic with the back of your knife and finely chop it. Sprinkle with the salt and continue chopping and scraping the garlic against the board with the flat side of the knife to make a paste. Scrape up and transfer the garlic paste to a small bowl. Add the oil, rosemary, sage, and pepper and stir well. Spread the rub on both sides of the chops. Allow the chops to stand at room temperature for 15 to 30 minutes before grilling.

3. Brush the cooking grates clean. Grill the chops over **direct medium heat**, with the lid closed as much as possible, until they are still slightly pink in the center, 8 to 10 minutes, turning once or twice. Remove from the grill and let rest for 3 to 5 minutes. Serve warm with grill-roasted plum tomatoes, if desired.

Access the grocery list for this recipe on your mobile device. timetogrill.mobi.

Pork Chops with White Bean Ragout

SERVES: 🜢🜢🜢🜢

PREP TIME: **15** MINUTES, PLUS ABOUT 25 MINUTES FOR THE RAGOUT

GRILLING TIME: **8** TO **10** MINUTES

// PASTE

- 2 tablespoons Dijon mustard
  Extra-virgin olive oil
  Kosher salt
  Ground black pepper

- 4 bone-in pork loin chops, each about 8 ounces and 1 inch thick, trimmed of excess fat

// RAGOUT

- 2 ounces pancetta, sliced ⅛ inch thick *or* 2 thick slices bacon, cut into ¼-inch dice
- 2 tablespoons minced shallot
- 2 cans (15 ounces each) white kidney (cannellini) beans, rinsed
- ¾ cup reduced-sodium chicken broth
- 1 ripe plum tomato, seeded and diced
- 3 tablespoons dry white wine *or* dry vermouth
- ½ teaspoon chopped fresh rosemary leaves
- ½ teaspoon chopped fresh sage leaves

- 2 slices whole-grain artisan bread, each about ½ inch thick, torn into pieces (1 cup)
- 1 garlic clove, finely chopped

1. In a small bowl mix the mustard with 3 tablespoons oil, 1 teaspoon salt, and ½ teaspoon pepper. Lightly brush the pork chops on both sides with the paste. Allow the chops to stand at room temperature for 15 to 30 minutes before grilling.

2. Prepare the grill for direct cooking over medium heat (350° to 450°F).

3. In a medium saucepan over medium heat, cook the pancetta in 2 teaspoons oil until it is lightly browned, about 5 minutes, stirring often. Add the shallot and cook until softened, about 2 minutes. Stir in the beans, broth, tomato, wine, rosemary, and sage and bring to a boil. Reduce the heat to medium-low and simmer until the liquid is reduced by half, about 15 minutes. Season with salt and pepper. Remove from the heat and cover.

4. In a food processor pulse the bread until coarse crumbs form. In a large skillet over medium heat, heat 2 tablespoons of oil and the garlic until the garlic begins to turn golden, about 3 minutes, stirring often. Add the bread crumbs and cook until the bread crumbs are crispy, about 2 minutes, stirring often.

5. Brush the cooking grates clean. Grill the chops over *direct medium heat*, with the lid closed as much as possible, until they are still slightly pink in the center, 8 to 10 minutes, turning once or twice. Remove from the grill and let rest for 3 to 5 minutes.

6. Serve the chops warm with the ragout and topped with bread crumbs.

Access the grocery list for this recipe on your mobile device. timetogrill.mobi.

Here you have arguably one of the easiest—and fastest—pork chop recipes ever. It's simply the meat, some readily available seasonings, good olive oil, and ripe pineapple. Now the fewer the ingredients you have, the more your technique matters, so focus on developing a nice, dark brown sear on the surface of the meat before it overcooks in the center. That requires keeping the lid closed as much as possible. If you happen to have a couple hours before dinner, take the time to soak your chops in a potent marinade of orange and pomegranate juices, and dial up the grilled pineapple accompaniment by mixing it with grilled apricots in a sweet and spicy salsa.

SERVES: 🧍🧍🧍🧍

PREP TIME: 10 MINUTES

GRILLING TIME: 8 TO 10 MINUTES

Simple Pork Chops
WITH GRILLED PINEAPPLE

// RUB
1½ teaspoons kosher salt
1 teaspoon dried oregano
¼ teaspoon granulated garlic
¼ teaspoon granulated onion
¼ teaspoon ground black pepper

4 bone-in pork loin chops, each about 8 ounces and 1 inch thick, trimmed of excess fat
   Extra-virgin olive oil

4 slices fresh pineapple, each about ½ inch thick

1. **Prepare the grill for direct cooking over medium heat (350° to 450°F).**

2. **In a small bowl combine the rub ingredients.** Lightly coat the chops on both sides with oil and season evenly with the rub. Allow the chops to stand at room temperature for 15 to 30 minutes before grilling.

3. **Brush the cooking grates clean.** Grill the chops over ***direct medium heat***, with the lid closed as much as possible, until they are still slightly pink in the center, 8 to 10 minutes, turning once or twice. At the same time, grill the pineapple over ***direct medium heat*** until well marked on both sides, 4 to 6 minutes, turning once. Remove the chops and the pineapple from the grill and let the chops rest for 3 to 5 minutes. Cut the pineapple slices into quarters and serve with the chops.

Access the grocery list for this recipe on your mobile device. timetogrill.mobi.

Marinated Pork Chops
WITH FRESH FRUIT SALSA

SERVES: 4

PREP TIME: **30** MINUTES

MARINATING TIME: **1** HOUR

GRILLING TIME: **14** TO **18** MINUTES

// MARINADE
- 1 cup refrigerated pomegranate juice
- Zest and juice of 1 orange
- 1 teaspoon pure chile powder
- 1 teaspoon kosher salt
- ½ teaspoon ground black pepper

- 4 bone-in pork loin chops, each about 8 ounces and 1 inch thick, trimmed of excess fat

// SALSA
- 4 slices fresh pineapple, each about ½ inch thick
- 4 fresh apricots, each one cut in half
- 1 teaspoon pure chile powder
- ½ teaspoon crushed red pepper flakes
- ½ teaspoon kosher salt

1. In a large bowl combine the marinade ingredients. Place the chops in the bowl, turn to coat them in the marinade, cover, and refrigerate for 1 hour. Allow the chops to stand at room temperature for 15 to 30 minutes before grilling.

2. Prepare the grill for direct cooking over medium heat (350° to 450°F).

3. Brush the cooking grates clean. Grill the pineapple and apricots over *direct medium heat*, with the lid closed as much as possible, until warm throughout, 6 to 8 minutes, turning once. Remove from the grill and coarsely

chop. Put the fruit in a food processor and add the remaining salsa ingredients. Pulse until you have a chunky salsa.

4. Remove the chops from the bowl and discard the marinade. Grill the chops over *direct medium heat*, with the lid closed as much as possible, until they are still slightly pink in the center, 8 to 10 minutes, turning once or twice. Remove from the grill and let rest for 3 to 5 minutes. Serve warm with the salsa.

Access the grocery list for this recipe on your mobile device. timetogrill.mobi.

THE BIRTH OF // the kettle

Back in 1952, a hankering for good barbecue lit a fire under George Stephen. George worked at Weber Brothers Metal Works, just outside of Chicago, welding metal buoys for a local yacht club. George loved to grill. With a growing family at home, he found it the perfect way to relax. Unfortunately, he didn't find the grills on the market at the time quite as perfect. The most popular grill of the day was an open, flat brazier—a product George found woefully under-engineered. If the wind kicked up, ashes blew onto your food, and if it began to rain, your meal was ruined. He knew there had to be a better way.

One day, George was about to weld two buoy halves together when the idea hit: Why not use the bottom half for the cooking bowl and the top half for the lid to create a grill? So he did. He added a handle and three legs and took his crazy looking contraption home to test.

The neighbors laughed and called it a UFO, but were surprised by how good the results were. George figured he was really on to something, so he packed up "George's Barbecue Kettle" and hit the road, demonstrating his funny looking creation at mom-and-pop hardware stores across the country. His invention became wildly popular and before long, his passion became America's pastime, sparking a backyard revolution that's lived on for generations.

George's Barbecue Kettle,
the precursor to today's Weber® kettle, 1952.

STEP 1

Discs of high-grade rolled steel are placed on a press. The press bends the metal into a bowl shape under 500 tons of pressure. The lid is pressed in a similar fashion.

poking some holes
IN GEORGE'S THEORY

As the story goes, when George first tried out the original kettle, it didn't work quite as he hoped. No matter how hard he tried, it just wouldn't stay lit. A neighbor peering over the back fence offered a little friendly advice, "Poke some holes in that thing so the fire can get some air!" So George did, and the rest is history. Today, Weber kettles are made in a state-of-the-art factory in suburban Chicago, not far from the birthplace of the original.

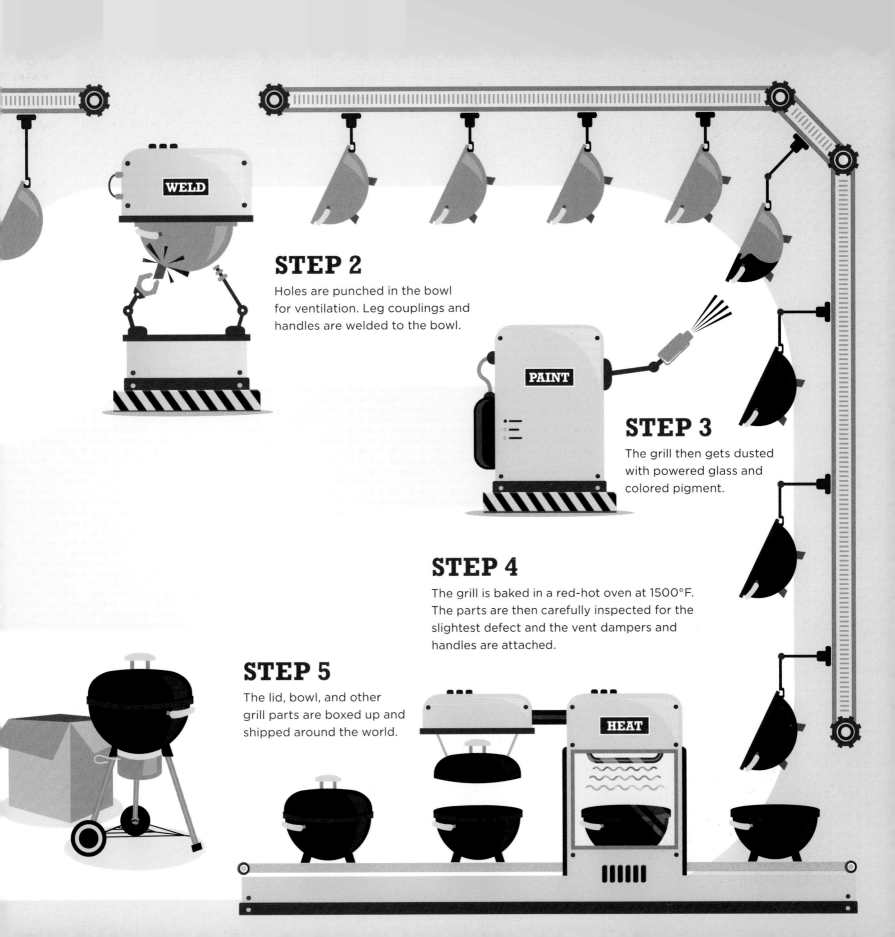

STEP 2

Holes are punched in the bowl for ventilation. Leg couplings and handles are welded to the bowl.

STEP 3

The grill then gets dusted with powered glass and colored pigment.

STEP 4

The grill is baked in a red-hot oven at 1500°F. The parts are then carefully inspected for the slightest defect and the vent dampers and handles are attached.

STEP 5

The lid, bowl, and other grill parts are boxed up and shipped around the world.

Au jus means "with juice" in French, and it usually refers to a simple sauce made from natural meat juices. In this easy recipe the pork juices that collect on the plate after it has been grilled are added to a white wine and chicken broth reduction, and the sauce is finished with a little butter. It's a good way to provide pork medallions with a spoonful of succulence. If you'd rather exercise your knife skills, consider the adventurous recipe that involves carefully cutting open pork tenderloins and pounding them out so you can fill them with lemony bread crumbs and herbs.

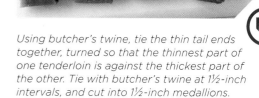

Using butcher's twine, tie the thin tail ends together, turned so that the thinnest part of one tenderloin is against the thickest part of the other. Tie with butcher's twine at 1½-inch intervals, and cut into 1½-inch medallions.

Marinated Pork Tenderloin Medallions Au Jus

SERVES: 👤👤👤👤

PREP TIME: **20** MINUTES, PLUS ABOUT 20 MINUTES FOR THE SAUCE

MARINATING TIME: **1** TO **4** HOURS

GRILLING TIME: **4** TO **6** MINUTES

SPECIAL EQUIPMENT:
BUTCHER'S TWINE

// MARINADE

- 2 cups dry white wine
- ½ cup chicken broth
- 2 tablespoons packed brown sugar
- 1 tablespoon finely chopped garlic
- 3 tablespoons finely chopped fresh rosemary leaves, divided

- 2 pork tenderloins, each ¾ to 1 pound, trimmed of excess fat and silver skin
- 1 tablespoon extra-virgin olive oil
- ½ teaspoon kosher salt
- ½ teaspoon ground black pepper
- 1 tablespoon unsalted butter

EASY

1. In a large bowl mix the wine, broth, sugar, garlic, and 2 tablespoons of the rosemary.

2. **Cut the tenderloins crosswise into 1½-inch medallions, starting at the thicker ends.** Tie the thinner ends together as shown above. Add the medallions to the bowl, turn to coat, cover, and refrigerate for 1 to 4 hours.

3. **Remove the medallions from the bowl, reserving the marinade.** Pat dry with paper towels and lightly brush both sides with the oil. Season evenly with the salt, pepper, and the remaining 1 tablespoon rosemary. Allow to stand at room temperature for 15 to 30 minutes before grilling.

4. **Prepare the grill for direct cooking over medium heat (350° to 450°F).**

5. **Brush the cooking grates clean.** Grill the medallions over ***direct medium heat***, with the lid closed as much as possible, until the outsides are evenly seared and the centers are barely pink, 4 to 6 minutes, turning once. Remove from the grill and let rest for 3 to 5 minutes, reserving the juices that accumulate.

6. **Strain the marinade into a small saucepan and bring it to a boil.** Lower the heat to maintain a steady simmer and cook until about 1 cup remains, skimming off any foam, 15 to 17 minutes. Remove from the heat. Add the reserved meat juices and stir in the butter. Serve the pork warm with the sauce.

Access the grocery list for this recipe on your mobile device. timetogrill.mobi.

Make a horizontal cut one-third of the way up the tenderloin so that the meat opens like a book, but do not cut all the way through the other side.

Make a second horizontal cut about halfway up the thicker section of meat, but stop before cutting all the way through, so you have a thin, flat piece of pork.

Pork Tenderloin Roulades
WITH GARLICKY SWEET POTATOES

SERVES: 👤👤👤👤

PREP TIME: **30** MINUTES

GRILLING TIME: **40** TO **45** MINUTES

SPECIAL EQUIPMENT: BUTCHER'S TWINE, INSTANT-READ THERMOMETER

1 tablespoon minced garlic
  Extra-virgin olive oil
  Kosher salt
  Ground black pepper
1½ pounds small sweet potatoes, cut crosswise into ¾-inch slices, skin left on

2 cups fresh bread crumbs
  Zest and ⅓ cup juice from 2 lemons
2 teaspoons finely chopped fresh thyme leaves

2 pork tenderloins, each ¾ to 1 pound, trimmed of excess fat and silver skin

1. In a medium bowl combine the garlic, 1 tablespoon oil, ½ teaspoon salt, and ¼ teaspoon pepper. Add the potatoes and turn to coat evenly. Place the potatoes on one long half of a 24-inch long piece of aluminum foil. Fold the other side of the foil over the potatoes and crimp the edges so that the potatoes are securely sealed in a packet.

2. To the same medium bowl add the bread crumbs, lemon zest and juice, thyme, ½ teaspoon salt, ¼ teaspoon pepper, and 2 tablespoons oil and toss until the bread crumbs are evenly moistened.

3. Butterfly the tenderloins using the techniques shown above. Cover the pork with plastic wrap and gently pound with the bottom of a small, heavy skillet, moving to different areas with every stroke until the pork is about ½ inch thick all over.

4. Prepare the grill for direct and indirect cooking over medium heat (350° to 450°F).

5. Press half of the stuffing onto each piece of meat, spreading it all the way to the edges. Roll the meat up from one long edge to the other so the tenderloins generally regain their original shape. Secure each roll with butcher's twine at 2-inch intervals. Brush with oil and season evenly with salt and pepper.

6. Brush the cooking grates clean. Grill the potato packet over *indirect medium heat* and the tenderloin rolls over *direct medium heat*, with the lid closed as much as possible, until the potatoes are tender and the outside of the pork is evenly seared and the internal temperature reaches 150°F, turning occasionally. The potatoes will take 40 to 45 minutes and the pork will take 25 to 30 minutes, so start the potatoes 15 to 20 minutes before the pork. Cut the pork into ½-inch slices. Serve with the hot potatoes.

Access the grocery list for this recipe on your mobile device. timetogrill.mobi.

Pork tenderloin's narrow, cylindrical shape means it cooks quickly, and because the cylinder has a lot of surface area, the searing heat of the grill has lots of opportunity to develop flavor on the outside of the meat. For a fast weeknight dinner, you will do well with the well-balanced chile powder rub in the easy recipe. If you are looking for a more substantial meal that still plays off a similar combination of pork and chiles, treat yourself to some posole, a traditional Mexican stew that often simmers for hours and hours with toasted, ground chilies. This quick and spicy version, made with grilled pork tenderloin and canned chipotle chile peppers, is easy to make any night of the week. Clove is the surprise ingredient that helps give this dish its indescribable flavor. You can have a mild version of the posole by limiting the number of chipotle peppers to just one.

Chile-Rubbed Pork Tenderloin

SERVES: 👤👤👤👤

PREP TIME: **10** MINUTES

GRILLING TIME: **15** TO **20** MINUTES

SPECIAL EQUIPMENT:
INSTANT-READ THERMOMETER

// RUB
1 tablespoon packed brown sugar
1 tablespoon pure chile powder
1 teaspoon ground cumin
¾ teaspoon kosher salt
½ teaspoon garlic powder
¼ teaspoon ground black pepper

2 pork tenderloins, each ¾ to 1 pound, trimmed of excess fat and silver skin
2 teaspoons extra-virgin olive oil
1 tablespoon finely chopped fresh oregano leaves

1. **In a small bowl combine the rub ingredients, mashing with a fork to mix thoroughly.** Coat the tenderloins with the oil and then season evenly with the rub. Allow the tenderloins to stand at room temperature for 15 to 30 minutes before grilling.

2. **Prepare the grill for direct cooking over medium heat (350° to 450°F).**

3. **Brush the cooking grates clean.** Grill the tenderloins over *direct medium heat*, with the lid closed as much as possible, until the outsides are evenly seared and the internal temperature reaches 150°F, 15 to 20 minutes, turning about every 5 minutes. Remove from the grill and let rest for 3 to 5 minutes. Season with the oregano and then cut into ½-inch slices. Serve warm.

Access the grocery list for this recipe on your mobile device. timetogrill.mobi.

EASY

SERVES: 🧍🧍🧍🧍 TO 🧍🧍🧍🧍🧍🧍

PREP TIME: **25** MINUTES, PLUS ABOUT 35 MINUTES ON THE STOVE TOP

GRILLING TIME: ABOUT **6** MINUTES

SPECIAL EQUIPMENT: PERFORATED GRILL PAN, 5- TO 7-QUART CAST-IRON DUTCH OVEN

2 pork tenderloins, each ¾ to 1 pound, trimmed of excess fat and silver skin *or* 1 boneless pork roast, about 1½ pounds, trimmed of excess fat
   Extra-virgin olive oil
1 teaspoon kosher salt, divided
¼ teaspoon ground black pepper
3 Anaheim chile peppers
1 medium onion, chopped
2 garlic cloves, minced
2 teaspoons ground cumin
¼ teaspoon ground cloves
2 canned chipotle chile peppers in adobo sauce, minced
1 tablespoon adobo sauce (from the canned chipotle chiles)
4 cups chicken broth
2 cans (15 ounces each) hominy, rinsed
1 can (15 ounces) crushed tomatoes

   Chopped avocado
   Thinly sliced cabbage
   Sour cream
   Lime wedges
   Corn tortillas

// To make grilled tortilla chips: Brush six corn tortillas on both sides with vegetable oil. Grill over *direct medium heat* for 2 to 3 minutes on each side, or until the edges darken and the tortillas are crisp. Season with salt.

Grilled Pork Posole

1. Prepare the grill for direct cooking over high heat (450° to 550°F) and preheat the grill pan.

2. Cut the pork into 1- to 1¼-inch pieces and then place them in a bowl. Add 1 tablespoon oil, ½ teaspoon of the salt, and the pepper and toss until evenly coated. Lightly brush the Anaheim chiles with oil.

3. Spread the pork in a single layer on the grill pan and cook over *direct high heat*, with the lid closed as much as possible, until the pork is seared but not completely cooked, 3 to 5 minutes, turning occasionally. At the same time, grill the chiles over *direct high heat* for about 6 minutes, turning occasionally to char all sides. Carefully remove the grill pan from the grill and transfer the pork to a bowl; set aside. Transfer the chiles to a medium bowl and cover tightly with plastic wrap to trap the steam. Let stand for 10 to 15 minutes.

4. Heat a large Dutch oven over medium heat. Add 1 tablespoon oil and the onion and cook until the onion is soft, about 10 minutes, stirring occasionally. Add the remaining ½ teaspoon salt, the garlic, cumin, cloves, chipotle peppers, and adobo sauce and cook for another minute, stirring constantly. Add the chicken broth, hominy, tomatoes, and pork, bring to a low boil, reduce the heat, and simmer for about 15 minutes. While the posole is simmering, peel, seed, and dice the Anaheim chiles and add them to the Dutch oven.

5. Serve the posole hot with avocado, cabbage, sour cream, lime wedges, and grilled tortilla chips.

Access the grocery list for this recipe on your mobile device. timetogrill.mobi.

Jerk is a fantastic style of cooking that originated in Jamaica, where small, scrubby pimento trees grow in the wild. Local cooks use pimento branches on charcoal grills to perfume all kinds of fish and meats that have been generously seasoned with chiles, garlic, thyme, nutmeg, and often allspice, because allspice berries are actually the dried fruit taken from pimento trees. You can get pretty close to the authentic flavors by using a store-bought jerk spice rub on pork tenderloin and cooling off the dish with a quick cucumber salad. Or you can blend your own jerk seasoning into a paste for the pork and make a colorful grilled corn salsa. Cutting the tenderloins into little medallions means they will cook a little faster and look a little fancier.

Jerk Pork Tenderloin
AND CUCUMBER-DILL SALAD

SERVES: 🧍🧍🧍🧍

PREP TIME: **15** MINUTES

GRILLING TIME: **15** TO **20** MINUTES

SPECIAL EQUIPMENT:
INSTANT-READ THERMOMETER

EASY

2 pork tenderloins, each ¾ to 1 pound, trimmed of excess fat and silver skin
4 tablespoons extra-virgin olive oil, divided
¼ cup jerk seasoning

2 tablespoons white wine vinegar
1 teaspoon granulated sugar
1 teaspoon Dijon mustard
2 tablespoons finely chopped fresh dill
1 English cucumber, 14 to 16 ounces, halved lengthwise and thinly sliced (about 4 cups)
½ small red bell pepper, finely diced
1¼ teaspoons kosher salt

1. **Brush the tenderloins all over with 2 tablespoons of the oil and season evenly with the jerk seasoning.** Allow the tenderloins to stand at room temperature for 15 to 30 minutes before grilling.

2. **Prepare the grill for direct cooking over medium heat (350° to 450°F).**

3. **In a medium bowl whisk the vinegar, sugar, mustard, dill, and the remaining 2 tablespoons of oil until the sugar dissolves.** Add the cucumber and bell pepper, toss to coat, and keep refrigerated until ready to serve.

4. **Brush the cooking grates clean.** Grill the tenderloins over **direct medium heat**, with the lid closed as much as possible, until the outsides are evenly seared and the internal temperature reaches 150°F, 15 to 20 minutes, turning every 5 minutes. Remove from the grill and let rest for 3 to 5 minutes. Cut the tenderloins crosswise into ½-inch slices.

5. **Season the cucumber salad with the salt and divide the salad and tenderloin slices evenly among serving plates.** Serve with rice, if desired.

Access the grocery list for this recipe on your mobile device. timetogrill.mobi.

Jerk Pork Medallions
WITH GRILLED CORN AND CUCUMBER SALSA

SERVES: ♦♦♦♦

PREP TIME: **30** MINUTES

GRILLING TIME: **14** TO **21** MINUTES

// SALSA
- 2 ears fresh corn, husked
  Extra-virgin olive oil
- ½ English cucumber, cut into medium dice
  (about 1½ cups)
- ½ medium red bell pepper, finely diced
- ½ cup crumbled feta cheese (2½ ounces)
- 2 tablespoons cider vinegar
- 2 tablespoons finely chopped fresh
  oregano leaves
- ½ teaspoon kosher salt
- ¼ teaspoon ground cayenne pepper
- ¼ teaspoon ground black pepper

// PASTE
- 3 tablespoons extra-virgin olive oil
- 2 tablespoons soy sauce
- 1 tablespoon onion powder
- 1 tablespoon packed brown sugar
- 2 teaspoons dried thyme
- 2 teaspoons ground allspice
- 1 teaspoon ground cayenne pepper
- 1 teaspoon ground black pepper
- 1 teaspoon garlic powder
- ½ teaspoon ground nutmeg
- ½ teaspoon ground cinnamon

- 2 pork tenderloins, each ¾ to 1 pound,
  trimmed of excess fat and silver skin

1. Prepare the grill for direct cooking over medium heat (350° to 450°F).

2. Lightly brush the ears of corn with oil. Brush the cooking grates clean. Grill the corn over *direct medium heat*, with the lid closed as much as possible, until the corn is browned in spots and tender, 10 to 15 minutes, turning occasionally. Remove from the grill and, when cool enough to handle, cut the corn kernels off the cobs into a medium bowl. Add the remaining salsa ingredients to the bowl, including 2 tablespoons oil, and set aside until ready to use.

3. In a small bowl mix the paste ingredients.

4. Cut off the thin, tapered end from each tenderloin and reserve for another use, or grill along with the medallions. Cut each tenderloin crosswise into six equal pieces, each about 1½ inches thick. Brush the paste all over the medallions, cover with plastic wrap, and let stand at room temperature for 15 to 30 minutes before grilling.

5. Grill the medallions over *direct medium heat*, with the lid closed as much as possible, until the outsides are evenly seared and the centers are barely pink, 4 to 6 minutes, turning once. Remove from the grill and let rest for 3 to 5 minutes. Serve warm with the salsa.

Access the grocery list for this recipe on your mobile device. timetogrill.mobi.

Vietnamese Pork Tenderloin Salad
WITH SPICY PEANUT VINAIGRETTE

Curly green leaf lettuce, crunchy peanuts, crisp carrots, and freshly sliced cucumber are hallmarks of a great Vietnamese salad. Here is an easy, satisfying version, topped with plenty of grilled pork tenderloin and peanut vinaigrette, which can be made seriously spicy or with just a mild kick. Dress the salad up a bit by slicing the carrots and cucumbers paper-thin with a mandoline. The sandwiches feature lots of the same tasty, fresh, healthy ingredients but assembled in a heartier way. You could use a bottled peanut sauce on the sandwiches, though the one in the recipe is so good, and making it yourself adds only a few minutes to your prep time.

SERVES: 👤👤👤👤

PREP TIME: **15** MINUTES

GRILLING TIME: **4** TO **6** MINUTES

// VINAIGRETTE
- ½ cup canola oil
- ¼ cup unsalted, chunky peanut butter
- 3 tablespoons rice vinegar
- 3 tablespoons finely chopped fresh cilantro leaves
- 2 teaspoons soy sauce
- 1 teaspoon hot chili-garlic sauce, such as Sriracha

- 2 pork tenderloins, each ¾ to 1 pound, trimmed of excess fat and silver skin, cut crosswise into medallions about 1½ inches thick

// SALAD
- 1 head green leaf lettuce, torn into bite-sized pieces
- 2 carrots, peeled and cut into matchsticks
- ½ English cucumber, very thinly sliced

1. **In a medium bowl whisk the vinaigrette ingredients.** Set aside ⅓ cup of the vinaigrette for basting the pork and ⅓ cup for serving. Brush the medallions all over with the remaining vinaigrette and allow to stand at room temperature for 15 to 30 minutes before grilling.

2. **Prepare the grill for direct cooking over medium heat (350° to 450°F).**

3. **Brush the cooking grates clean.** Grill the medallions over *direct medium heat*, with the lid closed as much as possible, until the outsides are evenly seared and the centers are barely pink, 4 to 6 minutes, turning and brushing with the reserved vinaigrette once. Remove from the grill and let rest for 3 to 5 minutes.

4. **Evenly divide the salad ingredients and the pork medallions among four plates.** Drizzle some of the vinaigrette over the top. Serve with any remaining vinaigrette and sliced scallions, if desired.

Access the grocery list for this recipe on your mobile device. timetogrill.mobi.

SERVES: 🧍🧍🧍🧍

PREP TIME: **20** MINUTES

GRILLING TIME: **16** TO **22** MINUTES

SPECIAL EQUIPMENT:
INSTANT-READ THERMOMETER

1 pork tenderloin, about 1 pound,
   trimmed of excess fat and silver skin
¼ cup plus 2 teaspoons canola oil, divided
½ teaspoon kosher salt
¼ teaspoon ground black pepper

½ cup unsalted, creamy peanut butter
¼ cup rice vinegar
2 teaspoons soy sauce
2 teaspoons hot chili-garlic sauce,
   such as Sriracha, divided
¼ cup mayonnaise
4 long sandwich rolls *or* baguette pieces
   8 inches long
4 leaves green leaf lettuce
2 carrots, peeled and coarsely grated
½ English cucumber, very thinly sliced
½ cup fresh cilantro leaves

Banh Mi Pork Tenderloin Sandwiches

1. Lightly coat the tenderloin with 2 teaspoons of the oil and season evenly with the salt and pepper. Allow the tenderloin to stand at room temperature for 15 to 30 minutes before grilling.

2. Prepare the grill for direct cooking over medium heat (350° to 450°F).

3. Brush the cooking grates clean. Grill the tenderloin over *direct medium heat*, with the lid closed as much as possible, until the outside is evenly seared and the internal temperature reaches 150°F, 15 to 20 minutes, turning about every 5 minutes. Remove from the grill and let rest for 3 to 5 minutes. Cut the tenderloin into ¼-inch slices.

4. In a small bowl whisk the remaining ¼ cup oil, the peanut butter, vinegar, soy sauce, and 1 teaspoon of the chili-garlic sauce until smooth. In another small bowl combine the remaining 1 teaspoon chili-garlic sauce and the mayonnaise.

5. Cut the rolls lengthwise almost in half, keeping one long side intact, so they open like a book. Toast the rolls, cut side down, over *direct medium heat*, 1 to 2 minutes. Remove from the grill and slather one cut side of each roll with a generous amount of the peanut sauce. Spread about 1 tablespoon of the mayonnaise mixture on the other side. Arrange equal amounts of lettuce, carrots, cucumber, cilantro, and sliced pork on each sandwich. Serve with any extra peanut sauce.

Access the grocery list for this recipe on your mobile device. timetogrill.mobi.

SERVES: 🍴🍴🍴🍴 TO 🍴🍴🍴🍴🍴🍴

PREP TIME: **15** MINUTES

GRILLING TIME: **15** TO **20** MINUTES

SPECIAL EQUIPMENT:
INSTANT-READ THERMOMETER

// SAUCE

1 cup ketchup
½ cup water
2 tablespoons unsalted butter
2 tablespoons cider vinegar
1 tablespoon molasses
1 tablespoon Worcestershire sauce
1 teaspoon granulated garlic
½ teaspoon ground black pepper

// RUB

1 teaspoon kosher salt
1 teaspoon prepared chili powder
¼ teaspoon granulated garlic
½ teaspoon ground black pepper

2 pork tenderloins, each ¾ to 1 pound,
  trimmed of excess fat and silver skin
2 tablespoons extra-virgin olive oil

On the opposite page you have a full-fledged recipe for one of American barbecue's proudest accomplishments: the pulled pork sandwich. As a pork shoulder cooks slowly over medium-low indirect heat, its bands of connective tissue melt and release luscious moisture into the meat. Bathed in sauce and topped with a crisp slaw, this cut of pig makes a mouthwatering sandwich. For days when you just don't have hours and hours to spend, turn to the recipe below, which calls for pork tenderloin instead. You will be pleasantly surprised at how easy it is to "pull" (shred) the pork after you have grilled and wrapped it in foil. Use it to make a quick version of a pulled pork sandwich or serve the tender meat over soft polenta.

Quick and Easy Pulled Pork Tenderloin

1. In a small saucepan whisk the sauce ingredients. Bring the sauce to a simmer over medium heat and simmer gently for about 5 minutes, whisking occasionally. Set aside to cool at room temperature.

2. In a small bowl mix the rub ingredients.

3. Lightly coat all sides of the tenderloins with the oil and season evenly with the rub, pressing the spices into the meat. Allow the tenderloins to stand at room temperature for 15 to 30 minutes before grilling.

4. Prepare the grill for direct cooking over medium heat (350° to 450°F).

5. Brush the cooking grates clean. Grill the tenderloins over **direct medium heat**, with the lid closed as much as possible, until the outsides are evenly seared and the internal temperature reaches 150°F, 15 to 20 minutes, turning about every 5 minutes. Remove from the grill and wrap with aluminum foil. Let rest for about 15 minutes or until cool enough to comfortably handle.

6. Cut the tenderloins crosswise into quarters. Pull the warm meat apart with your fingers or use two forks to shred the meat. In a large bowl moisten the pork with as much of the sauce as you like. Serve on a bed of soft polenta, if desired.

Access the grocery list for this recipe on your mobile device. timetogrill.mobi.

Pulled Pork Barbecue Sandwiches

SERVES: 10 TO 12

PREP TIME: 30 MINUTES

GRILLING TIME: 3 TO 4 HOURS

// SAUCE

- 2 cups ketchup
- ⅔ cup stout beer
- ½ cup cider vinegar
- ¼ cup packed brown sugar
- 2 tablespoons molasses
- 1 tablespoon Worcestershire sauce
- 1 tablespoon soy sauce
- 2 teaspoons Dijon mustard
- 1 teaspoon ground cayenne pepper

- 1 boneless pork shoulder roast (Boston butt), 4 to 5 pounds, rolled and tied
  Kosher salt
  Ground black pepper

// SLAW

- ½ head green cabbage, shredded
- 3 medium carrots, grated
- 1 red bell pepper, thinly sliced
- ½ sweet onion, thinly sliced
- ½ cup extra-virgin olive oil
- 2 tablespoons cider vinegar
- ¾ teaspoon Dijon mustard
- 2 tablespoons celery seed

  Kaiser rolls *or* hamburger buns

1. **In a small saucepan whisk the sauce ingredients.** Bring the sauce to a simmer over low heat and simmer gently for about 15 minutes, whisking occasionally. Set aside to cool at room temperature.

2. **Season all sides of the roast generously with salt and pepper.** Allow the roast to stand at room temperature for about 30 minutes before grilling.

3. **Prepare the grill for indirect cooking over medium-low heat (about 325°F).**

4. **Brush the cooking grates clean.** Grill the roast, fat side up, over ***indirect medium-low heat***, with the lid closed, keeping the temperature of the grill as close to 325°F as possible, until the internal temperature reaches 185° to 190°F, 3 to 4 hours. The meat should be so tender it pulls apart easily. Transfer to a cutting board, cover loosely with foil, and let rest for about 20 minutes. Toast the rolls over direct heat for about 1 minute.

5. **Meanwhile, in a large bowl combine the cabbage, carrots, pepper, and onion.** In a small bowl whisk the oil, vinegar, mustard, and celery seed. Add as much of the dressing to the slaw as you like. Mix well. Set aside.

6. **Using two forks or your fingers, pull the pork apart into shreds, discarding any pockets of fat.** In a large bowl moisten the pork with as much of the sauce as you like. Pile the warm pork on toasted buns and top with coleslaw.

Access the grocery list for this recipe on your mobile device. timetogrill.mobi.

Ham steaks develop nice, crispy edges on the grill in about ten minutes. By themselves, the steaks might taste a little dry, but you can assure yourself of juiciness by adding some grilled sweet pears and spooning a tangy vinegar glaze over the top. The glaze is also wonderful on ribs. Grilling a ham will let you serve more people with an equal amount of prep time. While the ham heats up on the grill, make the simple pear chutney here. Or make the chutney a day or so ahead. It is also a tasty condiment to spread on sandwiches of leftover ham and sliced Swiss cheese.

Ham Steaks with Grilled Pears
AND VINEGAR GLAZE

1. **Prepare the grill for direct cooking over medium heat (350° to 450°F).**

2. **Pat the ham steaks dry and then brush the ham and pears with the oil.**

3. **In a small saucepan over medium heat, combine the glaze ingredients.** Bring the mixture to a boil, and then reduce the heat to maintain a steady simmer. Cook until a syrupy glaze forms, 8 to 9 minutes.

4. **Brush the cooking grates clean.** Grill the ham and pears over *direct medium heat*, with the lid closed as much as possible, until the ham is hot and the pears are tender and nicely marked, 8 to 12 minutes, turning once. Remove from the grill as they are done. Cut the ham steaks into individual serving pieces. Arrange the pear quarters alongside the ham and serve hot, drizzled with the vinegar glaze.

Access the grocery list for this recipe on your mobile device. timetogrill.mobi.

SERVES: 👤👤👤👤

PREP TIME: **15** MINUTES

GRILLING TIME: **8** TO **12** MINUTES

2 ham steaks, each about 1 pound and ½ inch thick
2 ripe pears, such as Bosc, peeled, quartered, and cored
1 tablespoon vegetable oil

// GLAZE
¾ cup packed brown sugar
6 tablespoons cider vinegar
3 tablespoons Dijon mustard
⅛ teaspoon crushed red pepper flakes

SERVES: **6** TO **8**

PREP TIME: **15** MINUTES, PLUS ABOUT 20 MINUTES FOR THE CHUTNEY

GRILLING TIME: **30** TO **40** MINUTES

SPECIAL EQUIPMENT: LARGE DISPOSABLE FOIL PAN; 12-INCH, HEAVY-BOTTOMED SKILLET; INSTANT-READ THERMOMETER

1 boneless, cooked, smoked ham, 3 to 4 pounds
2 teaspoons vegetable oil
4 ripe pears, such as Bartlett or Anjou, peeled and cored, cut into bite-sized pieces
1½ cups packed brown sugar
¾ cup cider vinegar
1 tablespoon Dijon mustard
2 teaspoons peeled, grated fresh ginger
¼ teaspoon crushed red pepper flakes

Whole Ham with Pear Chutney

1. **Let the ham stand at room temperature for about 30 minutes before grilling.**

2. **Prepare the grill for indirect cooking over medium heat (350° to 450°F).**

3. **Brush the cooking grates clean.** Put the ham, flat side down, in a large disposable foil pan and add ½ cup of water to help prevent the ham from drying out. Place the pan over *indirect medium heat*, close the grill lid, and cook until the internal temperature reaches 160°F, 30 to 40 minutes.

4. **While the ham is cooking, make the chutney.** In a 12-inch, heavy-bottomed skillet over medium-high heat, warm the oil. Add the pears, cooking and stirring them until they are softened but not mushy, 4 to 5 minutes. Using a slotted spoon, remove about half of the pear pieces and set them aside. Add the sugar, vinegar, mustard, ginger, and red pepper flakes to the pears in the skillet, combining thoroughly. Cook until the mixture thickens and begins to darken in color, 8 to 10 minutes, stirring occasionally. Return the reserved pears and any accumulated juices to

the skillet and continue cooking for 5 minutes, stirring occasionally to prevent the chutney from sticking. Transfer to a serving dish and cool slightly.

5. **Remove the ham from the grill and let rest for 3 to 5 minutes.** Cut into slices and serve warm with the chutney.

Access the grocery list for this recipe on your mobile device. timetogrill.mobi.

Some barbecue purists will shudder at the thought of cooking ribs wrapped in foil, but if you want to make them in about one hour and fifteen minutes, as opposed to the usual three to four hours (or more), this is how. Seal each slab of ribs in two layers of foil so that on the grill the bubbling juices and fat steam the ribs to tenderness in about one hour. Then unwrap each slab and grill it directly on the cooking grate to brown the meat while you glaze it with sauce. To get one step closer to traditional barbecue, add some wood chips to the charcoal or the smoker box on a gas grill. If you feel compelled to maintain the low-and-slow approach, you will find a lot to love in the adventurous recipe, including a sweet and spicy glaze that reveals flavors of the Caribbean.

Foil-Wrapped Baby Back Ribs

1. **Prepare the grill for direct cooking over medium heat (350° to 450°F).**

2. **In a small bowl mix the rub ingredients.**

3. **Remove the membrane from the back of each rack of ribs (see photo at bottom right).** Cut each rack crosswise in the middle to create two smaller racks.

4. **Season each half rack evenly with the rub.** Using eight 18-by-24-inch sheets of heavy-duty aluminum foil, double wrap each half rack in its own packet.

5. **Brush the cooking grates clean.** Place the ribs on the grill over *direct medium heat* and cook for 1 hour, with the lid closed, occasionally turning the packets over for even cooking, making sure not to pierce the foil.

6. **Remove the packets from the grill and let rest for about 10 minutes.** Carefully open the foil packets, remove the ribs, and discard the rendered fat and foil.

7. **Drain and add the wood chips directly onto burning coals or to the smoker box of a gas grill, following manufacturer's instructions.** When the wood begins to smoke, return the ribs to the grill, bone side down. Grill over *direct medium heat*, with the lid closed as much as possible, until they are sizzling and lightly charred, 10 to 12 minutes, turning and basting once or twice with the sauce. Remove from the grill and let rest for about 5 minutes. Cut into individual ribs and serve warm with any remaining sauce.

Access the grocery list for this recipe on your mobile device. timetogrill.mobi.

SERVES: 👤👤👤👤

PREP TIME: **15** MINUTES

GRILLING TIME: ABOUT **1¼** HOURS

SPECIAL EQUIPMENT: 18-INCH-WIDE HEAVY-DUTY ALUMINUM FOIL

// RUB
- 1 tablespoon kosher salt
- 2 teaspoons paprika
- 2 teaspoons granulated garlic
- 2 teaspoons dried thyme
- ½ teaspoon ground black pepper

- 2 racks baby back ribs, each 2 to 2½ pounds

- 1 cup hickory wood chips, soaked in water for at least 30 minutes

- 1 cup prepared barbecue sauce

Caribbean Baby Back Ribs
WITH GUAVA GLAZE

SERVES: 🧍🧍🧍🧍

PREP TIME: **15** MINUTES

GRILLING TIME: **3** TO **4** HOURS

SPECIAL EQUIPMENT: RIB RACK

// RUB
- 1 tablespoon kosher salt
- 2 teaspoons dried oregano
- ½ teaspoon garlic powder
- ½ teaspoon onion powder
- ½ teaspoon ground black pepper

- 2 racks baby back ribs, each 2 to 2½ pounds

// GLAZE
- 1 cup guava jelly *or* apricot preserves
- ½ cup plus 1 tablespoon ketchup
- 3 tablespoons unsalted butter
- 3 scallions (white and light green parts only), minced
- 1 tablespoon peeled, grated fresh ginger
- 1½ teaspoons seeded and minced habanero chile pepper *or* 2 teaspoons minced jalapeño chile pepper
- 1 large garlic clove, grated

Using a dull dinner knife, slide the tip under the membrane covering the back of each rack of ribs. Lift and loosen the membrane until it breaks; grab a corner of it with a paper towel and pull it off.

1. **Prepare the grill for indirect cooking over low heat (250° to 300°F).**

2. **In a small bowl mix the rub ingredients.**

3. **Remove the membrane from the back of each rack of ribs (see photo at bottom left).** Season the ribs all over with the rub, putting more of it on the meaty sides than the bone sides. Arrange the ribs in a rib rack, all facing the same direction. Allow the ribs to stand at room temperature for about 30 minutes before grilling. Meanwhile, make the glaze.

4. **In a small saucepan over medium heat, mix the glaze ingredients.**

5. **Brush the cooking grates clean.** Place the ribs over *indirect low heat*, as far from the heat as possible, with the bone sides facing toward the heat. Close the lid. After 3 hours, check to see if any rack is ready to come off the grill. They are done when the meat has shrunk back from most of the bones by ½ inch or more. When you lift a rack by picking up one end with tongs, the rack should bend in the middle and the meat should tear easily (see page 23). If the meat does not tear easily, continue cooking for up to 4 hours.

6. **Remove the ribs from the rib rack and transfer to a sheet pan.** Lightly brush the ribs on both sides with the glaze. Lay the ribs flat on the cooking grate, with one rack at a time over direct heat. Grill them, with the lid closed as much as possible, until the ribs are a little crispy on the surface, 10 to 15 minutes, brushing them, turning them, and swapping their positions occasionally. Return the ribs to the sheet pan, give them one last coating of glaze, and cover with foil to keep warm for as long as 15 minutes. Cut the racks between the bones and serve right away.

Access the grocery list for this recipe on your mobile device. timetogrill.mobi.

The possibility of tender spareribs off the grill in under two hours might seem unthinkable, unless you are wise to this wonderfully easy and effective method of grilling them in foil. Sealed tightly in pouches with wine, garlic, and herbs, they steam in their own aromatic juices and turn tender in about one hour and fifteen minutes. Then take them out of their pouch and cook them on a sizzling cooking grate until crispy on the edges. The more adventurous approach isn't necessarily harder; you will just have to wait longer while a slow-cooking smoker softens the meat and seasons it with time.

SERVES: 👤👤👤👤

PREP TIME: 30 MINUTES

GRILLING TIME: ABOUT 1½ HOURS

SPECIAL EQUIPMENT: 18-INCH-WIDE HEAVY-DUTY ALUMINUM FOIL

Foil-Wrapped Spareribs

// PASTE

¼ cup dry white wine

2 tablespoons minced garlic

2 tablespoons finely chopped fresh oregano leaves

1 tablespoon finely chopped fresh rosemary leaves

1 tablespoon finely chopped fresh thyme leaves

1 tablespoon fennel seed

1 tablespoon kosher salt

2 teaspoons crushed red pepper flakes

1 teaspoon ground black pepper

⅓ cup extra-virgin olive oil

2 racks St. Louis-style spareribs, each 3 to 3½ pounds

1. **Prepare the grill for direct cooking over medium heat (350° to 450°F).**

2. **In a small bowl mix the paste ingredients.**

3. **Remove the thin membrane from the back of each rack of ribs (see photo on page 135).** Cut each rack crosswise in the middle to create two smaller racks.

4. **Season each half rack evenly with the paste.** Using eight 18-by-24-inch sheets of heavy-duty aluminum foil, double wrap each half rack in its own packet and seal tightly.

5. **Brush the cooking grates clean.** Place the foil-wrapped ribs on the grill over *direct medium heat*, close the lid, and cook for

1¼ hours, turning the packets over once or twice for even cooking, making sure not to pierce the foil.

6. **Remove the packets from grill and let rest for about 10 minutes.** Carefully open the foil packets, remove the ribs, and discard the rendered fat and foil. Return the ribs to the grill over *direct medium heat*, close the lid, and cook until they are sizzling and lightly charred, 8 to 10 minutes, turning once or twice. Remove from the grill and let rest for about 5 minutes. Cut the racks between the bones into individual ribs and serve warm with broccolini, if desired.

Access the grocery list for this recipe on your mobile device. timetogrill.mobi.

Slow Spareribs
WITH MEDITERRANEAN HERB BASTE

SERVES: 👤👤👤👤👤👤

PREP TIME: **30** MINUTES

GRILLING TIME: **3** TO **4** HOURS

// RUB

2 tablespoons kosher salt
2 tablespoons pure chile powder
2 tablespoons packed light brown sugar
1 tablespoon dried thyme
2 teaspoons ground black pepper

3 racks St. Louis-style spareribs,
  each 3 to 3½ pounds

// BASTE

2 cups fresh Italian parsley leaves and
  tender stems
½ cup fresh oregano leaves
3 ounces sun-dried tomatoes packed in oil
  (about ½ cup)
3 garlic cloves
1 teaspoon kosher salt
½ teaspoon crushed red pepper flakes
1½ cups dry white wine
¼ cup extra-virgin olive oil
2 tablespoons white wine vinegar

3 fist-size chunks hickory or apple
  wood (dry)

1. **Prepare your smoker, following the manufacturer's instructions, for cooking over low heat.**

2. **In a medium bowl mix the rub ingredients.**

3. **Using a dull dinner knife, slide the tip under the membrane covering the back of each rack of ribs (see photo on page 135).** Lift and loosen the membrane until it breaks, then grab a corner of it with a paper towel and pull it off. Season the ribs all over with the rub, putting more of the rub on the meaty sides than the bone sides.

4. **In a food processor or blender process the parsley, oregano, sun-dried tomatoes, garlic, salt, and red pepper flakes until the herbs are finely chopped.** Add the wine, oil, and vinegar. Process briefly to mix.

5. **Place the spareribs on the cooking grates and add two wood chunks to the coals.** Close the lid and smoke the spareribs, keeping the temperature inside the smoker between 250° to 300°F, until the meat has shrunk back from the bones at least ½ inch in several places and the meat tears easily when you lift each rack, 3 to 4 hours (not all racks will cook in the same amount of time). Maintain the temperature of the grill by opening and closing the vents. After the first hour, add the last wood chunk and then begin basting the ribs on both sides with the baste once every hour.

6. **Remove the racks from the smoker and let rest at room temperature for about 10 minutes.** If you cover them with foil, they will stay warm for about 30 minutes. If you wrap them tightly in foil, they will stay warm for at least 1 hour. When ready to serve, cut the racks between the bones into individual ribs. Serve warm.

Access the grocery list for this recipe on your mobile device. timetogrill.mobi.

EASY ADVENTUROUS

POULTRY

Herbed Chicken
WITH GRILLED CORN ON THE COB

On stressful nights when it seems like all the demands in your life are colliding and you're not sure how you will possibly get dinner on the table in time, stop right here and make a quick and easy meal based on chicken and corn. Fresh herbs bring just enough flavor to make it interesting. For a variation, try substituting herbs like oregano, marjoram, tarragon, or sage for the thyme and rosemary. The adventurous recipe builds on similar flavors with a New England-style chowder that is light enough for a summer evening. If the weather is chilly, substitute heavy cream for the milk or top the chowder with cooked, crumbled bacon. This can be made ahead and it is even better the second day.

EASY

SERVES: 👤👤👤👤

PREP TIME: **15** MINUTES

GRILLING TIME: **10** TO **15** MINUTES

¼ cup (½ stick) unsalted butter, softened
2 large garlic cloves, minced
4 boneless, skinless chicken breast halves, each about 6 ounces
2 tablespoons extra-virgin olive oil
2 tablespoons finely chopped mixed fresh herbs, such as rosemary and thyme
½ teaspoon kosher salt
¼ teaspoon ground black pepper
4 ears fresh corn, husked

1. Prepare the grill for direct cooking over medium heat (350° to 450°F).

2. In a small bowl mash the butter and garlic with a fork.

3. Lightly coat the chicken on both sides with the oil and season evenly with the herbs, salt, and pepper.

4. Brush the cooking grates clean. Grill the chicken, smooth (skin) side down first, over *direct medium heat*, with the lid closed as much as possible, until the meat is firm to the touch and opaque all the way to the center, 8 to 12 minutes, turning once or twice. At the same time, grill the corn over *direct medium heat* until the kernels turn brown in spots all over, 10 to 15 minutes, turning occasionally. Remove the chicken and corn from the grill and let the chicken rest for 3 to 5 minutes.

5. Spread the garlic butter on the corn and serve with the chicken.

Access the grocery list for this recipe on your mobile device. timetogrill.mobi.

Chicken and Corn Chowder
WITH PARMESAN-GARLIC TOAST

SERVES: 🧍🧍🧍🧍 TO 🧍🧍🧍🧍🧍🧍

PREP TIME: **30** MINUTES, PLUS ABOUT
30 MINUTES FOR THE CHOWDER

GRILLING TIME: **10** TO **16** MINUTES

3 boneless, skinless chicken breast halves,
  each about 6 ounces
1½ tablespoons extra-virgin olive oil
1½ tablespoons finely chopped fresh
  thyme leaves
  Kosher salt
  Ground black pepper
4 ears fresh corn, husked
2 tablespoons unsalted butter
1 medium yellow onion, finely chopped
2 teaspoons minced garlic
2 cups whole milk
3 large Yukon gold potatoes, about
  2 pounds total, cut into ½-inch cubes
4 cups chicken broth

// TOAST
¼ cup (½ stick) unsalted butter, melted
2 large garlic cloves, minced
½ baguette
¼ cup freshly grated Parmigiano-
  Reggiano® cheese

1. **Prepare the grill for direct cooking over medium heat (350° to 450°F).**

2. **Lightly coat the chicken on both sides with the oil and season evenly with the thyme, ½ teaspoon salt, and ¼ teaspoon pepper.**

3. **Brush the cooking grates clean.** Grill the chicken, smooth (skin) side down first, over *direct medium heat*, with the lid closed as much as possible, until the meat is firm to the touch and opaque all the way to the center, 8 to 12 minutes, turning once or twice. At the same time, grill the corn over *direct medium heat* until the kernels turn brown in spots all over, 8 to 10 minutes, turning occasionally. Remove from the grill.

4. **In a large saucepan over medium heat, melt the butter.** Add the onion and garlic, season with salt and pepper, and cook until soft, about 5 minutes, stirring occasionally. Add the milk, potatoes, and broth. Bring the soup to a simmer and then cook, uncovered, until the potatoes are tender, 15 to 20 minutes. For a thicker consistency, use an immersion blender to puree about a quarter of the soup, or transfer 2 to 3 cups of the soup to a blender and puree it. Return the pureed soup to the saucepan. While the chowder simmers, chop the chicken into ½-inch pieces, cut the kernels off the cobs, and make the toast.

5. **In a small bowl mash the butter and garlic with a fork.** Season with salt and pepper. Cut the baguette into slices about 1 inch thick and spread the butter mixture evenly on both sides of each slice. Grill over *direct medium heat*, with the lid open, until the slices are lightly toasted, 1 to 2 minutes (watch for flare-ups). Turn the slices over and sprinkle the toasted sides evenly with a thin layer of cheese. Grill until the cheese begins to melt, 1 to 2 minutes.

6. **Stir the chicken and corn into the soup.** Serve warm with the toast.

Access the grocery list for this recipe on your mobile device. timetogrill.mobi.

You can assemble grilled chicken panini (pressed sandwiches) an hour or so before you plan to serve them. When it's time to eat, warm them on the grill under a sheet pan weighted down with something heavy, such as a cast-iron skillet or heavy bricks. The toasted bread and compressed texture of the filling are easy to love. For something a little more lavish, blend grilled chicken with some creamy pasta, sweet cherry tomatoes, and fresh spinach topped with crispy bread crumbs. If you're using store-bought bread crumbs, just toast them in a skillet with a little grated lemon zest to perk them up.

Toasted Chicken Panini

WITH TOMATO AND ARUGULA

SERVES: 4

PREP TIME: 15 MINUTES

GRILLING TIME: 10 TO 13 MINUTES

SPECIAL EQUIPMENT: SHEET PAN, CAST-IRON SKILLET OR 2 FOIL-WRAPPED BRICKS

- 2 boneless, skinless chicken breast halves, each about 6 ounces
- Extra-virgin olive oil
- ½ teaspoon kosher salt
- ¼ teaspoon ground black pepper

- ½ cup herb and garlic spreadable cheese
- 1 cup baby arugula, rinsed and crisped
- 2 plum tomatoes, cut into ¼-inch slices
- 1 pound whole-grain artisan bread, cut into 8 slices, each about ¼ inch thick

1. **Prepare the grill for direct cooking over medium heat (350° to 450°F).**

2. **Remove the tenders from the underside of each chicken breast and save for another use.** Cut each breast in half lengthwise, creating two long strips. One at a time, place each breast strip, smooth side down, between two sheets of plastic wrap and pound to an even ¼-inch thickness. Brush both sides with oil and season evenly with the salt and pepper.

3. **Brush the cooking grates clean.** Grill the chicken breast strips over ***direct medium heat***, with the lid closed as much as possible, until firm to the touch and opaque all the way to the center, 4 to 5 minutes, turning once. Remove from the grill and let rest while you prepare the sandwiches.

4. **Reduce the temperature of the grill to low heat (250° to 350°F).**

5. **Spread the bread slices evenly with the cheese spread.** Top with some arugula, three slices of tomato, and a chicken breast strip. Press down on each sandwich so it is compacted and then lightly brush each sandwich on both sides with oil.

6. **Brush the cooking grates clean.** Place the sandwiches over ***direct low heat*** and put a sheet pan directly on top of the sandwiches; weigh it down with a cast-iron skillet or two foil-wrapped bricks. Grill until the bread is toasted and golden, 6 to 8 minutes, turning once (carefully remove the weight and the sheet pan before turning, then put the sheet pan and weight back in place). Remove the sandwiches from the grill and serve right away.

Access the grocery list for this recipe on your mobile device. timetogrill.mobi.

SERVES: 🧍🧍🧍🧍

PREP TIME: **30** MINUTES

GRILLING TIME: **10** TO **15** MINUTES

SPECIAL EQUIPMENT: PERFORATED GRILL PAN

2 slices whole-grain artisan bread, each about ½ inch thick, torn into pieces
Extra-virgin olive oil
1 tablespoon lemon zest
Kosher salt

¼ cup packed brown sugar
¼ cup dry sherry
2 cups grape tomatoes, about 10 ounces

4 boneless, skinless chicken breast halves, each about 6 ounces
½ teaspoon ground black pepper

½ pound dried linguine, fettuccine, or spaghetti
6 ounces baby spinach leaves, about 4 cups
1 container (4.4 ounces) herb and garlic spreadable cheese

 Creamy Chicken Linguine
WITH WILTED TOMATOES

1. Prepare the grill for direct cooking over medium heat (350° to 450°F) and preheat the grill pan.

2. In a food processor pulse the bread until coarse crumbs form. In a small skillet over medium-high heat, toss the crumbs with 1 tablespoon oil and toast until crisp and golden, 3 to 4 minutes. Remove from the heat and stir in the lemon zest and ¼ teaspoon salt. Set aside.

3. In a small bowl whisk the brown sugar and sherry until the sugar dissolves. In a medium bowl combine the tomatoes with 2 tablespoons of the brown sugar-sherry mixture and toss to coat. Set aside the rest of the brown sugar-sherry mixture to use for basting the chicken.

4. Using a slotted spoon, spread the tomatoes onto the preheated grill pan in a single layer. Grill over *direct medium heat*, with the lid open, just until the tomatoes are soft and caramelized, 2 to 3 minutes, stirring frequently. Using a spatula, remove the tomatoes from the grill and return to the medium bowl with the brown sugar-sherry mixture. Season with ¼ teaspoon salt and gently stir. Wearing insulated barbecue mitts, remove the grill pan from the grill.

5. Lightly coat the chicken on both sides with oil and season evenly with salt and pepper.

6. Brush the cooking grates clean. Grill the chicken, smooth (skin) side down first, over *direct medium heat*, with the lid closed as much as possible, until the meat is firm to the touch and opaque all the way to the center, 8 to 12 minutes, turning once or twice and basting with the reserved brown sugar-sherry mixture several times. Remove from the grill and let rest for 3 to 5 minutes. Cut the chicken into ½-inch cubes.

7. Meanwhile, cook the pasta in a large saucepan of boiling, salted water according to package directions. About 1 minute before the pasta is done, add the spinach to the saucepan and stir until wilted. Drain the pasta and spinach, reserving 1 cup of the pasta water, and then return the pasta and spinach to the saucepan. Immediately toss the hot pasta and spinach with the tomatoes, chicken, and cheese and stir to melt. If the sauce is too thick, add up to 1 cup of the reserved pasta water.

8. Divide the pasta evenly among serving plates and top with the bread crumbs. Serve immediately.

Access the grocery list for this recipe on your mobile device. timetogrill.mobi.

SERVES: 👤👤👤👤

PREP TIME: **15** MINUTES

GRILLING TIME: **16** TO **22** MINUTES

The sweet-hot dressing in this easy recipe fills two roles. It works first as a glaze for the chicken, peaches, and onions, and then as a dressing for the whole salad. You could use any tender greens you like for this salad, including mâche, arugula, and watercress. For the adventurous recipe, pick up bags of cleaned, sturdy greens like collard, mustard, or turnip greens. They simmer almost unattended while everything else is on the grill.

// DRESSING

⅔ cup honey Dijon mustard
2 teaspoons minced garlic
2 teaspoons hot pepper sauce, such as Cholula®
2 teaspoons fresh lemon juice
   Extra-virgin olive oil
   Kosher salt
   Ground black pepper

4 ripe peaches, each one cut in half
1 yellow onion, cut crosswise into ⅓-inch slices
4 boneless, skinless chicken breast halves, each about 6 ounces
5 ounces mâche *or* arugula

Chicken and Peach Salad
WITH SWEET-HOT DRESSING

1. In a medium bowl combine the mustard, garlic, hot sauce, and lemon juice. Gradually whisk in ½ cup of oil. Season with salt and pepper. Reserve ½ cup of the dressing to use for grilling; save the remainder to serve with the peaches, chicken, and greens.

2. Prepare the grill for direct cooking over medium heat (350° to 450°F).

3. Lightly brush both sides of the peach halves and onion slices with oil, and then brush the chicken on both sides with oil. Season the peaches, onion, and chicken evenly with salt and pepper.

4. Brush the cooking grates clean. Grill the peaches and onion over *direct medium heat*, with the lid closed as much as possible, until the peaches are slightly charred and the onion is tender, 8 to 10 minutes, turning once or twice and basting with the dressing during the last minute of grilling time. Remove from the grill and cut the peach halves into wedges and chop the onion slices.

5. Grill the chicken, smooth (skin) side down first, over *direct medium heat*, with the lid closed as much as possible, until the meat is firm to the touch and opaque all the way to the center, 8 to 12 minutes, turning and basting with the dressing once or twice. Remove from the grill and let rest for 3 to 5 minutes. Discard any remaining dressing used for basting. Cut the chicken on the diagonal into thin slices.

6. Divide the mâche among four bowls and add equal amounts of the chicken, peaches, and onion. Season with salt and pepper and serve with the reserved dressing to drizzle over the top.

Access the grocery list for this recipe on your mobile device. timetogrill.mobi.

EASY

Glazed Chicken, Peaches, and Sweet Potatoes
ON SOUTHERN GREENS

SERVES: 👤👤👤👤

PREP TIME: **30** MINUTES

GRILLING TIME: **8** TO **12** MINUTES

SPECIAL EQUIPMENT: LARGE,
DEEP SKILLET

// GLAZE

- 6 tablespoons honey
- 4 tablespoons fresh lemon juice
- 3-4 teaspoons minced canned chipotle chiles in adobo sauce
- ¼ teaspoon ground cayenne pepper
- ¼ teaspoon ground cloves
  Extra-virgin olive oil

  Kosher salt
  Ground black pepper

- 1 long, slender yam, about 1 pound and 2 inches in diameter
- 2 ripe peaches, each cut in half
- 4 boneless, skinless chicken breast halves, each about 6 ounces
- 6 slices apple wood smoked bacon, finely chopped
- 2 packages (12 ounces each) ready-to-use collard, mustard, or turnip greens
- ¼ cup water

1. Prepare the grill for direct cooking over medium heat (350° to 450°F).

2. In a small bowl whisk the glaze ingredients, including 6 tablespoons oil. Season with salt and pepper. Reserve ⅓ cup of the glaze to use for grilling; save the remainder to serve with the grilled chicken and greens.

3. Peel the yam and then cut it crosswise into ½-inch slices. Lightly brush the yam slices and peach halves with oil, and then brush the chicken on both sides with oil. Season the yam, peaches, and chicken evenly with salt and pepper.

4. In a large, deep skillet over medium-high heat, sauté the bacon until it begins to brown, about 4 minutes, stirring frequently. Add the greens to the skillet, a quarter of them at a time, tossing and cooking with the bacon until the greens are wilted, about 12 minutes total, cooking each addition for about 3 minutes. Season with salt and pepper. Add the water, cover the pan, and reduce the heat to medium. Simmer until the greens are just tender, about 10 minutes, stirring occasionally. Remove them from the heat and set aside.

5. Brush the cooking grates clean. Grill the yam slices, peach halves, and chicken over *direct medium heat*, with the lid closed as much as possible, until the yams and peaches are slightly charred and the chicken is firm to the touch and opaque all the way to the center, turning once. The yam and chicken will take 8 to 12 minutes and the peaches will take 8 to 10 minutes. During the last minute or so of grilling time, baste the yam, peaches, and chicken with the glaze. Remove from the grill as they are done. Cut the yams into quarters.

6. Divide the greens and yams equally among four plates. Serve with a chicken breast and peach half. Drizzle each plate generously with some of the remaining glaze and serve right away.

Access the grocery list for this recipe on your mobile device. timetogrill.mobi.

Packaged bags of romaine lettuce hearts save time when you want a quick lunch like this Caesar salad with grilled chicken. A perforated grill pan simplifies the process of toasting the croutons and softening the cherry tomatoes while you grill the chicken on the open area of the cooking grate. The adventurous recipe takes chicken salad in a slightly different direction by using grapes and walnuts instead of tomatoes and croutons, and then wrapping the salad in tortillas. Be sure to warm the tortillas so they wrap around the salad without cracking.

SERVES: ♦♦♦♦

PREP TIME: 15 MINUTES

GRILLING TIME: 8 TO 12 MINUTES

SPECIAL EQUIPMENT: PERFORATED GRILL PAN

Lemon Chicken Caesar Salad

EASY

// **DRESSING**
- ⅓ cup fresh lemon juice
- 3 large garlic cloves, smashed
- 1 tablespoon Dijon mustard
- 1 tablespoon Worcestershire sauce
- ¾ teaspoon kosher salt
- ½ teaspoon ground black pepper
- ¾ cup extra-virgin olive oil

- ½ pint small cherry tomatoes
- 3 slices country-style bread, cut into ½-inch cubes
- 4 boneless, skinless chicken breast halves, each about 6 ounces

- 1 large head romaine lettuce *or* 3 hearts of romaine, chopped
- 1 cup freshly grated Parmigiano-Reggiano® cheese

1. Prepare the grill for direct cooking over medium heat (350° to 450°F) and preheat the grill pan.

2. In a blender whirl the lemon juice, garlic, mustard, Worcestershire sauce, salt, and pepper until smooth. With the machine running, add the oil in a slow, steady stream, blending until emulsified.

3. In a medium bowl toss the tomatoes and bread cubes with 2 tablespoons of the dressing.

4. Pour 2 tablespoons of the dressing over the chicken and turn to coat them evenly.

5. Brush the cooking grates clean. Grill the chicken, smooth (skin) side down first, over **direct medium heat**, with the lid closed as

much as possible, until the meat is firm to the touch and opaque all the way to the center, 8 to 12 minutes, turning once or twice. During the last 2 to 3 minutes of grilling time, spread the tomatoes and bread cubes in a single layer on the grill pan and cook until the tomatoes start to blister and the bread is toasted, turning occasionally. Remove everything from the grill and let the chicken rest for 3 to 5 minutes. Cut the chicken crosswise into ½-inch slices.

6. In a large bowl toss the lettuce with the dressing and the cheese. Divide the salad, chicken, tomatoes, and croutons evenly among serving plates. Serve immediately.

Access the grocery list for this recipe on your mobile device. timetogrill.mobi.

Chicken Salad Wraps

WITH HERBED AIOLI AND WATERCRESS

SERVES: 🧍🧍🧍🧍 TO 🧍🧍🧍🧍🧍🧍

PREP TIME: **30** MINUTES

GRILLING TIME: **8** TO **12** MINUTES

3 boneless, skinless chicken breast halves, each about 6 ounces
  Extra-virgin olive oil
1 teaspoon chopped fresh thyme leaves
¼ teaspoon kosher salt
  Ground black pepper

12 flour tortillas (6 inches)

// AIOLI

⅓ cup mayonnaise
1 teaspoon Dijon mustard
1 small garlic clove, minced
1 tablespoon chopped fresh basil leaves
1 tablespoon chopped fresh parsley leaves

½ cup small red grapes, each one cut in half
½ cup chopped walnuts
2 scallions (white and light green parts only), thinly sliced
2 cups fresh watercress leaves and tender stems (1 small bunch)

1. Prepare the grill for direct cooking over medium heat (350° to 450°F). Preheat the oven to 200°F.

2. Lightly coat the chicken on both sides with oil and season evenly with the thyme, salt, and ⅛ teaspoon pepper.

3. Wrap the tortillas in a barely moist paper towel and then tightly in aluminum foil. Place the packet of tortillas in the oven to warm while grilling the chicken and preparing the aioli.

4. Brush the cooking grates clean. Grill the chicken, smooth (skin) side down first, over *direct medium heat*, with the lid closed as much as possible, until the meat is firm to the touch and opaque all the way to the center, 8 to 12 minutes, turning once. Remove from the grill and set aside to cool. Cut into ¼-inch cubes.

5. In a medium bowl whisk the mayonnaise, mustard, garlic, basil, parsley, 2 tablespoons oil, and ⅛ teaspoon pepper.

6. In a large bowl combine the chicken with the grapes, walnuts, and scallions and then add as much of the aioli as you like. Remove the tortillas from the oven. Divide the watercress and chicken salad among the tortillas. Wrap and serve.

Access the grocery list for this recipe on your mobile device. timetogrill.mobi.

In less than five minutes you can make a truly wonderful butter sauce with white wine and capers to instantly dress up ordinary chicken breasts. For a smooth, emulsified sauce, the key is making sure the butter does not get too hot. Otherwise the sauce will "break," meaning the fat will separate from everything else. So remove the skillet from the heat before you start adding bits of cold butter to the reduced white wine and shallots. The adventurous recipe involves cutting chicken breasts open like a book and stuffing them, which is a clever and uncomplicated way to give them some elegance. The filling can be customized with whatever flavors you like. For example, instead of olives and capers, you might prefer marinated artichoke hearts.

Chicken Breasts with White Wine-Caper Sauce

SERVES: ♦♦♦♦

PREP TIME: **10** MINUTES

GRILLING TIME: **8** TO **12** MINUTES

4 boneless, skinless chicken breast halves, each about 6 ounces
2 tablespoons extra-virgin olive oil
¾ teaspoon kosher salt
Ground black pepper

// **SAUCE**
¼ cup dry white wine
2 tablespoons minced shallot
2 teaspoons Dijon mustard
¼ cup (½ stick) unsalted butter, cut into 4 pieces
2 tablespoons nonpareil capers, rinsed
1 tablespoon finely chopped fresh Italian parsley leaves

EASY

1. **Prepare the grill for direct cooking over medium heat (350° to 450°F).**

2. **Lightly coat the chicken on both sides with the oil and season evenly with the salt and ½ teaspoon pepper.** Brush the cooking grates clean. Grill the chicken, smooth (skin) side down first, over *direct medium heat*, with the lid closed as much as possible, until the meat is firm to the touch and opaque all the way to the center, 8 to 12 minutes, turning once or twice. Remove from the grill and cover with foil to keep warm while you make the sauce.

3. **In a small skillet over medium heat, mix the wine, shallot, and mustard.** Cook until the mixture comes to a simmer. Simmer for about 30 seconds, and then remove the skillet from the heat. Add the butter, one piece at a time, whisking it into the sauce and waiting until it is almost completely melted before adding the next piece. After all the butter has been melted into the sauce, add the capers and parsley. Season with pepper.

4. **Transfer the chicken to serving plates, top with the sauce, and serve warm.**

Access the grocery list for this recipe on your mobile device. timetogrill.mobi.

Mediterranean Stuffed Chicken Breasts

SERVES: 👤👤👤👤

PREP TIME: **20** MINUTES

GRILLING TIME: **10** TO **14** MINUTES

// STUFFING
- ¼ cup pitted kalamata olives, rinsed
- ¼ cup sun-dried tomatoes packed in oil, drained
- 2 tablespoons nonpareil capers, rinsed
  Grated zest of 1 lemon
- ½ cup crumbled feta cheese (about 3 ounces)

- 4 thick boneless, skinless chicken breast halves, each about 8 ounces
  Extra-virgin olive oil
- ¾ teaspoon kosher salt
- ½ teaspoon ground black pepper

1. **In a food processor pulse the olives, sun-dried tomatoes, capers, and lemon zest until finely chopped, but not pureed.** Transfer the mixture to a bowl, stir in the cheese, and set aside.

2. **Prepare the grill for direct cooking over medium heat (350° to 450°F).**

3. **Place the chicken breasts on a cutting board, smooth (skin) side down.** Cut them in half horizontally, keeping the longer side intact, so they open like books (see page 18). Rub the outside of each breast with oil and season evenly with the salt and pepper. Open up each breast and spread 2 to 3 tablespoons of the filling (depending upon the size of the chicken breast) on one side of each breast, leaving a small border. Do not overstuff the chicken. Fold the other side of the chicken over, gently pressing around the edges to seal in the filling.

4. **Brush the cooking grates clean.** Grill the chicken, smooth (skin) side down first, over **direct medium heat**, with the lid closed as much as possible, until the meat is firm to the touch and opaque but still moist, 10 to 14 minutes, turning once (it's easiest to turn the chicken over on the uncut edge of the breast so the filling doesn't fall out). Remove from the grill and let rest for 3 to 5 minutes. Serve warm.

Access the grocery list for this recipe on your mobile device. timetogrill.mobi.

ADVENTUROUS

Here are two cases where curry-seasoned chicken is paired with Indian-style vegetables. In the first case, the pieces are boneless, skinless breasts so they cook on the grill in about ten minutes. You could just as easily use boneless breasts with the skin on, if you don't mind a little extra fat. Most of this dish's character comes from the eggplant and tomatoes cooked in a saucepan with sweet-and-sour juices. In the second case, the chicken breasts have bones still attached, so they take longer on the grill and they benefit from more complex curry seasonings. You will need a perforated grill pan for the accompanying vegetables, especially the green beans, or else you will lose nearly all of them through the grates.

SERVES:

PREP TIME: **15** MINUTES

GRILLING TIME: **8** TO **12** MINUTES

EASY

- 4 boneless, skinless chicken breast halves, each about 6 ounces
- 4 tablespoons canola oil, divided
- 4½ teaspoons curry powder, divided
- 1¼ teaspoons kosher salt, divided
- 2 medium Japanese eggplants, 12 to 16 ounces total, cut into ½-inch dice
- ¼ cup minced shallot
- 1 tablespoon minced serrano chile pepper (with seeds)
- 1 cup grape tomatoes, each cut into quarters
- ½ cup water
- 1 tablespoon honey
- 1 teaspoon red wine vinegar
- ¼ teaspoon ground black pepper
- 2 tablespoons finely chopped fresh cilantro leaves

Curry Chicken Breasts
WITH EGGPLANTS AND TOMATOES

1. Prepare the grill for direct cooking over medium heat (350° to 450°F).

2. Lightly coat the chicken on both sides with 1 tablespoon of the oil and season evenly with 4 teaspoons of the curry powder and ¾ teaspoon of the salt.

3. In a large skillet over medium-high heat, heat the remaining 3 tablespoons oil. Add the eggplants, shallot, chile, and the remaining ½ teaspoon curry powder. Sauté until the eggplants begin to brown, 4 to 6 minutes, stirring often. Add the tomatoes, water, honey, vinegar, pepper, and the remaining ½ teaspoon salt and cook until the eggplants are soft and the liquid has evaporated, about 4 minutes, stirring occasionally. Add the cilantro and mix well. Set aside.

4. Brush the cooking grates clean. Grill the chicken, smooth (skin) side down first, over **direct medium heat**, with the lid closed as much as possible, until the meat is firm to the touch and opaque all the way to the center, 8 to 12 minutes, turning once or twice. Remove from the grill and let rest for 3 to 5 minutes. Serve warm with the eggplants and tomatoes.

Access the grocery list for this recipe on your mobile device. timetogrill.mobi.

Roast Chicken

WITH CURRIED GREEN BEANS AND TOMATOES

SERVES: 👤👤👤👤

PREP TIME: **30** MINUTES

GRILL TIME: **35** TO **47** MINUTES

SPECIAL EQUIPMENT: PERFORATED
GRILL PAN

// PASTE

- 2 tablespoons canola oil
- 4 teaspoons curry powder
- 2 teaspoons minced garlic
- 1 teaspoon dry mustard
- 1 teaspoon honey
- 1 teaspoon kosher salt

- 4 chicken breast halves (with bone and skin), each 10 to 12 ounces

// DRESSING

- 3 tablespoons canola oil
- 1 tablespoon red wine vinegar
- 2 teaspoons minced serrano chile pepper (with seeds)
- ½ teaspoon curry powder
- ¼ teaspoon kosher salt
- ⅛ teaspoon ground black pepper

- ½ pound fresh skinny green beans, trimmed
- 1 pint grape tomatoes

1. **In a small bowl mix the paste ingredients.**

2. **Using your fingertips, carefully lift the skin from the chicken, leaving the skin closest to the breastbone attached.** Rub 1 teaspoon of the paste under the skin all over the exposed meat. Lay the skin back in place and rub the remaining paste evenly all over the chicken.

3. **Prepare the grill for direct and indirect cooking over medium heat (350° to 450°F) and preheat the grill pan.**

4. **In a small bowl whisk all of the dressing ingredients.**

5. **In a large bowl combine the green beans and tomatoes.** Use about one-half of the dressing to coat them lightly. Spread the vegetables in a single layer on the grill pan. Grill over **direct medium heat**, with the lid closed as much as possible, until the green beans are browned in spots and crisp-tender and the tomatoes are beginning to collapse, turning occasionally. The green beans will take 5 to 7 minutes and the tomatoes will take 2 to 3 minutes. Transfer the vegetables back into the large bowl to cool as they are done. Remove the grill pan from the grill.

6. **Brush the cooking grates clean.** Grill the chicken, skin side up, over **indirect medium heat**, with the lid closed as much as possible, until the meat is opaque all the way to the bone, 30 to 40 minutes. If desired, to crisp the skin, grill the breasts over **direct medium heat** during the last 5 to 10 minutes of grilling time, turning once. Transfer to a platter and let rest for 3 to 5 minutes.

7. **Whisk the remaining dressing.** Pour just enough of the dressing over the grilled vegetables to coat them very lightly. If desired, drizzle some of the remaining dressing over the chicken and serve right away with the green beans and tomatoes.

Access the grocery list for this recipe on your mobile device. timetogrill.mobi.

SERVES: 🧍🧍🧍🧍 TO 🧍🧍🧍🧍🧍🧍

PREP TIME: **15** MINUTES

GRILLING TIME: **8** TO **12** MINUTES

What's it going to be tonight: a simple barbecue chicken sandwich with pre-shredded coleslaw in about thirty minutes or slow-cooked, smoked chicken drumsticks and thighs with coleslaw made from scratch? Each one has its time and place. The first one features boneless chicken breasts and bottled barbecue sauce for the sake of speed. The second one calls for bone-in pieces that spend enough time on the grill that they can absorb a good amount of woodsy smoke. Plus, when you make your own sauce and slaw from scratch, the extra effort comes through in a boost of fresh flavors.

Shredded Barbecue Chicken Sandwiches
WITH QUICK COLESLAW

// RUB
1 teaspoon paprika
1 teaspoon granulated garlic
  Kosher salt
  Ground black pepper

4 boneless, skinless chicken breast halves, each about 6 ounces
  Vegetable oil

// SLAW
¼ cup mayonnaise
1 tablespoon cider vinegar
½ teaspoon granulated sugar
1 bag (8 ounces) shredded coleslaw blend of green cabbage, purple cabbage, and carrots (about 3 cups)

4–6 Kaiser rolls
½ cup prepared barbecue sauce, at room temperature

1. **Prepare the grill for direct cooking over medium heat (350° to 450°F).**

2. **In a small bowl combine the paprika, granulated garlic, 1 teaspoon salt, and ½ teaspoon pepper.** Lightly brush the chicken on both sides with oil and season evenly with the rub.

3. **In a large bowl whisk the mayonnaise, vinegar, sugar, ¼ teaspoon salt, and ⅛ teaspoon pepper to make a smooth dressing.** Add the coleslaw blend and mix well.

4. **Brush the cooking grates clean.** Grill the chicken, smooth (skin) side down first, over *direct medium heat*, with the lid closed as much as possible, until the meat is firm to the touch and opaque all the way to the center, 8 to 12 minutes, turning once or twice. During the last 30 seconds to 1 minute of grilling time, toast the rolls, cut side down, over direct heat. Remove the chicken and the rolls from the grill and let the chicken rest for 3 to 5 minutes. Shred or finely chop the chicken and put it in a large bowl. Add the barbecue sauce and mix well. Pile the chicken onto the rolls and top with the slaw.

Access the grocery list for this recipe on your mobile device. timetogrill.mobi.

EASY

SERVES: 👤👤👤👤 TO 👤👤👤👤👤👤

PREP TIME: **30** MINUTES

GRILLING TIME: **45** TO **50** MINUTES

// SAUCE

1 cup ketchup
¼ cup red wine vinegar
¼ cup molasses
2 tablespoons yellow mustard
1½ teaspoons Worcestershire sauce
1½ teaspoons pure ancho chile powder
½ teaspoon liquid smoke
½ teaspoon granulated garlic

Kosher salt
Ground black pepper

6 whole chicken legs, each 10 to 12 ounces, cut into thighs and drumsticks
Vegetable oil

2 handfuls hickory wood chips, soaked in water for at least 30 minutes

// SLAW

⅓ cup mayonnaise
1½ tablespoons cider vinegar
1 teaspoon granulated sugar
¼ teaspoon celery seed
2 cups very thinly sliced green cabbage
1 cup thinly sliced purple cabbage
1 cup peeled and coarsely grated carrot

 Smoked Chicken
WITH HOMEMADE COLESLAW

1. Prepare the grill for direct and indirect cooking over medium heat (350° to 450°F).

2. In a medium saucepan over medium heat, bring the sauce ingredients to a simmer. Season with salt and pepper. Set aside.

3. Lightly coat the chicken on all sides with oil and season evenly with salt and pepper.

4. Brush the cooking grates clean. Grill the chicken, skin side down first, over **direct medium heat**, with the lid closed as much as possible, until golden brown, about 10 minutes, turning once or twice. Watch for flare-ups. Move the chicken pieces over **indirect medium heat**. Drain and scatter the wood chips over the lit charcoal or put them in the smoker box of a gas grill, following manufacturer's instructions. Continue to grill the chicken, with the lid closed, for about 20 minutes. Meanwhile, make the coleslaw.

5. In a large bowl whisk the mayonnaise, vinegar, sugar, celery seed, ½ teaspoon salt, and ¼ teaspoon pepper. Add the green and purple cabbage and carrot and toss to coat. Refrigerate until ready to serve.

6. After the chicken pieces have cooked over indirect heat for 20 minutes, brush both sides with a thin layer of the sauce and continue cooking until the juices run clear and the meat is no longer pink at the bone, 15 to 20 minutes, occasionally turning and brushing with the sauce. Serve warm or at room temperature with the remaining sauce and the coleslaw on the side.

Access the grocery list for this recipe on your mobile device. timetogrill.mobi.

One easy aspect of this salad is the fact that only the duck is grilled; all the other ingredients and components come together quickly. If you don't have all of them, think about substituting mixed greens for the spinach, white cannellini beans for the garbanzo beans, and basil for the mint. You could even substitute chicken breasts for the duck breasts. The adventurous recipe is more of a main course with a strong Middle Eastern flair. The pomegranate glaze can be made a couple of hours ahead, if desired, but cook the pilaf while the duck is grilling and resting so that both will be ready and warm at the same time.

Duck and Spinach Salad

SERVES: ♈♈♈♈

PREP TIME: **15** MINUTES

GRILLING TIME: **8** TO **10** MINUTES

1 bag (5 ounces) baby spinach
1 can (15 ounces) garbanzo beans, rinsed
¾ cup thinly sliced red onion
½ cup coarsely chopped fresh mint leaves
½ cup crumbled feta cheese, divided

Extra-virgin olive oil
1 tablespoon red wine vinegar

2 duck breast halves, each 5 to 6 ounces, skin removed, patted dry
1 teaspoon ground cumin
Kosher salt
Ground black pepper

1. In a large bowl combine the spinach, garbanzo beans, onion, mint, and ¼ cup of the feta; cover and refrigerate.

2. In a small bowl whisk 3 tablespoons oil and the vinegar. Set aside.

3. Prepare the grill for direct cooking over medium-low heat (about 350°F).

4. Lightly brush the duck breasts on both sides with oil and season evenly with the **cumin and salt and pepper.** Brush the cooking grates clean. Grill the duck breasts, smooth (skin) side down first, over **direct medium-low heat**, with the lid closed as much as possible, until cooked to your desired doneness, 8 to 10 minutes for medium rare, turning once. Transfer to a cutting board and let rest for 3 to 5 minutes. Cut crosswise into ⅓-inch slices.

5. Add the duck slices to the salad. Whisk the oil and vinegar again and add enough of it to coat the ingredients lightly. Season with salt and pepper. Sprinkle the remaining ¼ of the feta over the salad and serve.

Access the grocery list for this recipe on your mobile device. timetogrill.mobi.

EASY

SERVES:

PREP TIME: **30** MINUTES, PLUS 10 TO 15 MINUTES FOR THE GLAZE

GRILLING TIME: **10** TO **12** MINUTES

1½ cups refrigerated pomegranate juice
¼ cup packed light brown sugar
2 tablespoons balsamic vinegar
1½ teaspoons ground cumin, divided

3 duck breast halves (with skin),
   each about 6 ounces, patted dry
½ teaspoon kosher salt
¼ teaspoon ground black pepper

// PILAF
1 tablespoon vegetable oil
¾ cup chopped yellow onion
¼ teaspoon ground turmeric
¼ teaspoon ground cardamom
1 cup basmati rice
1¾ cups low-sodium chicken broth
½ teaspoon kosher salt
⅓ cup raisins *or* currants
¼ cup chopped fresh mint leaves
¼ cup chopped unsalted pistachios

Glazed Duck Breasts
WITH SPICED MINT AND PISTACHIO PILAF

1. **In a small saucepan combine the pomegranate juice, brown sugar, and vinegar; bring to a boil over high heat, stirring until the sugar dissolves.** Lower the heat to a simmer and cook until the glaze is slightly thickened and reduced to ½ cup, 10 to 15 minutes, stirring often. Add ½ teaspoon of the cumin. Remove from the heat and reserve ¼ cup of the glaze to serve with the duck.

2. **Prepare the grill for direct cooking over medium-low heat (about 350°F).**

3. **Using a sharp knife, score the skin of each duck breast on the diagonal in a crisscross pattern (do not cut through the breast meat).** Rub both sides of each breast evenly with the remaining 1 teaspoon of the cumin, the salt, and pepper. Brush the duck with some of the glaze.

4. **In a heavy medium saucepan over medium-high heat, heat the oil.** Add the onion and sauté until tender and golden, 4 to 5 minutes. Add the turmeric and cardamom; stir for 15 seconds. Add the rice and stir for 30 seconds. Add the broth and salt and bring to a boil. Reduce the heat to low. Cover and simmer until the rice is tender and the liquid is absorbed, about 15 minutes. Remove from the heat and add the raisins. Let stand, covered, for 5 minutes.

5. **Brush the cooking grates clean.** Grill the duck breasts, skin side down first, over **direct medium-low heat**, with the lid closed as much as possible, until cooked to your desired doneness, 10 to 12 minutes for medium rare, turning once or twice and occasionally brushing the duck with the glaze (if flare-ups occur, move the breasts temporarily over indirect heat). Remove from the grill and let rest for 3 to 5 minutes.

6. **Divide the pilaf among four plates and top with the mint and pistachios.** Cut the duck breasts crosswise into ⅓-inch slices. Divide the duck slices among the plates. Serve warm with the reserved glaze.

Access the grocery list for this recipe on your mobile device. timetogrill.mobi.

Reach for the concentrated flavors in tomato paste when you only have a few minutes to marinate boneless chicken breasts. Nowadays you can buy the paste in convenient, resealable tubes, as opposed to those little cans that often end up half full and completely spoiled in the back of the refrigerator. The sweet paste balances nicely with the vinegar, red pepper flakes, and herbs in this quick marinade. The adventurous recipe takes a similar flavor profile but without the tomato paste. Instead it relies on lemon, red pepper flakes, and fresh herbs to flavor a whole butterflied chicken before it is grilled under bricks to ensure a crisp skin and evenly juicy interior, a recipe from Italy called *pollo al mattone*. For the accompanying salad, wash the greens ahead of time and keep them wrapped in paper towels inside a plastic bag in the refrigerator.

Tomato Red Chicken Breasts

SERVES: 👤👤👤👤

PREP TIME: **15** MINUTES

MARINATING TIME: **20** TO **30** MINUTES

GRILLING TIME: **8** TO **12** MINUTES

// MARINADE

  3 tablespoons extra-virgin olive oil
  2 tablespoons minced shallot
  1 tablespoon red wine vinegar
  2 teaspoons tomato paste
  1 teaspoon crushed red pepper flakes
  1 teaspoon kosher salt
  ½ teaspoon dried oregano *or* basil
  ¼ teaspoon ground black pepper

  4 boneless, skinless chicken breast halves, each about 6 ounces

1. In a large bowl whisk the marinade ingredients. Add the chicken breasts to the bowl and turn to coat them evenly. Allow the chicken to marinate at room temperature for 20 to 30 minutes before grilling.

2. Prepare the grill for direct cooking over medium heat (350° to 450°F).

3. Brush the cooking grates clean. Remove the chicken from the bowl and discard the marinade. Grill the chicken, smooth (skin) side down first, over *direct medium heat*, with the lid closed as much as possible, until the chicken is firm to the touch and opaque all the way to the center, 8 to 12 minutes, turning once or twice. Remove from the grill and let rest for 3 to 5 minutes. Serve warm with grilled eggplant, if desired (see note below).

Access the grocery list for this recipe on your mobile device. timetogrill.mobi.

// Grill eggplant slices for 4 minutes over *direct medium heat*. Turn them over, top each slice with about 1 teaspoon freshly grated Parmigiano-Reggiano® cheese, and continue to grill until the cheese is melted, about 4 minutes more.

 TIME TO GRILL // EASY

SERVES: 👤👤👤👤

PREP TIME: 30 MINUTES

MARINATING TIME: 30 MINUTES

GRILLING TIME: ABOUT 35 MINUTES

SPECIAL EQUIPMENT: POULTRY SHEARS, 2 FOIL-WRAPPED BRICKS OR CAST-IRON SKILLET, INSTANT-READ THERMOMETER

// MARINADE

1 teaspoon grated lemon zest
1 tablespoon fresh lemon juice
1 tablespoon minced garlic
1 tablespoon finely chopped fresh oregano *or* basil leaves
1 teaspoon crushed red pepper flakes
  Extra-virgin olive oil
  Kosher salt
  Ground black pepper

1 whole chicken, about 4 pounds, giblets and any excess fat removed

2 tablespoons red wine vinegar
1 tablespoon finely chopped shallots

2 navel oranges
4 cups loosely packed bite-sized pieces red leaf lettuce (from ½ medium head)

Pollo al Mattone

1. In a medium bowl whisk the marinade ingredients, including ¼ cup oil, 2 teaspoon salt, and ½ teaspoon pepper.

2. **Place the chicken, breast side down, on a work surface.** Using poultry shears, cut from the neck to the tail end, along either side of the backbone. Remove the backbone. Make a small slit in the cartilage at the bottom end of the breastbone. Then, placing both hands on the rib cage, crack the chicken open like a book. Run your fingers along either side of the cartilage in between the breast to loosen it from the flesh. Pull up on the bone to remove it along with the attached cartilage. The chicken should now lie flat (see page 18).

3. **Starting at the neck end of the chicken, carefully run your fingers over the breast meat and under the skin to loosen it.** Rub one quarter of the marinade directly on the breast meat and the remaining marinade all over the outside of the chicken. Let the chicken marinate at room temperature for 30 minutes.

4. **Prepare the grill for direct cooking over medium-low heat (about 350°F).**

5. **In a medium bowl whisk the vinegar, shallots, 3 tablespoons oil, ¼ teaspoon salt, and ⅛ teaspoon pepper to make a dressing.** Cut off all the peel and white pith from the oranges. Working over the bowl with the dressing, cut between the membranes to release the orange segments and let them fall into the bowl. Put the lettuce in a large bowl.

6. **Brush the cooking grates clean.** Place the chicken, breast side up, over **direct medium-low heat** and put two foil-wrapped bricks or a heavy cast-iron skillet directly on top. Close the lid and cook for 15 minutes. Remove the bricks and carefully turn the chicken over. Replace the bricks, close the lid, and cook until the juices run clear and an instant-read thermometer inserted into the thickest part of the thigh (not touching the bone) registers 160° to 165°F, about 20 minutes, adjusting the heat if needed to prevent burning. Remove from the grill and let rest for 5 to 10 minutes (the internal temperature will rise 5 to 10 degrees during this time). Cut into serving pieces.

7. **Remove the orange segments from the dressing and whisk the dressing one more time.** Lightly dress the lettuce and top with the orange segments. Serve the chicken warm with the salad.

Access the grocery list for this recipe on your mobile device. timetogrill.mobi.

ADVENTUROUS

WHAT'S THE DEAL WITH
// propane?

Propane, sometimes called liquefied petroleum gas, is one of the cleanest burning of all fossil fuels. One particularly interesting propane trait is that it's a gas that condenses into a liquid when compressed. This outstanding property makes it very easy to store in tanks and the perfect fuel source for firing up your gas grill.

C₃H₈

GAS WELL

GAS PLANT

SO HOW CAN YOU TELL HOW MUCH PROPANE IS LEFT IN YOUR TANK?

1 Use a built-in tank scale, which is available on certain grill makes and models.

2 Make sure your valve is closed and carefully pour hot water down the side of your tank. Then run your hand slowly along the tank where the hot water touched. The tank will feel noticeably cold up to the level where the propane stops.

3 Buy a liquid crystal sticker at a home improvement store. The sticker will change color to signal the fullness of your tank.

DID YOU KNOW?

The propane industry was born in 1910 when Dr. Walter O. Snelling, a chemistry and explosives expert for the U.S. Bureau of Mines, began experimenting with volatile fumes that formed in a jug of gasoline.

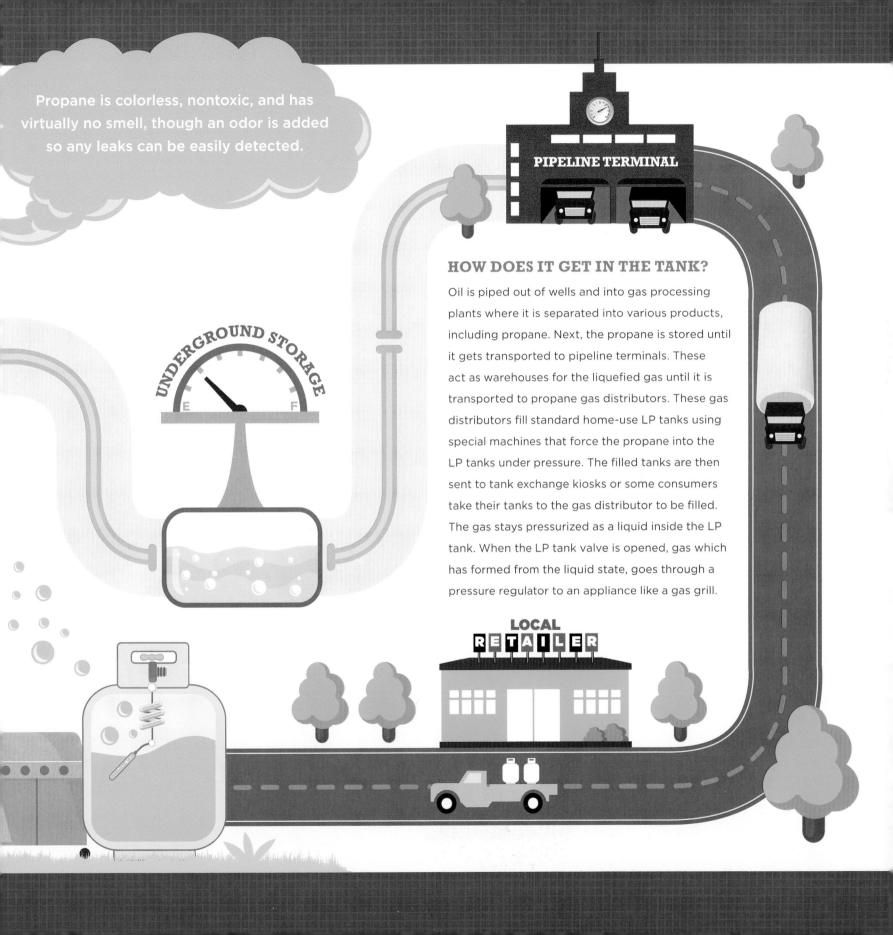

Propane is colorless, nontoxic, and has virtually no smell, though an odor is added so any leaks can be easily detected.

PIPELINE TERMINAL

UNDERGROUND STORAGE

E F

HOW DOES IT GET IN THE TANK?

Oil is piped out of wells and into gas processing plants where it is separated into various products, including propane. Next, the propane is stored until it gets transported to pipeline terminals. These act as warehouses for the liquefied gas until it is transported to propane gas distributors. These gas distributors fill standard home-use LP tanks using special machines that force the propane into the LP tanks under pressure. The filled tanks are then sent to tank exchange kiosks or some consumers take their tanks to the gas distributor to be filled. The gas stays pressurized as a liquid inside the LP tank. When the LP tank valve is opened, gas which has formed from the liquid state, goes through a pressure regulator to an appliance like a gas grill.

LOCAL RETAILER

When you are making brochettes or kabobs, avoid the common mistake of packing them with too many different ingredients, or else some of the ingredients are likely to end up either underdone or overdone. This easy recipe works out well because the chicken thighs and cubes of ham cook in exactly the same amount of time, and the kid-friendly sauce complements both types of meat. You can also grill the chicken pieces and ham cubes on their own skewers. The main-course salad picks up some of the same flavors in the brochettes and adds crunchy, colorful effects to them. You could substitute any kind of greens for the hearts of romaine, if you like. Baby spinach would be nice and healthy.

Chicken and Ham Brochettes
WITH HONEY-MUSTARD DIPPING SAUCE

SERVES: 🧍🧍🧍🧍🧍🧍

PREP TIME: **15** MINUTES

GRILLING TIME: **8** TO **10** MINUTES

SPECIAL EQUIPMENT: METAL OR BAMBOO SKEWERS (IF USING BAMBOO, SOAK IN WATER FOR AT LEAST 30 MINUTES)

3 tablespoons extra-virgin olive oil
1 teaspoon granulated garlic
   Kosher salt
   Ground black pepper
12 boneless, skinless chicken thighs, about 2 pounds total, cut into 1½-inch pieces
1 ham steak, about 1 pound and ¾ inch thick, cut into ¾-inch cubes

// SAUCE
⅔ cup mayonnaise
¼ cup Dijon mustard
3 tablespoons honey

1. Prepare the grill for direct cooking over medium heat (350° to 450°F).

2. In a large bowl whisk the oil, granulated garlic, ½ teaspoon salt, and ¼ teaspoon pepper. Add the chicken pieces and ham cubes and turn to coat them evenly. Thread the chicken and ham onto skewers, alternating the pieces and arranging them so they are touching (but not crammed together). You can also thread them separately on their own skewers.

3. In a small bowl whisk the sauce ingredients and then season with salt and pepper.

4. Brush the cooking grates clean. Grill the skewers over **direct medium heat**, with the lid closed as much as possible, until the chicken meat is firm and the juices run clear and the ham is heated through, 8 to 10 minutes, turning two or three times. Serve the kabobs immediately with the dipping sauce.

Access the grocery list for this recipe on your mobile device. timetogrill.mobi.

EASY

SERVES: ♦♦♦♦♦♦

PREP TIME: **35** MINUTES

MARINATING TIME: ABOUT **1** HOUR

GRILLING TIME: **8** TO **10** MINUTES

// MARINADE

- 2 tablespoons extra-virgin olive oil
- 2 tablespoons minced fresh rosemary leaves
- 1 tablespoon fresh lemon juice
- 1 tablespoon minced garlic
- 1½ teaspoons kosher salt
- ¼ teaspoon ground black pepper

- 6 boneless, skinless chicken thighs, about 3 ounces each

// DRESSING

- 1 cup mayonnaise
- 6 tablespoons Dijon mustard
- ¼ cup honey
- 2 tablespoons fresh lemon juice

  Kosher salt
  Ground black pepper

- 3 hearts of romaine, chopped
- 2 cups cherry tomatoes, each cut into quarters
- 2 large Hass avocados, diced
- ½ small red onion, finely diced
- 8 slices bacon, cooked and crumbled
- 3 hard-boiled eggs, cut into wedges

// To make hard-boiled eggs: Place eggs in a saucepan and completely cover with water. Bring to a boil, then turn off the heat, cover, and let stand for 15 minutes. Remove the eggs from the pan and run under cold water to stop the cooking.

Chopped Chicken Salad
WITH HONEY-MUSTARD DRESSING

1. In a small bowl whisk the marinade ingredients. Place the chicken in a large, resealable plastic bag and pour in the marinade. Press the air out of the bag and seal tightly. Turn the bag several times to distribute the marinade and refrigerate for about 1 hour.

2. Prepare the grill for direct cooking over medium heat (350° to 450°F).

3. In a small bowl combine the dressing ingredients. Season with salt and pepper.

4. Brush the cooking grates clean. Remove the thighs from the bag and discard the marinade. Grill the chicken, smooth (skin) side down first, over **direct medium heat**, with the lid closed as much as possible, until the meat is firm and the juices run clear, 8 to 10 minutes, turning once or twice. Remove from the grill and let rest for 3 to 5 minutes. Cut the meat into bite-sized pieces.

5. Divide the chicken, romaine, tomatoes, avocados, onion, bacon, and eggs evenly among six serving plates. Drizzle the salads with the dressing and serve immediately.

Access the grocery list for this recipe on your mobile device. timetogrill.mobi.

There is amazing flavor in this easy dish. It is a beautiful example of just the right balance between acidity, richness, saltiness, and a touch of sweetness. Serve these skewers alone or alongside couscous or stuffed into warm pita bread with a bit of hummus and chopped tomato. In the adventurous dish, the olives and lemons take on bigger roles, with green olives being the star and marinated lemon slices contributing fascinating flavors and color to the plate.

SERVES: 👤👤👤👤

PREP TIME: **15** MINUTES

MARINATING TIME: **5** TO **30** MINUTES

GRILLING TIME: **8** TO **10** MINUTES

SPECIAL EQUIPMENT: METAL OR BAMBOO SKEWERS (IF USING BAMBOO, SOAK IN WATER FOR AT LEAST 30 MINUTES)

EASY

// **MARINADE**

    2 tablespoons extra-virgin olive oil
    1 teaspoon finely grated lemon zest
    1 tablespoon fresh lemon juice
    1 teaspoon kosher salt
    ½ teaspoon ground black pepper

    6 boneless, skinless chicken thighs, each
       about 4 ounces, cut into 1½-inch pieces
    1 can (6 ounces) pitted, large black
       olives, drained

Lemon-Marinated Chicken and Olive Skewers

1. In a medium bowl combine the marinade ingredients. Add the chicken thigh pieces and toss to coat thoroughly. Let the chicken marinate at room temperature for 5 to 30 minutes before grilling.

2. Prepare the grill for direct cooking over medium heat (350° to 450°F).

3. Thread the chicken pieces onto skewers, alternating chicken pieces with olives. Brush the cooking grates clean. Grill the skewers over ***direct medium heat***, with the lid closed as much as possible, until the meat is firm and the juices run clear, 8 to 10 minutes, turning once or twice. Remove from the grill and let rest for 3 to 5 minutes. Serve warm.

Access the grocery list for this recipe on your mobile device. timetogrill.mobi.

Chicken Thighs and Olive-Fennel Salad
WITH GRILLED LEMON SLICES

SERVES: 4

PREP TIME: 20 MINUTES

MARINATING TIME: 1 HOUR OR MORE

GRILLING TIME: 8 TO 10 MINUTES

1 lemon, cut crosswise into ¼-inch slices
1 teaspoon granulated sugar
  Kosher salt

// SALAD
1 small fennel bulb
1 can (6 ounces) pitted green olives,
  rinsed and drained if very salty,
  each one cut in half
  Zest of 1 lemon, in long, thin shreds
1 tablespoon fresh lemon juice
1 teaspoon minced fresh oregano leaves
1 teaspoon minced garlic
½ teaspoon minced fresh rosemary leaves
  Extra-virgin olive oil
  Ground black pepper

6 boneless, skinless chicken thighs,
  each about 4 ounces

1. **In a medium bowl combine the lemon slices with the sugar and 1 tablespoon salt.** Mix well and let the slices marinate at room temperature for 1 hour or cover and refrigerate overnight.

2. **Prepare the grill for direct cooking over medium heat (350° to 450°F).**

3. **Cut off the thick stalks and the root end from the fennel bulb and discard them.** Cut the bulb lengthwise into quarters and then cut away and remove the thick triangular-shaped core. Cut the fennel vertically into ⅛-inch slices. Put the fennel in a medium bowl and add the remaining salad ingredients, including 1 tablespoon oil and ¼ teaspoon pepper. Set aside.

4. **Drain (don't rinse) the lemon slices and brush them on both sides with oil.** Then lightly brush the chicken on both sides with oil and season evenly with salt and pepper.

5. **Brush the cooking grates clean.** Grill the chicken thighs, smooth (skin) side down first, and the lemon slices over **direct medium heat**, with the lid closed as much as possible, until the meat is firm and the juices run clear and the lemon slices are nicely browned, 8 to 10 minutes, turning once or twice. Remove from the grill and let the chicken thighs rest for 3 to 5 minutes. Serve warm with the olive salad and lemon slices.

Access the grocery list for this recipe on your mobile device. timetogrill.mobi.

Store-bought garam masala is like curry powder in the sense that both are blends of various spices that vary in strengths and complexity from producer to producer. Literally translated, garam masala means "sweet mix" and it almost always features more of the sweet spices like cardamom and cloves, as opposed to the hot chile spices you might find in curry powder. Below it is used to season a dressing for a finely chopped grilled chicken spread. The recipe on the opposite page uses garam masala in a marinade for bone-in chicken thighs that are grilled and served with a tahini sauce for a more substantial dish.

Garam Masala Spiced Chicken Spread

SERVES: 🧍🧍🧍🧍;
🧍🧍🧍🧍🧍🧍 AS AN APPETIZER

PREP TIME: 15 MINUTES

GRILLING TIME: 8 TO 10 MINUTES

6 boneless, skinless chicken thighs,
  each about 3 ounces, or 1 pound total
  Extra-virgin olive oil
  Kosher salt
  Ground black pepper

¼ cup plain Greek yogurt
¼ cup mayonnaise
  Zest and juice of 1 lemon
1 teaspoon garam masala
¼ cup crumbled feta cheese
2 tablespoons finely chopped fresh
  Italian parsley leaves

  Pita chips
  Whole fresh basil leaves
  Sliced fresh vegetables, such as
  cucumber and red bell pepper

EASY

1. Prepare the grill for direct cooking over medium heat (350° to 450°F).

2. Lightly coat the chicken on both sides with oil and season evenly with salt and pepper.

3. Brush the cooking grates clean. Grill the chicken over **direct medium heat**, with the lid closed as much as possible, until the meat is firm and the juices run clear, 8 to 10 minutes, turning once or twice. Remove from the grill and let rest for 3 to 5 minutes. Coarsely chop the chicken.

4. In a medium bowl combine the yogurt, mayonnaise, lemon juice, garam masala, cheese, and parsley.

5. Put the chicken in a food processor and pulse until it is finely chopped. Add the chicken to the yogurt mixture and mix. Season with salt.

6. Serve the chicken spread warm or chilled with pita chips, whole basil leaves, and sliced fresh vegetables.

Access the grocery list for this recipe on your mobile device. timetogrill.mobi.

Marinated Chicken Thighs
WITH MINT-TAHINI SAUCE

SERVES: ♟♟♟♟

PREP TIME: **30** MINUTES

MARINATING TIME: **1** TO **2** HOURS

GRILLING TIME: **36** TO **40** MINUTES

// PASTE
- ½ cup plain Greek yogurt
- ¼ cup grated red onion
- 1 tablespoon fresh lemon juice
- 1 tablespoon garam masala
- 2 teaspoons minced garlic
- 2 teaspoons pure chile powder
- Kosher salt

- 8 chicken thighs (with bone and skin), each about 5 ounces, trimmed of excess fat and skin
- Extra-virgin olive oil

// SAUCE
- 1 large garlic clove
- ¼ cup plain Greek yogurt
- ¼ cup tahini
- ¼ cup water
- 2 tablespoons fresh lemon juice
- 1 cup packed fresh mint leaves

1. In a medium bowl combine the paste ingredients, including 1 teaspoon salt.

2. Place the chicken in a large, resealable plastic bag and spoon in the marinade. Press the air out of the bag and seal tightly. Turn the bag to distribute the marinade. Refrigerate for 1 to 2 hours, turning occasionally.

3. Prepare the grill for direct and indirect cooking over medium heat (350° to 450°F).

4. In a food processor, process the garlic until finely chopped. Add the yogurt, tahini, water, and lemon juice and process to combine. Add the mint and ½ teaspoon salt, and pulse until the mint is finely chopped and the sauce is smooth.

5. Remove the chicken from the bag and wipe off most of the marinade. Discard the marinade. Lightly brush the chicken on both sides with oil.

6. Brush the cooking grates clean. Grill the chicken, skin side down first, over *direct medium heat*, until golden brown, 6 to 10 minutes, turning once or twice. Then move the chicken over *indirect medium heat* and cook until the juices run clear and the meat is no longer pink at the bone, about 30 minutes. Keep the lid closed as much as possible during grilling. Remove from the grill and let rest for 3 to 5 minutes. Serve warm with the sauce.

Access the grocery list for this recipe on your mobile device. timetogrill.mobi.

A classic Mexican mole sauce made of ground chiles, nuts, chocolate, and many other ingredients is traditionally pooled on the plate, but you can also blend some of those complementary flavors into a spice rub for chicken, as you see here for the chicken breasts in the easy recipe. A similar rub also tastes great on a whole chicken that has been butterflied to lie flat on the grill for the adventurous version.

SERVES: 🧍🧍🧍🧍

PREP TIME: **10** MINUTES

GRILLING TIME: **33** TO **45** MINUTES

// **RUB**
- 2 tablespoons pure chile powder
- 2 teaspoons unsweetened cocoa powder
- 2 teaspoons packed brown sugar
- 1 teaspoon kosher salt
- 1 teaspoon ground black pepper

- 2 limes, each cut in half
- 4 plum tomatoes, each cut in half lengthwise
- 2 zucchini, each cut diagonally into ⅓-inch slices
- 4 chicken breast halves (with bone and skin), each 10 to 12 ounces
- 2 tablespoons extra-virgin olive oil

EASY

 Chicken Breasts with Mole Rub

1. **Prepare the grill for direct and indirect cooking over medium heat (350° to 450°F).**

2. **In a small bowl combine the rub ingredients.** Season the cut sides of the limes, the tomatoes, and the zucchini slices with the rub. Lightly coat the chicken on both sides with the oil and season evenly with the remaining rub.

3. **Brush the cooking grates clean.** Grill the chicken, bone side down, over *indirect medium heat*, with lid closed, until the meat is opaque all the way to the bone, 30 to 40 minutes. If desired, to crisp the skin, grill the chicken over *direct medium heat* during the last 5 to 10 minutes of grilling time, turning once. Remove from the grill and let rest for 3 to 5 minutes.

4. **While the chicken rests, grill the limes, tomatoes, and zucchini over *direct medium heat*, with the lid closed, until the limes and tomatoes are warm and the zucchini is crisp-tender, 3 to 5 minutes, turning once.

5. **Squeeze the grilled limes over the chicken and serve with the tomatoes and zucchini.

Access the grocery list for this recipe on your mobile device. timetogrill.mobi.

Mole-Rubbed Butterflied Chicken
WITH MEXICAN CREMA

SERVES: 👤👤👤👤

PREP TIME: **20** MINUTES

MARINATING TIME: **24** HOURS

GRILLING TIME: ABOUT **40** MINUTES

SPECIAL EQUIPMENT: INSTANT-READ
THERMOMETER, POULTRY SHEARS

// MARINADE
    Grated zest of 1 orange
½   cup fresh orange juice
¼   cup extra-virgin olive oil
3   tablespoons finely chopped fresh
    cilantro leaves and tender stems
1   tablespoon kosher salt
1   teaspoon ground black pepper

1   whole chicken, about 4 pounds,
    giblets and any excess fat removed

// RUB
2   tablespoons kosher salt
2   tablespoons pure chile powder
1   tablespoon unsweetened cocoa powder
1   tablespoon ground black pepper
1   tablespoon granulated sugar
1   teaspoon paprika

½   cup sour cream (thinned to drizzling
    consistency with milk)

1. **Whisk the marinade ingredients in a 13-by-9-inch glass baking dish.**

2. **Place the chicken, breast side down, on a cutting board.** Using poultry shears, cut from the neck to the tail end, along either side of the backbone. Remove the backbone. Once the backbone is out, you'll be able to see the interior of the chicken. Make a small slit in the cartilage at the bottom end of the breastbone. Then placing both hands on the rib cage, crack the chicken open like a book. Run your fingers along either side of the cartilage in between the breast to loosen it from the flesh. Grab the bone and pull up on it to remove it along with the attached cartilage. The chicken should now lie flat (see page 18).

3. **Place the chicken in the dish and turn to coat evenly with the marinade.** Cover with plastic wrap and refrigerate for 24 hours.

4. **In a small bowl mix the rub ingredients.**

5. **Prepare the grill for indirect cooking over medium heat (about 350°F).**

6. **Remove the chicken from the bowl and discard the marinade.** Coat the chicken all over with the rub. The rub will get wet and become a paste.

7. **Brush the cooking grates clean.** Grill the chicken, bone side down, over **indirect medium heat**, with the lid closed, until the juices run clear and an instant-read thermometer inserted into the thickest part of the thigh (not touching the bone) reaches 160° to 165°F, about 40 minutes. If desired, to crisp the skin, grill the chicken over **direct medium heat** during the last 5 to 10 minutes of grilling time, turning once. Remove from the grill and let rest for 5 to 10 minutes (the internal temperature will rise 5 to 10 degrees during this time).

8. **Cut the chicken into serving pieces.** Serve warm with the *crema* on the side and black beans and chopped avocado, if desired.

Access the grocery list for this recipe on your mobile device. timetogrill.mobi.

Caribbean flavors are at work in both of these recipes. On this page, fragrant spices such as allspice and cinnamon are spread in a paste under and over the chicken skin. Mince the onions and jalapeños as finely as you can and then mash them with the back of a fork to create a fairly smooth paste. On the opposite page, the seasonings on the chicken are simpler but the salsa brings a lot of tropical sweetness along with a bite of ginger and jalapeños. The longer you let the salsa sit before serving, the more juice the salt will draw out of the fruit.

SERVES: ♦♦♦♦

PREP TIME: **15** MINUTES

GRILLING TIME: **23** TO **35** MINUTES

// PASTE

  2 tablespoons extra-virgin olive oil
  2 tablespoons minced white onion
  2 small jalapeño chile peppers, stems and seeds removed, minced
  2 teaspoons dried thyme
  2 teaspoons ground allspice
  2 teaspoons ground black pepper
  ½ teaspoon ground cayenne pepper
  ½ teaspoon ground cinnamon
  ½ teaspoon kosher salt
     Juice of 1 lime

  4 chicken breast halves (with bone and skin), each 10 to 12 ounces

EASY

Barbados Chicken Breasts

1. Prepare the grill for direct and indirect cooking over medium heat (350° to 450°F).

2. In a medium bowl mix the paste ingredients. Using your fingertips, carefully lift the skin from the chicken breasts, leaving the skin closest to the breastbone attached. Run 1 teaspoon of the paste under the skin all over the exposed meat. Lay the skin back in place and spread the remaining paste evenly all over the chicken.

3. Brush the cooking grates clean. Grill the chicken, skin side down, over **direct medium heat**, with the lid closed, until the skin is browned, 3 to 5 minutes. Turn the chicken over and continue to grill over **indirect medium heat**, with the lid closed, until the meat is opaque all the way to the bone, 20 to 30 minutes. Remove from the grill and let rest for 3 to 5 minutes. Serve warm with rice and beans, if desired.

Access the grocery list for this recipe on your mobile device. timetogrill.mobi.

Roasted Chicken Breasts with Mango-Ginger Salsa

SERVES: 👤👤👤👤

PREP TIME: **30** MINUTES

GRILLING TIME: **23** TO **35** MINUTES

// SALSA

- 3 cups medium-diced ripe mangoes *or* peaches
- ½ cup finely diced red bell pepper
- ¼ cup finely diced white onion
- 1 medium jalapeño chile pepper, stem and seeds removed, minced
- 2 tablespoons finely chopped fresh cilantro leaves
- 1 tablespoon fresh lime juice
- 1 teaspoon peeled, grated fresh ginger
- ¼ teaspoon ground cayenne pepper
- ¼ teaspoon kosher salt

// RUB

- 1 teaspoon kosher salt
- 1 teaspoon dried thyme
- ½ teaspoon ground black pepper

- 4 chicken breast halves (with bone and skin), each 10 to 12 ounces
- 2 tablespoons extra-virgin olive oil

1. Prepare the grill for direct and indirect cooking over medium heat (350° to 450°F).

2. In a large bowl mix the salsa ingredients. Cover and refrigerate until ready to serve.

3. In a small bowl mix the rub ingredients. Lightly brush the chicken on both sides with the oil and season evenly with the rub.

4. Brush the cooking grates clean. Grill the chicken, skin side down first, over *direct medium heat*, with the lid closed, until the skin is browned, 3 to 5 minutes. Turn the chicken over and continue to grill over *indirect medium heat*, with the lid closed, until the meat is opaque all the way to the bone, 20 to 30 minutes. Remove from the grill and let rest for 3 to 5 minutes. Serve warm with the salsa.

Access the grocery list for this recipe on your mobile device. timetogrill.mobi.

Here is a bold, lemony wet rub (or is it a dry marinade?) that you can whip up from ingredients you are likely to have on hand. It works wonders on chicken parts, which you can have on the table within an hour of starting the recipe. If you have time to cook a whole bird, try it on a can of soda, which provides aromatic moisture inside the chicken, just as beer inside a beer can does. Lemon is the main flavor here, and is found in both the rub and in the soda. Another time, try orange zest and orange soda.

Lemon-Pepper Chicken

SERVES: 🧍🧍🧍🧍

PREP TIME: **15** MINUTES

GRILLING TIME: **30** TO **50** MINUTES

1. **Prepare the grill for indirect cooking over medium heat (350° to 450°F).**

2. **In a large bowl whisk all of the paste ingredients.**

3. **Cut the chicken into eight pieces: two breast halves, two thigh pieces, two**

drumsticks, and two wings (cut off and discard the wing tips). Add the chicken pieces to the bowl with the paste and turn to coat evenly.

4. **Brush the cooking grates clean.** Grill the chicken pieces, skin side down, over **indirect medium heat**, with the lid closed, until fully cooked. The breast and wing pieces will take 30 to 40 minutes. The drumstick and thigh pieces will take 40 to 50 minutes. If desired, to crisp the skin, grill the chicken over **direct medium heat** during the last 5 to 10 minutes of grilling time, turning once. Remove from the grill and let rest for 3 to 5 minutes. Serve warm with lemon wedges.

Access the grocery list for this recipe on your mobile device. timetogrill.mobi.

// PASTE

    Finely grated zest of 2 lemons
2 tablespoons fresh lemon juice
2 tablespoons extra-virgin olive oil
2 tablespoons whole-grain mustard
1½ teaspoons kosher salt
1 tablespoon dried oregano
2 garlic cloves, minced
¾ teaspoon crushed red pepper flakes

1 whole chicken, about 4 pounds, giblets and any excess fat removed
1 lemon, cut into 8 wedges

SERVES: ♦♦♦♦

PREP TIME: **10** MINUTES

GRILLING TIME: **1¼** TO **1½** HOURS

SPECIAL EQUIPMENT:
INSTANT-READ THERMOMETER

// PASTE

Grated zest of 2 lemons
2 tablespoons fresh lemon juice
2 tablespoons finely chopped
fresh oregano leaves
2 tablespoons finely chopped fresh
sage leaves
1½ teaspoons kosher salt
1 tablespoon packed brown sugar
½ teaspoon ground cayenne pepper
1 teaspoon ground black pepper
¼ cup extra-virgin olive oil

1 whole chicken, about 4 pounds,
giblets and any excess fat removed

1 can (12 ounces) lemon-lime soda (not
diet), at room temperature
2 handfuls hickory wood chips, soaked in
water for at least 30 minutes

Soda Can Chicken

1. In a small bowl combine all of the
paste ingredients.

**2. Using your fingers, gently separate the
skin from the meat, starting at the neck and
moving along the breasts.** Repeat to separate
the skin from the thighs and legs, starting at
the tail end.

**3. Spread the paste evenly on the meat
under the skin, making sure to coat as much
of it as you can.** Rub the remaining paste on
the outside of the chicken. Fold the wing tips
behind the chicken's back.

**4. Prepare the grill for indirect cooking over
medium heat (350° to 450°F).**

**5. Open the soda can and pour out about
half of the soda.** Using a can opener, make
four more holes in the top of the can. Place
the soda can on a solid surface. Plunk the
chicken cavity over the can.

6. Brush the cooking grates clean. Drain
and scatter the wood chips directly over
lit charcoal or put them in the smoker box
of a gas grill, following manufacturer's
instructions. When the wood chips begin to
smoke, transfer the chicken-on-a-can to the
grill, balancing the bird on its two legs and the

can, like a tripod. Grill over **indirect medium
heat**, with the lid closed, until the juices
run clear and an instant-read thermometer
inserted in the thickest part of the thigh (not
touching the bone) reaches 160° to 165°F, 1¼
to 1½ hours. Carefully remove the chicken-on-
a-can from the grill (do not spill the contents
of the soda can, as it will be very hot). Let the
chicken rest for 10 to 15 minutes (the internal
temperature will rise 5 to 10 degrees during
this time). Carefully lift the chicken from the
can and cut into serving pieces. Serve warm.

*Access the grocery list for this recipe
on your mobile device. timetogrill.mobi.*

Roasting chicken pieces rather than a whole chicken allows you to spread pastes like the one here with rosemary and mustard on all sides of the meat, meaning the flavors penetrate faster and more evenly. But if you are fortunate enough to have a rotisserie on your grill, nothing beats a brined whole chicken that turns slowly on a spit and bastes itself while the skin turns golden brown and delicious. Try adding some wood chips to the grill for even bigger flavor.

1. In a small bowl whisk all of the marinade ingredients.

2. Cut the chicken into six pieces: two breast halves, two whole legs (thigh and drumstick), and two wings (remove and discard the wing tips). Brush each chicken piece on both sides with the marinade. If you have time, marinate the chicken in the refrigerator for as long as 4 hours. If not, you can roast the chicken right away.

3. Prepare the grill for direct and indirect cooking over medium heat (350° to 450°F).

4. Brush the cooking grates clean. Grill the chicken pieces, skin side down, over *indirect medium heat*, with the lid closed as much as possible, until fully cooked, turning once or twice. The breasts and wing pieces will take 30 to 40 minutes and the whole legs will take 40 to 50 minutes. During the last 5 minutes of grilling time, move the chicken over *direct medium heat* and cook until well browned all over, turning once or twice. Remove from the grill and let rest for 3 to 5 minutes. Serve warm.

Access the grocery list for this recipe on your mobile device. timetogrill.mobi.

Easy Rosemary Roasted Chicken

EASY

SERVES: ††††

PREP TIME: **15** MINUTES

MARINATING TIME: UP TO **4** HOURS

GRILLING TIME: **30** TO **50** MINUTES

// MARINADE

- 2 tablespoons extra-virgin olive oil
- 1 tablespoon Dijon mustard
- 1 tablespoon Worcestershire sauce
- 1 tablespoon cider vinegar
- 1 tablespoon finely chopped fresh rosemary leaves
- ½ teaspoon kosher salt
- ¼ teaspoon ground black pepper

- 1 whole chicken, about 4 pounds, giblets and any excess fat removed

SERVES: ♦♦♦♦

PREP TIME: **20** MINUTES

BRINING TIME: **6** TO **12** HOURS

GRILLING TIME: **1¼** TO **1½** HOURS

SPECIAL EQUIPMENT:
BUTCHER'S TWINE, LARGE
DISPOSABLE FOIL PAN, ROTISSERIE,
INSTANT-READ THERMOMETER

// BRINE
- 1 gallon water
- ¾ cup kosher salt
- ½ cup granulated sugar
- 2 tablespoons dried rosemary
- 1 tablespoon caraway seed
- 1 tablespoon granulated garlic
- 2 teaspoons ground black pepper

- 1 whole chicken, about 4 pounds, giblets, wing tips, and any excess fat removed

 Rosemary-Brined
Rotisserie Chicken

1. **In a large pot combine the brine ingredients.** Stir well to dissolve the sugar and salt.

2. **Submerge the chicken in the brine, breast side down, and refrigerate for 6 to 12 hours.**

3. **Prepare the grill for indirect cooking over medium heat (350° to 450°F).**

4. **Remove the chicken from the pot and discard the brine.** Pat the chicken dry with paper towels. Truss the chicken with butcher's twine (see page 19).

5. **Following the grill's instructions, secure the chicken in the middle of a rotisserie spit,** put the spit in place, and turn on the motor. Place a large disposable foil pan underneath the chicken to catch the drippings. Cook the chicken over **indirect medium heat**, with the lid closed, for 1 hour.

6. **If your grill has an infrared burner at the back of the grill, after 1 hour of cooking, light that burner and set it to medium heat (leaving the regular outside burners on medium and the middle burners turned off).** If your grill does not have an infrared burner, continue to cook the chicken as you were doing. Either way, cook the chicken until the surface is deep golden brown and the internal temperature reaches 160° to 165°F in the thickest part of the thigh (not touching the bone). This should take 10 to 20 minutes with the infrared burner and 20 to 30 minutes without the infrared burner. Watch carefully that the chicken skin does not burn.

7. **When the chicken is fully cooked, turn off the rotisserie motor and remove the spit from the grill.** Tilt the chicken upright over the foil pan so that the liquid that has accumulated in the chicken's cavity pours into the pan. Let rest for 10 to 15 minutes (the internal temperature will rise 5 to 10 degrees during this time). Transfer the chicken from the spit to a cutting board. Cut into serving pieces. Serve warm.

Access the grocery list for this recipe on your mobile device. timetogrill.mobi.

Major Grey's chutney is a convenient little condiment to have waiting in the cabinet on evenings when you are racing against the clock. This sweet and tart dipping sauce includes mangoes, raisins, vinegar, and tamarind, which are all quite tasty with grilled turkey meatballs. To make an even more impressive dish, wrap the turkey in naan (Indian flat bread) and top it with fresh mint chutney and slices of ripe mango.

To avoid soaking bamboo skewers each time you need them, soak a big batch once for an hour or so, drain them, and then freeze them in a plastic bag. When it's time to grill, pull out as many skewers as you need.

Turkey Kofta
WITH MAJOR GREY'S CHUTNEY

SERVES: 👤👤👤👤 TO 👤👤👤👤👤👤

PREP TIME: **15** MINUTES

GRILLING TIME: ABOUT **6** MINUTES

SPECIAL EQUIPMENT: SHORT BAMBOO SKEWERS, SOAKED IN WATER FOR AT LEAST 30 MINUTES

EASY

// KOFTA

1¼ pounds ground turkey thigh meat
¼ cup finely chopped fresh cilantro leaves
1 tablespoon minced garlic
1 tablespoon curry powder
½ teaspoon ground cayenne pepper
1 teaspoon kosher salt

½ cup Major Grey's chutney

1. Prepare the grill for direct cooking over medium heat (350° to 450°F).

2. In a large bowl, using your hands, gently mix the *kofta* ingredients. Shape into 24 small meatballs, each about 1 inch in diameter. Place two meatballs side by side. Push a skewer through the meatballs and then another skewer parallel to the first one. Double skewer the remaining meatballs.

3. Brush the cooking grates clean. Grill the meatballs over ***direct medium heat***, with the lid closed as much as possible, until the meat is firm and fully cooked but still moist, about 6 minutes, turning once. Remove from the grill and serve warm with the chutney.

Access the grocery list for this recipe on your mobile device. timetogrill.mobi.

Turkey Wraps with Mint Chutney

SERVES: 4 TO 6

PREP TIME: **30** MINUTES

GRILLING TIME: ABOUT **6** MINUTES

1¼ pounds ground turkey thigh meat
2 teaspoons minced garlic
1 small jalapeño chile pepper, seeded and finely minced
1 tablespoon peeled, minced fresh ginger
1 tablespoon garam masala
1 teaspoon kosher salt

¼ cup extra-virgin olive oil

// CHUTNEY

1 cup loosely packed fresh mint leaves
1 cup coarsely chopped yellow onion
½ cup loosely packed fresh cilantro leaves
4 serrano chile peppers, seeded and coarsely chopped (about ⅓ cup)
2 tablespoons fresh lime juice
½ teaspoon ground cumin
½ teaspoon kosher salt

8 pieces naan
2 firm, ripe mangoes, peeled and cut into ¼-inch slices

1. **In a large bowl gently mix the ground turkey with the garlic, jalapeño, ginger, garam masala, and salt.**

2. **Pour the oil onto a sheet pan and brush it evenly all over the surface.** Using two spoons, shape the turkey mixture into 24 small ovals or quenelles, placing them on the oiled sheet pan as you make them. Turn them, making sure they are well coated with oil. Refrigerate until ready to grill.

3. **Prepare grill for direct cooking over medium heat (350° to 450°F).**

4. **In a food processor or blender combine the chutney ingredients and pulse until the mixture is blended but still chunky.**

5. **Brush the cooking grates clean.** Grill the quenelles over *direct medium heat*, with the lid closed as much as possible, until the meat is firm and fully cooked but still moist, about 6 minutes, turning once every 2 minutes. During the last minute of grilling time, lightly toast the naan over direct heat. Remove from the grill.

6. **Place three quenelles on each piece of naan.** Top generously with mint chutney and sliced mango.

Access the grocery list for this recipe on your mobile device. timetogrill.mobi.

EASY

Why don't we grill turkey cutlets more often? They cook on the grill in about five minutes and are so good—covered in garlic and sage and dipped in a cranberry sauce—that you can have a turkey dinner in about twenty minutes. Now, if you really want to dial it up, stuff a boneless turkey breast with sautéed apples and onions, and wrap the whole thing in bacon slices. It takes about an hour and a half to grill the turkey breast to perfection over indirect heat. Gobble gobble.

SERVES: 🧍🧍🧍🧍 TO 🧍🧍🧍🧍🧍🧍

PREP TIME: **15** MINUTES

GRILLING TIME: **4** TO **6** MINUTES

3 tablespoons extra-virgin olive oil
1 tablespoon minced fresh sage leaves
2 teaspoons minced garlic
1¾ teaspoons kosher salt, divided
½ teaspoon ground black pepper

8 turkey cutlets, each 3 to 4 ounces and about ½ inch thick

// SAUCE

1 Granny Smith apple, peeled, cored, and cut into ½-inch pieces
3 cups fresh cranberries, rinsed and drained (12 ounces)
½ cup apple juice
½ cup granulated sugar
¼ teaspoon ground cloves

Garlic-Sage Turkey Cutlets
WITH CRANBERRY SAUCE

1. Prepare the grill for direct cooking over medium heat (350° to 450°F).

2. In a shallow baking dish combine the oil, sage, garlic, 1½ teaspoons of the salt, and the pepper. Put the cutlets in the dish and turn to coat them evenly. Set aside at room temperature for as long as 20 minutes while you make the sauce.

3. In a medium saucepan combine the sauce ingredients, including the remaining ¼ teaspoon salt. Bring to a boil and then reduce to a simmer. Cover and cook until all the cranberries have popped, 6 to 10 minutes. Set aside to cool.

4. Brush the cooking grates clean. Grill the cutlets over ***direct medium heat***, with the lid closed as much as possible, until the meat is firm to the touch and no longer pink in the center, 4 to 6 minutes, turning once or twice. Remove from the grill and serve warm with the sauce spooned over the top.

Access the grocery list for this recipe on your mobile device. timetogrill.mobi.

Bacon-Wrapped Turkey Breast
WITH APPLE-SAGE STUFFING

SERVES: ††††††

PREP TIME: **30** MINUTES

GRILLING TIME: ABOUT **1½** HOURS

SPECIAL EQUIPMENT: BUTCHER'S TWINE, LARGE DISPOSABLE FOIL PAN, INSTANT-READ THERMOMETER

// STUFFING

- 3 tablespoons unsalted butter
- 1 medium yellow onion, roughly chopped
- 1 large apple, peeled, cored, and roughly chopped
- 1 tablespoon minced fresh sage leaves
- 1 tablespoon minced garlic
- ½ teaspoon kosher salt
- ¼ teaspoon ground black pepper

- 1 boneless, skinless turkey breast, about 3 pounds, butterflied
- 12 slices bacon

// SAUCE

- 2 cups fresh cranberries, rinsed and drained (8 ounces)
- 1 cup apple juice
- 3 tablespoons packed dark brown sugar
- ¼ teaspoon kosher salt
- ¼ teaspoon ground black pepper

1. In a large skillet over medium-high heat, melt the butter. Add the onion and apple and cook for 3 to 4 minutes, stirring occasionally. Add the sage, garlic, salt, and pepper. Cook for 2 more minutes, stirring occasionally. Transfer to a medium bowl and let cool for a few minutes.

2. Place the butterflied turkey breast on a work surface between two sheets of plastic wrap and pound to an even thickness. Evenly spread the stuffing over the turkey breast and then roll up the breast lengthwise to create a cylinder. Wrap the turkey in the bacon as shown in the photo below and tie it with butcher's twine to create a uniform roast and to secure the bacon.

3. Before you light the grill, place a large disposable foil pan underneath the cooking grate to catch the bacon grease. Prepare the grill for indirect cooking over medium heat (about 400°F).

4. Brush the cooking grates clean. Center the turkey over the foil pan and grill over *indirect medium heat*, with the lid closed, until the internal temperature reaches 160° to 165°F, about 1½ hours, turning once or twice to ensure the bacon gets crispy on all sides. Meanwhile, make the sauce.

5. In a medium saucepan over medium-high heat, bring the sauce ingredients to a boil. Lower the heat to a simmer and cook until the cranberries pop and the sauce thickens, 10 to 12 minutes, stirring occasionally. Let cool to room temperature.

6. Transfer the turkey to a carving board and let rest for 5 to 10 minutes (the internal temperature will rise 5 to 10 degrees during this time). Remove the twine and carve into 1-inch slices. Serve warm or at room temperature with the sauce.

Access the grocery list for this recipe on your mobile device. timetogrill.mobi.

Arrange the bacon slices on a work surface in six tightly spaced parallel stripes, overlapping the ends of two slices to make each stripe. Place the rolled turkey breast in the center of the bacon and then crisscross the bacon around the turkey.

Bacon and mayonnaise together in one sauce may seem excessively rich, but you use only a little for dipping these quick-cooking turkey tenderloins. The glaze would also be good on chicken or pork, though it's pretty sweet (and could burn), so brush it on only during the last five to ten minutes. The longer recipe uses a brine, which contributes a lot of flavor, but you could skip it on a busy day; just season the tenderloins with salt and pepper. There are plenty of flavors in the corn and pepper salad—a version of a Louisiana side dish called *maque choux*.

Bourbon-Glazed Turkey Tenderloins

SERVES: 👤👤👤👤

PREP TIME: **15** MINUTES

GRILLING TIME: **13** TO **16** MINUTES

SPECIAL EQUIPMENT:
INSTANT-READ THERMOMETER

// AIOLI

2 slices apple wood smoked bacon, coarsely chopped
2 garlic cloves
1 scallion, root end trimmed, chopped
1 tablespoon sherry
½ cup mayonnaise
Kosher salt

// GLAZE

2 tablespoons packed brown sugar
2 tablespoons ketchup
2 tablespoons cider vinegar
2 tablespoons bourbon
1 teaspoon Worcestershire sauce

2 turkey tenderloins, about 1¼ pounds total
Ground black pepper

1. In a small sauté pan over medium-high heat, fry the chopped bacon until crisp but not burned, about 6 minutes, stirring occasionally. Drain the bacon on paper towels and reserve the bacon drippings.

2. In the bowl of a food processor or blender whirl the garlic until finely chopped. Add the bacon, scallion, sherry, mayonnaise, and ¼ teaspoon salt and pulse until well combined.

3. Prepare the grill for direct cooking over medium heat (350° to 450°F).

4. In a medium bowl whisk the glaze ingredients until the sugar has dissolved.

5. Lightly brush the tenderloins on both sides with the reserved bacon drippings (if you do not have enough bacon drippings, you can add, or substitute, vegetable oil). Season evenly with salt and pepper.

6. Brush the cooking grates clean. Grill the tenderloins over *direct medium heat*, with the lid closed as much as possible, for about 8 minutes, turning once. Brush the tenderloins generously with the glaze and continue cooking until the meat is no longer pink in the center and the internal temperature reaches 160° to 165°F, 5 to 8 minutes, turning and basting frequently with the glaze. Remove from the grill and let rest for 5 to 10 minutes (the internal temperature will rise 5 to 10 degrees during this time). Cut the tenderloins crosswise into slices and serve warm with the bacon aioli.

Access the grocery list for this recipe on your mobile device. timetogrill.mobi.

SERVES: †††††

PREP TIME: **30** MINUTES

BRINING TIME: **2** HOURS

GRILLING TIME: **10** TO **12** MINUTES

SPECIAL EQUIPMENT:
INSTANT-READ THERMOMETER

// BRINE

½ cup bourbon
½ cup water
¼ cup packed brown sugar
2 tablespoons kosher salt
½ teaspoon crushed red pepper flakes
1 cup ice cubes

2 turkey tenderloins,
about 1¼ pounds total
Extra-virgin olive oil

// SALAD

4 slices bacon, finely chopped
1 cup finely diced red bell pepper
½ cup finely diced red onion
¼ cup sherry
4 cups frozen corn kernels *or* fresh corn
(from 4–5 ears)
1 cup heavy whipping cream
½ teaspoon kosher salt
¼ teaspoon ground cayenne pepper
¼ cup chopped fresh Italian parsley leaves

1. In a medium saucepan over medium heat, combine the bourbon, water, sugar, salt, and red pepper flakes. Stir until the sugar and salt dissolve. Remove from the heat and stir in the ice cubes to quickly cool the brine.

2. Place the turkey tenderloins in a large, resealable plastic bag and pour in the brine. Press the air out of the bag and seal tightly.

Brined Turkey Tenderloins
WITH CORN AND PEPPER SALAD

Place the bag in a bowl or a rimmed dish and refrigerate for 2 hours, turning the bag every 30 minutes.

3. Remove the tenderloins from the bag and discard the brine. Rinse the tenderloins under cold water and pat dry with paper towels. Lightly brush the tenderloins on both sides with oil.

4. Prepare the grill for direct cooking over medium heat (350° to 450°F).

5. In a large sauté pan over medium-high heat, fry the bacon until crisp but not burned, about 6 minutes, stirring occasionally. Transfer the bacon to paper towels and pour off all but 1 tablespoon of the drippings. Add the bell pepper and onion to the pan and sauté until the onion is tender, 4 to 5 minutes. Stir in the sherry, scraping any browned bits from the bottom of the pan, and cook until

the sherry evaporates, 2 to 3 minutes. Add the corn and cream and simmer until the cream reduces and the mixture has the consistency of creamed corn, about 5 minutes, stirring frequently. Season with salt and cayenne; remove from the heat and cover to keep warm. Just before serving, add the bacon and parsley and stir to combine.

6. Brush the cooking grates clean. Grill the tenderloins over *direct medium heat*, with the lid closed as much as possible, until the meat is no longer pink in the center and the internal temperature reaches 160° to 165°F, 10 to 12 minutes, turning once. Remove from the grill and let rest for 5 to 10 minutes (the internal temperature will rise 5 to 10 degrees during this time). Cut the tenderloins crosswise into slices and serve on top of the salad.

Access the grocery list for this recipe on your mobile device. timetogrill.mobi.

Ask just about anyone who has grilled a turkey, and they'll say there is no turning back, especially if they have taken the time to brine it first. This recipe calls for brining the bird in an ice chest, a sensible alternative to taking up half the space in your refrigerator. One other key is making a full-blown pan gravy from (almost) homemade turkey stock. For regular days, when you just want some nicely roasted turkey, stick to the easy recipe here. Fresh whole turkey breasts are usually sold as two connected breast sections with the ribs still attached. Frozen whole turkey breasts may also include the back of the turkey. For this recipe, remove the back and save it for another use. Salsa verde is very easy to prepare. Make extra to have on hand for perking up other simply grilled poultry, as well as meat and seafood. Pour a thin layer of olive oil over the top to keep it bright green and add the vinegar right before serving or the verdant sauce will turn cloudy.

Turkey Breast
WITH ITALIAN SALSA VERDE

SERVES: **6** TO **8**

PREP TIME: **15** MINUTES

GRILLING TIME: **1½** TO **2** HOURS

SPECIAL EQUIPMENT: LARGE DISPOSABLE FOIL PAN, INSTANT-READ THERMOMETER

// SALSA VERDE

2 cups tightly packed fresh Italian parsley leaves
2 tablespoons nonpareil capers, rinsed
1 teaspoon anchovy paste
1 garlic clove, minced
Kosher salt
Ground black pepper
Extra-virgin olive oil

1 whole turkey breast (with bone and skin), 6 to 7 pounds, thawed if necessary
2 tablespoons red wine vinegar

1. **Carefully place a large disposable foil pan underneath the cooking grate to catch the turkey drippings.** Prepare the grill for indirect cooking over medium-low heat (about 350°F).

2. **In a food processor combine the parsley, capers, anchovy paste, garlic, ¼ teaspoon salt, and ¼ teaspoon pepper and pulse until the parsley is finely chopped.** With the machine running, gradually add ½ cup oil and process to a fairly smooth sauce. Transfer to a bowl, cover, and set aside at room temperature while the turkey is grilling.

3. **Brush the turkey breast all over with oil and season evenly with salt and pepper.** Brush the cooking grates clean. Center the turkey above the foil pan and grill over *indirect medium-low heat*, with the lid closed, until an instant-read thermometer inserted into the thickest part of the breast (not touching the bone), reaches 160° to 165°F, 1½ to 2 hours. Keep the temperature of the grill as close to 350°F as possible. Transfer to a cutting board and let rest for 5 to 10 minutes (the internal temperature will rise 5 to 10 degrees during this time).

4. **Remove each half of the turkey breast by cutting lengthwise along both sides of the breastbone.** Pull each breast half away from the breastbone, using a sharp knife to carefully release the meat from the rib cage. Cut the meat across the grain into ½-inch slices. Stir the vinegar into the salsa verde. Serve the turkey warm or at room temperature with the salsa verde on the side.

Access the grocery list for this recipe on your mobile device. timetogrill.mobi.

EASY

Brined Turkey
WITH HERBED PAN GRAVY

Place the turkey, breast side down, inside a large, sturdy plastic bag. Put the bag in an ice chest lined with ice. Then pour the brine over the turkey.

SERVES: **8** TO **12**

PREP TIME: **15** MINUTES, PLUS 2 HOURS TO MAKE AND COOL THE BRINE, 1 HOUR AND 10 MINUTES TO MAKE THE STOCK, 30 MINUTES TO MAKE THE GRAVY AND CARVE THE BIRD

BRINING TIME: **12** TO **14** HOURS

GRILLING TIME: ABOUT **2¾** HOURS

SPECIAL EQUIPMENT: LARGE STOCKPOT OR CLEAN BUCKET THAT CAN HOLD AT LEAST 10 QUARTS, STURDY PLASTIC BAG, LARGE ICE CHEST, BUTCHER'S TWINE, 2 LARGE DISPOSABLE FOIL PANS, ROASTING RACK, INSTANT-READ THERMOMETER, GRAVY SEPARATOR

// BRINE
- 1¼ cups kosher salt
- 1 cup packed light brown sugar
- 1 tablespoon whole black peppercorns
- 3 quarts water
- 6 quarts ice water

- 1 whole turkey, 12 to 14 pounds, thawed if necessary
- 2 bags (5 pounds each) ice cubes

- 2 small onions, chopped, divided
- 1 tablespoon vegetable oil
- 2 quarts reduced-sodium chicken broth
- 3 tablespoons unsalted butter, melted, if needed
- ½ cup all-purpose flour
- 2 teaspoons chopped fresh herbs, such as rosemary, thyme, or sage, or a combination
  Kosher salt
  Ground black pepper

1. The night before grilling, brine the turkey: In a large non-reactive stockpot combine the salt, brown sugar, peppercorns, and 3 quarts water. Bring to a boil over high heat, stirring to dissolve the salt. Remove the brine from the heat and cool it until tepid. Add the ice water. (If your stockpot is not large enough to hold 10 quarts of liquid, pour the brine and the ice water into a clean bucket.) The brine should be very cold.

2. Remove the giblets, neck, and lumps of fat from the tail area of the turkey. Place them in a bowl, cover with plastic wrap, and refrigerate. Remove and discard the pop-up timer if there is one. Place the turkey inside the sturdy plastic bag. Arrange a thin layer of ice on the bottom of the ice chest and set the turkey on top of it. Pour enough of the cold brine into the bag to cover the turkey as much as possible when the bag is closed and tightly tied. Discard any extra brine. Add ice and/or thermal ice packs to cover and surround the turkey, keeping it cold. Close the ice chest and brine the turkey for 12 to 14 hours, no longer.

 Pull the bag up and around the turkey to submerge as much of the meat as possible in the brine. Then seal the bag and close the ice chest.

3. Remove the turkey from the bag and discard the brine. Pat the turkey dry inside and outside with paper towels. Tuck the wing tips behind the turkey's back. Add 1 cup of the chopped onion to the body cavity. Tie the drumsticks together with butcher's twine. Place one large disposable foil pan inside the other. Place the turkey on a roasting rack set inside the pans and let stand at room temperature for 1 hour before grilling.

4. Prepare the grill for indirect cooking over medium-low heat (about 350°F). Place the reserved lumps of fat in the roasting pan. Grill the turkey over *indirect medium-low heat*, with the lid closed, keeping the grill's temperature as close to 350°F as possible, until an instant-read thermometer inserted in the thickest part of the thigh (not touching the bone) reaches 160° to 165°F, about 2¾ hours. Occasionally during grilling, tilt the bird so the juices run out of the cavity into the roasting pan. The juices will reduce and turn dark brown, adding color and rich flavor for the gravy.

5. Meanwhile, in a large saucepan on the stove top, heat the oil over medium-high heat. Using a heavy knife or cleaver, chop the reserved neck into 2-inch chunks. Add the neck and giblets to the saucepan and cook, turning occasionally, until well browned, 5 to 6 minutes. Add the remaining chopped onion and cook until softened, about 3 minutes. Add the broth and bring the mixture to a low boil. Reduce the heat to low and simmer gently until reduced by half, about 1 hour. Drain, discard the solids, and set the stock aside.

6. When the turkey is done, transfer it to a platter and let it rest for 20 to 30 minutes (the internal temperature will rise 5 to 10 degrees during this time). While it is resting, strain the pan juices into a gravy separator. Let stand for 3 minutes so the fat rises to the top of the separator. Pour the pan juices into a 1-quart measuring cup, reserving the fat. Add more of the stock as needed to make 1 quart.

7. Measure the fat. You should have ½ cup. Add melted butter if needed. In a medium saucepan, heat the fat (and butter) over medium heat. Whisk in the flour and let bubble for 1 minute, stirring constantly. Whisk in the stock mixture and bring the gravy to a boil. Reduce the heat to medium-low, simmer for 5 minutes and then pour the gravy into the roasting pan. Scrape up any browned bits with a rubber spatula, taking care not to pierce the foil pan. Return the gravy to the saucepan and add the fresh herbs. Simmer to blend the flavors for 5 minutes, whisking often. Taste and season carefully with salt and pepper (the brine may have seasoned the gravy enough).

8. Carve the turkey and serve with the gravy.

Access the grocery list for this recipe on your mobile device. timetogrill.mobi.

Indirect heat is essential for a moist, evenly cooked turkey. Create two beds of charcoal on opposite sides of the charcoal grate and leave a wide area open in middle.

Once every hour, add 5 to 8 briquettes to each bed of charcoal. This helps to maintain a fairly even level of heat. Drop the briquettes into the grill gently so they don't send ashes onto the turkey.

While the grill lid is open, tilt the turkey so that the juices accumulating in the center will pour into the pan and flavor the base of the gravy.

EASY　　　　**ADVENTUROUS**

SEAFOOD

When you are dealing with ingredients as special as lobster, the cooking should be so straightforward that it doesn't distract from the amazing, natural flavors. Basting the lobster and sweet corn with garlic butter is all you really need to do. But if you would rather cut down on last-minute prep work, grill the lobster ahead of time and set aside the meat while you make an elegant bisque based on the lobster shells. When it is time to serve, combine the bisque and lobster meat, reheating them gently. Serve with slices of grilled bread brushed with garlic.

Lobsters and Corn

SERVES: 👤👤👤👤

PREP TIME: **15** MINUTES

GRILLING TIME: **10** TO **15** MINUTES OR **20** TO **30** MINUTES

1 cup (2 sticks) unsalted butter
2 garlic cloves, finely chopped
  Kosher salt
  Ground black pepper
4 live lobsters, each 1½ to 2 pounds
4 ears fresh corn, husked
2 tablespoons finely chopped fresh Italian parsley leaves

1. **In a small saucepan over low heat, cook the butter with the garlic, ½ teaspoon salt, and ¼ teaspoon pepper until the butter is melted.** Set aside.

2. **Prepare the grill for direct and indirect cooking over medium heat (350° to 450°F).**

3. **Place a lobster on a cutting board, shell side down.** Insert the tip of a large, sharp knife into the lobster's body just below the head (no need to be shy about this process—it takes some strength), and cut the lobster open down the center, cutting through the body but not through the back shell. (The shell will hold the juices as it cooks.) Remove and discard the head sac and intestines. Rinse the lobster under cold running water. To help the lobster stay flat on the grill, insert a bamboo skewer through the tail meat. Remove the rubber bands on the claws. Brush the inside of the lobster with some of the butter. Repeat with the remaining lobsters.

4. **Brush the cooking grates clean.** Grill the lobsters, shell side down, over *direct medium heat*, with the lid closed as much as possible, until the tail meat is firm and white, 10 to 15 minutes, brushing occasionally with additional butter. (Soft-shell lobsters will cook more quickly than hard-shell lobsters.) At the same time, if your grill is big enough, grill the corn. If not, grill the corn after the lobsters. Brush the corn with some of the butter and grill over *direct medium heat*, with the lid closed as much as possible, until browned in spots and tender, 10 to 15 minutes, turning occasionally. Season the corn with salt and pepper.

5. **Transfer the lobsters and corn to a large platter.** Heat the butter mixture over medium heat until it comes to a simmer. Add the parsley. Serve the lobsters with the corn and the remaining butter mixture.

Access the grocery list for this recipe on your mobile device. timetogrill.mobi.

EASY

SERVES: **6** TO **8**

PREP TIME: **20** MINUTES, PLUS ABOUT 45 MINUTES TO COOK THE BISQUE

GRILLING TIME: **7** TO **11** MINUTES

SPECIAL EQUIPMENT: KITCHEN SHEARS

4 lobster tails, each 6 to 8 ounces, thawed if necessary
　Extra-virgin olive oil
3 cups fish stock *or* clam juice
2 tablespoons unsalted butter
1 medium yellow onion, finely chopped
2 ribs celery, cut into ¼-inch dice
2 carrots, peeled and cut into ¼-inch dice
2 garlic cloves, finely chopped
　Kosher salt
　Ground black pepper
½ cup white wine
½ teaspoon smoked paprika
1 tablespoon tomato paste
2 cups half-and-half
2 tablespoons finely chopped fresh chives

Lobster Bisque

1. **Prepare the grill for direct cooking over medium heat (350° to 450°F).**

2. **Using kitchen shears, split each tail in half lengthwise.** (If desired, to prevent the lobster meat from curling on the grill, thread a skewer lengthwise through the center of the meat.) Lightly brush the exposed meat with oil.

3. **Brush the cooking grates clean.** Grill the lobster tails, meat side down, over **direct medium heat**, with the lid closed, until lightly marked, 2 to 3 minutes (watch for flare-ups). Turn the tails over and cook until the meat is white and firm but not dry, 5 to 8 minutes, brushing occasionally with oil. Remove from the grill and let cool.

4. **Remove the lobster meat from the shells and cut the meat into bite-sized pieces.** Reserve the shells.

5. **In a medium saucepan over medium heat, heat the fish stock and add the lobster shells.** Lower the heat and gently simmer for about 20 minutes. Remove from the heat and strain the liquid over a medium bowl. Discard the shells.

6. **In a large pot over medium heat, melt the butter.** Add the onion, celery, carrots, garlic, ½ teaspoon salt, and ¼ teaspoon pepper. Cook until all the vegetables begin to soften and lightly brown, about 5 minutes, stirring occasionally. Add the wine and cook until

it evaporates, about 3 minutes, stirring to scrape up any browned bits. Add the paprika and tomato paste and stir to combine. Stir in the fish stock and then the half-and-half. Bring to a simmer and cook until the vegetables are tender, about 10 minutes. Transfer to a blender (in two batches), or use an immersion blender, and puree until smooth. Return the bisque to the pot and simmer until it has the consistency you like. Add the lobster meat and cook until warm, 3 to 5 minutes. Season with salt and pepper. Ladle into bowls and garnish with chives. Serve warm.

Access the grocery list for this recipe on your mobile device. timetogrill.mobi.

Either one of these recipes works well with scallops in place of the shrimp. Nice accompaniments for the easy recipe include grilled eggplant and steamed rice. If you like, mix some boiled edamame into the adventurous recipe for a little more color and healthy protein.

SERVES: 4; 6 AS AN APPETIZER

PREP TIME: 15 MINUTES

GRILLING TIME: 2 TO 4 MINUTES

// SAUCE

¼ cup soy sauce
1 scallion (white and light green parts only), thinly sliced
1 tablespoon rice vinegar
1 teaspoon chili oil

// GLAZE

3 tablespoons honey
1 tablespoon rice vinegar
1 teaspoon peeled, grated fresh ginger

2 pounds large shrimp (21/30 count), peeled and deveined, tails left on
2 tablespoons vegetable oil
Kosher salt
Ground black pepper

Ginger-Honey Glazed Shrimp

1. **Prepare the grill for direct cooking over high heat (450° to 550°F).**

2. **In a small serving bowl combine the sauce ingredients.**

3. **In a large bowl whisk the glaze ingredients until smooth.**

4. **In another large bowl coat the shrimp with the vegetable oil and season evenly with salt and pepper.**

5. **Brush the cooking grates clean.** Grill the shrimp over ***direct high heat***, with the lid closed as much as possible, until they are firm to the touch and just turning opaque in the center, 2 to 4 minutes, turning once or twice. Transfer the shrimp to the large bowl with the glaze and toss to coat.

6. **Arrange the shrimp on a platter and serve warm with the sauce.**

Access the grocery list for this recipe on your mobile device. timetogrill.mobi.

Shrimp and Shiitake Mushrooms with Soba

SERVES: 👤👤👤👤

PREP TIME: **30** MINUTES

GRILLING TIME: **2** TO **4** MINUTES

SPECIAL EQUIPMENT: PERFORATED
GRILL PAN

// SAUCE
- ¼ cup soy sauce
- 2 tablespoons sake
- 1 tablespoon rice vinegar
- 1 tablespoon peeled, grated fresh ginger
- 1 teaspoon toasted sesame oil
- 1 teaspoon wasabi paste
- 1 garlic clove, minced

- 1 package (8 ounces) soba noodles

- ¼ pound fresh shiitake mushrooms, stems removed
- 1¼ pounds large shrimp (21/30 count), peeled and deveined, tails removed
  Vegetable oil
  Kosher salt
  Ground black pepper

- 3 scallions, thinly sliced
- 1 tablespoon toasted sesame seeds
- 1 sheet pre-toasted, ready-to-use nori, cut into ⅛-inch strips (optional)

1. In a medium bowl whisk the sauce ingredients until the wasabi paste dissolves.

2. In a large pot of salted water cook the soba noodles according to package directions. Drain, and then rinse with cold water to stop the cooking process.

3. Prepare the grill for direct cooking over high heat (450° to 550°F) and preheat the grill pan.

4. Brush the mushrooms and shrimp all over with vegetable oil and season evenly with salt and pepper.

5. Spread the mushrooms and shrimp in a single layer on the grill pan. Grill over *direct high heat*, with the lid closed as much as possible, until the mushrooms are lightly browned and tender and the shrimp are firm to the touch, lightly charred, and just turning opaque in the center, 2 to 4 minutes, turning once or twice. Remove from the grill and thinly slice the mushrooms.

6. In a large bowl toss the soba noodles and mushrooms with the sauce. Divide evenly among serving plates and top with grilled shrimp, scallions, sesame seeds, and nori, if using. Serve immediately.

Access the grocery list for this recipe on your mobile device. timetogrill.mobi.

This easy shrimp recipe makes a colorful, zesty, and healthy first course. Wrap the marinated shrimp in tortillas or serve them with a side of Mexican rice and black beans for a main course. The marinade is good on just about everything—fish, chicken, pork, and even beef—so consider making a large batch of it and freezing portions of it in plastic bags for future use. Marinated shrimp also makes for a tasty change of pace from the usual chicken in tortilla soup. Be sure to have extra tortilla chips and cheese on hand because people are likely to ask for second helpings.

Cilantro-Marinated Shrimp

SERVES: 4

PREP TIME: 20 MINUTES

MARINATING TIME: 10 TO 15 MINUTES

GRILLING TIME: 2 TO 4 MINUTES

SPECIAL EQUIPMENT: METAL OR BAMBOO SKEWERS (IF USING BAMBOO SOAK IN WATER FOR AT LEAST 30 MINUTES)

// MARINADE
½ cup coarsely chopped yellow onion
½ cup loosely packed fresh cilantro leaves
2 tablespoons vegetable oil
2 tablespoons fresh lime juice
1 jalapeño chile pepper, seeded and coarsely chopped
1 tablespoon minced garlic
1½ teaspoons kosher salt
1 teaspoon ground cumin

1¼ pounds large shrimp (21/30 count), peeled and deveined, tails left on

Your favorite salsa

1. Prepare the grill for direct cooking over high heat (450° to 550°F).

2. In a blender combine the marinade ingredients and process until smooth. Put the shrimp in a large, resealable plastic bag and pour in the marinade. Press the air out of the bag and seal tightly. Turn the bag to distribute the marinade, place in a bowl, and marinate at room temperature for 10 to 15 minutes while the grill preheats.

3. Remove the shrimp from the bag and discard the marinade. Thread the shrimp onto skewers. Brush the cooking grates clean. Grill the shrimp over **direct high heat**, with the lid closed as much as possible, until the shrimp are firm to the touch, lightly charred, and just turning opaque in the center, 2 to 4 minutes, turning once or twice. Remove from the grill and serve warm with your favorite salsa.

Access the grocery list for this recipe on your mobile device. timetogrill.mobi.

Begin by skewering one shrimp through both the head and tail ends. Skewer the next shrimp through the head end only, with the tail end pointing in the opposite direction. Skewer the remaining shrimp just like the second one, with all the tails facing the same way.

Shrimp Tortilla Soup
WITH AVOCADO AND CILANTRO

SERVES: 👤👤👤👤👤👤

PREP TIME: **20** MINUTES, PLUS
ABOUT 30 MINUTES FOR THE SOUP

GRILLING TIME: **2** TO **4** MINUTES

4   tablespoons vegetable oil, divided
2   cups finely chopped yellow onion
2   teaspoons minced garlic
1   tablespoon tomato paste
1   tablespoon pure chile powder
1   teaspoon ground cumin
½   teaspoon dried Mexican oregano
2   quarts low-sodium chicken broth
1   can (14.5 ounces) diced tomatoes
1   can (4 ounces) diced, roasted
      green chiles
1½ cups frozen corn *or* fresh corn kernels
      (from 2 ears of corn)

1¼ pounds large shrimp (21/30 count),
      peeled and deveined
      Kosher salt
      Ground black pepper

2   tablespoons fresh lime juice
1   bag (8 ounces) tortilla chips
1½ cups grated Monterey Jack cheese
2   large Hass avocados, diced
4–6 tablespoons finely chopped fresh
      cilantro leaves

1. **Heat a large saucepan over medium heat until hot but not smoking.** Add 2 tablespoons of the oil and swirl to coat the bottom of the saucepan. Add the onion and sauté for about 5 minutes, or until it begins to soften. Add the garlic and cook for 1 to 2 minutes, or until softened. Stir in the tomato paste, chile powder, cumin, and oregano, and sauté for another 1 to 2 minutes, or until fragrant. Add the broth, tomatoes, green chiles, and corn kernels, bring to a boil, and simmer for 20 to 25 minutes.

2. **Prepare the grill for direct cooking over high heat (450° to 550°F).**

3. **Lightly brush the shrimp with the remaining 2 tablespoons of oil and season evenly with salt and pepper.**

4. **Brush the cooking grates clean.** Grill the shrimp over *direct high heat*, with the lid closed as much as possible, until the shrimp are firm to the touch, lightly charred, and just turning opaque in the center, 2 to 4 minutes, turning once or twice. Remove from the grill.

5. **Season the soup with lime juice, salt, and pepper.** Put one handful of tortilla chips in each of six soup bowls. Top with equal amounts of cheese and shrimp. Ladle the soup into the bowls and finish with avocados and cilantro.

Access the grocery list for this recipe on your mobile device. timetogrill.mobi.

You have reached a fork in the road. Either recipe here will take you to some great Spanish food. It's just a matter of how much time you want to spend. In a matter of minutes you can whirl together some pantry ingredients, like jarred roasted peppers, slivered almonds, and sherry vinegar, for a fun romesco sauce that tastes great with grilled shrimp and sausages. Or you can make a masterpiece of a meal by combining very similar ingredients with rice and clams in a big skillet. Either way, the smokiness of the grilled shrimp and sausages will lift the flavors of the finished dish.

SERVES: ♀♀♀♀ TO ♀♀♀♀♀♀

PREP TIME: **15** MINUTES

GRILLING TIME: **2** TO **4** MINUTES

SPECIAL EQUIPMENT: 8 METAL OR BAMBOO SKEWERS (IF USING BAMBOO, SOAK IN WATER FOR AT LEAST 30 MINUTES)

// SAUCE
- 2 garlic cloves
- 1 cup roasted red bell peppers (from a jar), drained (about 3 peppers)
- 1–2 slices country-style bread, crusts removed, cubed (to make ¾ cup)
- ⅓ cup slivered almonds, toasted
- 1 tablespoon sherry vinegar
- 1 teaspoon smoked paprika
- ½ teaspoon kosher salt
  Extra-virgin olive oil

- 1 pound large shrimp (21/30 count), peeled and deveined, tails left on
- 1 pound fully cooked andouille sausages, cut crosswise into ½-inch pieces

- 1 lemon, cut into wedges

EASY

Shrimp and Andouille Skewers
WITH ROMESCO SAUCE

1. **In a food processor or blender process the garlic until finely chopped.** Add the peppers, bread, and almonds and process to combine. Add the vinegar, paprika, and salt and, with the motor running, slowly add ¼ cup oil. Blend until almost smooth. If the sauce is too thick, add about 1 tablespoon of water.

2. **Prepare the grill for direct cooking over high heat (450° to 550°F).**

3. **Thread the shrimp and sausage pieces alternately onto skewers.** Lightly brush with oil.

4. **Brush the cooking grates clean.** Grill the skewers over ***direct high heat***, with the lid closed as much as possible, until the shrimp are firm to the touch and just turning opaque in the center, 2 to 4 minutes, turning once or twice. Remove from the grill and serve warm with the sauce and lemon wedges.

Access the grocery list for this recipe on your mobile device. timetogrill.mobi.

Shrimp, Sausage, and Clam Paella

SERVES: 👤👤👤👤👤👤

PREP TIME: **30** MINUTES

GRILLING TIME: **33** TO **39** MINUTES

SPECIAL EQUIPMENT: 12-INCH
CAST-IRON SKILLET

½ pound large shrimp (21/30 count),
   peeled and deveined, tails left on
3 tablespoons extra-virgin olive
   oil, divided
   Kosher salt
   Ground black pepper

½ pound fully cooked andouille sausages

2 cups finely diced yellow onion
1 cup finely diced red bell pepper
1 tablespoon minced garlic
1 teaspoon smoked paprika
¼ teaspoon crushed saffron threads
2 cups medium-grain rice, such as Arborio
1 quart chicken broth
1 bottle (8 ounces) clam juice

½ cup small pimento-stuffed green olives
12 littleneck clams, rinsed and scrubbed

1. Prepare the grill for direct cooking over medium heat (350° to 450°F).

2. In a medium bowl combine the shrimp with 1 tablespoon of the oil and toss to coat. Season with salt and pepper.

3. Brush the cooking grates clean. Grill the shrimp and sausages over *direct medium heat*, with the lid closed as much as possible, until the shrimp are cooked halfway and the sausages are beginning to color, about 2 minutes, turning once. Remove from the grill and set aside to cool. When the sausage is cool enough to handle, cut crosswise into ½-inch slices.

4. Place a 12-inch cast-iron skillet over *direct medium heat*. Heat the remaining 2 tablespoons of oil in the skillet. Add the onion and pepper and cook until the onion is tender, about 5 minutes, stirring occasionally and rotating the pan for even cooking. Stir in the garlic, paprika, saffron, rice, and 1 teaspoon salt and cook until the rice is well coated, 1 to 2 minutes. Slowly stir in the broth and clam juice. Close the grill lid and let the mixture cook at a brisk simmer until the rice is al dente, about 15 minutes. Nestle the shrimp, sausage, and olives into the rice. Bury the clams. Continue cooking, with the grill lid closed, until the clams open and the shrimp are opaque in the center, 10 to 15 minutes. Discard any clams that have not opened.

5. Wearing insulated barbecue mitts, transfer the skillet from the grill to a heatproof surface. Serve the paella hot from the skillet.

Access the grocery list for this recipe on your mobile device. timetogrill.mobi.

Skewering shrimp means having to turn only each skewer, rather than each individual shrimp, which is convenient, especially when you are grilling dozens of shrimp. To prevent the shrimp from spinning, skewer each one twice—once near the head and once near the tail end. For the fried rice, be sure to use rice that has been cooked ahead of time and chilled; otherwise the grains tend to stick to the wok and get gooey. As with any stir-fry, have all your ingredients prepped and close at hand before you start cooking.

SERVES:

PREP TIME: **15** MINUTES

MARINATING TIME: **10** TO **15** MINUTES

GRILLING TIME: **2** TO **4** MINUTES

SPECIAL EQUIPMENT: METAL OR BAMBOO SKEWERS (IF USING BAMBOO, SOAK IN WATER FOR AT LEAST 30 MINUTES)

EASY

// VINAIGRETTE
¼ cup fresh lime juice
2 tablespoons peanut oil
1 tablespoon seasoned rice vinegar
1 teaspoon grated lime zest
1 teaspoon prepared chili powder
1 teaspoon soy sauce

1 pound large shrimp (21/30 count), peeled and deveined, tails left on
2 cups fresh pineapple chunks
1 bunch scallions, cut into 2-inch sections (white and light green parts only)
2 tablespoons finely chopped fresh mint leaves

Pineapple Shrimp Kabobs

1. **In a large bowl whisk the vinaigrette ingredients.** Pour ¼ cup into a serving bowl and set aside.

2. **Prepare the grill for direct cooking over high heat (450° to 550°F).**

3. **Put the shrimp, pineapple, and scallions in the large bowl with the vinaigrette.** Toss to coat evenly. Marinate at room temperature for 10 to 15 minutes while the grill preheats.

4. **Thread the shrimp, pineapple, and scallions alternately onto skewers.** Discard the vinaigrette in the large bowl.

5. **Brush the cooking grates clean.** Grill the kabobs over *direct high heat*, with the lid closed as much as possible, until the shrimp are firm to the touch and just turning opaque in the center and the pineapple and scallions are lightly charred, 2 to 4 minutes, turning once or twice. Remove from the grill and drizzle with the reserved vinaigrette. Garnish with the mint. Serve warm.

Access the grocery list for this recipe on your mobile device. timetogrill.mobi.

Pineapple Fried Rice with Grilled Shrimp

SERVES: 🧍🧍🧍🧍 TO 🧍🧍🧍🧍🧍🧍

PREP TIME: **30** MINUTES

GRILLING TIME: **16** TO **21** MINUTES

SPECIAL EQUIPMENT: 12-INCH
CAST-IRON SKILLET OR WOK

1½ pounds large shrimp (21/30 count),
    peeled and deveined, tails left on
    Peanut oil
    Kosher salt
    Ground black pepper
1 cup slivered red onion
1 tablespoon minced garlic
2 teaspoons minced serrano chile pepper,
   seeds removed
2 large eggs, lightly beaten
4 cups cooked jasmine rice, chilled
3 tablespoons soy sauce
1 teaspoon toasted sesame oil
2 cups coarsely chopped fresh pineapple
¼ cup finely chopped fresh mint leaves
¼ cup finely chopped fresh cilantro leaves
½ cup roughly chopped roasted cashews

!

// Warm or room temperature rice tends
to break down and get gooey/starchy
when it cooks in the pan/wok. Chilled
rice does not.

1. Prepare the grill for direct cooking over high heat (450° to 550°F).

2. In a large bowl lightly coat the shrimp with peanut oil and season evenly with salt and pepper.

3. Brush the cooking grates clean. Grill the shrimp over *direct high heat*, with the lid closed as much as possible, until firm to the touch and just turning opaque in the center, 2 to 4 minutes, turning once or twice. Remove from the grill and set aside. Decrease the temperature of the grill to medium heat (350° to 450°F).

4. In a 12-inch cast-iron skillet over *direct medium heat*, heat ¼ cup peanut oil. Add the onion, garlic, and chile and cook until the onion is tender, about 5 minutes, stirring occasionally and rotating the pan for even cooking. Stir in the eggs and cook for 1 to 2 minutes. Add the rice, soy sauce, and sesame oil, mix thoroughly, and cook until lightly browned, 8 to 10 minutes, stirring occasionally. Keep the lid closed as much as possible during grilling.

5. Remove from the heat and add the shrimp, pineapple, mint, and cilantro. Toss to combine and season with salt and pepper. Top with the cashews. Serve hot from the skillet.

Access the grocery list for this recipe on your mobile device. timetogrill.mobi.

A bottled Italian dressing based on oil, vinegar, and spices makes a fine marinade for many kinds of seafood and poultry. Likewise, a bottled marinara sauce can be absolutely wonderful and convenient, especially if you only need a cup or so. A general rule for store-bought marinades and sauces like these is, the fewer the ingredients, the higher the quality. Thaw frozen scallops overnight in the refrigerator. If you are really in a hurry, run cold water (not warm or hot) over them while they are in a bowl in the sink.

Seared Scallops
WITH PROSCIUTTO BITS

1. **Prepare the grill for direct cooking over medium heat (350° to 450°F).**

2. **Remove and discard the small, tough side muscle that might be left on each scallop.** Lightly brush the scallops with the oil and season evenly with the salt and pepper.

3. **Brush the cooking grates clean.** Grill the prosciutto over *direct medium heat*, with the lid open, until the meat browns on the edges and turns crispy, 1 to 3 minutes, turning once or twice. Remove from the grill and let cool. Roughly chop the prosciutto into pieces.

4. **Grill the scallops over *direct medium heat*, with the lid closed as much as possible, until just opaque in the center, 4 to 6 minutes, turning once or twice.** Remove from the grill.

5. **In a small saucepan over medium heat, warm the marinara sauce.** To serve, divide the marinara sauce evenly among four plates. Arrange three scallops on top. Garnish with the chopped prosciutto and fresh herbs. Serve warm.

Access the grocery list for this recipe on your mobile device. timetogrill.mobi.

SERVES: 👤👤👤👤

PREP TIME: **10** MINUTES

GRILLING TIME: **5** TO **9** MINUTES

EASY

12 sea scallops, each 1 to 1½ ounces
 1 tablespoon extra-virgin olive oil
½ teaspoon kosher salt
¼ teaspoon ground black pepper
 2 paper-thin slices prosciutto
 1 cup good-quality marinara sauce
 2 tablespoons finely chopped fresh Italian
       parsley *or* basil leaves

1. **Prepare the grill for direct cooking over medium heat (350° to 450°F).**

2. **Bring a large pot of water to a boil for the fettuccine.**

3. **In a large skillet over medium-low heat, cook the bacon until crisp, 6 to 10 minutes, turning occasionally.** Remove the bacon with a slotted spoon and transfer to a plate lined with a paper towel. Pour off all but ¼ cup bacon grease. Raise the heat to medium-high. Add the onion and cook until tender, 4 to 6 minutes. Carefully add the wine (not directly from a bottle) and cook for 1 minute to burn off the alcohol. Turn off the heat while you grill the scallops.

4. **Remove and discard the small, tough side muscle that might be left on each scallop.** Lightly brush the scallops with the oil and season evenly with ½ teaspoon salt and ¼ teaspoon pepper. Brush the cooking grates clean. Grill the scallops over *direct medium heat*, with the lid closed as much as possible, until they are golden brown, 2 to 4 minutes, turning once. Remove from the grill and add them to the skillet with the onion.

5. **Cook the pasta according to the package instructions.** Drain the pasta and transfer it immediately to the skillet with the scallops. Turn the heat on high and cook the pasta and the sauce together for 1 minute. Turn off the heat, add the parsley, lemon juice, and bacon, and toss again to combine. Season with salt and pepper. Serve warm.

Access the grocery list for this recipe on your mobile device. timetogrill.mobi.

Fettuccine
WITH SCALLOPS, BACON, AND ONIONS

SERVES: 👤👤👤👤

PREP TIME: **25** MINUTES

GRILLING TIME: **2** TO **4** MINUTES

6	thick slices apple wood smoked bacon, cut into 1-inch segments
1	large yellow onion, halved and cut crosswise into thin slices
½	cup dry white wine
12	sea scallops, each 1 to 1½ ounces
1	tablespoon extra-virgin olive oil
	Kosher salt
	Ground black pepper
½	pound dried fettuccine
⅓	cup packed whole fresh Italian parsley leaves
1–2	tablespoons fresh lemon juice

Scallop Salad
WITH CITRUS VINAIGRETTE

Garlic-marinated scallops meet a light and zesty vinaigrette in this easy salad for alfresco dining. You can embellish the vinaigrette by adding the zest and segments of oranges or grapefruit. To create a more substantial meal, tuck the scallops along with shredded cabbage and onions into corn tortillas. The avocado sauce has a little kick, but chile spice lovers might also want to keep a bottle of hot sauce within reach.

SERVES: 🧍🧍🧍🧍

PREP TIME: 15 MINUTES

GRILLING TIME: 4 TO 6 MINUTES

6 tablespoons extra-virgin olive oil, divided
 Finely grated zest of 1 lime
3 tablespoons fresh lime juice
2 tablespoons honey
2 tablespoons minced shallot
1 tablespoon finely chopped fresh Italian parsley leaves
 Kosher salt
 Ground black pepper
16 large sea scallops, each about 2 ounces
4 ounces mixed greens (3 to 4 cups)

1. Prepare the grill for direct cooking over high heat (450° to 550°F).

2. In a small bowl whisk 4 tablespoons of the oil, the lime zest and juice, honey, shallot, and parsley. Season with salt and pepper.

3. Remove and discard the small, tough side muscle that might be left on each scallop. Lightly brush the scallops with the remaining 2 tablespoons of oil and season evenly with salt and pepper.

4. Brush the cooking grates clean. Grill the scallops over *direct high heat*, with the lid closed as much as possible, until lightly browned and just opaque in the center, 4 to 6 minutes, turning once or twice. Remove from the grill.

5. Whisk the vinaigrette again. In a medium bowl toss the greens with just enough of the vinaigrette to coat the leaves lightly. Arrange equal amounts of the greens and scallops on individual serving plates. Serve with the remaining vinaigrette.

Access the grocery list for this recipe on your mobile device. timetogrill.mobi.

SERVES: 4

PREP TIME: 30 MINUTES

MARINATING TIME: 15 TO 20 MINUTES

GRILLING TIME: 4 TO 6 MINUTES

Scallop Tacos

WITH CABBAGE SLAW AND AVOCADO SAUCE

// SAUCE

- 1 large Hass avocado, diced
- ½ cup water
- ¼ cup loosely packed fresh cilantro leaves and tender stems
- 1 large jalapeño chile pepper, seeded
- 1 tablespoon fresh lime juice
- 1 large garlic clove

Kosher salt
Ground black pepper

// MARINADE

- 3 tablespoons extra-virgin olive oil
- Grated zest of 1 lime
- 2 tablespoons fresh lime juice
- 2 large garlic cloves, grated or minced

- 24 sea scallops, each 1 to 1½ ounces
- 1 cup thinly sliced green cabbage, rinsed under cold water
- ⅓ cup thinly sliced red onion, rinsed under cold water
- 8 corn or flour tortillas (6 inches)

!

// To take the "bite" out of the onion and mellow out the taste of the cabbage, rinse them in a sieve under cold running water.

1. **In a blender combine the sauce ingredients and process until smooth.** Season with salt and pepper. Transfer to a small serving bowl. Set aside at room temperature until ready to serve.

2. **In a large bowl whisk the marinade ingredients, including 1 teaspoon salt and ¼ teaspoon pepper.** Remove the small, tough side muscle that might be left on each scallop. Add the scallops to the marinade and turn to coat evenly. Cover and marinate at room temperature for 15 to 20 minutes while the grill preheats.

3. **Prepare the grill for direct cooking over high heat (450° to 550°F).**

4. **In a medium bowl combine the cabbage and onion.**

5. **Brush the cooking grates clean.** Lift the scallops one at a time from the marinade, letting the excess marinade drip back into the bowl. Discard the marinade. Grill the scallops over ***direct high heat***, with the lid closed as much as possible, until lightly browned and just opaque in the center, 4 to 6 minutes, turning once or twice. Remove from the grill.

6. **Warm the tortillas over *direct high heat* for about 10 seconds on each side.**

7. **Fill each tortilla with some of the cabbage mixture and three scallops.** Top with the sauce. Serve right away.

Access the grocery list for this recipe on your mobile device. timetogrill.mobi.

Although many farmed mussels don't develop large "beards," the small bunch of threads that connect them to their habitat, most wild ones do. Just before cooking, prepare wild mussels by first soaking them for thirty minutes to one hour in cold, salted water (this removes any extra sand), then scrubbing them and removing the beards, discarding any mussels that are chipped or that don't close when you tap the shells. To "debeard" a mussel, use your thumb and first finger to grasp the beard, and pull sharply, perpendicular to the mussel. To clean clams, rinse and scrub them under cold water, then soak in cold, salted water for one hour to remove any sand and grit.

Roasted Mussels
WITH GARLIC-PARSLEY BUTTER

SERVES: 👤👤;
👤👤👤👤 AS AN APPETIZER

PREP TIME: 10 MINUTES

SOAKING TIME FOR WILD MUSSELS:
30 MINUTES TO 1 HOUR

GRILLING TIME: 21 TO 25 MINUTES

SPECIAL EQUIPMENT: 12-INCH
CAST-IRON SKILLET

¼ cup (½ stick) unsalted butter, softened
4 large garlic cloves, minced
¼ cup minced fresh Italian parsley leaves

2 tablespoons extra-virgin olive oil
1 small yellow onion, minced
¼ teaspoon kosher salt
⅛ teaspoon ground black pepper
¾ cup dry white wine
2 pounds live mussels, scrubbed and
   beards removed

1. **In a small bowl mash the butter, garlic, and parsley with a fork until evenly blended.** Set aside.

2. **Prepare the grill for direct cooking over medium heat (350° to 450°F).**

3. **In a 12-inch cast-iron skillet combine the oil, onion, salt, and pepper.** Place the skillet over **direct medium heat**, close the grill lid, and cook until the onion begins to soften, about 5 minutes, stirring once or twice. Add the wine, stir to combine, and cook, with the grill lid closed, until the wine comes to a boil. Simmer for 5 minutes.

4. **Add the mussels to the skillet, cover the skillet with a sheet pan (or use foil), close the grill lid, and cook for 8 to 10 minutes.** Check to see if the mussels are open. If not, continue to cook 3 to 5 minutes more. Wearing insulated barbecue mitts, carefully remove the sheet pan from the skillet and remove the skillet from the grill. Remove and discard any unopened mussels. Add the butter mixture to the skillet, dropping bits of it all over, and use a large spoon to stir the mussels around as the butter melts. Serve the mussels and sauce in bowls with crusty bread, if desired.

Access the grocery list for this recipe on your mobile device. timetogrill.mobi.

 Creamy Linguine
WITH MUSSELS AND CLAMS

SERVES: 👤👤👤👤

PREP TIME: **30** MINUTES

SOAKING TIME FOR WILD MUSSELS
AND CLAMS: **30** MINUTES TO **1** HOUR

GRILLING TIME: **20** TO **25** MINUTES

SPECIAL EQUIPMENT: 12-INCH
CAST-IRON SKILLET

3 tablespoons unsalted butter
1 small onion, finely chopped
3 large garlic cloves, finely chopped
¼ teaspoon kosher salt
¼ teaspoon ground black pepper
¼ teaspoon crushed red pepper flakes
2 tablespoons all-purpose flour
1 cup heavy whipping cream
1½ pounds live mussels, scrubbed and
    beards removed
1½ pounds manila or littleneck clams, rinsed
    and scrubbed
¾ pound dried linguine
¼ cup chopped fresh basil leaves
    Finely grated zest and juice of 1 lemon

1. **Prepare the grill for direct cooking over medium heat (350° to 450°F).**

2. **Bring a large pot of water to a boil for the linguine.**

3. **Place a 12-inch cast-iron skillet over *direct medium heat*. Melt the butter in the skillet.** Add the onion, garlic, salt, pepper, and red pepper flakes; stir to coat with the butter and continue cooking until the onion begins to soften, 5 minutes, stirring once or twice. Add the flour and cook for 1 to 2 minutes. Add the cream, stir to combine, and cook until the mixture comes to a simmer and thickens. Keep the grill lid closed as much as possible during grilling.

4. **Add the mussels and clams to the sauce, cover the skillet with a sheet pan (or use foil), close the grill lid, and cook for 10 minutes.** Meanwhile, cook the linguine in the boiling water until al dente, according to package instructions. Drain and set aside.

5. **Carefully remove the sheet pan from the skillet.** Using tongs, transfer the mussels and clams that have opened to a large mixing bowl, pouring any liquid in the shells back into the skillet (allow the sauce to continue simmering as you work). As you transfer, the shellfish will continue to open as you make more room in the pan. Carefully pick the meat out of the shells of the mussels and clams, reserving it in another bowl, and discard the shells. Throw away any shellfish that haven't opened by the time you've finished picking out all of the meat.

6. **When all the meat is collected, add it, along with the cooked pasta and any remaining juices from the meat, to the skillet.** Toss to combine. Divide evenly among four large bowls and top with basil, lemon zest, and lemon juice. Serve immediately.

Access the grocery list for this recipe on your mobile device. timetogrill.mobi.

flavor food?

Long before the days of refrigeration, smoking was a matter of life and death. It was how our ancestors preserved meat, fish, and game birds to have on hand when fresh food was scarce. While other means of preservation eventually made smoking obsolete in the sense of survival, there was no way to replace the wonderfully layered taste of smoked foods. Cooks all over the world have sustained the art of smoking and refined how we can use it today primarily for flavor.

Inside a grill or smoker, smoldering wood fills the air with aromatic smoke, and food inherits the unique flavors of the wood, be it hickory, apple, mesquite, or any other type. Hardwoods are most commonly used for smoking because their molecules burn and caramelize to create a milder, more palatable taste than softwoods. Smokers are easy to find these days, and many of them do a great job of slow-cooking big hunks of meat like beef brisket and pork shoulder, but you can also smoke just about anything in a charcoal grill or a gas grill equipped with a smoker box.

DOES SMOKE
really follow you?

Yes, actually. As all the miniscule particles that make up a smoke cloud float through the air, they react to changes in the airflow around them. To explain, a campfire or smoking grill will be taking in air from every direction. Your body's presence in the line of airflow creates a vacuum, thus drawing smoke toward you. So no matter what side of the fire you move to, the vacuum effect will come with you, making the smoke come with you, too.

DID YOU KNOW?

When the Chinese were constructing the Great Wall, they used smoke signals to communicate with each other from tower to tower.

Although salmon goes particularly well with the fennel tapenade on this page and the silky orange sauce on the opposite page, feel free to substitute any type of grilled fish in either recipe. The top candidates include swordfish, tuna, and grouper. Their firm textures make them a little easier to grill than the more tender halibut, mackerel, and sea bass, but tender fillets are an option, too, if you have a knack for grilling fish.

Salmon Fillets with Fennel-Olive Tapenade

SERVES: 🧍🧍🧍🧍🧍🧍

PREP TIME: **15** MINUTES

GRILLING TIME: **8** TO **12** MINUTES

// TAPENADE

1 medium fennel bulb, about 1¼ pounds, with stalks attached
1 cup garlic-stuffed green olives (about 20)
Finely grated zest of 1 medium orange
2 tablespoons fresh orange juice
2 teaspoons roughly chopped fresh tarragon leaves
Extra-virgin olive oil
Kosher salt
Ground black pepper

6 salmon fillets (with skin), each 6 to 8 ounces and about 1¼ inches thick, pin bones removed

1. **Cut the stalks from the fennel bulbs.** If desired, finely chop and reserve the fronds for garnish. Cut out and discard the tough core from the bulb. Roughly chop the bulb. In a medium pot of boiling, salted water, cook the fennel for 3 minutes. Drain in a sieve and then run cold water over it to stop the cooking.

2. **In the bowl of a food processor combine the fennel with the olives, orange zest and juice, tarragon, and 3 tablespoons oil.** Pulse the mixture and scrape down the sides of the bowl occasionally until you have a coarse texture. Season with salt and pepper.

3. **Prepare the grill for direct cooking over high heat (450° to 550°F).**

4. **Generously coat the fillets with oil and season evenly with salt and pepper.**

5. **Brush the cooking grates clean.** Grill the salmon over ***direct high heat***, with the lid closed as much as possible, until you can lift the fillets off the cooking grate with tongs without sticking, 6 to 8 minutes. Turn the fillets over and continue cooking to your desired doneness, 2 to 4 minutes for medium rare. Slip a spatula between the skin and the flesh and transfer the fillets to serving plates. Serve warm with the tapenade and garnish with chopped fennel fronds, if desired.

Access the grocery list for this recipe on your mobile device. timetogrill.mobi.

EASY

Salmon with Creamy Citrus Sauce

SERVES: 👤👤👤👤 TO 👤👤👤👤👤👤

PREP TIME: **30** MINUTES

GRILLING TIME: **3** TO **6** MINUTES

SPECIAL EQUIPMENT: 12 METAL OR
BAMBOO SKEWERS (IF USING
BAMBOO, SOAK IN WATER FOR
AT LEAST 30 MINUTES)

// SAUCE

- 1 medium orange
- 1 teaspoon cornstarch
- ½ cup bottled clam juice
- 4 large egg yolks
- 2 tablespoons finely chopped fresh
  tarragon leaves
- 1 tablespoon unsalted butter
  Finely grated zest of 1 lemon
- 2 tablespoons fresh lemon juice
  Kosher salt
  Ground black pepper

- 1 center cut, skinless salmon fillet,
  about 2 pounds, pin bones removed
  Extra-virgin olive oil

**1. Finely grate the zest from the orange
and set aside.** Squeeze ½ cup juice from the
orange and pour it into a heavy-bottomed,
medium saucepan. Add the cornstarch and
whisk until the cornstarch has dissolved.
Whisk in the clam juice and egg yolks. Cook
over medium heat until the sauce thickens
and comes to a gentle boil, about 4 minutes,
whisking almost constantly. Remove from the
heat and stir in the tarragon, butter, grated
orange and lemon zests, and the lemon
juice. Stir to melt the butter. Season with
salt and pepper. Cover to keep warm; whisk
the sauce occasionally.

**2. Prepare the grill for direct cooking over
high heat (450° to 550°F).**

3. Cut the fillet into ¾-inch slices. Thread
the slices onto skewers. Generously brush the
salmon on all sides with oil and season evenly
with salt and pepper.

4. Brush the cooking grates clean. Grill the
salmon skewers over ***direct high heat***, with
the lid closed as much as possible, until you
can lift them off the cooking grate with tongs
without sticking, 2 to 4 minutes. Turn the
salmon skewers over and continue cooking
to your desired doneness, 1 to 2 minutes for
medium. Reheat the sauce gently over low
heat and whisk again. Spoon the sauce over
the salmon. Serve warm.

*Access the grocery list for this recipe
on your mobile device. timetogrill.mobi.*

Not every type of fish can stand up to the bold, smoky flavors of chipotle chiles, but salmon can. In the recipe below, the chiles are blended into a seasoned butter, which you melt over the top of simply grilled salmon fillets. Consider making a double batch of the butter and freezing some of it for use at a moment's notice. In the adventurous recipe on the next page, the chipotle flavors star in a southwestern cream sauce that you simmer with fresh corn and poblano chiles while cooking the pasta. Just add flaked pieces of grilled salmon to create that same winning combination in a filling dish.

SERVES: ♔♔♔♔

PREP TIME: **10** MINUTES

GRILLING TIME: **8** TO **11** MINUTES

EASY

Salmon with Chipotle Butter

// BUTTER

- 6 tablespoons (¾ stick) unsalted butter, softened
- 2-3 canned chipotle chiles in adobo sauce, excess sauce wiped off, seeded and minced
- 1 teaspoon minced garlic
  Kosher salt

- 4 salmon fillets (with skin), each 6 to 8 ounces and about 1 inch thick, pin bones removed
- 2 tablespoons vegetable oil
  Ground black pepper
- 1 lime, cut into wedges

1. In a medium bowl combine the butter ingredients, including ½ teaspoon salt.

2. Prepare the grill for direct cooking over high heat (450° to 550°F).

3. Generously brush the salmon fillets on both sides with the oil and season evenly with salt and pepper. Brush the cooking grates clean. Grill the salmon over **direct high heat**, with the lid closed as much as possible, until you can lift the fillets off the cooking grate with tongs without sticking, 6 to 8 minutes. Turn the fillets over and continue cooking to your desired doneness, 2 to 3 minutes for medium rare. Slip a spatula between the skin and the flesh, and lift the salmon from the grill. Smear some chipotle butter on top of each fillet and serve warm with lime wedges.

Access the grocery list for this recipe on your mobile device. timetogrill.mobi.

SERVES: 👤👤👤👤👤👤

PREP TIME: **30** MINUTES

GRILLING TIME: **8** TO **11** MINUTES

---

3 large poblano chile peppers
3 salmon fillets (with skin), each 6 to
   8 ounces and about 1 inch thick,
   pin bones removed
2 tablespoons vegetable oil
   Kosher salt
   Ground black pepper

// SAUCE

1½ cups heavy whipping cream
3–4 canned chipotle chiles in adobo
   sauce, excess sauce wiped off, seeded
   and minced
2 tablespoons tomato paste
2 teaspoons minced garlic
¼ teaspoon ground cumin
¼ teaspoon dried Mexican oregano

1 pound dried linguine

2 cups fresh corn kernels
   (from 2–3 ears corn)
1 tablespoon fresh lime juice
¾ cup crumbled cotija cheese (3 ounces)

↗ Chipotle Salmon Linguine

1. Prepare the grill for direct cooking over high heat (450° to 550°F).

2. Grill the poblanos over *direct high heat*, with the lid closed as much as possible, until charred and blackened on all sides, about 10 minutes, turning occasionally. Transfer to a bowl, cover with plastic wrap, and set aside for at least 10 minutes. Remove the peppers from the bowl and peel away and discard the charred skins. Cut off the tops and remove the seeds. Cut into bite-sized pieces.

3. Bring a large pot of water to a boil for the linguine.

4. Brush the salmon fillets on both sides with the oil and season evenly with salt and pepper. Brush the cooking grates clean. Grill the salmon, skin side up, over *direct high heat*, with the lid closed as much as possible, until you can lift the fillets off the cooking grate with tongs without sticking, 6 to 8 minutes. Turn the fillets over and continue cooking to your desired doneness, 2 to 3 minutes for medium rare. Slip a spatula between the skin and the flesh, and lift the salmon from the grill. Transfer to a plate and tent with foil to keep warm.

5. In a large, heavy sauté pan combine the sauce ingredients, bring to a boil, and simmer for about 6 minutes, or until thickened and saucy.

6. Meanwhile, cook the linguine according to the package directions. Drain and reserve ½ cup of the pasta water.

7. Add the poblanos and corn kernels to the sauce and cook for 3 to 4 minutes, or until the corn turns bright yellow. Stir in the lime juice and season with salt.

8. Toss the drained pasta with the sauce and ¼ cup of the reserved pasta water. Add additional pasta water, about 1 tablespoon at a time, as needed to coat the pasta. Flake the salmon into bite-sized pieces and gently fold into the pasta. Top with the cheese and serve right away.

Access the grocery list for this recipe on your mobile device. timetogrill.mobi.

SEAFOOD

CHIPOTLE SALMON LINGUINE

ADVENTUROUS

Sun-dried tomatoes deserve a place in the refrigerator right beside other essential condiments like olives and Dijon mustard. These brick-red, sweet-tart morsels bring a taste of summer to the table any time of year, and an easy vinaigrette takes advantage of all that taste to dress up simple, grilled salmon. Cooking en papillote, where all the juices, flavors and mouthwatering smells are trapped inside a tightly sealed packet, seems more adventurous, but it is certainly not hard. In fact, one very nice feature of cooking this way is that the fish is guaranteed not to stick to the cooking grate.

Salmon Steaks with Sun-Dried Tomato Dressing

SERVES: 👤👤👤👤

PREP TIME: **10** MINUTES

GRILLING TIME: **8** TO **11** MINUTES

1 tablespoon red wine vinegar
2 teaspoons chopped fresh oregano leaves
⅛ teaspoon crushed red pepper flakes
   Kosher salt
   Extra-virgin olive oil
6 tablespoons sun-dried tomatoes in olive oil, drained, patted dry, and roughly chopped

4 salmon steaks, each 6 to 8 ounces and about 1 inch thick, pin bones removed
   Ground black pepper

1. **Prepare the grill for direct cooking over high heat (450° to 550°F).**

2. **In a small bowl whisk the vinegar, oregano, red pepper flakes, and ¼ teaspoon salt.** Gradually whisk in ¼ cup oil. Stir in the sun-dried tomatoes. Set the dressing aside until ready to use.

3. **Brush the salmon on both sides with oil and season evenly with salt and pepper.**

4. **Brush the cooking grates clean.** Grill the salmon over **direct high heat**, with the lid closed as much as possible, until you can lift the steaks off the cooking grate without sticking, 6 to 8 minutes. Turn the steaks over and cook to your desired doneness, 2 to 3 minutes for medium rare.

5. **Transfer each salmon steak to a dinner plate.** Spoon the dressing evenly over the top and serve right away.

Access the grocery list for this recipe on your mobile device. timetogrill.mobi.

EASY

Salmon and Sun-Dried Tomatoes en Papillote

SERVES: 👤👤👤👤

PREP TIME: **20** MINUTES

GRILLING TIME: **27** TO **35** MINUTES

1 red bell pepper
3 tablespoons sun-dried tomatoes in olive oil, drained and chopped
3 tablespoons chopped kalamata olives
2 tablespoons nonpareil capers, drained
2 teaspoons finely chopped fresh oregano leaves
1 garlic clove, minced

4 salmon steaks, each 6 to 8 ounces and about 1 inch thick, pin bones removed
Kosher salt
Ground black pepper
1 large zucchini, ends trimmed, cut in half lengthwise and then cut into ¼-inch half-moons
4 teaspoons extra-virgin olive oil
1 lemon, quartered

1. **Prepare the grill for direct cooking over medium heat (350° to 450°F).**

2. **Brush the cooking grates clean.** Grill the pepper over **direct medium heat**, with the lid closed as much as possible, until it is blackened and blistered all over, 12 to 15 minutes, turning occasionally. Place the pepper in a bowl and cover with plastic wrap to trap the steam. Set aside for 10 minutes. Remove from the bowl, peel away and discard the skin, cut off and discard the stem and seeds, and then roughly chop the pepper.

3. **In a medium bowl combine the pepper, tomatoes, olives, capers, oregano, and garlic.**

4. **Season the salmon evenly with ½ teaspoon salt and ½ teaspoon pepper.** Put the zucchini in a medium bowl and add ¼ teaspoon salt and ⅛ teaspoon pepper. Toss to coat evenly.

5. **Tear four 18-inch lengths of heavy-duty aluminum foil.** Place one piece of foil on a work surface. Fold the foil in half crosswise to make a crease and re-open the foil to lie flat. Pour 1 teaspoon of oil in the center of the bottom half of the foil. Place a salmon steak in the oil and turn to coat on both sides. Add one-fourth of the red pepper mixture and one-fourth of the zucchini over and around the salmon. Fold the foil over and crimp the three open sides tightly. Repeat with the remaining foil and ingredients.

6. **Brush the cooking grates clean.** Grill the packets over **direct medium heat**, with the lid closed as much as possible, until the salmon is barely opaque in the thickest part of the flesh (cut a small hole in the top of one packet and pull the fish apart with the tip of a knife to check), 15 to 20 minutes. Remove the packets from the grill.

7. **Open each packet and transfer its contents to a dinner plate.** Squeeze a lemon quarter over each salmon steak and serve warm.

Access the grocery list for this recipe on your mobile device. timetogrill.mobi.

In this easy recipe the coconut milk in the marinade is here not so much for flavor as it is for added moisture as the fish grills, though you will certainly taste the Thai green curry paste in the marinade and the sauce. Curry paste can be found in the Asian foods aisle of the supermarket. The little stacked sandwiches on the opposite page make great party food. To save time, have the salmon skinned at the fish counter. Be sure to blot the fish as dry as possible so the patties will be firm enough to handle with ease. A mandoline or one-millimeter slicing blade on a food processor makes it quick and easy to cut the cucumbers paper-thin for the pickled vegetables.

SERVES: 🕴🕴🕴🕴

PREP TIME: **15** MINUTES

MARINATING TIME: **15** TO **30** MINUTES

GRILLING TIME: **14** TO **19** MINUTES

// MARINADE

- 1 can (14 ounces) coconut milk (not lite)
  Grated zest and juice of 2 large limes
- 2 tablespoons packed light brown sugar
- 2 tablespoons Thai green curry paste
- 1 tablespoon soy sauce
- 1 teaspoon hot chili-garlic sauce, such as Sriracha

- 4 salmon fillets (with skin), each 6 to 8 ounces and about 1 inch thick, pin bones removed

- 1¼ pounds small pattypan squash, each cut in half lengthwise
- 1 teaspoon extra-virgin olive oil

Coconut-Curry Salmon
WITH PATTYPAN SQUASH

1. Prepare the grill for direct cooking over high heat (450° to 550°F).

2. In a glass baking dish just large enough to hold all the salmon fillets, combine the marinade ingredients. Add the fillets and turn to coat all sides. Marinate at room temperature for 15 to 30 minutes while the grill preheats.

3. Remove the fillets from the dish, allowing any excess marinade to drip off. Reserve the marinade. Brush the cooking grates clean. Grill the salmon, flesh side down, over **direct high heat**, with the lid closed as much as possible, until you can lift the fillets off the cooking grate with tongs without sticking, 6 to 8 minutes. Turn the fillets over and continue cooking to your desired doneness, 2 to 3 minutes for medium rare. Slip a spatula between the skin and the flesh, and transfer the fillets to serving plates.

4. While the salmon is cooking, pour the reserved marinade into a small saucepan. Bring to a boil over medium-high heat.

Reduce the heat to maintain a steady simmer and cook until the sauce has thickened and coats the back of a spoon, 6 to 8 minutes, stirring occasionally.

5. Lightly brush the squash with the oil. Grill over **direct high heat**, with the lid closed as much as possible, until crisp-tender and lightly browned, 6 to 8 minutes, turning occasionally. Serve the squash and salmon drizzled with the coconut sauce.

Access the grocery list for this recipe on your mobile device. timetogrill.mobi.

EASY

Salmon Sliders

WITH SPICY GINGER SAUCE AND PICKLED VEGETABLES

SERVES: **6** TO **8**

PREP TIME: **30** MINUTES

MARINATING TIME: **1** HOUR

CHILLING TIME: **30** MINUTES

GRILLING TIME: **6** TO **8** MINUTES

1 cup rice vinegar
2 tablespoons granulated sugar
1 teaspoon kosher salt
½ English cucumber, cut into paper
   thin slices
½ medium red onion, cut in half
1 small red bell pepper

// SAUCE

½ cup mayonnaise
2 teaspoons peeled, grated fresh ginger
1 teaspoon hot chili-garlic sauce,
   such as Sriracha

1 skinless salmon fillet, about 2 pounds,
   pin bones removed, patted dry, cut into
   1-inch pieces
¾ cup thinly sliced scallions (white and
   light green parts only)
½ cup finely chopped fresh cilantro leaves
1 tablespoon peeled, grated fresh ginger
2 tablespoons fresh lime juice
2 tablespoons soy sauce
1 tablespoon toasted sesame oil
1 teaspoon hot chili-garlic sauce,
   such as Sriracha
1 large egg
½ cup panko bread crumbs

18 small buns, each about 2 inches
    in diameter
    Canola oil spray

1. In a medium bowl stir the vinegar, sugar, and salt. Squeeze the cucumber slices until they are crushed and releasing liquid. Cut the onion into ⅛-inch slices, and then cut them into 1-inch pieces. Cut the bell pepper lengthwise into ⅛-inch slices, remove the seeds, and then cut into 1-inch pieces. Place the cucumber, onion, and pepper in the vinegar mixture. Let marinate at room temperature for 1 hour, stirring occasionally. Drain well before assembling the sliders.

2. In a small bowl combine the sauce ingredients. Cover and refrigerate.

3. In a food processor pulse the salmon pieces until coarsely chopped. Add the scallions, cilantro, ginger, lime juice, soy sauce, sesame oil, chili-garlic sauce, and egg. Pulse a few times until just blended, being careful not to puree the mixture. Some texture should remain. Transfer the mixture to a large bowl, gently stir in the bread crumbs, and form into ½-inch-thick patties roughly the size of the buns. Arrange the patties on a sheet pan and refrigerate for 30 minutes before grilling.

4. Prepare the grill for direct cooking over medium heat (350° to 450°F).

5. Brush the cooking grates clean. Lay a single layer of heavy-duty aluminum foil over the grates. Generously spray the sliders on both sides with the canola oil spray. Grill over *direct medium heat*, with the lid closed as much as possible, until you can lift the patties easily from the foil with a spatula, 6 to 8 minutes, turning once after about 4 minutes. During the last minute of grilling time, grill the buns, cut side down, until lightly toasted.

6. To assemble the sliders, slather the bottom of each bun with the sauce, place a patty on top, and finish with some pickled vegetables. Serve immediately.

Access the grocery list for this recipe on your mobile device. timetogrill.mobi.

When a recipe like the easy one here calls for both lemon zest and juice, be sure to zest the lemon first, while the fruit is still whole. The other recipe builds on the affinities between swordfish and tomato, and incorporates a classic Sicilian combination of currants and pine nuts. If you happen to have some crusty day-old bread, you can skip the step of grilling the bread. Just finely chop it and add it to the "salsa," which will soften it as it absorbs the dressing.

Swordfish and Tomato Kabobs

SERVES: 👤👤👤👤

PREP TIME: **15** MINUTES

MARINATING TIME: **15** TO **30** MINUTES

GRILLING TIME: **8** TO **10** MINUTES

SPECIAL EQUIPMENT: 8 METAL OR BAMBOO SKEWERS (IF USING BAMBOO, SOAK IN WATER FOR AT LEAST 30 MINUTES

// MARINADE

- ¼ cup finely chopped fresh Italian parsley leaves
  Grated zest and juice of 1 lemon
- 1 tablespoon red wine vinegar
- 1 small shallot, minced
- 1 teaspoon kosher salt
- ½ teaspoon ground black pepper

- 4 swordfish steaks, each 8 to 10 ounces and about 1 inch thick, cut into 1-inch pieces
- 2 cups (about 24) grape tomatoes

1. **Prepare the grill for direct cooking over medium heat (350° to 450°F).**

2. **In a medium bowl combine the marinade ingredients.** Put the swordfish steaks in the bowl, cover, and marinate at room temperature for 15 to 30 minutes while the grill preheats.

3. **Thread the swordfish and tomatoes alternately on the skewers.** Discard any remaining marinade.

4. **Brush the cooking grates clean.** Grill the kabobs over *direct medium heat*, with the lid closed as much as possible, until the swordfish is opaque in the center but still juicy, 8 to 10 minutes, turning several times. Remove from the grill and serve right away.

Access the grocery list for this recipe on your mobile device. timetogrill.mobi.

EASY

What are currants? They are just a small version of raisins made from Zante grapes.

SERVES: 👤👤👤👤

PREP TIME: **30** MINUTES

GRILLING TIME: **8** TO **10** MINUTES

// SALSA

1 large slice country white bread,
1½ to 2 ounces
Extra-virgin olive oil

2 cups grape tomatoes, each halved or
quartered, depending on their size

¼ cup pine nuts, lightly toasted

¼ cup finely chopped fresh Italian
parsley leaves

¼ cup minced red onion

2 tablespoons dried currants *or* raisins
Finely grated zest of 1 lemon

2 tablespoons fresh lemon juice

1 tablespoon red wine vinegar
Kosher salt

4 swordfish steaks, each 8 to 10 ounces
and about 1 inch thick
Ground black pepper

Swordfish Steaks with Sicilian Salsa

1. Prepare the grill for direct cooking over medium heat (350° to 450°F).

2. Brush the bread on both sides with oil. Set aside. In a medium bowl mix the remaining salsa ingredients, including 1 teaspoon salt.

3. Brush the swordfish steaks on both sides with oil and season evenly with salt and pepper.

4. Brush the cooking grates clean. Grill the bread and swordfish steaks over ***direct medium heat***, with the lid closed as much as possible, until the bread is golden brown and crispy and the swordfish is just opaque in the center but still juicy, turning once. The bread will take 4 to 6 minutes and the swordfish will take 8 to 10 minutes. Remove from the grill as they are done.

5. Cut the bread into ¼-inch dice and add to the bowl with the salsa. Serve the swordfish steaks warm with the salsa.

Access the grocery list for this recipe on your mobile device. timetogrill.mobi.

Here's a quick way to prepare fresh tuna for a casual weeknight dinner. Brushing the fish with a lemony vinaigrette before grilling gives it more oomph than oil alone can provide. You could make the vinaigrette even stronger with about a teaspoon of Dijon mustard or soy sauce, or both. If you double the vinaigrette and divide it into two bowls, you will have some to drizzle over the cooked tuna. In the other recipe, the tuna is grilled rare and served with a lemony salad of beans and coarsely chopped olives and peppers. Any leftover salad is also nice spooned on grilled baguette slices for an appetizer.

A fine grater can quickly remove the outermost skin of a lemon. The oil-rich zest holds a wealth of flavor, but avoid the bitter, white pith.

Tuna Steaks
WITH LEMON VINAIGRETTE

SERVES: 👤👤👤👤

PREP TIME: **15** MINUTES

GRILLING TIME: ABOUT **8** MINUTES

EASY

// VINAIGRETTE
- 2 tablespoons extra-virgin olive oil
  Finely grated zest and juice of 1 lemon
- 1 small shallot, finely diced

- 4 tuna steaks, each about 8 ounces and 1 inch thick
- ½ teaspoon kosher salt
- ¼ teaspoon ground black pepper
  Lemon wedges
- ¼ cup small fresh basil leaves *or* roughly chopped fresh basil leaves

1. **Prepare the grill for direct cooking over high heat (450° to 550°F).**

2. **In a small bowl whisk the vinaigrette ingredients until well blended.** Coat the tuna steaks on both sides with the vinaigrette and season evenly with the salt and pepper.

3. **Brush the cooking grates clean.** Grill the tuna over **direct high heat**, with the lid closed as much as possible, until just turning opaque throughout, about 8 minutes, turning once. Remove from the grill.

4. **Serve warm with lemon wedges and fresh basil sprinkled on top.**

Access the grocery list for this recipe on your mobile device. timetogrill.mobi.

Tuna with Cannellini Bean and Olive Salad

SERVES: 4 TO 6

PREP TIME: **30** MINUTES

GRILLING TIME: ABOUT **4** MINUTES

1 tablespoon white balsamic vinegar
Extra-virgin olive oil
1 cup ½-inch-diced roasted red bell peppers (from a jar), drained
½ cup ½-inch-diced pitted brine-cured green olives
½ cup ½-inch-diced pitted kalamata olives
½ cup finely chopped red onion
2 teaspoons finely grated lemon zest
1 can (15 ounces) cannellini beans, rinsed
Kosher salt
Ground black pepper

2 tuna steaks, each about 1 pound and 1¼ inches thick
¼ cup roughly chopped fresh basil leaves
1 head Boston or butter lettuce

1. In a large bowl whisk the vinegar with 2 tablespoons oil until well blended. Add the red peppers, olives, onion, and lemon zest; stir to combine. Add the beans and stir gently to incorporate all the ingredients. Season with salt and pepper. Set aside.

2. Prepare the grill for direct cooking over high heat (450° to 550°F).

3. Coat the tuna steaks on both sides with oil and lightly season with salt and pepper. Brush the cooking grates clean. Grill the tuna over ***direct high heat***, with the lid closed as much as possible, until cooked to your desired doneness, about 4 minutes for rare, turning once. Remove from the grill and cut each tuna steak into ⅓-inch slices. Add the basil to the salad.

4. To serve, arrange two lettuce leaves on each plate. Spoon equal amounts of the bean salad onto the center of the leaves and arrange the tuna slices on top of the bean salad.

Access the grocery list for this recipe on your mobile device. timetogrill.mobi.

The first recipe here requires so little in the way of actual cooking that it might just be the quickest recipe in this book. The key is to buy fresh, sushi-grade tuna and sear it on a blazing hot grill, leaving the center raw. The second recipe calls for cooking the tuna on a cedar plank, which of course takes some more time but pays off with deep, woodsy aromas. If you prefer to eat the smoked tuna warm, make the vegetable salad first and dress it just before serving.

Seared Tuna with Cucumber-Radish Salad

SERVES: 👤👤👤👤

PREP TIME: **15** MINUTES

GRILLING TIME: **2** TO **4** MINUTES

// SALAD
- 1 shallot, thinly sliced into rings
- 1 English cucumber, cut crosswise into ⅛-inch slices
- 6 radishes, thinly sliced
- 1 tablespoon whole-grain mustard
  Kosher salt

// SAUCE
- 1 tablespoon balsamic vinegar
- 1 tablespoon honey

- 4 tuna fillets, each 6 to 8 ounces and 1 to 1½ inches thick
  Vegetable oil
  Ground black pepper

EASY

A mandoline or one-millimeter slicing blade on a food processor makes it quick and easy to cut the cucumbers paper-thin for the salad.

1. In a large bowl combine the salad ingredients and then season with salt. Set aside at room temperature until ready to serve, stirring occasionally.

2. **Prepare the grill for direct cooking over high heat (450° to 550°F).**

3. **In a small bowl combine all of the sauce ingredients.**

4. **Lightly brush the tuna fillets with oil and season evenly with salt and pepper.**

5. **Brush the cooking grates clean.** Grill the tuna over **direct high heat**, with the lid open, just until seared on both sides but still raw inside, 2 to 4 minutes, turning once. Remove from the grill and cut the tuna crosswise into ¼-inch slices. Divide the salad evenly among serving plates and top with sliced tuna. Drizzle the sauce over the top.

Access the grocery list for this recipe on your mobile device. timetogrill.mobi.

Cedar-Smoked Tuna with Crisp Vegetables

SERVES: 🧍🧍🧍🧍

PREP TIME: **20** MINUTES

GRILLING TIME: **21** TO **28** MINUTES

SPECIAL EQUIPMENT: 1 UNTREATED CEDAR PLANK, 12 TO 15 INCHES LONG AND ½ TO ¾ INCH THICK, SOAKED IN WATER FOR AT LEAST 1 HOUR

// DRESSING
2 tablespoons balsamic vinegar
2 tablespoons fresh lemon juice
1 tablespoon whole-grain mustard
Kosher salt
Ground black pepper
Extra-virgin olive oil

1 pound asparagus

4 tuna steaks, each about 8 ounces and 1 inch thick
½ teaspoon paprika

4 scallions (white and light green parts only), thinly sliced
4-6 radishes, thinly sliced
2 cups tightly packed baby arugula

1. **Prepare the grill for direct cooking over medium heat (350° to 450°F).**

2. **In a small bowl whisk the vinegar, lemon juice, mustard, ¼ teaspoon salt, and ½ teaspoon pepper.** Then slowly whisk in ¼ cup oil until the dressing is emulsified. Set aside.

3. **Remove and discard the tough bottom of each asparagus spear by grasping each end and bending it gently until it snaps at its natural point of tenderness, usually two-thirds of the way down the spear.** Lightly coat the asparagus with oil and season evenly with salt and pepper.

4. **Brush the tuna steaks on both sides with oil and season evenly with 1 teaspoon salt, ½ teaspoon pepper, and the paprika.**

5. **Place the soaked plank over *direct medium heat* and close the lid.** After 5 to 10 minutes, when the plank begins to smoke and char, turn the plank over. Place the tuna in a single layer on the plank. Close the lid and cook until the tuna is firm but still juicy, about 10 minutes. If the plank catches on fire, use a spray bottle to mist out the flames. Transfer the tuna to a serving platter. Discard the charred cedar plank once it cools.

6. **Brush the cooking grates clean.** Grill the asparagus over *direct medium heat*, with the lid closed as much as possible, until crisp-tender, 6 to 8 minutes, turning once. Remove from the grill and cut into 1-inch pieces.

7. **In a large bowl combine the asparagus with the scallions, radishes, and arugula.** Drizzle with the dressing and toss to coat. Put the vegetables on the serving platter with the tuna and serve right away.

Access the grocery list for this recipe on your mobile device. timetogrill.mobi.

Wrapping fish in a slice or two of bacon imparts rich, meaty flavors and makes it easier to flip on the grill. Just be vigilant about the likelihood of flare-ups over direct heat, and reserve an area of the grill with indirect heat just in case. With a little more time, you could grill some potatoes and incorporate them with crispy bacon and pepper for a winning salad to serve with halibut or almost any kind of fish you like. Either mahi mahi or red snapper would be great.

Bacon-Wrapped Halibut Fillets

SERVES: 👤👤👤👤

PREP TIME: **10** MINUTES

MARINATING TIME: **5** TO **30** MINUTES

GRILLING TIME: ABOUT **10** MINUTES

// MARINADE

- 2 tablespoons extra-virgin olive oil
- 1 teaspoon minced fresh rosemary leaves
- 1 teaspoon minced fresh oregano leaves
- 1 teaspoon minced garlic
- ¼ teaspoon kosher salt
- ¼ teaspoon ground black pepper

- 4 skinless halibut fillets, each about 6 ounces and 1 inch thick
- 1 lemon, thinly sliced
- 8 thin slices bacon

1. **Prepare the grill for direct and indirect cooking over medium heat (350° to 450°F).**

2. **In a medium bowl combine the marinade ingredients.** Add the halibut and turn to coat each fillet thoroughly. Let marinate at room temperature for 5 to 30 minutes.

3. **Place one or two lemon slices on each fillet.** Using two slices of bacon, wrap a fillet by starting with one end of a bacon slice on the underside of the fillet. Wrap it around in a slight spiral, bringing it back to the bottom so the edges of the bacon slice overlap only minimally. Wrap the second slice the same way to cover the rest of the fillet as much as possible. Secure the bacon with toothpicks. Repeat with the remaining fillets.

4. **Brush the cooking grates clean.** Grill the halibut, underside down, over *direct medium heat*, with the lid closed as much as possible, until the bacon is browned and the halibut is opaque in the center, about 10 minutes, turning once or twice (when flare-ups occur, move the halibut temporarily over indirect heat). Remove from the grill and serve warm.

Access the grocery list for this recipe on your mobile device. timetogrill.mobi.

EASY

SERVES: 👤👤👤👤

PREP TIME: **20** MINUTES

GRILLING TIME: **23** TO **27** MINUTES

4 medium Yukon Gold potatoes, about
1¼ pounds total, cut into ½-inch slices
4 halibut fillets (with or without skin), each
6 to 8 ounces and about 1 inch thick
Extra-virgin olive oil
Kosher salt
Ground black pepper

12 sprigs fresh rosemary, each 5 to
6 inches long, soaked in water for
about 30 minutes

4 thick slices bacon, cooked and
coarsely chopped
½ cup finely diced red bell pepper
¼ cup finely chopped fresh Italian
parsley leaves
1 tablespoon nonpareil capers, drained
and coarsely chopped
2 tablespoons cider vinegar

Halibut
WITH WARM POTATO AND BACON SALAD

*Sprigs of fresh rosemary protect the
delicate flesh of the halibut from the flames of
the grill. As the sprigs burn, they also give the
fish a gentle smoky (and rosemary) flavor.*

**1. Prepare the grill for direct and indirect
cooking over medium heat (350° to 450°F).**

**2. Brush the potato slices and halibut fillets
on all sides with oil; season the potatoes
with salt and the fillets with salt and pepper.**
Drain the rosemary sprigs and organize them
into four beds of three sprigs each. Place one
fish fillet, skin or skinned side down, on top of
each bed of sprigs.

3. Brush the cooking grates clean. Grill
the potato slices over ***direct medium heat***,
with the lid closed as much as possible, until
marked by the grill, 3 to 5 minutes, turning
once. Then move them over ***indirect medium
heat*** and continue cooking until golden brown
and tender, about 10 minutes, turning once or

twice. Remove from the grill and cut into
bite-sized pieces.

**4. In a medium bowl combine the potatoes,
bacon, pepper, parsley, and capers.** Add 2
tablespoons oil and the vinegar. Toss gently
to combine. Season with pepper.

**5. Grill the rosemary-bedded halibut over
indirect medium heat, with the lid closed,
until the flesh is opaque in the center and
just beginning to flake, 10 to 12 minutes (do
not turn).** Lift the fillets off the rosemary and
serve warm with the salad.

*Access the grocery list for this recipe
on your mobile device. timetogrill.mobi.*

In the time it takes to make fresh guacamole, you can marinate mahi mahi fillets with some exciting and authentic Mexican flavors. Your dinner plates will already show the colors of the Mexican flag (red, green, and white); nevertheless some rice steamed with a little achiote powder for its red color would be nice. The other recipe dials up the overall effect by brushing the fish fillets with a Mexican pesto and serving them with an avocado sauce made smooth with tangy buttermilk.

1. Prepare the grill for direct cooking over high heat (450° to 550°F).

2. In a glass baking dish combine the beer, jalapeño, and 3 tablespoons of the lime juice. Place the fillets in the dish, cover, and let marinate at room temperature for 15 minutes, turning once. (Do not leave the fillets in the marinade longer than 15 minutes as the lime juice will begin to cook the fish.)

3. Meanwhile, make the guacamole. Cut the avocados in half, remove the pits, and scoop the flesh into a medium bowl. Add the remaining 2 tablespoons lime juice, the tomato, cilantro, ½ teaspoon salt, and ⅛ teaspoon pepper. Mash with the back of a fork.

4. Remove the fillets from the dish and discard the marinade. Lightly brush the fillets on both sides with oil and season evenly with salt and pepper. Brush the cooking grates clean. Grill the fillets over **direct high heat**, with the lid closed as much as possible, until the flesh is opaque in the center but still moist, 6 to 8 minutes, turning once. Remove from the grill and serve warm with the guacamole.

Access the grocery list for this recipe on your mobile device. timetogrill.mobi.

Beer-Marinated Mahi Mahi
WITH GUACAMOLE

SERVES: ♟♟♟♟

PREP TIME: **15** MINUTES

GRILLING TIME: **6** TO **8** MINUTES

EASY

// You can substitute the mahi mahi with other firm white fillets, such as striped bass or grouper.

1 cup beer
1 medium jalapeño chile pepper, thinly sliced
5 tablespoons fresh lime juice, divided
4 skinless mahi mahi fillets, each 6 to 8 ounces and ¾ inch thick

2 medium Hass avocados
1 medium plum tomato, diced
1 tablespoon roughly chopped fresh cilantro leaves
Kosher salt
Ground black pepper
Extra-virgin olive oil

Mahi Mahi with Pepita Pesto
AND AVOCADO CREAM

SERVES: 👤👤👤👤

PREP TIME: **30** MINUTES

GRILLING TIME: **6** TO **8** MINUTES

2 garlic cloves, roughly chopped, divided
2 jalapeño chile peppers, stems and seeds
   removed, roughly chopped, divided
1 medium Hass avocado
½ cup buttermilk
1 tablespoon white wine vinegar
1 tablespoon fresh lime juice
¼ teaspoon ground cumin
   Kosher salt

// PESTO
½ cup shelled pumpkin seeds
½ cup packed fresh cilantro leaves
½ cup packed fresh Italian parsley leaves
2 tablespoons freshly grated Parmigiano-
   Reggiano® cheese
2 teaspoons fresh lime juice
¼ teaspoon Tabasco® sauce
   Extra-virgin olive oil

4 skinless mahi mahi fillets, 6 to 8 ounces
   and about ¾ inch thick
   Ground black pepper

1. **Prepare the grill for direct cooking over high heat (450° to 550°F).**

2. **In a blender or food processor pulse half the garlic and half the jalapeño until finely chopped.** Add the avocado, buttermilk, vinegar, lime juice, cumin, and ½ teaspoon salt. Process until smooth. Add 2 to 4 tablespoons of water, if desired, for a smoother, looser consistency. Transfer to a serving bowl, cover, and refrigerate until ready to serve.

3. **In a large skillet over medium heat, toast the pumpkin seeds until lightly browned, 1 to 2 minutes, stirring occasionally.** Remove from the heat and set aside to cool.

4. **In a food processor or blender combine the remaining garlic and jalapeño with the pumpkin seeds, cilantro, parsley, cheese, lime juice, Tabasco, and ⅛ teaspoon salt.** Pulse until finely chopped. With the motor running, add in ⅓ cup oil in a steady stream.

5. **Lightly brush the fillets on both sides with oil and season evenly with salt and pepper.** Brush the cooking grates clean. Grill the fillets over **direct high heat**, with the lid closed, until nice grill marks appear and the fillets release easily from the cooking grate, 4 to 5 minutes. Turn the fillets over and generously spoon the tops of the fillets with the pesto. Continue cooking, with the lid closed, until the flesh is opaque in the center but still moist, 2 to 3 minutes. Remove from the grill.

6. **Spoon 3 to 4 tablespoons of the avocado sauce on each plate and top with a fillet.** Serve with any remaining sauce on the side.

Access the grocery list for this recipe on your mobile device. timetogrill.mobi.

SERVES: 🧍🧍🧍🧍

PREP TIME: **15** MINUTES

MARINATING TIME: ABOUT
20 MINUTES

GRILLING TIME: ABOUT **6** MINUTES

SPECIAL EQUIPMENT: PERFORATED
GRILL PAN

As a stand-alone sauce or condiment, store-bought pesto falls way short of the version you make yourself with fresh, fragrant basil leaves, but it sure can give a quick zip of flavor to a white wine marinade for striped bass. Cooking tomatoes on a grill pan next to the fish saves you the time and effort of skewering them. If you are a little nervous about the fish falling apart, grill that on the pan, too. Another good (and more impressive) approach is to cook tender fish in a parchment envelope with potatoes, carrots, peas, zucchini, and tomatoes—all flavored by pesto and natural juices.

Pesto-Marinated Striped Bass
WITH WARM TOMATOES

EASY

// MARINADE

½ cup white wine
¼ cup prepared pesto
1 teaspoon crushed red pepper flakes
½ teaspoon kosher salt

4 striped bass fillets (with skin),
   each about 6 ounces and ½ inch thick
3 cups grape tomatoes

1. In a small bowl mix the marinade ingredients. Place the fillets on a sheet pan and spoon the marinade over the fillets. Allow the fish to marinate at room temperature for about 20 minutes while you preheat the grill.

2. Prepare the grill for direct cooking over medium heat (350° to 450°F) and preheat the grill pan.

3. Using a spatula, transfer the fillets from the sheet pan directly to the grill and discard any remaining marinade left on the sheet pan. Arrange the tomatoes on the grill pan in a single layer and grill the fish and tomatoes over **direct medium heat**, with the lid closed as much as possible, until the fish is just opaque at the center and the tomatoes are warm and have collapsed, about 6 minutes, turning the tomatoes once or twice. Do not turn the fish. Remove from the grill and serve the fillets warm with the tomatoes.

Access the grocery list for this recipe on your mobile device. timetogrill.mobi.

SERVES: ††††

PREP TIME: **35** MINUTES

GRILLING TIME: **20** TO **25** MINUTES

// PESTO

- 1 tablespoon plus ½ cup extra-virgin olive oil, divided
- 1 garlic clove
- ¼ cup pine nuts
- 2 cups fresh basil leaves
- ½ cup freshly grated Parmigiano-Reggiano® cheese
- ¼ teaspoon crushed red pepper flakes
  Kosher salt

- 4 medium Yukon gold potatoes, cut into ⅛-inch slices
- 4 skinless sea bass fillets, each about 6 ounces and ½ inch thick
- 1 carrot, cut into matchsticks
- ½ cup sugar snap peas, cut into short, thin strips
- 1 zucchini, cut into matchsticks
- 2 cups grape tomatoes
  Ground black pepper

Sea Bass in Parchment
WITH PESTO AND VEGETABLES

1. In a small skillet over medium heat, warm **1 tablespoon of the oil.** Add the garlic and sauté for about 2 minutes. Add the pine nuts and cook until golden, 2 to 3 minutes. Remove from the heat and let cool.

2. In a food processor combine the cooled garlic and pine nuts, the basil, cheese, red pepper flakes, and ½ teaspoon salt. Pulse for about 30 seconds. With the motor running, slowly add the remaining ½ cup oil and process until you have a pesto consistency.

3. Prepare the grill for indirect cooking over medium heat (350° to 450°F).

4. Cut four pieces of parchment paper, **each about 15 by 15 inches.** On the lower half of each piece of parchment, layer sliced potatoes from one whole potato, then top with one fillet, and equal amounts of the pesto, thinly cut vegetables, and tomatoes. Season with salt and pepper. Fold the parchment over and crimp the three open sides tightly.

5. Brush the cooking grates clean. Grill the pouches over *indirect medium heat*, with the lid closed, until the potatoes are cooked, 20 to 25 minutes. To check for doneness, using tongs, gently unfold one of the pouches and carefully remove a potato, being careful not to puncture the bottom of the parchment. Gently pierce the potato with a knife to ensure doneness. When everything is cooked, remove the pouches from the grill. Carefully open each pouch to let the steam escape and then arrange on serving plates. Serve immediately.

Access the grocery list for this recipe on your mobile device. timetogrill.mobi.

ADVENTUROUS

Red Snapper
WITH CAPER-PARSLEY BUTTER

When you plan to make a recipe as simple as the one below, focus on your techniques. They can affect the final results as much as the ingredients. For example, grill the fillets longer on the first side than the second. This assures you a nicely developed crust on the first side that will release easily from the cooking grate. For the whole fish, check the doneness by the appearance of the flesh along the backbone, cutting a little slit there with the tip of a thin-blade knife. When the color turns from translucent to opaque, the fish is ready to come off the grill.

1. **Prepare the grill for direct cooking over high heat (450° to 550°F).**

2. **In a small saucepan over medium heat, melt the butter.** Add the parsley, lemon juice, and capers and stir to combine. Remove from the heat and keep warm while you grill the fillets.

3. **Lightly brush both sides of the fillets with oil and season evenly with salt and pepper.** Brush the cooking grates clean. Grill the fillets, flesh side down first, over **direct high heat**, with the lid closed as much as possible, until the fish just barely begins to flake when you poke it with the tip of a knife, 4 to 5 minutes, carefully turning with a spatula after 3 minutes of grilling time. Remove from the grill and serve the fillets warm over a bed of sautéed spinach, if desired, with the butter sauce spooned over the top.

Access the grocery list for this recipe on your mobile device. timetogrill.mobi.

EASY

SERVES: 👤👤👤👤

PREP TIME: **10** MINUTES

GRILLING TIME: **4** TO **5** MINUTES

½   cup (1 stick) unsalted butter
2   tablespoons finely chopped fresh Italian parsley leaves
1   tablespoon fresh lemon juice
1   tablespoon nonpareil capers, rinsed

4   red snapper fillets (with skin), each 4 to 5 ounces and about ½ inch thick
    Extra-virgin olive oil
    Kosher salt
    Ground black pepper

SERVES: 👤👤👤👤

PREP TIME: **30** MINUTES

GRILLING TIME: **53** MINUTES TO **1** HOUR

SPECIAL EQUIPMENT:
BUTCHER'S TWINE

// SAUCE

- 1 large shallot, cut in half through the root and stem ends
- 7 plum tomatoes, about 1 pound total, each halved lengthwise
  Extra-virgin olive oil
- ½ cup tightly packed fresh Italian parsley leaves
- ¼ cup toasted pine nuts
- 2 tablespoons fresh lemon juice
- 1 tablespoon sherry vinegar
- ¼ teaspoon ground cayenne pepper
  Kosher salt

- 1 whole red snapper, 3 to 3¼ pounds, gutted and scaled
  Ground black pepper
- 1 tablespoon tomato paste
- 1 lemon, cut into 4 slices
- ½ cup tightly packed fresh Italian parsley leaves

Carefully remove the backbone from the fish.

Lemon-Stuffed Snapper
WITH ROASTED TOMATO SAUCE

1. Prepare the grill for direct and indirect cooking over medium heat (350° to 450°F).

2. Lightly brush the shallot and tomatoes with oil. Brush the cooking grates clean. Grill them over *direct medium heat*, with the lid closed as much as possible, until the tomato skins blister and the shallot is tender, 8 to 10 minutes, turning once or twice. Cut off and discard the root ends of the shallot halves and then roughly chop the shallot. In a food processor combine the shallot and tomatoes with the parsley, pine nuts, lemon juice, vinegar, and cayenne pepper. Pulse until you have a smooth consistency. Season with salt.

3. Season the inside of the fish evenly with 1 teaspoon salt and 1 teaspoon pepper and then spread with the tomato paste. Fill the fish with lemon slices and the parsley. Tie the fish with butcher's twine to hold it closed. Lightly brush the fish with oil.

4. Brush the cooking grates clean. Grill the fish over *indirect medium heat*, with the lid closed, until the flesh is opaque near the bone but still juicy, 45 to 50 minutes, turning once. Transfer to a cutting board and let rest for 3 to 5 minutes.

5. Carefully remove the twine from the fish and then cut off the head and tail. Cut along the backbone and then open the fish like a book. Remove the bones, and lift the flesh off the skin. Serve the fish warm with the sauce.

Access the grocery list for this recipe on your mobile device. timetogrill.mobi.

EGGS

Some weekend mornings call for a rich indulgence of buttery eggs and sizzling steaks. The easy approach is to sear the steaks first, so they pick up some smoky flavors from the grill, and then fry your eggs alongside the meat in a cast-iron skillet. If you are in the mood for something more adventurous, try making steak-and-egg quesadillas, where the eggs cook right on top of grilled tortillas before you add cheese, chiles, and tender slices of beef. Keep the grill lid closed as much as possible so the cheese melts thoroughly before the tortillas are toast.

Steak and Eggs

SERVES: 4

PREP TIME: 10 MINUTES

GRILLING TIME: 10 TO 14 MINUTES

SPECIAL EQUIPMENT: 12-INCH CAST-IRON SKILLET

2 New York strip steaks, each 10 to 12 ounces and about 1 inch thick, trimmed of excess fat
Extra-virgin olive oil
Kosher salt
Ground black pepper
¾ teaspoon smoked paprika
2 tablespoons unsalted butter, divided
8 large eggs

1. **Prepare the grill for direct cooking over high heat (450° to 550°F).**

2. **Lightly brush the steaks on both sides with oil and season evenly with salt, pepper, and the paprika.** Allow the steaks to stand at room temperature for 15 to 30 minutes before grilling.

3. **Brush the cooking grates clean.** Grill the steaks over ***direct high heat***, with the lid closed as much as possible, until cooked to your desired doneness, 6 to 8 minutes for medium rare, turning once or twice (if flare-ups occur, move the steaks temporarily over indirect heat). When you turn the steaks, place a 12-inch cast-iron skillet on the cooking grate to preheat. Remove the steaks from the grill and let rest for 3 to 5 minutes. Lower the temperature of the grill to medium heat (350° to 450°F).

4. **Coat the skillet with the butter.** Crack the eggs into the skillet and season them with salt and pepper. Cook over ***direct medium heat***, with the lid closed as much as possible, until cooked as desired, 4 to 6 minutes for partially runny yolks. Transfer to plates and serve right away with the steak.

Access the grocery list for this recipe on your mobile device. timetogrill.mobi.

EASY

Brunch Quesadillas

SERVES: 🤵🤵🤵🤵 TO 🤵🤵🤵🤵🤵🤵

PREP TIME: **30** MINUTES

GRILLING TIME: **6** TO **8** MINUTES FOR THE STEAKS AND ABOUT **4** MINUTES PER BATCH FOR THE QUESADILLAS

- 2 New York strip steaks, each 10 to 12 ounces and about 1 inch thick, trimmed of excess fat
  Extra-virgin olive oil
- 1 teaspoon ground cumin
- ¼ teaspoon kosher salt
- ¼ teaspoon ground black pepper

- 6 large eggs
- 2 cups grated Mexican-style cheese
- 1 can (4 ounces) diced green chiles, well drained
- 6 tablespoons finely chopped fresh cilantro leaves
- 6 flour tortillas (8 to 9 inches)
  Salsa
  Sour cream
  Lime wedges
  Guacamole

1. Lightly brush the steaks on both sides with oil and season evenly with the cumin, salt, and pepper. Allow the steaks to stand at room temperature for 15 to 30 minutes before grilling.

2. Prepare the grill for direct cooking over high heat (450° to 550°F).

3. Brush the cooking grates clean. Grill the steaks over **direct high heat**, with the lid closed as much as possible, until cooked to your desired doneness, 6 to 8 minutes for medium rare, turning once or twice (if flare-ups occur, move the steaks temporarily over indirect heat). Remove from the grill and then lower the temperature of the grill to medium heat (350° to 450°F). Let the steaks rest for 3 to 5 minutes. Cut the steaks into small cubes and then divide into six equal portions.

4. Crack each egg into a small bowl and whisk to blend. Divide the cheese into six equal portions. Set the steak, eggs, cheese, chiles, and cilantro on a large tray and place it near the grill.

5. When the grill temperature has reached medium, brush the cooking grates clean. Working in batches of two (or three at the most), arrange the tortillas on the grill and cook them over **direct medium heat**, with the lid open, until grill marks appear, 20 to 30 seconds. Flip the tortillas over. Working quickly, pour one beaten egg onto each tortilla and use a fork to spread the egg over as much of the surface as possible. Deflate the puffy spots of the tortillas as needed to make spreading the egg easier. If the egg begins to spill off the side, bend the edges upward with tongs or use a piece of steak to contain it. Don't worry if a little runs into the flame anyway. Scatter the chiles over the egg on all the tortillas and then top each with a portion of the steak cubes and the grated cheese. Close the lid and cook until the egg is set and the cheese is melted, 3 to 4 minutes. The egg will begin to look puffy and the tortilla may be quite brown. Carefully transfer each tortilla to a plate, sprinkle with 1 tablespoon cilantro, and fold it in half. Tongs makes this job easier. Repeat with the remaining ingredients.

6. Cut the quesadillas into wedges and serve them immediately with salsa, sour cream, lime wedges, and guacamole on the side.

Access the grocery list for this recipe on your mobile device. timetogrill.mobi.

ADVENTUROUS

Simmering eggs in a tomato-based sauce is a low-risk, straightforward way to prepare them on a grill. You can make them either very Provençal, with a garlic-infused tomato sauce, or take them in a bolder direction inspired by the Veracruz region of Mexico, where peppers, olives, and capers strengthen the sauce. If you have time, layer the eggs on tortillas and top them with cilantro and crumbled cotija cheese. However you go, keep in mind that by the time the yolks have clouded over, they are firm in the center. If you like your eggs on the runny side, remove them from the sauce when the whites are opaque but the yolks are still bright yellow and soft.

Eggs Provençal

SERVES: ♦♦♦♦

PREP TIME: 15 MINUTES

GRILLING TIME: 22 TO 25 MINUTES

SPECIAL EQUIPMENT: 12-INCH CAST-IRON SKILLET

EASY

1 can (28 ounces) crushed tomatoes
1 tablespoon extra-virgin olive oil
1 teaspoon minced garlic
2 teaspoons finely chopped fresh basil leaves
2 teaspoons finely chopped fresh thyme leaves
1 teaspoon finely chopped fresh rosemary leaves
  Kosher salt
  Ground black pepper
8 large eggs
4 thick slices toasted bread
2 ounces goat cheese, crumbled

1. **Prepare the grill for direct cooking over medium heat (350° to 450°F).**

2. **In a 12-inch cast-iron skillet combine the tomatoes, oil, garlic, all the herbs, ¼ teaspoon salt, and ⅛ teaspoon pepper.**

3. **Brush the cooking grates clean.** Place the skillet over ***direct medium heat***, close the lid, and cook the sauce for 15 minutes, stirring once or twice. Stir the sauce again, and then, using the back of a large spoon, make eight shallow wells in the mixture so the skillet is barely visible through the sauce. The liquid from the sauce may begin to refill the indentations, but the wells should at least partially remain. Crack one egg into each indentation, close the lid, and cook over ***direct medium heat***, with the lid closed, until the egg yolks have just started to cloud over and the whites are set as desired, 7 to 10 minutes.

4. **Scoop the eggs and sauce onto thick slices of toast.** Top with the cheese and season with salt and pepper. Serve hot.

Access the grocery list for this recipe on your mobile device. timetogrill.mobi.

Huevos Veracruz

SERVES: 4

PREP TIME: 30 MINUTES

GRILLING TIME: 17 TO 20 MINUTES

SPECIAL EQUIPMENT: 12-INCH CAST-IRON SKILLET

8 corn tortillas (6 inches)
2 tablespoons extra-virgin olive oil
2 tablespoons finely chopped shallot
1 green bell pepper, stemmed, seeded, and finely diced
1 tablespoon finely diced jalapeño nacho slices (from a can or jar)
2 teaspoons minced garlic
1 bay leaf
 Kosher salt
 Ground black pepper
1 can (15 ounces) petite-cut diced tomatoes
¼ cup pitted, chopped green olives
2 tablespoons nonpareil capers, drained
8 large eggs
2 tablespoons finely chopped fresh cilantro leaves
¼ cup crumbled cotija cheese
4 lime wedges

1. **Prepare the grill for direct cooking over medium heat (350° to 450°F).** Preheat the skillet on the grill for 3 minutes.

2. **Wrap the tortillas in a foil packet.**

3. **To a 12-inch cast-iron skillet add the oil and then the shallot, bell pepper, jalapeño, garlic, bay leaf, ¼ teaspoon salt, and ¼ teaspoon pepper, mixing thoroughly.** Cook over *direct medium heat* until the peppers are softened, about 5 minutes, stirring once or twice. Add the whole can of diced tomatoes and its juice, the olives, and capers and cook until the tomatoes are heated through, about 5 minutes, stirring occasionally. Keep the lid closed as much as possible during grilling.

4. **Using the back of a large spoon, make eight shallow wells in the mixture so the skillet is just visible through the sauce.** Crack one egg into each indentation, close the lid, and cook over *direct medium heat* until the yolks have just started to cloud over and the whites are set as desired, 7 to 10 minutes. During the last 1 to 2 minutes of cooking time, warm the tortillas over direct heat, turning once.

5. **To serve, remove the bay leaf from the sauce.** Set two warm tortillas on each plate, spoon some sauce on top and then two eggs. Season with salt and pepper and garnish with cilantro, cheese, and a squeeze of lime.

Access the grocery list for this recipe on your mobile device. timetogrill.mobi.

A farmhouse breakfast is best done the old-fashioned way, with bacon fried in a heavy skillet and eggs cooked in the glorious drippings. Doing all this on the grill leaves the lingering bacon smell and splatters outside. For an even more filling dish that still requires just one skillet, fry diced beets and potatoes in the bacon fat and finish them with tangy goat cheese and champagne vinegar. It's nice to peel the beets and potatoes before cooking for a smooth texture, but leaving them on is fine and will save you several minutes of prep time.

Farmhouse Breakfast

EASY

SERVES: 👤👤👤👤

PREP TIME: **15** MINUTES

GRILLING TIME: **19** TO **26** MINUTES

SPECIAL EQUIPMENT: 12-INCH
CAST-IRON SKILLET

8 large eggs
  Butter
4 slices crusty bread, each about
  1 inch thick
8 thick slices bacon
¼ teaspoon kosher salt
¼ teaspoon ground black pepper
1 garlic clove, cut in half *or* jam

1. **Prepare the grill for direct cooking over medium heat (350° to 450°F).**

2. **Crack all the eggs gently into a large bowl.** Butter the bread slices on both sides.

3. **Brush the cooking grates clean.** Arrange the bacon in a single layer in a 12-inch cast-iron skillet, with pieces on the bottom and around the sides. Grill over *direct medium heat*, with the lid closed as much as possible, until crisp, 15 to 20 minutes, turning and rearranging the bacon as it cooks and shrinks. Drain the bacon on paper towels and then wrap in foil and keep warm on the grill's warming rack or in a low oven.

4. **Use a large serving spoon to scoop out about half of the bacon grease from the skillet, leaving a ⅛-inch layer on the bottom.** Gently pour all the eggs into the skillet at once and season with the salt and pepper. Place the bread directly on the grill and cook both the eggs and the bread over *direct medium heat*, with the lid closed as much as possible, until the eggs begin to cloud over on top (the yolks will be partially runny) and the bread is toasted. The eggs will take 4 to 6 minutes and the toast will take 3 to 4 minutes. Turn the bread once during grilling. Transfer the toast to the warming rack or oven with the bacon.

5. **Using a serving spoon or spatula, cut the eggs apart and scoop them out of the skillet one at a time.** If savory toast is desired, rub each side with the cut side of the garlic clove while the toast is still warm. If sweet toast is preferred, spread it with jam. Serve the eggs and toast immediately with the bacon.

Access the grocery list for this recipe on your mobile device. timetogrill.mobi.

Red Flannel Hash

SERVES: 4 TO 6

PREP TIME: **30** MINUTES

GRILLING TIME: **50** TO **57** MINUTES

SPECIAL EQUIPMENT: 12-INCH CAST-IRON SKILLET

8 thick slices bacon, coarsely chopped
½ yellow onion, thinly sliced
2 red beets, about 1 pound total, cut into ½-inch pieces
1 teaspoon kosher salt
½ teaspoon ground black pepper
2 tablespoons chopped fresh thyme leaves
1 large garlic clove, finely chopped
2 russet potatoes, about 1½ pounds total, cut into ½-inch pieces
3 tablespoons champagne vinegar *or* white wine vinegar
4 ounces goat cheese, crumbled

8 large eggs, scrambled or fried (optional)

1. **Prepare the grill for direct cooking over medium heat (350° to 450°F).**

2. **Brush the cooking grates clean.** Spread the bacon out in a 12-inch cast-iron skillet. Grill over **direct medium heat**, with the lid closed as much as possible, until crisp, 15 to 17 minutes, stirring the bacon pieces occasionally. Using a slotted spoon, transfer the bacon to paper towels to drain. Carefully remove about 2 tablespoons of the bacon grease from the skillet and discard.

3. **Combine the onion, beets, salt, pepper, and thyme in the skillet and cook over direct medium heat,** with the lid closed as much as possible, for 10 minutes, stirring once. Add the garlic and potatoes and cook, with the lid closed, until the beets and potatoes are tender and there are browned bits sticking to the skillet, 25 to 30 minutes, stirring and scraping the bottom of the skillet occasionally.

4. **Stir in the vinegar and all but ¼ cup of the bacon pieces.** Top the hash with the cheese and the remaining ¼ cup of bacon. Serve immediately with scrambled or fried eggs and fresh fruit, if desired.

Access the grocery list for this recipe on your mobile device. timetogrill.mobi.

Using a long-handled spoon, stir and scrape the bottom of the skillet occasionally.

You could certainly make French toast with a cast-iron skillet or griddle, but if you grill the soaked slices of bread directly on the cooking grates, the toast takes on a crisper crust and cooks a little faster, too. For the best results, use high-quality artisanal bread—the kind you slice yourself. If you have access to buttery brioche, fill the slices with jam and cream cheese, and soak them in a batter spiked with orange zest before grilling. They make a decadent, creamy meal—great for entertaining. To save time in the morning, make the toast sandwiches and whisk the soaking batter the night before, and refrigerate them separately. Feel free to substitute other fruits for the jam and topping.

Cinnamon French Toast

SERVES: 𝌆𝌆𝌆𝌆

PREP TIME: **15** MINUTES

STANDING TIME: **10** MINUTES

GRILLING TIME: **6** TO **8** MINUTES

    6 large eggs
 1½ cups whole milk
    1 tablespoon pure vanilla extract
    1 tablespoon ground cinnamon
    2 tablespoons granulated sugar
 ⅛ teaspoon kosher salt
    8 slices country-style white bread,
        each about ¾ inch thick
        Canola oil spray
        Confectioners' sugar
        Butter
        Maple syrup

1. In a large bowl whisk the eggs, milk, vanilla, cinnamon, sugar, and salt. Arrange the bread in one layer in a large baking dish and pour the egg mixture over the bread. Let the bread stand for 10 minutes at room temperature, turning the bread occasionally so that all the slices get a chance to sit in the liquid on both sides.

2. Prepare the grill for direct cooking over medium-low heat (about 350°F).

3. Brush the cooking grates clean. Tip one slice of bread on its side so that any extra liquid runs off. Spray both sides with the oil and then place on the grill. Repeat with the remaining slices. Grill over **direct medium-low heat**, with the lid closed as much as possible, until firm on both sides and golden brown, 6 to 8 minutes, turning once. Remove from the grill and dust with confectioners' sugar. Serve immediately with butter and syrup.

Access the grocery list for this recipe on your mobile device. timetogrill.mobi.

1. **Arrange six slices of the brioche in a baking pan large enough to fit them all comfortably in one layer.** Spread each slice with 1 ounce of cream cheese, leaving a one-half-inch border at the edges. Spread each of the other six slices with a heaping tablespoon of jam, and then invert them onto the halves with the cream cheese, making sandwiches.

2. **In a large bowl whisk the eggs, milk, half-and-half, sugar, vanilla, orange zest, and salt.** Pour the mixture over the sandwiches, and let stand at room temperature for 20 minutes, turning the sandwiches once.

3. **Lightly spray the peaches with oil.**

4. **Prepare the grill for direct and indirect cooking over medium-low heat (about 350°F).**

5. **Brush the cooking grates clean.** Tip one sandwich on its side so that any extra liquid runs off. Spray both sides with oil and then place on the grill. Repeat with the remaining sandwiches. Grill over *direct medium-low heat*, with the lid closed as much as possible until browned on both sides, 6 to 8 minutes, turning once. Move the sandwiches onto a piece of foil placed over *indirect medium-low heat*, close the lid, and continue cooking until the sandwiches are firm in the center, about 5 minutes. At the same time, grill the peaches over *direct medium-low heat* until the flesh is marked and the peaches are warm, 5 to 10 minutes, turning once or twice. Remove from the grill and cut the peach quarters in half lengthwise.

6. **Serve the sandwiches hot with the peaches on top.**

Access the grocery list for this recipe on your mobile device. timetogrill.mobi.

Stuffed Brioche French Toast

SERVES: ♙♙♙♙♙♙

PREP TIME: **30** MINUTES

STANDING TIME: **20** MINUTES

GRILLING TIME: **11** TO **18** MINUTES

12 slices brioche, each about ¾ inch thick
6 ounces cream cheese, softened
6 heaping tablespoons peach jam
8 large eggs
1 cup whole milk
1 cup half-and-half
2 tablespoons granulated sugar
1 tablespoon pure vanilla extract
   Finely grated zest of 1 orange
¼ teaspoon kosher salt

4 large, ripe freestone peaches, quartered
   Canola oil spray

If cooking isn't at the top of your wish list first thing in the morning, here are two breakfast ideas that require very little last-minute effort. One is to grill slices of sturdy, ripe plum tomatoes topped with Parmesan cheese and basil. They make a savory side dish for eggs cooked any way you like. Another is to assemble a strata the night before. This is just bread, cheese, eggs, and tomatoes layered into a cast-iron skillet with sausages that you have grilled ahead of time. In the morning, you simply set the skillet on the grill and let the strata cook for thirty minutes or so, until the bread is toasty, the eggs are set, and the cheese is bubbling.

SERVES: ♟♟♟♟ TO ♟♟♟♟♟♟

PREP TIME: 15 MINUTES

GRILLING TIME: 5 TO 8 MINUTES

EASY

3 tablespoons extra-virgin olive oil, divided
1 tablespoon finely chopped fresh thyme leaves
1 teaspoon finely chopped fresh oregano leaves
½ teaspoon kosher salt
¼ teaspoon ground black pepper
6 plum tomatoes, about 1½ pounds total, cut into ½-inch slices
1 baguette, cut crosswise on the diagonal into ½-inch slices
¼ cup freshly grated Parmigiano-Reggiano® cheese
1 teaspoon balsamic vinegar
¼ cup finely chopped fresh basil leaves

Breakfast Tomatoes

1. Prepare the grill for direct cooking over medium heat (350° to 450°F).

2. In a large bowl combine 1 tablespoon of the oil, the thyme, oregano, salt, and pepper. Add the tomato slices to the bowl and turn them gently to coat each slice thoroughly.

3. Lightly brush the baguette slices with the remaining 2 tablespoons of oil. Brush the cooking grates clean. Grill the baguette slices over **direct medium heat**, with the lid closed as much as possible, until toasted, 1 to 2 minutes, turning once. Transfer to a sheet pan and arrange in a single layer.

4. Grill the tomatoes over **direct medium heat**, with the lid closed as much as possible, until they are nicely marked on the first side, 3 to 4 minutes. Turn the slices over and sprinkle each with cheese. Close the lid and grill the second side until the tomatoes are soft but not falling apart and the cheese has begun to melt, 1 to 2 minutes. Remove from the grill and place each tomato on a piece of grilled bread. Drizzle each tomato slice with a few drops of the vinegar. Sprinkle with the basil and serve immediately.

Access the grocery list for this recipe on your mobile device. timetogrill.mobi.

Tomato and Sausage Strata

SERVES: 8

PREP TIME: 20 MINUTES

REFRIGERATION TIME: OVERNIGHT

GRILLING TIME: 10 TO 12 MINUTES FOR THE SAUSAGES, PLUS 30 TO 40 MINUTES FOR THE STRATA

SPECIAL EQUIPMENT: 12-INCH CAST-IRON SKILLET

2-3 fresh mild Italian sausages, each about 4 ounces, pierced a few times with a fork
8 large eggs
1⅔ cups whole milk
2 teaspoons finely chopped fresh rosemary leaves
2 teaspoons finely chopped fresh oregano leaves
½ teaspoon kosher salt
¼ teaspoon ground black pepper
1 loaf Italian bread, cut into ¾-inch cubes (to make 8 cups)
1 pint small grape tomatoes
1 roasted red bell pepper (from a jar), cut lengthwise into ¼-inch slices
6 ounces mozzarella cheese, cut into ¼- to ½-inch cubes
1½ teaspoons unsalted butter
½ cup freshly grated Parmigiano-Reggiano® cheese

1. **Prepare the grill for direct cooking over medium heat (350° to 450°F).**

2. **Brush the cooking grates clean.** Grill the sausages over *direct medium heat*, with the lid closed as much as possible, until they are cooked through and no longer pink in the center, 10 to 12 minutes, turning occasionally. Remove from the grill and turn off the grill.

3. **Cut the cooked sausages in half lengthwise and then cut them crosswise into thin slices.** In a large bowl whisk the eggs, milk, rosemary, oregano, salt, and pepper. Add the sausage slices, bread cubes, tomatoes, bell pepper, and mozzarella cheese to the bowl and toss to coat evenly.

4. **Grease a 12-inch cast-iron skillet with the butter.** Put the mixture in the skillet and top with the Parmesan cheese. Cover with foil and refrigerate overnight. Allow the skillet to stand at room temperature for about 30 minutes before grilling.

5. **Prepare the grill for direct cooking over medium-low heat (about 350°F).**

6. **Remove and discard the foil from the skillet.** Grill over *direct medium-low heat*, with the lid closed as much as possible, until the center of the strata is firm (a knife inserted into the center should come out free of uncooked egg) and the bread is toasted, 30 to 40 minutes. Toward the end of the cooking time some liquid may accumulate as the cheese melts. The liquid will reabsorb upon resting. Remove from the grill and let the strata cool for about 10 minutes. Serve warm.

Access the grocery list for this recipe on your mobile device. timetogrill.mobi.

Bursting with flavor, this easy asparagus salad with juicy tomatoes and creamy cheese makes a great addition to a weekend brunch with eggs. Although it's most delicious warm, the salad can be assembled ahead of time and dressed just before serving, which makes it a great choice for a potluck or a picnic. Consider doubling or tripling the recipe for a crowd. The frittata draws on some of the same ingredients but they are cooked instead in a nonstick skillet with eggs. This recipe serves as a great template for any grilled frittata. In place of the asparagus or tomatoes, use ready-to-go pantry items like drained artichoke hearts, roasted red peppers, or sun-dried tomatoes.

Asparagus and Tomato Salad
WITH FETA

SERVES: ♟♟♟♟ TO ♟♟♟♟♟♟

PREP TIME: **10** MINUTES

GRILLING TIME: **6** TO **8** MINUTES

SPECIAL EQUIPMENT: PERFORATED GRILL PAN

// VINAIGRETTE

- 1 tablespoon Dijon mustard
- 2 tablespoons champagne vinegar
- ¼ teaspoon kosher salt
- ⅛ teaspoon ground black pepper
- ½ cup extra-virgin olive oil

- 1½ pounds asparagus
- 1 pint cherry tomatoes
- 3 slices country-style white bread, about 3 ounces total, cut into ½-inch cubes (you should have about 2 cups)
- ½ cup crumbled feta cheese
- 2 tablespoons chopped fresh chives

1. Prepare the grill for direct cooking over medium heat (350° to 450°F) and preheat the grill pan.

2. In a small bowl whisk the mustard, vinegar, salt, and pepper. Slowly drizzle and whisk in the oil until it is emulsified.

3. Remove and discard the tough bottom of each asparagus spear by grasping at each end and bending it gently until it snaps at its natural point of tenderness, usually about two-thirds of the way down the spear.

4. Spread the asparagus on a large plate. Drizzle with 2 tablespoons of the vinaigrette and turn the spears until they are evenly coated. In a medium bowl toss the tomatoes and bread cubes with 2 tablespoons of the vinaigrette.

5. Brush the cooking grates clean. Spread the tomatoes and bread cubes in a single layer on the grill pan and lay the asparagus on the cooking grate. Grill over **direct medium heat**, with the lid closed as much as possible, until the asparagus is tender, the tomatoes begin to soften, and the bread cubes are toasted, turning often. The asparagus will take 6 to 8 minutes and the tomatoes and bread cubes will take 2 to 4 minutes.

6. Arrange the asparagus on a platter and top with the tomatoes, croutons, feta, and chives. Serve with the remaining vinaigrette.

Access the grocery list for this recipe on your mobile device. timetogrill.mobi.

EASY

Asparagus, Tomato, and Feta Frittata

SERVES: 👤👤👤👤👤👤

PREP TIME: **20** MINUTES

GRILLING TIME: ABOUT **17** MINUTES

SPECIAL EQUIPMENT:
10-INCH OVENPROOF SKILLET,
PREFERABLY NONSTICK

  6 large eggs
 ¼ cup half-and-half
 ¼ cup freshly grated Parmigiano-
     Reggiano® cheese
 ¼ teaspoon kosher salt
 ¼ teaspoon ground black pepper
  1 tablespoon extra-virgin olive oil
 ½ pound asparagus, ends trimmed,
     cut into 1-inch pieces
  2 garlic cloves, finely chopped
  1 cup cherry tomatoes, each cut in half
 ¾ cup crumbled feta cheese

1. **In a blender whirl the eggs, half-and-half, Parmesan cheese, salt, and pepper for 10 seconds.** Set aside.

2. **Prepare the grill for direct cooking over medium heat (350° to 450°F) and preheat the skillet on the cooking grate for 3 minutes.**

3. **Add the oil to the skillet and then the asparagus; stir briefly.** Cook over *direct medium heat*, with the lid closed, for 2 minutes. Wearing barbecue mitts, remove the skillet from the grill and roll the asparagus around in the skillet so that the oil coats the bottom and sides of the pan evenly. Place the skillet back on the cooking grate, arrange the asparagus in an even layer, and then scatter the garlic, tomatoes, and feta on top of the asparagus. Pour the egg mixture into the skillet. Grill the frittata over *direct medium heat*, with the lid closed as much as possible, until the eggs are puffed, browned, and firm in the center, about 15 minutes. Remove from the grill and serve immediately.

Access the grocery list for this recipe on your mobile device. timetogrill.mobi.

VEGETABLES

Choose asparagus spears about as thick as your finger, as they do better on the grill than pencil-thin ones, and grill over medium heat, not high heat, so they cook through without charring. A cool green goddess dip, brightly colored with fresh parsley, scallions, and tarragon, pairs brilliantly with the asparagus. Use any leftover dip as a salad dressing. The Napoleons heighten the flavors—literally and figuratively—by stacking them high with golden grilled potatoes and goat cheese. For a vegetarian main course, double the recipe and serve two Napoleons per person.

1. Prepare the grill for direct cooking over medium heat (350° to 450°F).

2. In a food processor pulse the parsley, scallions, and tarragon until finely chopped. Add the sour cream, mayonnaise, and lemon juice and process until smooth. Add the capers and pulse until combined. Transfer to a serving bowl and refrigerate until ready to serve.

3. Remove and discard the tough bottom of each asparagus spear by grasping at each end and bending it gently until it snaps at its natural point of tenderness, usually about two-thirds of the way down the spear.

4. Spread the asparagus on a platter. Drizzle with the oil and season with the salt. Roll the spears until they are evenly coated.

5. Brush the cooking grates clean. Grill the asparagus (perpendicular to the grate) over **direct medium heat**, with the lid closed as much as possible, until browned in spots but not charred, 6 to 8 minutes, turning occasionally. Remove from the grill and serve warm with the dip.

Access the grocery list for this recipe on your mobile device. timetogrill.mobi.

Asparagus
WITH GREEN GODDESS DIP

EASY

SERVES: 👤👤👤👤👤👤

PREP TIME: **10** MINUTES

GRILLING TIME: **6** TO **8** MINUTES

// DIP

¼ cup loosely packed fresh Italian parsley leaves

2 scallions (white and light green parts only), coarsely chopped

2 tablespoons roughly chopped fresh tarragon leaves

⅔ cup sour cream

⅓ cup mayonnaise

2 tablespoons fresh lemon juice

2 tablespoons nonpareil capers, rinsed

2 pounds asparagus

2 tablespoons extra-virgin olive oil

1 teaspoon kosher salt

Asparagus and Potato Napoleons
WITH TARRAGON VINAIGRETTE

SERVES: 🧍🧍🧍🧍🧍🧍

PREP TIME: **20** MINUTES

GRILLING TIME: **6** TO **8** MINUTES

// VINAIGRETTE
- 3 tablespoons fresh lemon juice
- 2 tablespoons finely chopped fresh tarragon leaves
- 1 teaspoon Dijon mustard
- Kosher salt
- Ground black pepper
- Extra-virgin olive oil

- 1 pound asparagus
- 4 large russet potatoes, peeled
- 3 ounces goat cheese, crumbled
- 1 tablespoon nonpareil capers, rinsed

1. Prepare the grill for direct cooking over medium heat (350° to 450°F).

2. In a medium bowl whisk the lemon juice, tarragon, mustard, ¼ teaspoon salt, and ⅛ teaspoon pepper. While whisking, gradually add ½ cup oil to make a smooth emulsion.

3. Remove and discard the tough bottom of each asparagus spear by grasping at each end and bending it gently until it snaps at its natural point of tenderness, usually about two-thirds of the way down the spear.

4. Bring a medium saucepan of salted water to a boil over high heat. Trim the bottom off one end of each potato so it can stand vertically on the cutting board without rolling.

Cut the potatoes lengthwise into ¼-inch slices. Reserve the twelve largest slices, and discard the remainder or save for another use. Add the potato slices to the water and reduce the heat to medium. Simmer just until almost tender, about 3 minutes (do not overcook). Drain carefully, rinse the potato slices under cold water, and pat dry with paper towels. Drizzle 2 tablespoons of oil on a sheet pan. Add the potatoes and asparagus to the pan and turn to coat them with the oil; season with salt.

5. Brush the cooking grates clean. Grill the potatoes and asparagus over **direct medium heat**, with the lid closed as much as possible, until the asparagus is browned in spots but not charred and the potatoes are golden

brown and tender, 6 to 8 minutes, turning once after about 4 minutes. Remove the vegetables from the grill as they are done. Cut the asparagus into bite-sized pieces.

6. Place one potato slice on each of six dinner plates and build the Napoleons evenly with half of the asparagus, another potato slice, the remaining asparagus, cheese, and capers. Whisk the vinaigrette again and drizzle about 1½ tablespoons on and around each Napoleon. Serve warm.

Access the grocery list for this recipe on your mobile device. timetogrill.mobi.

Everyone seems to have a strong opinion about brussels sprouts, usually negative. Some people protest about their sulfurous taste and smell, but that's because they have had overcooked brussels sprouts. If you roast them in a single layer on a perforated grill pan just until they are barely tender, they have a subtle sweetness with none of that harsh sulfurous effect. Look for the smallest buds possible so they cook quickly. If you still taste some bitterness, add salt (or bacon or Parmesan cheese).

Cut a slash in the root end of each brussels sprout to help it cook evenly.

Roasted Brussels Sprouts

EASY

SERVES: 👤👤👤👤

PREP TIME: **10** MINUTES

GRILLING TIME: **10** TO **15** MINUTES

SPECIAL EQUIPMENT: PERFORATED GRILL PAN

// **MARINADE**

1 tablespoon lemon-infused olive oil
1 teaspoon finely chopped fresh thyme leaves
½ teaspoon kosher salt
¼ teaspoon ground black pepper

1 pound brussels sprouts, each one trimmed at the root end and cut in half lengthwise

Finely grated zest of 1 lemon
1 teaspoon champagne vinegar

1. **Prepare the grill for direct cooking over low heat (250° to 350°F) and preheat the grill pan.**

2. **In a medium bowl mix the marinade ingredients.** Add the brussels sprouts and turn to coat them evenly.

3. **Spread the brussels sprouts in a single layer on the grill pan and grill over *direct low heat*, with the lid closed as much as possible, until crisp-tender, 10 to 15 minutes, turning several times.** Transfer to a serving bowl and add the lemon zest and vinegar. Toss to coat evenly. Season with salt, if desired. Serve warm.

Access the grocery list for this recipe on your mobile device. timetogrill.mobi.

Pasta with Brussels Sprouts, Tomatoes, and Bacon

SERVES: 🧍🧍🧍🧍🧍🧍

PREP TIME: **30** MINUTES

GRILLING TIME: **10** TO **15** MINUTES

SPECIAL EQUIPMENT: PERFORATED GRILL PAN

MARINADE
- 1 tablespoon extra-virgin olive oil
- 1 teaspoon chopped fresh thyme leaves
- 1 teaspoon kosher salt
- ½ teaspoon ground black pepper

- 1½ pounds brussels sprouts, each one trimmed at the root end and cut into quarters
- 3 cups grape tomatoes

- ½ pound dried penne
- 2 large eggs, beaten well
- 6 thick slices bacon, cooked and crumbled
- ½ cup freshly grated Parmigiano-Reggiano® cheese

1. Prepare the grill for direct cooking over low heat (250° to 350°F) and preheat the grill pan. Bring a large pot of salted water to a boil for the pasta.

2. In a medium bowl mix the marinade ingredients. Add the brussels sprouts and turn to coat them evenly.

3. Spread the brussels sprouts in a single layer on the grill pan and grill over *direct low heat*, with the lid closed as much as possible, until crisp-tender, 10 to 15 minutes, turning several times. Add the tomatoes to the grill pan during the last 5 minutes of cooking time and cook until warmed and softened. Transfer the brussels sprouts and tomatoes to a medium bowl.

4. While the brussels sprouts and tomatoes are on the grill, cook the pasta according to package directions. Drain and reserve 1 cup of the pasta water.

5. Add the hot pasta, ½ cup of the pasta water, the beaten eggs, bacon, and cheese to the bowl with the brussels sprouts and tomatoes and stir to combine the ingredients. Add more pasta water if needed. Let the pasta sit at room temperature for 3 minutes to let the flavors meld.

6. Divide the pasta evenly among six bowls. Serve with more cheese on the side, if desired.

Access the grocery list for this recipe on your mobile device. timetogrill.mobi.

Butternut Squash Soup

SERVES: 🧍🧍🧍🧍

PREP TIME: **20** MINUTES

GRILLING TIME: ABOUT **20** MINUTES

SPECIAL EQUIPMENT: PERFORATED GRILL PAN

2 tablespoons extra-virgin olive oil
1 teaspoon minced fresh sage leaves
   Kosher salt
   Ground black pepper
1 butternut squash, about 2 pounds, peeled, seeded, and cut into 1-inch cubes
1 large Granny Smith apple, peeled, cored, and chopped
1 small shallot, peeled and cut into quarters

2 cups chicken broth
1 tablespoon champagne vinegar
¼ cup heavy whipping cream
   Finely grated zest of 1 small orange
   Minced fresh chives (optional)

Perhaps the most challenging part of each of these recipes is cutting the hard butternut squash. Begin by cutting off about one-half inch from the bottom and top ends of each squash to make flat surfaces. Peel each squash lengthwise with a vegetable peeler. Then, with the squash standing up on its flat bottom end so it won't wobble, use a heavy, sharp knife and some elbow grease to cut from the top through the bottom. Finally scoop out the seeds and dice the squash.

1. **Prepare the grill for direct cooking over low heat (250° to 350°F) and preheat the grill pan.**

2. **In a large bowl whisk the oil, sage, 1 teaspoon salt, and ½ teaspoon pepper.** Add the squash, apple, and shallot and toss to coat evenly.

3. **Spread the squash, apple, and shallot in a single layer on the grill pan.** Grill over *direct low heat*, with the lid closed as much as possible, until the vegetables and apple are fork tender, about 20 minutes, turning occasionally. Remove the squash mixture from the grill and place in a food processor or blender; pulse until finely chopped.

4. **In a medium saucepan over medium heat, warm the broth.** Add the broth, vinegar, cream, and orange zest to the food processor and process until smooth. Pour the soup back into the saucepan and season with salt and pepper. Keep warm over low heat. Serve the soup warm, garnished with chives, if desired.

Access the grocery list for this recipe on your mobile device. timetogrill.mobi.

EASY

Botanically speaking, butternut squash is a fruit that happens to have a tough outer skin that preserves it for months. There is no need to refrigerate it.

SERVES: 👤👤👤👤

PREP TIME: **35** MINUTES

GRILLING TIME: **20** TO **30** MINUTES

SPECIAL EQUIPMENT: PERFORATED GRILL PAN

¼ cup extra-virgin olive oil
1 tablespoon minced fresh sage leaves
1 tablespoon minced fresh thyme leaves
1 teaspoon kosher salt
1 teaspoon ground black pepper

1 butternut squash, about 2 pounds, peeled, seeded, and cut into 1-inch chunks
1 large Granny Smith apple, peeled, cored, and cut into 1-inch chunks
1 medium sweet potato, peeled and cut into 1-inch chunks
1 medium red onion, peeled and cut into wedges

Finely grated zest of 1 orange

Roasted Butternut Squash Hash

1. Prepare the grill for direct cooking over low heat (250° to 350°F) and preheat the grill pan.

2. In a large bowl whisk the oil, sage, thyme, salt, and pepper. Add the squash, apple, sweet potato, and onion pieces and toss to coat evenly.

3. Spread the vegetables and apple in a single layer on the grill pan. Grill over *direct low heat*, with the lid closed as much as possible, until tender, 20 to 30 minutes, turning occasionally. Transfer to a serving bowl and stir in the orange zest. Serve warm.

Access the grocery list for this recipe on your mobile device. timetogrill.mobi.

ADVENTUROUS

Here's an easy salad that makes very good use of pre-washed spinach, bite-size mozzarella balls, and store-bought pesto. You can have everything prepped in the time it takes to preheat the grill. The sandwich reworks similar ingredients into a more filling and sophisticated recipe that stars burrata cheese. This wonderful style of mozzarella cheese has an especially soft, creamy interior. *Burrata* means "buttered" in Italian, which should give you some idea of the decadence oozing inside this sandwich.

Spinach Salad with Grilled Tomatoes and Onions

SERVES: 🧍🧍🧍🧍

PREP TIME: **10** MINUTES

GRILLING TIME: ABOUT **8** MINUTES

// DRESSING
½ cup store-bought pesto
3 tablespoons buttermilk
½ teaspoon ground black pepper

1 red onion, cut crosswise into ½-inch slices
6 plum tomatoes, each cut in half lengthwise

1 container (8 ounces) fresh mozzarella balls
4 cups baby spinach

1. **Prepare the grill for direct cooking over medium heat (350° to 450°F).**

2. **In a small bowl whisk the dressing ingredients.** Cover and refrigerate until ready to use.

3. **Brush the cooking grates clean.** Grill the onion and tomatoes over *direct medium heat*, with the lid closed as much as possible, until the onion is tender and the tomatoes are warmed through, about 8 minutes, turning once or twice. Remove from the grill and cut the onion slices into bite-sized pieces.

4. **Place one cup of spinach on each plate and top with equal amounts of the onion, tomatoes, and mozzarella balls.** Drizzle with the dressing. Serve right away.

Access the grocery list for this recipe on your mobile device. timetogrill.mobi.

EASY

Warm Focaccia Sandwiches with Burrata Cheese

SERVES: 🯄🯄🯄🯄🯄🯄

PREP TIME: **30** MINUTES

GRILLING TIME: **9** TO **10** MINUTES

SPECIAL EQUIPMENT: SHEET PAN

// PESTO

2 cups tightly packed fresh basil leaves
¾ cup freshly grated Parmigiano-Reggiano® cheese
¼ cup pine nuts, lightly toasted and cooled
1 large garlic clove
Extra-virgin olive oil
3 tablespoons white balsamic vinegar
Kosher salt
Ground black pepper

// SANDWICH

2 large bell peppers, 1 red and 1 yellow, each cut into 4 planks
1 large red onion, cut crosswise into ⅓-inch slices
6 ciabatta rolls, cut in half horizontally
3 ripe tomatoes, preferably heirloom, cut into ⅓-inch slices
1 ball (8 ounces) *burrata* cheese *or* fresh mozzarella cheese, cut into irregular ⅓-inch slices
1 cup baby arugula

1. In a food processor combine the basil, Parmesan cheese, pine nuts, and garlic and process to a coarse puree. With the motor running, gradually add ½ cup oil through the feed tube and process until almost smooth. Transfer the pesto to a small bowl. Stir in the vinegar and season with salt and pepper.

2. Prepare the grill for direct cooking over medium heat (350° to 450°F).

3. Lightly brush both sides of the peppers and onion and the cut side of the rolls with oil.

4. Brush the cooking grates clean. Grill the peppers and onion over *direct medium heat*, with the lid closed as much as possible, until browned in spots and tender, about 8 minutes, turning once or twice. During the last minute of grilling time, toast the rolls over direct heat, cut side down, just until lightly browned and grill marks appear.

5. Place the bottom half of the rolls, grilled side up, on a sheet pan. Spread a layer of pesto on the rolls. Top with the grilled bell peppers and onion slices, then the tomato slices, slightly overlapping. Dollop the *burrata* cheese over the tomatoes. Place the sandwiches on the sheet pan back on the grill, topping side up. Grill over *direct medium heat*, with the lid closed, until the cheese softens and begins to melt slightly, 1 to 2 minutes. Remove the sandwiches from the grill. Put the arugula on top of the cheese. Spread some of the remaining pesto (you may not need all of it) on the cut side of the top half of the rolls. Serve right away.

Access the grocery list for this recipe on your mobile device. timetogrill.mobi.

One quick and easy way to make a side dish for a favorite steak or fish fillet is to grill some russet potato wedges until golden brown and tender, which takes only about ten minutes, and they need only a little butter and some fresh herbs to make them memorable. To amp up the flavors and texture a bit, add some grilled cabbage wedges, onion slices, and a ham steak to the grill and roughly chop the whole lot until it has a hash consistency. Some grilled mushrooms or zucchini would also be good.

Grilled Potato Wedges
WITH FRESH HERBS AND BUTTER

SERVES: 👤👤👤👤

PREP TIME: **10** MINUTES

GRILLING TIME: **8** TO **10** MINUTES

 2 tablespoons extra-virgin olive oil
½ teaspoon kosher salt
½ teaspoon ground black pepper
 2 large russet potatoes, each cut into 8 wedges
 2 tablespoons unsalted butter, melted
 1 teaspoon Dijon mustard
¼ cup minced fresh herbs, such as rosemary, thyme, chive, dill, and Italian parsley

1. Prepare the grill for direct cooking over medium heat (350° to 450°F).

2. In a medium bowl combine the oil, salt, and pepper. Add the potato wedges to the bowl and toss to coat evenly.

3. Brush the cooking grates clean. Grill the potatoes over *direct medium heat*, with the lid closed as much as possible, until they are golden brown and quite tender, 8 to 10 minutes, turning occasionally. Transfer the potatoes back to the medium bowl.

4. In a small bowl mix the butter and mustard. Drizzle over the potatoes. Add the herbs and stir to coat the potatoes evenly. Serve warm.

Access the grocery list for this recipe on your mobile device. timetogrill.mobi.

EASY

Potato Hash with Cabbage, Ham, and Onions

SERVES: 👤👤👤👤

PREP TIME: **20** MINUTES

GRILLING TIME: **10** TO **12** MINUTES

4 tablespoons extra-virgin olive
oil, divided
1 teaspoon kosher salt
½ teaspoon onion powder
½ teaspoon ground black pepper

2 russet potatoes, about 1½ pounds total,
cut lengthwise into ⅓-inch slices
½ head green cabbage, quartered
1 red onion, cut crosswise into
½-inch slices

2 tablespoons unsalted butter, melted
1 teaspoon whole-grain mustard
2 teaspoons minced fresh thyme leaves

1 ham steak, 8 to 12 ounces and about
½ inch thick

**1. Prepare the grill for direct cooking over
medium heat (350° to 450°F).**

**2. In a medium bowl mix 2 tablespoon of
the oil, the salt, onion powder, and pepper.**
Brush all sides of the potato slices, cabbage
quarters, and onion slices with the oil mixture.

**3. In a small bowl combine the remaining
2 tablespoons oil, the butter, mustard, and
thyme to make a dressing.** Set aside.

4. Brush the cooking grates clean. Grill the
potatoes, cabbage, onion, and ham steak over
direct medium heat, with the lid closed as
much as possible, until the potatoes are
tender, the cabbage and onion are crisp-
tender, and the ham is warmed through,
10 to 12 minutes, turning once or twice.
Remove from the grill and roughly chop.

**5. Place the chopped veggies and ham in a
serving bowl and drizzle with the dressing;
stir until well combined.** Serve warm.

*Access the grocery list for this recipe
on your mobile device. timetogrill.mobi.*

*Green cabbage fades in color as it is stored,
so buy the darkest green heads you can. Avoid
any that have cracks at the stem end.*

"Baking" potatoes directly on coals imparts an earthy smokiness, even through the foil, and the skins turn wonderfully crisp in this dish. To shave some time off this recipe, choose smaller potatoes that will cook faster. The salad is a better choice for getting parts done ahead of time. You can boil the potatoes and make the vinaigrette up to a day in advance.

Foil-Wrapped Baked Potatoes

WITH SAUTÉED WILD MUSHROOMS

SERVES: 4

PREP TIME: 20 MINUTES

GRILLING TIME: 40 TO 50 MINUTES

- 4 large russet potatoes, pricked several times
- 1 pound mixed mushrooms, such as chanterelle, shiitake, porcini, portabello, cremini, or white button
- 2 tablespoons extra-virgin olive oil
- Kosher salt
- 10 garlic cloves, peeled and thinly sliced
- 6 tablespoons dry white wine
- 2 tablespoons unsalted butter
- 1 tablespoon fresh thyme leaves

- ¼ cup freshly shaved Parmigiano-Reggiano® cheese
- ½ cup crème fraîche *or* sour cream

1. **Fill a chimney starter to the rim with charcoal and burn the charcoal until it is lightly covered with ash.** Spread the charcoal in a tightly packed, single layer across one-half of the charcoal grate. Close the lid. Leave all the vents open. If using a gas grill, prepare the grill for direct cooking over high heat (450° to 550°F).

2. **Scrub the potatoes under cold running water and, while they're still wet, wrap each individually in heavy-duty aluminum foil.** Place the potatoes directly on the coals of a charcoal grill or on the cooking grates over ***direct high heat*** on a gas grill. Close the lid, and cook until the potatoes are tender when pierced with a fork or the tip of a knife, 40 to 50 minutes, turning occasionally.

3. **While the potatoes are cooking, clean the mushrooms and cut them into 1½- to 2-inch pieces.**

4. **In a large sauté pan over high heat, heat the oil until it is shimmering, 2 to 3 minutes.** Add the mushrooms, season with 1 teaspoon of salt, and stir them quickly to coat with oil. Sauté until they are nicely browned, 5 to 6 minutes, stirring as little as possible. Reduce the heat to medium, add the garlic, and cook until fragrant, 1 to 2 minutes, stirring constantly to prevent browning. Add the wine and bring quickly to a boil. Stir in the butter until it melts. Turn off the heat. Add the thyme.

5. **Remove the potatoes from the grill and carefully unwrap them.**

6. **To serve, cut the potatoes down the middle and put each on a plate.** Squeeze them open and use a fork to fluff up the insides. Season with salt. Spoon the mushrooms evenly over the potatoes, and then top with the cheese and crème fraîche. Serve warm.

Access the grocery list for this recipe on your mobile device. timetogrill.mobi.

Warm Potato Salad
WITH ARUGULA, RED ONION, AND GRAINY MUSTARD

SERVES: 4

PREP TIME: **20** MINUTES

GRILLING TIME: **15** TO **20** MINUTES

SPECIAL EQUIPMENT: PERFORATED GRILL PAN

// VINAIGRETTE

- 1 tablespoon sherry vinegar *or* red wine vinegar
- ½ small shallot, finely chopped (about 2 teaspoons)
- 1½ teaspoons fresh lemon juice
- ¾ teaspoon whole-grain mustard
- ½ teaspoon minced garlic
  Kosher salt
  Ground black pepper
  Extra-virgin olive oil

- 1 pound small new potatoes, each 1½ to 2 inches in diameter, scrubbed and cut in half
- 4 cups baby arugula
- ¼ medium red onion, very thinly sliced into half-moons (about ½ cup)
- 1 pint cherry tomatoes, each halved or quartered, depending on their size
- ¼ cup freshly shaved Parmigiano-Reggiano® cheese

1. **Prepare the grill for direct cooking over medium heat (350° to 450°F) and preheat the grill pan.**

2. **In a large bowl whisk the vinaigrette ingredients, including ¼ teaspoon salt, and ⅛ teaspoon pepper.** Slowly add 3 tablespoons of oil, whisking constantly to emulsify the vinaigrette. Set aside.

3. **In a large bowl lightly coat the potatoes with oil and season them with salt.** Spread the potatoes in a single layer on the grill pan. Grill over **direct medium heat**, with the lid closed as much as possible, until they are golden brown and tender, 15 to 20 minutes, turning with a wide spatula about every 5 minutes. Remove from the grill.

4. **In a large bowl combine the arugula, onion, and tomatoes.** Drizzle the salad with 3 tablespoons of the vinaigrette, season with salt and pepper, and toss gently. Divide the salad among four plates.

5. **Put the potatoes in the bowl with the remaining vinaigrette and toss to coat them well.** Using a slotted spoon to allow excess vinaigrette to drip off, mound an equal portion of the potatoes on top of each salad and then top with the cheese. Drizzle more vinaigrette over the salads, if desired, and serve immediately.

Access the grocery list for this recipe on your mobile device. timetogrill.mobi.

THE FUNDAMENTALS // of fire

Fire is a side effect of a rapid chemical reaction (oxidation) that produces energy in the form of heat and light. It is created from the interplay of three basic elements: fuel, heat, and oxygen. When combined together in the right amounts, they form an essential combination for combustion.

CHAIN REACTION

FUEL

Solid fuels (like wood and charcoal) and liquid fuels (like oil and propane) do not burn. Instead, it's the vapors or gases that are produced when these materials are heated that burn. Some fuels burn completely, leaving nothing behind. Other fuels such as wood don't burn completely and leave carbon (or char) and non-combustible minerals (ash) behind.

OXYGEN O₂

Oxygen is an invisible gas in the air. Its role in fire is to sustain combustion. A fire can't burn or sustain itself without oxygen, and it has to be mixed with the right amount of fuel to ignite. Oxygen makes up about 21 percent of the atmosphere.

A CASE OF
the vapors

Gas molecules break apart and rearrange themselves, combining with oxygen to form water and carbon dioxide in a process called oxidation. This "burning" releases energy creating heat, light, and sound.

A burning fire creates a sustaining chemical reaction that feeds a fire more heat so that it can continue until oxygen or fuel is depleted. Without this chain reaction, the fire goes out.

heat
+ fuel
———
vapor

vapor [vey-per] noun:
visible particles of moisture floating or suspended in the air, as smoke, fog, steam

HEAT 〜

The minimum temperature it takes to reach the point at which a material produces enough vapors to burn is called the flash point. The ignition point is the temperature at which the vapor will ignite when exposed to a spark, flame, or ignition source.

Wood Ignition Point: 500°F
Charcoal Ignition Point: ≈660°F

DID YOU KNOW?

A crackling fire is often considered a thing of beauty. But oddly enough, Hephaestus, the Greek god of fire and metalworking, is considered the only "ugly" god in ancient mythology.

This easy salad embellishes the famous *caprese* salad of tomatoes, basil, and mozzarella cheese with the addition of grilled eggplant. Look for eggplants with firm, glossy skins. As eggplants age, they lose their shine and their texture turns soft. It is also nice if the eggplants are about the same diameter from tip to end, so all the slices will be about the same size. The version of eggplant Parmesan on the other page is lighter than the traditional, fried version, but it is every bit as satisfying.

Eggplant and Tomato Salad

SERVES: 🚶🚶🚶🚶

PREP TIME: **10** MINUTES

GRILLING TIME: ABOUT **8** MINUTES

2 globe eggplants, cut crosswise into ½-inch slices
2 beefsteak tomatoes, cut crosswise into ½-inch slices
Extra-virgin olive oil
Kosher salt
Ground black pepper

1 pound fresh mozzarella cheese, cut into ⅓-inch slices
10 fresh basil leaves

1. Prepare the grill for direct cooking over medium heat (350° to 450°F).

2. Brush the eggplant and tomato slices with oil and season evenly with salt and pepper. Brush the cooking grates clean. Grill over **direct medium heat**, with the lid closed as much as possible, until the vegetables are tender and nicely marked, turning once. The eggplant will take about 8 minutes and the tomatoes will take 2 to 4 minutes. Remove from the grill as they are done.

3. Divide the eggplants, tomatoes, cheese, and basil among four plates. Drizzle with a little more olive oil or your favorite salad dressing, if desired.

Access the grocery list for this recipe on your mobile device. timetogrill.mobi.

EASY

Eggplant Parmesan

SERVES: 👤👤👤👤

PREP TIME: **20** MINUTES

GRILLING TIME: **8** TO **10** MINUTES

- 1 jar (15 ounces) good-quality marinara sauce
- 2 large egg whites
- ¾ cup freshly grated Parmigiano-Reggiano® cheese
- ½ cup plus 2 tablespoons panko bread crumbs
- 1 large globe eggplant, cut into 12 slices, each about ⅓ inch thick and 3 to 4 inches in diameter
  Kosher salt
  Ground black pepper
  Olive oil spray
- 2½ cups grated fontina cheese
- 12 large fresh basil leaves

1. In a small, heavy saucepan over medium heat, warm the marinara sauce. Set aside.

2. Prepare the grill for direct cooking over medium-high heat (400° to 500°F).

3. In a shallow bowl whisk the egg whites until very light and foamy. In another shallow bowl combine the Parmesan cheese and bread crumbs.

4. Dip one eggplant slice into the egg whites, covering thoroughly, and then place it in the bread crumb mixture. Turn to coat, patting the crumbs to help them adhere, then gently shake off the excess. Place on a large sheet pan and repeat with the remaining eggplant slices. Season with salt and pepper. Generously spray both sides with olive oil.

5. Brush the cooking grates clean. Grill the eggplant slices over *direct medium-high heat*, with the lid closed as much as possible, until the bottoms are golden, 4 to 5 minutes. Using a thin spatula, turn the slices over. Place ¼ cup of fontina cheese on each eggplant slice. Continue cooking, with the lid closed, until the eggplant bottoms are golden brown and the cheese is melted, 4 to 5 minutes.

6. Slightly overlap three eggplant slices on each of four plates. Serve warm with the sauce spooned over the eggplant and a basil leaf on top of each slice.

Access the grocery list for this recipe on your mobile device. timetogrill.mobi.

ADVENTUROUS

Whole eggplants roasting over a hot fire collapse and concentrate their flavors. Then all you need to do is peel them and mash them with some lemon, garlic, herbs, and salt for a delicious Middle Eastern dip. You might want to add some fresh tomato and good olive oil, too. If that combination is appealing and you want a main course rather than an appetizer, consider the pasta recipe on the other page.

1. Prepare the grill for direct cooking over high heat (450° to 550°F).

2. Pierce each eggplant approximately 10 times with a fork. Brush the pita with oil and season evenly with 1 teaspoon of the salt.

3. Brush the cooking grates clean. Grill the eggplants over *direct high heat*, with the lid closed as much as possible, until the skins are charred and they begin to collapse, 15 to 20 minutes, turning every 5 minutes. During the last 2 to 4 minutes of grilling time, grill the pita over direct heat, turning once. Remove them from the grill.

4. When the eggplants are cool enough to handle, cut them in half lengthwise and scoop out the pulp, discarding any clumps of seeds that could turn the dip bitter. Place the pulp in a medium bowl and mash with a fork (you may need to run a sharp knife through the pulp to break up the fibers) and then add the remaining 1 teaspoon of salt, the parsley, lemon juice, and garlic and mix well.

5. Cut the pita pockets into wedges (keep the minis whole) and serve with the eggplant.

Access the grocery list for this recipe on your mobile device. timetogrill.mobi.

Eggplant Caviar with Pita

SERVES: TO
AS AN APPETIZER

PREP TIME: **10** MINUTES

GRILLING TIME: **15** TO **20** MINUTES

EASY

2 medium globe eggplants
4 whole-wheat pita bread pockets *or* 1 bag (6 ounces) mini pita bread
Extra-virgin olive oil
2 teaspoons kosher salt, divided
3 tablespoons chopped fresh Italian parsley leaves
2 tablespoons fresh lemon juice
1½ teaspoons minced garlic

Eggplant and Tomato Pasta
WITH TOASTED SESAME SEEDS

A male eggplant (left) will often have fewer seeds than a female eggplant (right).

SERVES: 🧍🧍🧍🧍 TO 🧍🧍🧍🧍🧍🧍

PREP TIME: **25** MINUTES

GRILLING TIME: **8** TO **10** MINUTES

2 medium globe eggplants, cut crosswise into ½-inch slices
1 medium yellow onion, cut crosswise into ½-inch slices
¼ cup extra-virgin olive oil
Kosher salt
6 plum tomatoes

12 ounces dried gemelli (or any short pasta)

⅓ cup chopped fresh Italian parsley leaves
1 tablespoon minced garlic
⅓ cup nonpareil capers, rinsed
¼ cup toasted sesame seeds

1. Prepare the grill for direct cooking over medium heat (350° to 450°F).

2. Brush the eggplant and onion slices with the oil and season with salt. Brush the cooking grates clean. Grill the eggplants, onion, and tomatoes over ***direct medium heat***, with the lid closed as much as possible, until the vegetables are tender, 8 to 10 minutes, turning as needed. Remove from the grill. Slip the tomatoes from their skins and then chop the tomatoes, eggplants, and onion into a medium dice.

3. Bring a large saucepan of salted water to a boil. Add the pasta and cook until al dente, following package instructions. Drain well.

4. In a large bowl combine the chopped vegetables with the parsley, garlic, and capers. Add the hot pasta and toss to combine. Sprinkle with toasted sesame seeds. Serve right away.

Access the grocery list for this recipe on your mobile device. timetogrill.mobi.

ADVENTUROUS

You will be pleasantly surprised how easy and effective it is to grill tofu on aluminum foil. The heat of the grill passes through the foil and browns the tofu, but at the same time the foil holds the tender slices together. The tofu and vegetables may be left in the marinade for up to 12 hours, so feel free to start dinner before leaving for work in the morning. Vegetarians and carnivores alike will love the mixture of nuts and crunch in the adventurous, healthy soba salad. Leftovers also make an easy lunch for the next day. If the noodles seem a little dry, add a little hot water to moisten things up.

SERVES: 👤👤👤👤

PREP TIME: **15** MINUTES

MARINATING TIME: **3** TO **12** HOURS

GRILLING TIME: **12** TO **16** MINUTES

EASY

// MARINADE
½ cup reduced-sodium soy sauce
½ cup vegetable oil
¼ cup rice vinegar
3 tablespoons toasted sesame oil
2 teaspoons hot chili-garlic sauce,
   such as Sriracha

2 packages (14 ounces each) extra-firm
   tofu, drained
6 ounces button or cremini mushrooms,
   cleaned, ends trimmed flat
2 small zucchini, cut lengthwise into
   4 quarters
2 red bell peppers, cut into 1-inch strips

Spicy Grilled Tofu
WITH MARINATED VEGETABLES

1. In a small bowl combine the marinade ingredients, whisking until combined. Cut each tofu block lengthwise into four slices, each about ¾ inch thick. Place the tofu in a large glass baking dish. Place the mushrooms, zucchini, and peppers in a large bowl. Pour half of the marinade into the dish with the tofu and the remainder into the bowl with the vegetables. Cover and refrigerate at least 3 hours or up to 12 hours, turning the tofu and vegetables once or twice.

2. Prepare the grill for direct cooking over high heat (450° to 550°F).

3. Brush the cooking grates clean. Lay a large sheet of heavy-duty aluminum foil, about 12 by 16 inches, directly on the cooking grates. Lift the tofu slices out of the dish, letting any extra marinade drip off, and arrange them in a single layer on the foil. Reserve the marinade. Grill the tofu over *direct high heat*, with the

lid closed as much as possible, until both sides are nicely browned and the slices are hot, 6 to 8 minutes, turning once with a wide spatula and brushing occasionally with some of the reserved marinade. Transfer the tofu slices to a serving plate and tent them with foil to keep them warm while grilling the vegetables. Remove the foil from the grill.

4. Grill the mushrooms, zucchini, and peppers over *direct high heat*, with the lid closed as much as possible, until nicely marked, 3 to 4 minutes. Turn, brush with the reserved marinade, and continue cooking until tender, 3 to 4 minutes. Remove from the grill and cut the zucchini and peppers into bite-sized pieces. Transfer the vegetables to the serving plate with the tofu and serve immediately.

Access the grocery list for this recipe on your mobile device. timetogrill.mobi.

Soba Noodles with Grilled Tofu and Peanuts

SERVES: 🧍🧍🧍🧍 TO 🧍🧍🧍🧍🧍🧍

PREP TIME: **30** MINUTES

GRILLING TIME: **6** TO **8** MINUTES

1 package (9.5 ounces) soba noodles
   or 1 box (12 to 13.25 ounces) dried
   whole-grain spaghetti
1 cup roasted, unsalted peanuts
1 cup grated carrots
2 cups sugar snap peas, about 6 ounces,
   cut diagonally into ¼-inch pieces
3 scallions (white and light green parts
   only), thinly sliced

1 tablespoon toasted sesame oil
1 tablespoon soy sauce
¼ teaspoon garlic powder
1 package (14 ounces) extra-firm tofu,
   drained and cut in half horizontally

// SAUCE
¾ cup creamy peanut butter
¾ cup boiling water
¼ cup chopped fresh cilantro leaves
3 tablespoons fresh lime juice
3 tablespoons soy sauce
2 tablespoons toasted sesame oil
1 tablespoon peeled, minced fresh ginger
1 teaspoon hot chili-garlic sauce,
   such as Sriracha

1. **Bring a large pot of water to a boil for the noodles, and boil water for the peanut sauce.**

2. **Prepare the grill for direct cooking over high heat (450° to 550°F).**

3. **Cook the noodles according to package directions, rinsing well with cold water when they're done.** Transfer the noodles to a large bowl and add the peanuts, carrots, snap peas, and scallions.

4. **In a small bowl whisk the sesame oil, soy sauce, and garlic powder.** Brush the oil mixture on both sides of the tofu.

5. **Brush the cooking grates clean.** Lay a large sheet of heavy-duty aluminum foil, about 12 by 16 inches, directly on the cooking grates and arrange the tofu on the foil. Grill over ***direct high heat***, with the lid closed as much as possible, until lightly browned, 6 to 8 minutes, turning once.

6. **While the tofu is grilling, combine the sauce ingredients in a food processor or blender and process until smooth.** Add the sauce to the noodles and vegetables and mix gently with tongs until all the noodles are coated. Remove the tofu from the grill and cut into 1-inch cubes. Add the tofu to the noodles and serve right away.

Access the grocery list for this recipe on your mobile device. timetogrill.mobi.

SERVES: 4

PREP TIME: 15 MINUTES

GRILLING TIME: 16 TO 21 MINUTES

Between the chipotle aioli, grilled mushrooms, fresh spinach, and melted Swiss cheese, these unique quesadillas deliver a fantastic punch. Be sure to grill them over low heat so the cheese has time to melt and the tortillas don't burn. You can make the aioli up to two days in advance. Flavors abound in the tostado recipe, too—and without an ounce of meat. Serve them already assembled or with the components on the side so your guests can make their own.

Portabello, Spinach, and Swiss Cheese Quesadillas

// AIOLI

- ½ cup mayonnaise
- 2 tablespoons fresh lime juice
- 1 tablespoon minced chipotle chiles in adobo sauce
- 1 tablespoon honey
- 1 teaspoon minced garlic

// QUESADILLAS

- 4 large portabello mushrooms, stems and gills removed
- Extra-virgin olive oil
- 4 cups grated Swiss cheese
- 8 flour tortillas (8 inches)
- 1 bag (5 ounces) baby spinach

1. **In a medium serving bowl whisk the aioli ingredients until smooth.** Cover and refrigerate until ready to serve.

2. **Prepare the grill for direct cooking over medium heat (350° to 450°F).**

3. **Generously brush the mushroom caps with oil.** Brush the cooking grates clean. Grill the mushrooms over ***direct medium heat***, with the lid closed as much as possible, until tender, 12 to 15 minutes, turning occasionally and, if necessary to prevent them from drying out, brushing with a bit more oil. Remove from the grill and cut them into thin slices.

4. **Decrease the temperature of the grill to low heat (250° to 350°F).**

5. **Assemble the quesadillas by spreading ¼ cup cheese on one half of each tortilla.** Top the cheese with one quarter of the spinach, one quarter of the sliced mushrooms, and another ¼ cup of cheese. Fold the empty side of the tortillas over the fillings.

6. **Brush the outside of the tortillas lightly with oil and grill over *direct low heat*, with the lid closed as much as possible, until golden on both sides, 4 to 6 minutes, turning once.** Cut the quesadillas into wedges and serve warm with the aioli.

Access the grocery list for this recipe on your mobile device. timetogrill.mobi.

EASY

SERVES: 👤👤👤👤

PREP TIME: **30** MINUTES

GRILLING TIME: **12** TO **15** MINUTES

// CREMA
1 ripe Hass avocado, diced
½ cup sour cream
2 tablespoons fresh lime juice

Kosher salt

// SALSA
1 cup finely chopped ripe tomato
¼ cup thinly sliced red onion
1 small jalapeño chile pepper,
  seeded and minced
2 tablespoons finely chopped fresh
  cilantro leaves
1 tablespoon red wine vinegar

4 large portabello mushrooms,
  stems and gills removed
1 large red onion, cut crosswise into
  ½-inch slices
  Extra-virgin olive oil
2 tablespoons prepared fajita seasoning
2 large bell peppers, 1 red and 1 yellow,
  each cut into 4 planks
8 flour tortillas (8 inches)
2 cups grated Monterey Jack cheese

Portabello Tostados
WITH AVOCADO CREMA AND TOMATO SALSA

1. In a food processor blend the crema ingredients until smooth. Season with salt. Cover and refrigerate until ready to serve.

2. In a medium bowl mix all of the salsa ingredients and season with salt. Set aside at room temperature.

3. Prepare the grill for direct cooking over medium heat (350° to 450°F).

4. Generously brush the mushroom caps and onion slices with oil and season evenly with the fajita seasoning.

5. Brush the cooking grates clean. Grill the mushrooms, onion, and peppers over *direct medium heat*, with the lid closed as much as possible, until browned and tender, turning occasionally. The mushrooms will take 12 to 15 minutes, the onion will take 8 to 10 minutes, and the bell pepper will take 6 to 8 minutes. If necessary, to prevent the mushrooms from drying out, occasionally brush them with a bit more oil. Remove the vegetables from the grill and scrape off any blackened areas of the peppers. Cut the vegetables into thin strips.

6. Grill the tortillas on one side over *direct medium heat*, with the lid open, just until warm, 10 to 20 seconds. Turn them over, top each one with ¼ cup of the cheese, and grill just until the cheese melts. Remove from the grill and assemble the tostados with the grilled vegetables, salsa, and crema.

Access the grocery list for this recipe on your mobile device. timetogrill.mobi.

EASY   **ADVENTUROUS**

DESSERTS

This recipe couldn't be simpler. With just a handful of ingredients, you can have a light, homemade dessert off the grill in minutes. Greek yogurt, which is thicker than regular yogurt, is now available at most supermarkets, but if you can't find it, you can make your own thick yogurt by placing two cups of regular plain yogurt in a cheesecloth-lined strainer set over a bowl and then refrigerating it overnight. The liquid will drain from the yogurt and the yogurt will have thickened. If you feel up for baking a more substantial dessert on the grill, try the wonderful pound cake on the other page. Some cornmeal in the batter gives the cake a toothsome texture that complements the soft, juicy plums. The whipped cream topping can be made ahead and refrigerated.

Plums with Honey-Lemon Yogurt

SERVES: 🧍🧍🧍🧍🧍🧍

PREP TIME: **15** MINUTES

GRILLING TIME: ABOUT **6** MINUTES

1 cup plain Greek yogurt
2 tablespoons honey
2 teaspoons fresh lemon juice
¼ teaspoon ground cardamom

6 plums, firm but ripe, about 2 pounds
   total, each cut in half
   Vegetable or canola oil
1 tablespoon granulated sugar
⅓ cup coarsely chopped pistachios

1. In a small bowl whisk the yogurt, honey, lemon juice, and cardamom. Refrigerate until ready to use.

2. Prepare the grill for direct cooking over medium heat (350° to 450°F).

3. Lightly brush the cut side of each plum half with oil. Brush the cooking grates clean. Grill the plum halves, cut side down first, over *direct medium heat*, with the lid open, until slightly charred and grill marks appear, about 3 minutes. Turn the plums over, sprinkle evenly with the sugar, and continue cooking for 3 more minutes.

4. To serve, place two plum halves in each of six cups or bowls. Spoon the honey yogurt over the plums. Sprinkle the pistachios on top.

Access the grocery list for this recipe on your mobile device. timetogrill.mobi.

Plums with Lemon Polenta Cake

SERVES: 6 TO 8

PREP TIME: 30 MINUTES

BAKING TIME: 1 HOUR TO 1 HOUR AND 10 MINUTES

GRILLING TIME: ABOUT 6 MINUTES

SPECIAL EQUIPMENT: 9-BY-5-INCH LOAF PAN

1¼ cups all-purpose flour
1½ teaspoons baking powder
½ teaspoon kosher salt
¾ cup medium grind cornmeal, such as Bob's Red Mill®
1 cup granulated sugar
1 cup (2 sticks) unsalted butter, softened
1 tablespoon packed finely grated lemon zest
1 tablespoon fresh lemon juice
2 teaspoons pure vanilla extract
4 large eggs
½ cup plain Greek yogurt

4 plums, firm but ripe, about 1½ pounds total, each cut in half
Vegetable or canola oil
2 tablespoons honey
¼ teaspoon ground cardamom

1 cup chilled heavy whipping cream
2-3 tablespoons granulated sugar

1. Position the oven rack in the center of the oven and preheat to 350°F. Grease a 9-by-5-inch loaf pan. Dust the pan with flour; tap out the excess.

2. In a medium bowl whisk the flour, baking powder, salt, and cornmeal. In the bowl of an electric mixer beat 1 cup sugar, the butter, lemon zest and juice, and vanilla until fluffy, 2 to 3 minutes. Add the eggs, one at a time, and beat until well blended after each addition. Add the flour mixture in three additions alternately with the yogurt, beginning and ending with the flour mixture. Transfer the batter to the prepared loaf pan and smooth the top.

3. Bake at 350°F until the cake is deep golden and a toothpick inserted into the center of the cake comes out clean, 1 hour to 1 hour and 10 minutes. Transfer the cake to a rack and let cool in the pan for 15 minutes, then turn the cake out onto the rack and cool completely. While the cake is cooling, prepare the plums and the whipped cream.

4. Prepare the grill for direct cooking over medium heat (350° to 450°F).

5. Lightly brush the cut side of each plum half with oil. Brush the cooking grates clean. Grill the plum halves, cut side down first, over *direct medium heat*, with the lid open, until slightly charred and grill marks appear, about 6 minutes, turning once after about 3 minutes. Transfer the plums to a cutting board. Cool slightly, then cut each plum half into four wedges. Place the plums in a medium bowl. Add the honey and cardamom. Gently stir to combine.

6. In a medium bowl beat the whipping cream with 2 to 3 tablespoons sugar until soft peaks form.

7. Cut the cake into ½-inch slices. Spoon some of the plum mixture over each slice. Top with dollops of whipped cream.

Access the grocery list for this recipe on your mobile device. timetogrill.mobi.

Of all the fruits you could grill, pineapple slices are the easiest because they are so firm and flat. Served warm and juicy, they work deliciously with something rich like whipped cream or ice cream. Feel free to substitute toasted almonds or peanuts if you can't find macadamia nuts. Many of the same tropical flavors are remixed in the adventurous dessert, including coconut in the cake, but on busy days, just use pound cake from the store instead.

Pineapple with Toasted Coconut
AND RASPBERRY CREAM

SERVES: 🤵🤵🤵🤵

PREP TIME: **15** MINUTES

GRILLING TIME: **4** TO **6** MINUTES

¼ cup shredded coconut
¼ cup chopped macadamia nuts
½ cup chilled heavy whipping cream
2 tablespoons raspberry jelly
1 fresh pineapple, peeled, cored, and cut into ½-inch slices

1. Prepare the grill for direct cooking over medium heat (350° to 450°F).

2. In a small skillet over low heat, toast the coconut, about 3 minutes. Watch it closely; it can burn quickly. Pour the coconut into a small bowl. To the same skillet, add the nuts and cook until golden, about 3 minutes, shaking the skillet occasionally. Pour the nuts into the bowl with the coconut.

3. In a medium bowl whisk the cream for about 2 minutes. Add the jelly and continue whisking until soft peaks form, 2 to 3 minutes more.

4. Brush the cooking grates clean. Grill the pineapple slices over *direct medium heat*, with the lid open, until nicely marked, 4 to 6 minutes, turning once. Remove from the grill and cut into bite-sized pieces.

5. Divide the pineapple among four dessert dishes. Top with coconut, nuts, and cream.

Access the grocery list for this recipe on your mobile device. timetogrill.mobi.

1. **Preheat the oven to 350°F.** Lightly grease the inside of a 9-by-5-inch loaf pan.

2. **In a small bowl sift the flour, baking powder, and salt.** In another small bowl mix the buttermilk and sour cream.

3. **In a large bowl using an electric mixer on medium speed, cream the butter and granulated sugar until the mixture is light and fluffy, about 5 minutes.** Add the eggs, one at a time, beating well after each addition. Add the dry ingredients alternately with the wet ingredients, beginning and ending with the dry ingredients. Mix just until the batter is smooth. Stir in the coconut. Evenly spread the batter into the prepared loaf pan and smooth the top. Bake at 350°F until a toothpick inserted into the center comes out clean, about 50 minutes. Remove from the oven and let cool. Cut into ¾-inch slices (you won't need all of the cake).

4. **Prepare the grill for direct cooking over medium heat (350° to 450°F).**

5. **In a blender puree the sauce ingredients.** Pour the sauce into a small saucepan and cook over medium heat until thickened, about 3 minutes. Strain the sauce through a sieve into a small bowl and discard the seeds left behind. Set aside until ready to serve.

6. **Brush the cooking grates clean.** Grill the pineapple over ***direct medium heat***, with the lid open, until nicely marked, 4 to 6 minutes, turning once. During the last 2 minutes of grilling time, grill the cake until lightly marked, turning once. Remove the pineapple and cake from the grill and cut the pineapple into bite-sized chunks.

7. **Place a slice of the cake on each serving plate and top with pineapple chunks and raspberry sauce.**

Access the grocery list for this recipe on your mobile device. timetogrill.mobi.

Pineapple with Coconut Pound Cake
AND RASPBERRY SAUCE

SERVES: 👤👤👤👤👤👤

PREP TIME: **40** MINUTES

BAKING TIME: ABOUT **50** MINUTES

GRILLING TIME: **4** TO **6** MINUTES

SPECIAL EQUIPMENT: 9-BY-5-INCH LOAF PAN

// CAKE
- 1½ cups cake flour
- ¼ teaspoon baking powder
- ½ teaspoon kosher salt
- ½ cup buttermilk
- ¼ cup sour cream
- ¾ cup (1½ sticks) unsalted butter, softened
- ¾ cup granulated sugar
- 2 large eggs, at room temperature
- ½ cup toasted shredded coconut

// SAUCE
- 1 pint fresh raspberries
- 3 tablespoons packed brown sugar
- 2 tablespoons balsamic vinegar
- 2 teaspoons cornstarch

- 1 fresh pineapple, peeled, cored, and cut into ½-inch slices

Warm fruit pie à la mode is a quintessential summertime pleasure, and this recipe delivers all the taste without all the work. Sweet, tart apricots and crunchy cookie crumbs stand in for the pie, while ice cream and caramel sauce add the finishing touches. For something more adventurous, try individual apricot tarts that look so professional they could have been purchased at a bakery. Frozen puff pastry shells are a real time saver, and the homemade caramel sauce made with apricot nectar plays up the summery fruit flavor. The sauce takes a bit of watching, but it is not difficult and is well worth the effort. Both the pastry shells and the caramel sauce can be made ahead, which makes the final assembly pretty simple.

Apricot Pie à la Mode Sundaes

SERVES: 👤👤👤👤👤👤

PREP TIME: **15** MINUTES

GRILLING TIME: **6** TO **8** MINUTES

1 cup plus 2 tablespoons caramel sauce
2 tablespoons Scotch whiskey *or* rum
6 apricots, firm but ripe, each cut in half lengthwise
2 tablespoons unsalted butter, melted
  Vanilla ice cream
¾ cup coarsely crushed shortbread *or* sugar cookies
¼ cup sliced almonds, toasted and chopped

1. **Prepare the grill for direct cooking over medium heat (350° to 450°F).**

2. **In a medium bowl mix the caramel sauce and whiskey.** Set aside. In a medium bowl toss the apricots with the melted butter.

3. **Brush the cooking grates clean.** Grill the apricots, cut side down first, over **direct medium heat**, with the lid closed as much as possible, until heated through, 6 to 8 minutes, turning once.

4. **In each of six ice cream dishes, arrange two apricot halves over two scoops of ice cream.** Drizzle with 2 to 3 tablespoons of caramel-whiskey sauce and top with about 2 tablespoons cookie crumbs. Garnish with a sprinkle of almonds and serve right away.

Access the grocery list for this recipe on your mobile device. timetogrill.mobi.

SERVES: 🜊🜊🜊🜊🜊🜊

PREP TIME: **15** MINUTES, PLUS ABOUT 45 MINUTES FOR THE PASTRY AND CARAMEL

GRILLING TIME: **6** TO **8** MINUTES

SPECIAL EQUIPMENT: PASTRY BRUSH

1 package (6 shells, 10 ounces) frozen puff pastry shells

// SAUCE
1 cup granulated sugar
3 tablespoons water
½ cup heavy whipping cream
½ cup canned apricot nectar
2 tablespoons unsalted butter
½ teaspoon pure vanilla extract

½ cup mascarpone cheese
1 tablespoon confectioners' sugar

9 apricots, firm but ripe, each cut in half lengthwise
2 tablespoons unsalted butter, melted
¼ teaspoon ground nutmeg
3 tablespoons sliced almonds, toasted and chopped

Apricot Mascarpone Tarts
WITH CARAMEL SAUCE

1. Preheat the oven to 400°F. Prepare the grill for direct cooking over medium heat (350° to 450°F).

2. Place the pastry shells, top sides up and about 2 inches apart, on a baking sheet. Bake until puffed and golden brown, 20 to 25 minutes. Remove from the oven and cool for 5 minutes. Remove the centers of the pastries to make shells. Return the shells to the oven to crisp, 3 to 5 minutes. Cool completely.

3. In a medium, heavy-bottomed saucepan combine the granulated sugar and water. Cook over high heat, stirring constantly, until the sugar is just dissolved. Then cook, without stirring, occasionally swirling the pan and using a pastry brush dipped in cold water to brush down the sugar crystals that form on the side of the pan, until the caramel is medium-dark amber, 3 to 5 minutes. The caramel should have a sharp aroma without being acrid. Watch the sauce carefully because once it begins to darken, it caramelizes quickly. Remove from the heat.

4. In a small saucepan over medium-low heat, heat the cream and the apricot nectar until steaming. Carefully pour the hot cream mixture into the saucepan of caramel. It will bubble up and some solid pieces may form. Return the mixture to medium-low heat and stir constantly until the caramel is completely melted, about 1 minute. Simmer, stirring occasionally, until the sauce is slightly reduced, about 3 minutes. Remove from the

heat. Whisk in 2 tablespoons butter until it is completely incorporated. Stir in the vanilla. Set aside at room temperature to cool and thicken.

5. In a small bowl combine the mascarpone and confectioners' sugar. Set aside.

6. In a large bowl toss the apricots, melted butter, and nutmeg. Brush the cooking grates clean. Grill the apricots, cut side down, over **direct medium heat**, with the lid closed as much as possible, until heated through, 6 to 8 minutes, turning once. Remove from the grill and cut each apricot piece in half lengthwise.

7. Place each pastry shell on a plate and spoon in some of the mascarpone mixture. Top with apricot pieces. Drizzle caramel sauce over and around each tart and finish with almonds. Serve immediately.

Access the grocery list for this recipe on your mobile device. timetogrill.mobi.

The hardest part of the easy recipe below might just be finding soft, ripe peaches. After that the key is mostly a matter of watching them carefully on the grill so the brown sugar and butter get good and dark but not too dark. The tart combines many of the same flavors in a skillet. If you don't have a twelve-inch cast-iron skillet, you can use one with a ten-inch diameter. The crust will just be a little higher around the edges. If peaches are not looking particularly good, use apricots instead.

Caramelized Peaches
WITH BRIE AND ALMONDS

SERVES: 👤👤👤👤

PREP TIME: **10** MINUTES

GRILLING TIME: **8** TO **10** MINUTES

¼ cup packed brown sugar
2 tablespoons unsalted butter, melted
4 ripe peaches, each cut in half
2 tablespoons vegetable oil
5 ounces Brie cheese, cut into 8 slices, each about ¼ inch thick
2 tablespoons chopped toasted almonds

1. Prepare the grill for direct cooking over medium heat (350° to 450°F).

2. In a small bowl combine the brown sugar and butter.

3. Lightly brush the peaches with the oil. Brush the cooking grates clean. Grill the peaches, cut side down, over *direct medium heat*, with the lid closed as much as possible, until the peaches are lightly charred and beginning to soften, 5 to 6 minutes. Turn the peaches over and top evenly with the brown sugar-butter mixture. Continue to grill until the peaches are tender, 3 to 4 more minutes.

4. Remove the peaches from the grill and top each with a slice of cheese. Let the cheese melt as the peaches cool, about 5 minutes. Serve with almonds sprinkled on top.

Access the grocery list for this recipe on your mobile device. timetogrill.mobi.

EASY

Skillet Peach Tart

WITH CARDAMOM

SERVES: 8 TO 10

PREP TIME: 30 MINUTES

GRILLING TIME: 1 TO 1¼ HOURS

SPECIAL EQUIPMENT: 12-INCH
CAST-IRON SKILLET

// CRUST
- ¼ cup toasted almonds
- 1½ cups all-purpose flour
- ½ cup granulated sugar
- ½ teaspoon ground cardamom
- ½ teaspoon kosher salt
- ½ cup (1 stick) unsalted butter, cold, cut into pieces
- 1 large egg

// FILLING
- ¼ cup all-purpose flour
- ½ cup packed brown sugar
- 1 teaspoon ground cardamom
- 4 peaches, firm but ripe, about 2 pounds total, thinly sliced

1. **In the bowl of a food processor finely grind the almonds.** Add the flour, sugar, cardamom, and salt and blend. Add the butter and pulse until the mixture resembles fine bread crumbs. With the machine running, add the egg and let it whirl until the dough pulls away from the sides of the bowl.

2. **Spoon the dough into a 12-inch cast-iron skillet.** With lightly floured fingers, press the dough to cover the bottom of the skillet and one and one-half inches up the sides.

3. **Prepare the grill for indirect cooking over medium heat (350° to 450°F).**

4. **In a large mixing bowl combine the flour, brown sugar, and cardamom.** Measure ¼ cup of the mixture and set aside. Add the sliced peaches to the bowl and toss to coat.

5. **Sprinkle the crust with the reserved ¼ cup sugar mixture.** Pour the sliced peaches into the crust and spread them out evenly.

6. **Brush the cooking grates clean.** Place the skillet over *indirect medium heat*, close the lid, and cook until the crust is golden and the filling thickens, 1 to 1¼ hours. Wearing insulated barbecue mitts, remove the skillet from the grill and let cool for at least 30 minutes before cutting into serving pieces.

Access the grocery list for this recipe on your mobile device. timetogrill.mobi.

Stop right there. If berries are in season, you must make this very French, very delicious dessert now. Really, you can substitute any kind of ripe berries you like for the blueberries and raspberries. The crisp is a little more adventurous because it calls for crème anglaise, which can be a challenging sauce for beginners. The trickiest part is cooking the sauce long enough that it thickens properly but not so long that the eggs overcook. Of course you could skip that part altogether and just serve the crisp with ice cream, which is really just frozen crème anglaise.

SERVES: **6** TO **8**

PREP TIME: **15** MINUTES

GRILLING TIME: **35** TO **45** MINUTES

SPECIAL EQUIPMENT: 10-INCH SPRINGFORM PAN

EASY

1 lemon
1 cup fresh blueberries
1 cup fresh raspberries
2 tablespoons orange liqueur, such as Grand Marnier

5 tablespoons unsalted butter
½ cup plus 1 tablespoon granulated sugar, divided
¼ teaspoon ground cardamom
2 large eggs
2 large egg whites
1 cup all-purpose flour
2 tablespoons confectioners' sugar (optional)

Summer Berry Clafoutis

1. Prepare the grill for indirect cooking over medium heat (about 375°F). Generously grease the inside of a 10-inch springform pan.

2. Finely grate the zest from the lemon and set aside. Squeeze 2 teaspoons juice from the lemon and add to a medium bowl with the berries and liqueur. Stir gently to combine. Set aside.

3. In a large bowl using an electric mixer, cream the butter, ½ cup of the granulated sugar, the lemon zest, and cardamom, beating for about 3 minutes. Beat in the eggs and egg whites until well incorporated, about 1 minute. Scrape down the sides of the bowl and add the flour, mixing well for about 30 seconds.

4. Spread the batter into the prepared springform pan. Using a slotted spoon, remove the berries from the liquid and place on top of the batter. Mix the remaining 1 tablespoon of granulated sugar with the liquid and drizzle over the berries.

5. Brush the cooking grates clean. Bake the cake over **indirect medium heat**, with the lid closed, until light golden, 35 to 45 minutes (check the cake after 30 minutes). Keep the grill's temperature as close to 375°F as possible. Wearing insulated barbecue mitts, carefully remove the cake from the grill and allow to cool for 10 minutes. Sprinkle with confectioners' sugar before serving, if desired.

Access the grocery list for this recipe on your mobile device. timetogrill.mobi.

SERVES: **6** TO **8**

PREP TIME: **30** MINUTES

GRILLING TIME: **35** TO **40** MINUTES

SPECIAL EQUIPMENT: 10-INCH
CAST-IRON SKILLET

Mixed Berry Crisp
WITH CRÈME ANGLAISE

// FILLING
- ¾ cup granulated sugar
- 2 tablespoons cornstarch
- ¼ teaspoon ground cinnamon
- ¼ teaspoon ground cardamom
- ¾ cup water
- 2 cups fresh blueberries
- 1 cup fresh raspberries
- 1 cup thinly sliced fresh strawberries

// TOPPING
- ¼ cup plus 2 tablespoons all-purpose flour
- 3 tablespoons packed light brown sugar
- ½ teaspoon ground cinnamon
- 2 tablespoons unsalted butter, cold, cut into pieces

// CRÈME ANGLAISE
- 4 large egg yolks
- ⅓ cup granulated sugar
- 1 cup heavy whipping cream
- 2 teaspoons pure vanilla extract

The crème anglaise is ready when you run your fingertip down the middle of the spoon and it makes a "road."

1. Prepare the grill for indirect cooking over medium heat (about 400°F).

2. In a medium saucepan combine the sugar, cornstarch, cinnamon, and cardamom. Slowly stir in the water and then bring to a boil over medium-high heat, stirring constantly. Remove from the heat.

3. Place the berries in a 10-inch cast-iron skillet. Pour the liquid over the berries. Brush the cooking grates clean. Bake the berries over *indirect medium heat*, with the lid closed, for about 10 minutes.

4. Meanwhile, in a medium bowl combine the flour, brown sugar, and cinnamon. Using a fork, cut the butter into the flour mixture until it has the consistency of fine bread crumbs. Carefully remove the skillet from the grill and sprinkle the topping evenly over the berries. Place the skillet over *indirect medium heat*, close the lid, and continue to bake until the berries are bubbling and the topping is just

beginning to brown, 25 to 30 minutes. Keep the grill's temperature as close to 400°F as possible. Carefully remove the skillet from the grill and allow to cool for about 15 minutes.

5. In a medium bowl whisk the egg yolks and sugar to a rich yellow color. In a medium saucepan over medium heat, heat the cream until scalded but not boiling (bubbles will begin to form around the edge of the pan). Whisking constantly, slowly pour ½ cup of the hot cream into the egg-sugar mixture. Then, using a wooden spoon and stirring constantly, gradually add the egg mixture into the saucepan containing the cream, stirring constantly. Cook until the mixture thickens and coats the back of the spoon, 1 to 2 minutes. Remove the saucepan from the heat. Stir in the vanilla. Spoon the warm crisp into bowls and top with the crème anglaise.

Access the grocery list for this recipe on your mobile device. timetogrill.mobi.

When you need a surefire grilled dessert that requires a minimum effort, look no further than this crowd pleaser: bananas in warm caramel sauce served over ice cream with chocolate and pecans. To reduce your last-minute efforts, scoop balls of ice cream ahead of time onto a baking sheet, cover with plastic wrap, and freeze until serving. Likewise, one nice thing about the pudding is that you can make it in the morning or the night before, so all that's left to do at dessert time is to strain the raspberry jam and grill the bananas.

Warm Banana Chocolate Sundaes

1. **Prepare the grill for direct cooking over medium heat (350° to 450°F).**

2. **Tear off two 12-inch lengths of heavy-duty aluminum foil.** Working with one piece of foil at a time, place a sliced banana in the center of the foil. Sprinkle with ¼ cup brown sugar, then 2 tablespoons each cream and brandy. Fold in the sides of the foil, then the top and bottom to enclose the banana mixture. Repeat with the other banana.

3. **Brush the cooking grates clean.** Grill the foil packets, seam side up, over **direct medium heat**, with the lid closed, until the brown sugar is melted and the liquid is simmering and combined into a sauce (open a packet to check), 5 to 7 minutes. Transfer the packets to a sheet pan and let rest for 5 minutes to cool slightly.

4. **Put two scoops of ice cream into each of four serving bowls.** Snip the foil packets open with scissors. Pour the contents of the packets evenly over the ice cream in each bowl. Sprinkle each with equal amounts of the chocolate and then top with the nuts. Serve immediately.

Access the grocery list for this recipe on your mobile device. timetogrill.mobi.

SERVES: 🙂🙂🙂🙂

EASY

PREP TIME: **15** MINUTES

GRILLING TIME: **5** TO **7** MINUTES

2 bananas, peeled and cut crosswise into ½-inch slices
½ cup packed brown sugar
¼ cup heavy whipping cream
¼ cup brandy *or* bourbon *or* fresh orange juice
Vanilla ice cream
1 ounce bittersweet chocolate, finely grated
⅓ cup finely chopped pecans

SERVES: 🧍🧍🧍🧍🧍🧍

PREP TIME: **20** MINUTES

CHILLING TIME: AT LEAST **8** HOURS

GRILLING TIME: **2** TO **3** MINUTES

SPECIAL EQUIPMENT: SIX 6-OUNCE RAMEKINS OR CUSTARD CUPS

// PUDDING

- 1 envelope (about 2¼ teaspoons) unflavored gelatin powder
- ¼ cup cold water
- 1½ cups heavy whipping cream
- ¾ cup whole milk
- ¼ cup granulated sugar
- 6 ounces semisweet chocolate, finely chopped (or chips)
- ½ teaspoon pure vanilla extract

- 1 cup raspberry jam
- 3 bananas
  Vegetable oil

Chocolate Pudding
WITH GRILLED BANANAS

1. In a small bowl sprinkle the gelatin over the water and let stand until the gelatin softens, about 5 minutes.

2. In a medium saucepan over medium-high heat, bring the cream, milk, and sugar to a simmer, stirring to dissolve the sugar. Remove the saucepan from the heat and add the softened gelatin; stir constantly until the gelatin is completely dissolved, 2 full minutes. Put the chocolate in a medium bowl (or even better, a Pyrex® 4-cup measure with a spout) and pour the hot cream mixture over the chocolate. Let stand 3 minutes and then whisk until the chocolate is completely melted. Whisk in the vanilla. Let cool at room temperature.

3. Pour equal amounts of the chocolate mixture into each ramekin. Place the ramekins on a sheet pan and loosely cover with plastic wrap. Refrigerate until the puddings are chilled and set, at least 8 hours or up to 1 day.

4. In a small saucepan over medium heat, heat the raspberry jam and stir until warmed through and melted. Place a small sieve over a bowl and strain the seeds out of the jam, extracting by pressing the jam with a spoon. Set aside.

5. Prepare the grill for direct cooking over medium heat (350° to 450°F).

6. Cut each banana in half lengthwise, but do not peel. The skins will help the bananas hold their shape on the grill. Lightly brush the cut side of the bananas with oil. Brush the cooking grates clean. Grill the bananas, cut side down, over ***direct medium heat***, with the lid open, until warmed and well marked but not too soft, 2 to 3 minutes. Remove from the grill. Peel the banana halves and cut them into ½-inch slices.

7. Serve the puddings with banana slices and strained raspberry jam over the top.

Access the grocery list for this recipe on your mobile device. timetogrill.mobi.

Bread and chocolate make an amazing combination that you don't see often enough. Both the sandwiches and the chocolate fondue are made with quality bittersweet chocolate. If you are not a fan of dark chocolate, or to make the sandwiches for children, substitute milk chocolate for the dark chocolate, and creamy, sweetened peanut butter for the orange marmalade. Because the sandwiches are grilled over lower heat than you would use to grill meats, it's a good way to use the coals as they are cooling down from having grilled your dinner entrée. The grilled bread for the fondue is tossed in olive oil rather than the more predictable butter. It's a sophisticated combination that you have to taste to believe.

Grilled Chocolate Sandwiches

SERVES: 4 TO 8

PREP TIME: 5 MINUTES

GRILLING TIME: 4 TO 5 MINUTES

8 slices country-style white bread, each about ½ inch thick (from a large loaf, slices should be roughly 6½ by 4 inches)
2 tablespoons plus 2 teaspoons orange marmalade
2 bars (4 ounces each) good-quality bittersweet chocolate
6 tablespoons (¾ stick) unsalted butter, melted
2 tablespoons confectioners' sugar

1. **Prepare the grill for direct cooking over medium-low heat (about 350°F).**

2. **Lay four of the bread slices on a work surface.** Spread 2 teaspoons of marmalade on each of them. Place one-fourth of the chocolate on each of the four slices, breaking the chocolate into pieces to fit the shape of the bread. Top each sandwich with one of the remaining slices of bread and brush melted butter onto both sides of each sandwich.

3. **Brush the cooking grates clean.** Grill the sandwiches over *direct medium-low heat*, with the lid closed as much as possible, until the bread is a golden brown and crispy and the chocolate is melted, 4 to 5 minutes, turning once. Remove the sandwiches from the grill and let them rest for about 1 minute. Using a large serrated knife, cut each sandwich in half on the diagonal or into three pieces. Lightly dust the sandwiches with confectioners' sugar and serve.

Access the grocery list for this recipe on your mobile device. timetogrill.mobi.

EASY

Toasted Bread and Pears with Chocolate Fondue

SERVES: 🧍🧍🧍🧍🧍🧍

PREP TIME: **15** MINUTES

GRILLING TIME: **3** TO **5** MINUTES

// FONDUE

- 8 ounces good-quality bittersweet chocolate, finely chopped
- ½ cup heavy whipping cream
- 1 tablespoon Grand Marnier *or* whiskey *or* 2 teaspoons pure vanilla extract

- 3 ripe pears, such as Anjou or Comice
- ¼ cup extra-virgin olive oil
  Finely grated zest of 1 large orange
- 8 ounces country-style white bread, cut into 1½-inch chunks
- 1 teaspoon flaky sea salt *or fleur de sel*

// To serve the fondue later, let it cool to room temperature, transfer to an airtight container, and refrigerate until you're ready to serve (for up to a week). Warm the fondue over low heat, stirring constantly, or heat at low power in a microwave oven for 3 to 5 minutes, stirring halfway through.

1. Put the chocolate in a medium bowl. Using a microwave oven, heat the cream in a small bowl until it just begins to bubble, about 1 minute on high. Add the warm cream to the chocolate and stir constantly until the chocolate is melted and the sauce is smooth. Stir in the Grand Marnier. Keep warm.

2. Cut the pears in half lengthwise, core, and then cut each half lengthwise into thirds.

3. Prepare the grill for direct cooking over high heat (450° to 550°F).

4. In a large bowl whisk the oil and orange zest. Add the bread chunks and carefully toss to coat them evenly.

5. Brush the cooking grates clean. Grill the bread chunks over **direct high heat**, with the lid open, until golden brown and crunchy, 3 to 5 minutes, turning occasionally. Remove from the grill and sprinkle with the sea salt.

6. Serve the fondue in bowls with the bread and pear slices on the side for dipping.

Access the grocery list for this recipe on your mobile device. timetogrill.mobi.

Chocolate Brownies

It is fitting that we end this chapter with two of the easiest and most satisfying desserts the world has ever known. Both of them can, and should, be made hours ahead of time. Both use a bit of orange to complement the deep, dark chocolate flavors. The cake just takes a little longer to make, and its looks give it a much bigger wow factor. To simplify matters, you could replace the glaze with whipped cream.

SERVES: 8

PREP TIME: **15** MINUTES

GRILLING TIME: **25** TO **35** MINUTES

SPECIAL EQUIPMENT:
8-INCH-SQUARE BAKING PAN

EASY

⅓ cup unsweetened cocoa powder
½ cup all-purpose flour
¼ teaspoon kosher salt
¼ teaspoon baking powder
2 large eggs
½ cup granulated sugar
½ teaspoon vanilla extract
½ teaspoon orange extract
½ cup (1 stick) unsalted butter, melted and cooled slightly
3 tablespoons orange marmalade

1. Prepare the grill for indirect cooking over medium heat (about 350°F). Generously grease an 8-inch-square baking pan.

2. In a medium bowl sift the cocoa, flour, salt, and baking powder. In another medium bowl beat the eggs with a wooden spoon. Beat in the sugar and the vanilla and orange extracts. Slowly add in the melted butter and beat until completely incorporated.

3. Add the sifted dry ingredients to the butter mixture. Stir well until all the dry ingredients are completely moistened.

4. Scrape the batter into the prepared baking pan. Drop spoonfuls of the marmalade onto the top of the batter at even intervals across the center of the batter. Drag the tip of a knife through each marmalade mound and pull it randomly through the batter.

5. Place the pan over *indirect medium heat*, close the lid, and bake until the brownies pull slightly away from the edges of the pan and a toothpick inserted into the center comes out clean, 25 to 35 minutes. Keep the grill's temperature as close to 350°F as possible. Carefully remove the pan from the grill. Cool for about 15 minutes. Cut into 16 squares.

Access the grocery list for this recipe on your mobile device. timetogrill.mobi.

Chocolate Cake
WITH ORANGE GLAZE

SERVES: 8

PREP TIME: 30 MINUTES

GRILLING TIME: 40 TO 50 MINUTES

SPECIAL EQUIPMENT: 9-INCH-ROUND CAKE PAN

// CAKE
- 1⅓ cups granulated sugar
- ½ cup unsweetened cocoa powder
- 1¾ cups all-purpose flour
- 1 teaspoon baking soda
- 1 teaspoon baking powder
- ¼ teaspoon kosher salt
- 3 large eggs
- 1 cup buttermilk
- 1 cup sour cream
- 6 tablespoons (¾ stick) unsalted butter, melted and cooled slightly

// GLAZE
- 1 orange
- 1 cup confectioners' sugar

1. **Prepare the grill for indirect cooking over medium heat (about 375°F).**

2. **Grease a 9-inch-round cake pan and line the bottom with parchment paper.**

3. **In a medium bowl sift the granulated sugar, cocoa, flour, baking soda, baking powder, and salt.** Set aside.

4. **In the bowl of an electric mixer fitted with the paddle attachment, beat the eggs on medium speed until frothy, about 1 minute.** Beat in the buttermilk and sour cream until well combined. Slowly beat in the sugar mixture. Remove the bowl from the mixer and fold in the melted butter by hand, working slowly so it is completely incorporated.

5. **Pour the batter into the greased cake pan.** Place the pan on the grill over *indirect medium heat*, close the lid, and bake until the edges pull slightly away from the sides and a toothpick inserted in the center comes out clean, 40 to 50 minutes. Keep the grill's temperature as close to 375°F as possible. Wearing insulated barbecue mitts, remove the cake from the grill and cool completely. Once cool, invert the cake onto a platter and make the glaze.

6. **Finely grate the zest from the orange and set aside.** Squeeze 3 tablepoons juice from the orange. In a medium bowl combine 2 tablespoons of the juice with the confectioners' sugar. Mix, and add another tablespoon of juice, if necessary, until you have a spreadable consistency. Stir in the orange zest.

7. **Glaze the top of the cake and refrigerate until ready to eat.**

Access the grocery list for this recipe on your mobile device. timetogrill.mobi.

RESOURCES

// red meat grilling guide

The cuts, thicknesses, weights, and grilling times are meant to be guidelines rather than hard and fast rules. Cooking times are affected by such factors as altitude, wind, outside temperature, and desired doneness. Two rules of thumb: Grill steaks and kabobs using the direct method for the time given on the chart or to your desired doneness, turning once. Grill roasts and thicker cuts using the indirect method for the time given on the chart or until an instant-read thermometer reaches the desired internal temperature. Let roasts, larger cuts of meat, and thick steaks rest for 5 to 10 minutes before carving. The internal temperature of the meat will rise 5 to 10 degrees during this time.

CUT	THICKNESS/WEIGHT	APPROXIMATE GRILLING TIME
Steak: New York strip, porterhouse, rib eye, T-bone, and filet mignon (tenderloin)	¾ inch thick	**4 to 6 minutes** direct high heat
	1 inch thick	**6 to 8 minutes** direct high heat
	1¼ inches thick	**8 to 10 minutes** direct high heat
	1½ inches thick	**10 to 14 minutes:** sear 6 to 8 minutes direct high heat, grill 4 to 6 minutes indirect high heat
	2 inches thick	**14 to 18 minutes:** sear 6 to 8 minutes direct high heat, grill 8 to 10 minutes indirect high heat
Beef, ground	¾ inch thick	**8 to 10 minutes** direct high heat
Flank steak	1½ to 2 pounds, ¾ inch thick	**8 to 10 minutes** direct medium heat
Flat iron steak	1 inch thick	**8 to 10 minutes** direct medium heat
Hanger steak	1 inch thick	**8 to 10 minutes** direct medium heat
Kabob	1-inch cubes	**4 to 6 minutes** direct high heat
	1½-inch cubes	**6 to 7 minutes** direct high heat
Rib roast (prime rib), boneless	5 to 6 pounds	**1¼ to 1¾ hours** indirect medium heat
Rib roast (prime rib), with bone	8 pounds	**2½ to 3 hours:** sear 10 minutes direct medium heat, grill 2⅓ to 3 hours indirect low heat
Skirt steak	¼ to ½ inch thick	**4 to 6 minutes** direct high heat
Strip loin roast, boneless	4 to 5 pounds	**50 to 60 minutes:** sear 10 minutes direct medium heat, grill 40 to 50 minutes indirect medium heat
Tenderloin, whole	3½ to 4 pounds	**35 to 45 minutes:** sear 15 minutes direct medium heat, grill 20 to 30 minutes indirect medium heat
Tri-tip	2 to 2½ pounds	**30 to 40 minutes:** sear 10 minutes direct medium heat, grill 20 to 30 minutes indirect medium heat
Veal loin chop	1 inch thick	**6 to 8 minutes** direct high heat

Note: All cooking times are for medium-rare doneness, except ground beef (medium).

Access this grilling guide on your mobile device. timetogrill.mobi.

// TYPES OF RED MEAT FOR THE GRILL

Tender Cuts for Grilling

Beef New York strip

Beef porterhouse steak

Beef rib steak/rib eye steak

Beef T-bone steak

Beef tenderloin (filet mignon) steak

Lamb loin chop

Lamb sirloin chop

Veal loin chop

Moderately Tender Cuts for Grilling

Beef flank steak

Beef flatiron steak

Beef hanger steak

Beef skirt steak

Beef top sirloin

Lamb shoulder blade chop

Lamb sirloin chop

Veal shoulder blade chop

Bigger Cuts for Searing and Grill-roasting

Beef standing rib roast (prime rib)

Beef strip loin

Beef tri-tip roast

Beef whole tenderloin

Leg of lamb

Rack of lamb

Rack of veal

Tougher Cuts for Barbecuing

Beef ribs

Brisket

// red meat doneness

DONENESS	CHEF STANDARDS	USDA
Rare	120° to 125°F	n/a
Medium rare	125° to 135°F	145°F
Medium	135° to 145°F	160°F
Medium well	145° to 155°F	n/a
Well done	155°F +	170°F

// lamb grilling guide

CUT	THICKNESS/WEIGHT	APPROXIMATE GRILLING TIME
Chop: loin, rib, shoulder, or sirloin	¾ to 1½ inches thick	**8 to 12 minutes** direct medium heat
Lamb, ground	¾ inch thick	**8 to 10 minutes** direct medium heat
Leg of lamb, boneless, rolled	2½ to 3 pounds	**30 to 45 minutes:** sear 10 to 15 minutes direct medium heat, grill 20 to 30 minutes indirect medium heat
Leg of lamb, butterflied	3 to 3½ pounds	**30 to 45 minutes:** sear 10 to 15 minutes direct medium heat, grill 20 to 30 minutes indirect medium heat
Rack of lamb	1 to 1½ pounds	**15 to 20 minutes:** sear 5 minutes direct medium heat, grill 10 to 15 minutes indirect medium heat
Rib crown roast	3 to 4 pounds	**1 to 1¼ hours** indirect medium heat

Note: All cooking times are for medium-rare doneness, except ground lamb (medium).

Access this grilling guide on your mobile device. timetogrill.mobi.

// pork grilling guide

The cuts, thicknesses, weights, and grilling times are meant to be guidelines rather than hard and fast rules. Cooking times are affected by such factors as altitude, wind, outside temperature, and desired doneness. Two rules of thumb: Grill chops and brats using the direct method for the time given on the chart or to your desired doneness, turning once. Grill roasts and thicker cuts using the indirect method for the time given on the chart or until an instant-read thermometer reaches the desired internal temperature. The USDA recommends that pork is cooked to 160°F, but most chefs today cook it to 145°F or 150°F, when it still has some pink in the center and all the juices haven't been driven out. Of course, the doneness you choose is entirely up to you. Let roasts, larger cuts of meat, and thick chops rest for 5 to 10 minutes before carving. The internal temperature of the meat will rise 5 to 10 degrees during this time.

CUT	THICKNESS/WEIGHT	APPROXIMATE GRILLING TIME
Bratwurst, fresh	3 ounce link	**20 to 25 minutes** direct medium heat
Bratwurst, pre-cooked	3 ounce link	**10 to 12 minutes** direct medium heat
Chop, boneless or bone-in	¾ inch thick	**6 to 8 minutes** direct high heat
	1 inch thick	**8 to 10 minutes** direct medium heat
	1¼ to 1½ inches thick	**10 to 12 minutes:** sear 6 minutes direct high heat, grill 4 to 6 minutes indirect high heat
Loin roast, boneless	2½ pounds	**40 to 50 minutes** direct medium heat
Loin roast, bone-in	3 to 5 pounds	**1¼ to 1¾ hours** indirect medium heat
Pork shoulder (Boston butt), boneless	5 to 6 pounds	**5 to 7 hours** indirect low heat
Pork, ground	½ inch thick	**8 to 10 minutes** direct medium heat
Ribs, baby back	1½ to 2 pounds	**3 to 4 hours** indirect low heat
Ribs, spareribs	2½ to 3½ pounds	**3 to 4 hours** indirect low heat
Ribs, country-style, boneless	1½ to 2 pounds	**12 to 15 minutes** direct medium heat
Ribs, country-style, bone-in	3 to 4 pounds	**1½ to 2 hours** indirect medium heat
Tenderloin	1 pound	**15 to 20 minutes** direct medium heat

Access this grilling guide on your mobile device. timetogrill.mobi.

// TYPES OF PORK FOR THE GRILL

Tender Cuts for Grilling

Center-cut chop

Loin chop

Tenderloin (whole or in medallions)

Moderately Tender Cuts for Grilling

Ham steak

Shoulder blade steak

Sirloin chop

Bigger Cuts for Searing and Grill-roasting

Center loin roast

Center rib roast

Country-style ribs

Cured ham

Rack of pork

Sirloin loin roast

Tougher Cuts for Barbecuing

Baby back ribs

Shoulder (Boston butt)

Spareribs

// poultry grilling guide

The cuts, weights, and grilling times are meant to be guidelines rather than hard and fast rules. Cooking times are affected by such factors as altitude, wind, and outside temperature. Cooking times are for the USDA's recommendation of 165°F. Let whole poultry rest for 5 to 10 minutes before carving. The internal temperature of the meat will rise 5 to 10 degrees during this time.

CUT	WEIGHT	APPROXIMATE GRILLING TIME
Chicken breast, bone-in	10 to 12 ounces	**23 to 35 minutes:** 3 to 5 minutes direct medium heat, 20 to 30 minutes indirect medium heat
Chicken breast, boneless, skinless	6 to 8 ounces	**8 to 12 minutes** direct medium heat
Chicken drumstick	3 to 4 ounces	**36 to 40 minutes:** 6 to 10 minutes direct medium heat, 30 minutes indirect medium heat
Chicken thigh, bone-in	5 to 6 ounces	**36 to 40 minutes:** 6 to 10 minutes direct medium heat, 30 minutes indirect medium heat
Chicken thigh, boneless, skinless	4 ounces	**8 to 10 minutes** direct medium heat
Chicken thigh meat, ground	¾ inch thick	**12 to 14 minutes** direct medium heat
Chicken, whole	4 to 5 pounds	**1 to 1¼ hours** indirect medium heat
Chicken, whole leg	10 to 12 ounces	**48 minutes to 1 hour:** 8 to 10 minutes direct medium heat, 40 to 50 minutes indirect medium heat
Chicken wing	2 to 3 ounces	**35 to 43 minutes:** 5 to 8 minutes direct medium heat, 30 to 35 minutes indirect medium heat
Cornish game hen	1 to 1¼ hours indirect medium heat	**50 to 60 minutes** indirect high heat
Duck breast, boneless	10 to 12 ounces	**9 to 12 minutes:** grill 3 to 4 minutes direct low heat, grill 6 to 8 minutes indirect high heat
Duck, whole	5½ to 6 pounds	**40 minutes** indirect high heat
Turkey breast, boneless	2½ pounds	**1 to 1¼ hours** indirect medium heat
Turkey, whole, not stuffed	10 to 12 pounds	**2½ to 3½ hours** indirect low heat

Access this grilling guide on your mobile device. timetogrill.mobi.

// seafood grilling guide

The types, thicknesses, weights, and grilling times are meant to be guidelines rather than hard and fast rules. Cooking times are affected by such factors as altitude, wind, outside temperature, and desired doneness. The general rule of thumb for grilling fish: 4 to 5 minutes per ½-inch thickness; 8 to 10 minutes per 1-inch thickness.

TYPE	THICKNESS/WEIGHT	APPROXIMATE GRILLING TIME
Fish, fillet or steak Includes halibut, red snapper, salmon, sea bass, swordfish, and tuna	¼ to ½ inch thick	**3 to 5 minutes** direct high heat
	½ to 1 inch thick	**5 to 10 minutes** direct high heat
	1 to 1¼ inches thick	**10 to 12 minutes** direct high heat
Fish, whole	1 pound	**15 to 20 minutes** indirect medium heat
	2 to 2½ pounds	**20 to 30 minutes** indirect medium heat
	3 pounds	**30 to 45 minutes** indirect medium heat
Clam (discard any that do not open)	2 to 3 ounces	**6 to 8 minutes** direct high heat
Lobster tail	6 ounce tail	**7 to 11 minutes** direct medium heat
Mussel (discard any that do not open)	1 to 2 ounces	**5 to 6 minutes** direct high heat
Oyster	3 to 4 ounces	**2 to 4 minutes** direct high heat
Scallop	1½ ounces	**4 to 6 minutes** direct high heat
Shrimp	1½ ounces	**2 to 4 minutes** direct high heat

// TYPES OF SEAFOOD FOR THE GRILL

Firm Fillets and Steaks
Grouper
Salmon
Squid
Swordfish
Tuna

Medium-firm Fillets and Steaks
Chilean sea bass
Halibut
Mackerel
Mahi mahi
Monkfish
Red snapper

Tender Fillets
Bluefish
Striped bass
Trout

Whole Fish
Bluefish
Grouper
Mackerel
Red snapper
Striped bass
Trout

Shellfish
Clams
Lobster
Mussels
Oysters
Scallops
Shrimp

Access this grilling guide on your mobile device. timetogrill.mobi.

// vegetable and fruit grilling guide

Just about everything from apples to zucchini tends to cook best over direct medium heat. The temperature on the grill's thermometer should be somewhere between 350° and 450°F.

TYPE	THICKNESS/SIZE	APPROXIMATE GRILLING TIME
Apple	whole	**35 to 40 minutes** indirect medium heat
	½-inch slices	**4 to 6 minutes** direct medium heat
Apricot	halved	**6 to 8 minutes** direct medium heat
Artichoke hearts	whole	**14 to 18 minutes:** boil 10 to 12 minutes; cut in half and grill 4 to 6 minutes direct medium heat
Asparagus	½-inch diameter	**6 to 8 minutes** direct medium heat
Banana	halved lengthwise	**6 to 8 minutes** direct medium heat
Bell pepper	whole	**10 to 15 minutes** direct medium heat
Carrot	1-inch diameter	**7 to 11 minutes:** boil 4 to 6 minutes, grill 3 to 5 minutes direct high heat
Corn, husked		**10 to 15 minutes** direct medium heat
Corn, in husk		**25 to 30 minutes** direct medium heat
Eggplant	½-inch slices	**8 to 10 minutes** direct medium heat
Garlic	whole	**45 minutes to 1 hour** indirect medium heat
Mushroom, button or shiitake		**8 to 10 minutes** direct medium heat
Mushroom, portabello		**10 to 15 minutes** direct medium heat
Onion	halved	**35 to 40 minutes** indirect medium heat
	½-inch slices	**8 to 12 minutes** direct medium heat
Peach/Nectarine	halved lengthwise	**8 to 10 minutes** direct medium heat
Pear	halved lengthwise	**10 to 12 minutes** direct medium heat
Pineapple	½-inch slices or 1-inch wedges	**4 to 8 minutes** direct medium heat
Potato, new	halved	**15 to 20 minutes** direct medium heat
Potato, russet	whole	**45 minutes to 1 hour** indirect medium heat
	½-inch slices	**9 to 11 minutes;** simmer 3 minutes, grill 6 to 8 minutes direct medium heat
Scallion	whole	**3 to 4 minutes** direct medium heat
Squash, acorn (1½ pounds)	halved	**40 minutes to 1 hour** indirect medium heat
Tomato, garden or plum	halved	**6 to 8 minutes** direct medium heat
	whole	**8 to 10 minutes** direct medium heat
Zucchini	½-inch slices	**3 to 5 minutes** direct medium heat

Access this grilling guide on your mobile device. timetogrill.mobi.

// grill maintenance

A little TLC is all it takes to ensure that you get years of use from your grill. Maintenance is the key. Each time you use the grill, remember to clean the cooking grates. With the grill on high (either right before cooking or right after) brush the cooking grates with a long-handled, stainless steel brush. Be sure to get in between the grates with your brush, too.

Monthly Maintenance Plan for Gas Grills

1. When your grill is warm, but not hot, use a wet, soapy sponge or dishcloth to wipe the inside of the lid. This will help keep natural carbon build-up from accumulating inside the lid.

2. Remove the grates and brush the metal bars that shield the burners. A good brush, like the one you use to brush the cooking grates, will work well. This will help to eliminate flare-ups. (If you grill often, you may need to do this a little more frequently than once a month.)

3. Gently clean the burner tubes with a steel brush. Brush side-to-side along the burner tubes and take care not to damage the openings themselves by brushing too hard.

4. Use a plastic putty knife or spatula to scrape the grease from the bottom of the grill. If your grill has a collection tray, scrape the bits into it. Then dispose of the contents of the collection tray.

5. Wash the inside of the grill with warm, soapy water. Take care not to get water in the burner tubes.

6. Reassemble, wait a month, and repeat.

Monthly Maintenance Plan for Charcoal Grills

1. When the grill is cold, remove the ash from the bowl. Because the ash naturally contains a small amount of moisture, it is important to get the ash out of the bowl each time you use it and before storing your grill. If your grill has an ash catcher, empty after each use.

2. Wipe the inside of the bowl with a warm, wet sponge. This will help keep natural carbon build-up from accumulating inside the lid.

Monthly Maintenance Plan for Electric Grills

1. When your grill is warm, but not hot, use a wet, soapy sponge or dishcloth to wipe the inside of the lid. This will help keep natural carbon build-up from accumulating inside the lid.

2. Remove the grates. Use a plastic putty knife or spatula to scrape the grease from the bottom of the grill. If your grill has a collection tray, scrape the bits into it. Then dispose of the contents of the collection tray.

3. Wipe the inside of the grill with a warm, damp sponge, being very careful not to get the heating element wet.

TIME TO GRILL

// safety

Please read your owner's guide and familiarize yourself with and follow all "dangers," "warnings," and "cautions." Also follow the grilling procedures and maintenance requirements contained in your owner's guide. If you cannot locate the owner's guide for your grill model, please contact the manufacturer prior to use.

If you have any questions concerning the "dangers," "warnings," and "cautions" contained in your Weber® gas or charcoal owner's guide, or if you do not have an owner's guide for your specific grill model, please contact Weber-Stephen Products LLC Customer Service at 1.800.446.1071 before using your grill. You can also access your owner's guide online at www.weber.com.

General Notes

1. Gas and charcoal grills are designed for outdoor use only. If used indoors, toxic fumes will accumulate and cause serious bodily injury or death.

2. Grills radiate a lot of heat, so always keep the grill at least five feet away from any combustible materials, including the house, garage, deck rails, etc. Combustible materials include, but are not limited to, wood or treated wood decks, wood patios, and wood porches. Never use a grill indoors or under a covered patio.

3. Keep the grill in a level position at all times.

4. Use proper barbecuing tools with long, heat-resistant handles.

5. Don't wear loose or highly flammable clothing when grilling.

6. Do not leave infants, children, or pets unattended near a hot grill.

7. Use insulated barbecue mitts to protect hands while cooking or using the grill or adjusting the vents.

Gas Grill Safety

1. Always check the bottom tray and grease tray before cooking. They should be clean and free of debris. It prevents dangerous grease fires and deters visits from unwanted critters.

2. If a flare-up should occur, make sure the lid is closed. Then, if necessary, move the food over indirect heat until the flare-up subsides. Never use water to extinguish flames on a gas grill.

3. Do not line the funnel-shaped bottom tray with foil. This could prevent grease from flowing into the grease catch pan. Grease is also likely to catch in the tiny creases of the foil and start a fire.

4. Never store propane tanks or spares indoors (that means the garage, too).

5. For the first few uses, the temperature of a new gas grill may run hotter than normal. Once your grill is seasoned and the inside of the cooking box is less reflective, the temperature will return to normal.

Charcoal Grill Safety

1. Do not add charcoal starter fluid or charcoal impregnated with charcoal starter fluid to hot or warm charcoal.

2. Do not use gasoline, alcohol, or other highly volatile fluids to ignite charcoal. If using charcoal starter fluid, remove any fluid that may have drained through the bottom vents before lighting the charcoal.

3. Do not use a grill unless all parts are in place. Make sure the ash catcher is properly attached to the legs underneath the bowl of the grill.

4. Remove the lid from the grill while lighting and getting the charcoal started.

5. Always put charcoal on top of the charcoal grate, not into the bottom of the bowl.

6. Do not place a chimney starter on or near any combustible surface.

7. If a flare-up should occur, place the lid on the grill and close the top vent about halfway. If the flames are still threatening, open the lid and move the food over indirect heat. Do not use water to extinguish the flames.

8. Never touch the cooking or charcoal grate or the grill to see if it is hot.

9. Use the hook on the inside of the lid to hang the lid on the side of the bowl of the grill. Avoid placing a hot lid on carpet or grass. Do not hang the lid on the bowl handle.

10. Keep electrical cords away from the hot surfaces of the grill.

11. To extinguish the coals, place the lid on the bowl and close all of the vents (dampers). Make sure that the vents on the lid and the bowl are completely closed. Do not use water, as it will damage the porcelain finish.

// index

INDEX

// sources

"Propane." How Products are Made. Ed. Stacey L. Blachford. Gale Cengage, 2002. eNotes.com. 2006. http://www.enotes.com/how-products-encyclopedia/propane (accessed January 19, 2011).

"Propane." need.org. http://www.need.org/needpdf/infobook_activities/SecInfo/PropaneS.pdf (accessed January 19, 2011).

"Smoke in Your Eyes." CampFish.net. http://campfish.net/campfire-smoke.php (accessed January 19, 2011).

"Smoke Follows Beauty." "bodhi." newsgroups.derkeiler.com. 2005. http://newsgroups.derkeiler.com/Archive/Alt/alt.gathering.rainbow/2005-11/msg00669.html (accessed January 19, 2011).

dictionary.com. http://dictionary.reference.com/browse/vapor (accessed January 14, 2011).

merriam-webster.com. http://www.merriam-webster.com/dictionary/vapor (accessed January 14, 2011).

"Fire." wikipedia.org. http://en.wikipedia.org/wiki/Fire (accessed January 19, 2011).

"Fire Physics." mb-soft.com. http://mb-soft.com/juca/print/317.html (accessed January 19, 2011).

"Chapter 1—Chemistry and Physics of Fire." maiif.org. http://www.maiif.org/pdf/fire_chapter1.pdf (accessed January 19, 2011).

"Charcoal." wikipedia.org. http://en.wikipedia.org/wiki/Charcoal (accessed January 19, 2011).

"What Is Charcoal?" Tiffany Maleshefski. 2007. chow.com. http://www.chow.com/food-news/53975/what-is-charcoal (accessed January 19, 2011).

"All About Charcoal." virtualweberbullet.com. http://www.virtualweberbullet.com/charcoal.html (accessed January 19, 2011).

"Charcoal, The original source of the cookout." Derrick Riches. about.com. http://bbq.about.com/od/charcoal/a/aa071997.htm (accessed January 19, 2011).

TOP TEN TIPS //
for saving time

(1) Sharpen your knives.
Much of the time required to make a recipe is spent slicing and dicing. Dull knives will slow you down and sharp knives will speed you up.

(2) Stock your pantry with ingredients that you can quickly turn into sauces and side dishes.
Get to know convenient items like peeled garlic cloves in jars and store-bought pizza dough.

(3) Shop for more than just today.
To cut down on trips to the supermarket, pick up ingredients for tomorrow and the next day, too.

(4) Read the whole recipe before you grill.
Be prepared for any times required for marinating meats or letting charcoal burn down to low temperatures. Plan to use those times for other steps.

(5) Prep the food while preheating your grill.
You can get a lot done in those fifteen minutes. Just don't forget to light the grill first.

(6) Before you grill, assemble all your ingredients and tools nearby.
Running back into the kitchen might waste time, and it can be risky to leave your food unattended.

(7) Prepare your grill with more than just one heat zone.
Two or three areas of various heat levels mean you can grill two or three things simultaneously.

(8) Brush the cooking grates clean while they're hot.
It's much faster and easier to brush a hot grate than a cold one, so do this after you preheat the grill or when you have just finished grilling.

(9) Grill with the lid closed as much as possible.
The heat reflecting off the lid helps to cook food from both sides, which shortens the grilling time.

(10) Don't overcrowd your grill.
You should always leave about one-third of the grill free for maneuvering your food from place to place. Otherwise, you might need to take food off the grill and slow down the cooking.